THE PLACE TO BE

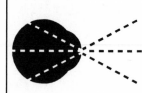

This Large Print Book carries the
Seal of Approval of N.A.V.H.

THE PLACE TO BE

WASHINGTON, CBS, AND THE
GLORY DAYS OF TELEVISION NEWS

ROGER MUDD

THORNDIKE PRESS
A part of Gale, Cengage Learning

GALE
CENGAGE Learning™

Detroit • New York • San Francisco • New Haven, Conn • Waterville, Maine • London

GALE
CENGAGE Learning

Thorndike Press® Large Print Biography.
The text of this Large Print edition is unabridged.
Other aspects of the book may vary from the original edition.
Set in 16 pt. Plantin.
Printed on permanent paper.

LIBRARY OF CONGRESS CATALOGING-IN-PUBLICATION DATA

Mudd, Roger, 1928–
   The place to be : Washington, CBS, and the glory days of
television news / by Roger Mudd. — Large print ed.
      p. cm.
   Originally published: New York : Public Affairs, c2008.
   Includes bibliographical references.
   ISBN-13: 978-1-4104-0936-2 (hbk. : lg. print : alk. paper)
   ISBN-10: 1-4104-0936-8 (hbk. : lg. print : alk. paper)
   1. Mudd, Roger, 1928– 2. Television journalists—United
States—Biography. 3. CBS News—History. 4. Large type books.
I. Title.
PN4874.M75A3 2008b
070'.92—dc22
   [B]   2008022369

Published in 2008 by arrangement with Public Affairs™, a member of
Perseus Books Group.

Printed in the United States of America
1 2 3 4 5 6 7 12 11 10 09 08

For E. J., Daniel, Maria,
Jonathan, and Matthew

CONTENTS

PROLOGUE

There was a time when journalism had no metes or bounds and almost everybody could take a turn at being a journalist — Benjamin Franklin, Walt Whitman, Georges Clemenceau, Johann Wolfgang von Goethe, Charles Dickens, even Benito Mussolini.

Today — with the help of a technological revolution — almost anybody is taking a turn at journalism. There are Web site reporters like Matt Drudge, revolving-door journalists like Tim Russert, and talking-head journalists like John McLaughlin, and there are bloggers — political bloggers, travel bloggers, financial bloggers.

In the 1920s, with a growing sense of professionalism, journalism began to embrace ethical standards and dignity among the newspaper reporters. Such men as Richard Oulahan of the *New York Times,* Fred Essary of the *Baltimore Sun,* and Paul Y. Anderson of the *St. Louis Post-Dispatch*

11

were indeed "gentlemen of the press." Tailored suits, fedoras, canes, and calling cards were as much a part of their equipment as their notepads and typewriters. Under Harding, Coolidge, and Hoover, covering Washington was genteel, collegial, unhurried, and formal. Between press and politician there was an unspoken trust. The federal government was small; press credentials and security clearances were unheard of; members of Congress, cabinet secretaries, even presidents were available and often without appointment; the city and its government could be covered with a two-man bureau, three at most.

Then in 1933 came Roosevelt and radio coverage of the White House. Life in Washington was never the same. Almost overnight the capital became one of the world's most important datelines. The city finally had a real newsmaker — fireside chats, two presidential press conferences a week, five or six stories every day, four times the traffic on the wire services. The old formalities broke down. Gone was the requirement that questions for the president had to be written and submitted in advance. This president knew everyone's first name. With Roosevelt's informalities came the intimacy and immediacy of radio, and with radio

12

came White House radio reporters. They were unlike the newspapermen. They were not ink-stained wretches: they did not write; they talked. Men like Robert Trout, John Charles Daly, and Carleton Smith were more announcer than reporter, ad-libbing some but mainly putting the president on and off the air. The press boys said they were actors, a different breed. They did not play poker because, said Walter Trohan of the *Chicago Tribune,* they were out in the woods brushing up on their Shakespeare.

How galling it was for the press when FDR's press secretary moved the newspaper reporters from their privileged second car in the presidential motorcade to the third car. In their place went the radio men, because radio had more listeners than the *New York Times* had readers.[1] It was hard to argue with the numbers: 25 million radios and an audience of 64 million.

In 1933 there were three evening news broadcasts: at 6:45 on NBC, Lowell Thomas, former professor of oratory, editor, and globetrotter; at 7:15 on the Mutual Broadcasting System, Gabriel "Ah, There's Good News Tonight" Heatter; at 7:45 on CBS, Boake Carter, British-born poseur and Anthony Eden look-alike, whom FDR grew to despise.[2] Unlike the mellow-voiced

White House announcers, many of the radio commentators of the 1930s were ex-newspaper reporters or columnists. Gabriel Heatter began on the *New York Evening Journal;* Walter Winchell — "Good Evening, Mr. and Mrs. North America and all the ships at sea" — was a gossip columnist for the *New York Daily Mirror;* Fulton Lewis Jr., with his nightly anti-New Deal rant on Mutual, was the former city editor of the *Washington Herald;* Floyd Gibbons, with his machine-gun delivery on CBS, was an heroic foreign correspondent for the *Chicago Tribune;* and Drew Pearson, with his "Predictions of Things to Come," started as the Washington bureau chief of the *Baltimore Sun.* They all had a gimmick or a catchy phrase to set them apart. H. R. Baukhage of ABC began with a growled "Baukhage Talking." Earl Godwin of NBC closed his broadcast with "God bless you, one and all." Norman Brokenshire on CBS opened with "How do you do, ladies and gentlemen?" But when he heard that other announcers were using the line, he added a second "How DO you do?"

On March 13, 1938, the gimmickry and flummery of radio news ended with the birth of the news roundup concept on CBS. It had been spliced together in a crisis —

Hitler's seizure of Austria. That night the American radio audience heard Robert Trout anchoring from New York, calling in Edward R. Murrow from Vienna, William L. Shirer from London, Edgar Ansel Mowrer from Paris, Pierre Huss from Berlin, and Frank Gervasi from Rome. Only Murrow and Shirer were CBS employees. The others — newspaper and wire-service men — had been pressed into service.[3] The news roundup was extraordinary — journalists, without a single "How do you do" or "God bless," reporting live on what they were seeing and learning. Despite the crackling wireless radio connections from Europe, what came through was extraordinary. The country had never heard anything like it. These were not radio showmen with their "Ah, there's good news tonight" rigamarole; they were serious, believable observers of a Europe about to descend into chaos.

As Europe descended, Americans sat by their radios mesmerized, listening to a group of men Murrow hired who could do it all — write, report, and broadcast: Bill Shirer, Eric Sevareid, Larry LeSueur, Charles Collingwood, Winston Burdett, Bill Downs, Richard C. Hottelet, and Howard K. Smith. They were the foundation blocks of what became known as The House of

Murrow, broadcasting's most respected news organization. They came home after the war as celebrities, as men of authority like Shirer, men of bravery like LeSueur and Hottelet, and men of such unbelievable good looks, like Murrow, Sevareid, Collingwood, and Smith, that they were wrapped in glamour.

They came home, however, to hear the rumblings of what eventually became an upheaval in their world of journalism brought on by television. Television news was being created day by day. It had no rules on the use of pictures, on the dangers of visual exaggeration, on its showbiz tendencies. Radio it was not. TV was a toy and Murrow's Boys were not sure they wanted to play. But Murrow realized the awesome power of the tube and in 1951 he joined with Fred Friendly to produce the great documentary series of *See It Now,* followed in 1959 by *CBS Reports.* With William S. Paley's glittering entertainment schedule on CBS — Ed Sullivan, Arthur Godfrey, Jackie Gleason, and Lucille Ball — and with David Sarnoff's landmark shows on NBC like *Today, Tonight,* and *Your Show of Shows,* the 1950s became the Golden Age of Television. But they were not the Golden Age of Television News — not even with Murrow's groundbreaking documentary work.

The first regular Monday-to-Friday CBS evening news broadcast, started in 1948, was fifteen minutes long and carried in only four cities: New York, Boston, Philadelphia, and Washington, D.C. The anchorman, Douglas Edwards, unsure about a future in TV, had to be coaxed away from radio. To watch a kinescope of those early shows is to laugh out loud: no news film, no cameras crews, no interviews, no field correspondents, perhaps a map or two and some still photographs, and that was about all.

Technology improved through the 1950s, of course, but not until 1963, when the *CBS Evening News with Walter Cronkite* expanded to thirty minutes, did the Golden Age of Television News really begin. For the next twenty years, CBS News set a standard for thoroughness, balance, credibility, commitment, and journalistic skill that has not been equaled.

At the heart of the CBS News operation was its Washington bureau — a proud, competitive, and talented cadre of reporters, correspondents, producers, editors, and executives who so dominated the network's news division that it became almost an independent duchy.

This is a memoir, but it is mostly the story

of the men and women of the great CBS Washington bureau. For more than two decades, as they will still tell you, it was the place to be.

CHAPTER 1
THE GLORY YEARS

The story was on every newscast and front page in the country; thousands of editorial writers and columnists weighed in over Valentine's Day weekend, 1980.

The story was that Dan Rather and not I would succeed Walter Cronkite — not necessarily as the most trusted man in America, but at least as the appointed leader of the finest television news organization in America.

Bill Leonard, the president of CBS News, urged me to stay, promising first refusal on stories, documentaries, specials, election-night coanchoring, and freedom to teach one day a week. I knew I could not stay. On November 7, 1980, I went to work for NBC. After twenty years of beating the stuffing out of what we sneeringly called the National Biscuit Company, it felt strange just saying, "Roger Mudd, NBC News, Washington." I hoped I hadn't made a mistake, but I wasn't sure.

Decades later, total strangers still tell me it was CBS that made the mistake, in picking Dan Rather. But in my heart of hearts, I remain glad they did, given what was about to happen to TV news in general and to CBS News in particular in the 1980s — the encroachment of entertainment values, the firings, and the budget cuts, the sappy definition of news as "moments," the greedy takeover by Larry Tisch, the crushed and brokenhearted staff.

My life at CBS News, which began on May 31, 1961, ended on November 6, 1980 — that is, my last paycheck was dated November 6.

During those nineteen years, five months, and seven days at CBS News, working in its Washington bureau was the central experience of my professional life. There was no news bureau like it anywhere in television or, with two or three exceptions, in print. Of the hundred or so reporters and producers who worked in the bureau during those two decades, almost all of us were college graduates. Three or four went to the Ivy schools, a few more to other private colleges, but most attended the big public universities — Illinois, Indiana, Michigan State, Missouri, Wisconsin, Massachusetts,

City College of New York, and Rutgers. We were the sons and daughters of bakers, electrical engineers, ditch diggers, mapmakers, roofers, preachers, maids, architects, house painters, professors, coal miners, mill workers, deli owners, nurses, salesmen, bankers, and manufacturers. Only two were from wealthy parents.

Very few of us had wandered into journalism. Most of us aimed directly at it. Several dozen of us were delayed getting started by military service. But once started — as many started on newspapers as on radio or television — we became better broadcasters, better writers, better investigators, better editors than scores of our colleagues still languishing at the local stations and newspapers.

Being assigned to the Washington bureau was never automatic; it meant that you either were of top network quality or showed signs of it. We all felt privileged and lucky to be in the bureau, but each of us knew that, given the competition within and without, we wouldn't stay long if we didn't measure up. This was no hiding place or dumping grounds for losers.

Once in the bureau, though, believing we were the best, we tended to swagger; we were aggressive; we out-covered, out-wrote,

21

and out-filmed our competition. We laughed at the gentlemanly, pipe-smoking NBC bureau, which sniffed at our hard-charging ways. They claimed their follow-up stories were superior to our breaking stories — not much of a claim if you're in the news business. We were quietly proud of each other's work, although compliments were rare, egos and vanity being obstacles.

As a rule, we didn't give out compliments except when new reporters made their debut on the Cronkite show. We would gather around the big monitor in the newsroom to watch and to give the rookie a welcoming round of applause. The camaraderie was rough-and-tumble but genuine. Bob Schieffer felt he wasn't part of the bureau until the night we all hooted at him for pronouncing it "tenderhooks" instead of "tenterhooks."

The stories the bureau was witness to and got to cover enabled us to nearly monopolize the output of CBS News for twenty years — our dawn-to-dusk coverage of the great March on Washington in 1963; our superlative work during the funeral of John F. Kennedy; the Senate's civil rights filibuster in 1964; the civil rights movement and Washington's response to it; the impact on the government of the Vietnam War and the rising protests against it; the unequaled reporting of the bureau during the Watergate scandal; the last, bitter days of Richard Nixon's presidency and the rise of the unelected Gerald Ford; the arrival and quick departure of Jimmy Carter; and, in between, five presidential campaigns. That twenty-year stretch was unlike any in our history for the changes it wrought, its political upheavals, the growing distrust of government it produced, and the sheer excitement it generated.

What I've set out is not a retelling of those events but an account of the men and women who covered them and how they covered them under enormous pressures — not only from their own standards of journalism, but also from a hostile White House, an ill-tempered Congress, and a politically jumpy corporate headquarters in New York.

Coupled with such great stories was the ascendancy of television news and Washington's fitful attempts to accommodate it. The federal government for years had been geared to newspaper deadlines — ten or eleven o'clock at night. But TV forced the White House to change its clocks and readjust its rhythm. The TV deadlines of 6 and 6:30 PM meant the administration had to deal with TV first — to reschedule its briefings and its press releases. And once the White House set its clock to the TV clock, the rest of the government had to follow. For the newspapers, it meant no longer being first; for television it meant being able to bring an entire government to a halt each night to watch the tube.

We knew that the White House and the Hill and the agencies were all tuned to the three network news shows, but we also knew they were watching CBS the most closely.

For me and the hundreds of others in the Washington bureau, those twenty years were the glory years of television news.

CHAPTER 2
GIMME REWRITE

My adventure into journalism began in the spring of 1953 on the rewrite desk of the *Richmond* (Virginia) *News Leader,* where I was hired as a temporary replacement for a woman on maternity leave. I had applied at the paper not so much to become a journalist as to learn about journalism. My advisers at the University of North Carolina, where I had gotten my master's degree in history, had encouraged me to keep working toward a Ph.D.; but since the subject of my graduate research was the relationship of the press with Franklin D. Roosevelt's New Deal, a period of newspapering seemed to make the most sense. A year or two as a reporter certainly wouldn't hurt if indeed I returned to graduate school; and if I didn't, then journalism might be a good fit.

Peyton Winfree, the editor of the *Lynchburg News,* said he would take me on as a cub reporter at forty-five dollars a week.

Charles Rowe, editor of the Fredericks-
burg *Free Lance-Star,* offered me a job as
sports editor, but he admitted that sports
was more or less a blind alley.

Charles Hamilton, the managing editor of
the *News Leader,* said he would hire me as
a summer replacement. Fifty-two dollars a
week, he said, with a chance of being kept
on after September.

I took the job and started work on June
15, 1953. Douglas Southall Freeman, the
vaunted editor of the *News Leader* and
biographer of Robert E. Lee, had died the
day before I started and was succeeded by
the *enfant terrible* of Virginia journalism,
James Jackson "Kilpo" Kilpatrick.

At first my main job was to rewrite hand-
outs from Kiwanis, Rotary, Knights of
Columbus, and the local department stores.
This was one of my earliest efforts:

SALVATION ARMY WANTS MAT-
TRESSES

The Salvation Army has announced that
mattresses of all sizes and infants' cloth-
ing are in heavy demand at its industrial
center. Women having layettes to donate
are asked to call the Army immediately.

As I slowly got the hang of things, the city desk gave me a telephone headset and occasionally let me take dictation from the paper's beat reporters, who called in from the Hustings Court, the police court, city hall, or the state capitol. Because the *News Leader* was an evening paper and always approaching a deadline — the Blue Streak, the home edition, the makeover, and the final — some reporters who hadn't the time to polish their stories told me to "fix 'em." Little did they know what a slow fixer I was. I had no idea what I was doing. My typing skills were nonexistent; I had to ask everyone to slow down; I could feel an editor standing at my shoulder watching me botch one story after another.

The *News Leader* was trying very hard to keep its reputation as a statewide paper with a network of stringers all over the state. They were called "stringers" because they worked part-time for a string of other papers, dailies and weeklies. We had stringers in Massaponax, Short Pump, Petersburg, Cuckoo, and Gum Springs, and we had Isabel Gough in Ditchley.

Ditchley was barely a village in Northumberland County on Virginia's Northern Neck, and Isabel covered it like the dew. No women's club meeting or board of supervisors' vote or county agent's report was beyond her reach. That summer I learned more — about Reedville and menhaden, about Heathsville and oysters — listening to Isabel on my headset than had I been on the Northern Neck itself. Nobody on the rewrite desk knew exactly where Ditchley was, but if you had read the *News Leader* back then and seen the space the state editor gave Isabel's stuff, you would have thought Ditchley was a major East Coast urban center.

I thought I could cope with most southern accents, but the stringers from Southside, Virginia, threw me. One stringer phoned in an obituary from Emporia with a list of survivors, including the "Miseries" Edith Perkins, Gloria Bagwell, and Clarissa Muse. I didn't know what to think about the word "miseries." Maybe it meant they were into heavy grieving. Too embarrassed to ask the stringer to spell it, I turned in my copy, "Miseries" and all.

Dick Payne, the assistant city editor, took one look at it and started laughing. "That's the way they pronounce 'Mrs.' down in Hopewell," he said

Whoops! But I was learning. On my first day, I had been issued a style book that instructed reporters never to hyphenate the

News Leader, never to use the word "contact" to describe the process of getting in touch with someone, and never to refer to a black minister as "The Reverend," which was a title reserved for whites. A black minister got only a plain "Reverend" in the *News Leader.* And I learned that the *Times-Dispatch* — like the *News Leader,* owned by the Bryan family of Richmond for four generations — was known to the *Leader* people as the *Times-Disgrace.*

The copy desk was run by Mr. Fitzgerald (no one ever called him anything but "Mr. Fitz") — a slender, courtly southerner who always wore a white shirt to work. After my first month on the rewrite, he paid me a major compliment. He said I was the only reporter he had ever seen who knew that "not only" had to be followed by "but also."

Charles Hamilton, the managing editor, spent most of the day in his glass-walled office in the southeast corner of the newsroom on Fourth Street. He was the one who hired me, but he rarely spoke to me after that.

The city editor was John Leard, who was very quick, very efficient, at times inscrutable, but always helpful. I missed a deadline one morning, and after watching me struggle for thirty minutes and turn in my copy an hour late, he said, "Next time, try a martini first."

Several times a week, Mr. Leard would give me a feature assignment, which got me out of the office, or a chance to work the phones on something other than "The West End Men's Club will hold its monthly meeting. . . ."

The first story of my own ran on June 19. It was about a seventy-nine-year-old man who had been Richmond's director of public utilities during the Depression and had recently ridden his bicycle from Washington, D.C., to Ithaca, New York, for a Cornell reunion. It was not exactly what editors today would call a "holy shit" story, but much to the amusement of the city room it locked me in as the *News Leader*'s bike specialist. For the next three months, anything with the flimsiest connection to bikes landed on my desk.

I became such a total bike specialist that the desk rewarded me with my first byline.

"BIKE TRIP TO FLORIDA," the June 20 headline read, "by ROGER MUDD."

The story was about two teenaged Richmond boys who were biking to Florida. The lead sentence read, "They crossed Lee Bridge at 7:15 AM today." The desk taught us to keep our leads short and snappy. James Thurber, when he was a police reporter, once wrote: "Dead. That's what the man was police found yesterday. . . ."

But for me the story was *my* byline. To read for the first time your own name in boldface caps is to know euphoria firsthand. It was an announcement to the 125,000 readers of the *News Leader* that Roger Mudd existed. It was an acknowledgment by the editorial superstructure that you were professionally competent, that your hard work deserved public notice, and that, as low as the pay was, there were other forms of compensation.

Through the summer of 1953 I happily came to work at 7 AM and churned out feature stories about the collector of Civil War ordnance who hated his collection, about a bullfrog that was keeping the 200 block of West Thirty-Fourth Street awake, about Mary Lyle's hundredth birthday, about the effect of the Korean War on the local scrap-metal market, and, finally, my great triumph about the repercussions in Richmond of the Mau Mau revolt in East Africa.

On an evening paper, everything had to have a local angle, and this was the local angle: Calabar bass fiber, extracted from the palm trees in the Calabar region of Nigeria, was used to make the stiff push brooms for sweeping streets. The Mau Mau revolt had cut off the world's supply of the black fiber. Henry A. Brizzolara, the owner of the Old Dominion Brush Company, which produced the six gross of brooms the city of Richmond used each year, told me he had only a small quantity on hand and his Vermont supplier was about to run out.

"REVOLT BRUSHES CITY," read the tantalizing page one headline.

My lead sentence read, "Unless the revolting Mau Mau of British East Africa calm down soon, the cleanliness of Richmond's streets might suffer."

The Mau Mau story was a true exclusive, and the *Times-Disgrace* had to rewrite me. So talked-about was my broom story that every week through the summer the desk would send the clip back to me with the note: "Pls. update." Two of the office wits had made for my desk a small sign that read: "*News Leader* Mau-Mau Editor."

Each Tuesday I would call the brush company and check on Mr. Brizzolara and his brooms. When I called on a Tuesday in September, the secretary said, "Oh, Mr. Mudd. I'm so sorry. Mr. Brizzolara died over the weekend." I expressed my condolences to the secretary and sent the desk a note: "Broom source dead. What next?"

The desk replied: "Have you thought about an obit?" Duh.

Living in Richmond in the early 1950s was easy. I took the bus to work and was able to save about ten dollars a week from my paycheck. Like most bachelors, I lived around, sharing apartments in the city's West End, on the Northside, on Baltimore Row in the historic part of town, and finally in a row house that is now part of the Virginia Commonwealth University. The city was highly stratified socially, but the young newspapermen and -women, some married but most single, were able to create their own separate society of picnics, pasta-and-salad dinners, and softball games. There was a certain pleasure, if not pride, in being outside Richmond's inner circles. After all, we believed, as journalists, we were supposed to stand on the curb and watch the parade go by, not march in it.

Charlie McDowell, a Washington and Lee University classmate, and an established byline reporter on the *Times-Dispatch*, lived in downtown Richmond on Franklin Street in one of those English basement flats. He and his wife, Annie, watched out for and took good care of young rewrite men.

Soon after Labor Day, Mr. Hamilton let

me know that the reporter would be returning from maternity leave and that he would
not keep me on. It came as no surprise.
Though my typing had improved, my writing speed had not. Charlie McDowell has
kindly insisted over the years that my happy
life at the *News Leader* was not brief because
I didn't know how to write but because my
fingers were too big to fit the keys.

Mr. Hamilton said he would gladly recom-
mend me elsewhere if I wanted to stay in
newspapering. His telephone call generated
an offer to work on the *Virginian Pilot,* in
Norfolk, at sixty dollars a week. Before I
could say "yes" or "no" to the *Pilot,* Mr.
Hamilton told me that WRNL, the
company-owned radio station right across
the street, was looking for a full-time news
director. It wasn't that I was dying to get
into radio; it was that I didn't want to leave
Richmond. So I applied to WRNL (the call
letters stood for *Richmond News Leader*),
took an audition, and was hired at sixty-five
dollars a week.

CHAPTER 3
PIPE POEUS

Getting started at the radio station was rocky at first; in fact, it was a disaster.

I was twenty-five years old. Even though I had no experience and very little preparation, I was assigned to do the noon broadcast. On my first day, everything was moving along reasonably well until I hit an item from Rome about the declining health of Pope Pius XII and the Swiss doctors who had been called in.

To my horror, I heard myself saying, "The condition of Pipe Poeus has grown steadily worse and they have summoned to the Vatican bedside the Pipe's doctor and two Swish spesulists."

I burst into laughter and lunged for the cough-box, the little gizmo on my desk designed to kill the microphone for a cough or a throat clearing. Of course, I had never used the box before. Hitting what I thought was the cut-off switch, I kept laughing. What the audience heard for the next few minutes, however, were brief bursts of insane laughter followed by ten and fifteen seconds of dead air. I had hit the wrong switch. Not until a frantic engineer took the controls away from me did *The News at Noon* get back on track.

I was not fired. I was not even reprimanded, but probably would have been had Richmond's radio-listening Catholic population been any larger.

It seems funny now. Back then it was a disaster.

Coming from the newspaper, I thought I knew what news was and what news wasn't, but because I had no editor at my shoulder to help me I had to work very hard to master the basics of Richmond's politics, neighborhoods, organizations, folklore, and *patois.*

I used my days off to learn where the seven hills of Richmond were and why the statue of General A. P. Hill wasn't on a horse (his Civil War veterans couldn't raise the money) and how to pronounce all those new and mysterious Virginia names: Poquoson and Taliaferro and Smythe and Wythe and Fauquier and Loudoun and Henrico and Toano and Mattaponi.

I learned that "The River" was not the Cowpasture but the James, that "The Club" was not Kiwanis but the Country Club of Virginia, and that "The University" was not my university — Washington and Lee — but the University of Virginia.

Above all — especially because I was interested in politics — I learned about the Byrds and their oligarchic machine, which had dominated state politics since the '20s. Unless you've lived in Virginia or have run for office or covered those who have, it's hard to imagine what it must have been like running against a Byrd. Not only would your opponent be named Byrd or be married to a Byrd or be a Byrd "lieutenant," which is what the Richmond newspapers politely called a member of the Byrd "organization," which is what the papers politely called the Byrd machine, but also there was the Byrd airport and the Harry Flood Byrd Highway and Byrd Park and the Byrd Theater and Byrd High School and Byrd apples and Byrd Apple Juice.

The management at the station gave me a week to learn the system — how to keep up to date using the Associated Press wire machine, how to clear the machine and put the latest national copy on the national hook and the local copy on the local hook, how to put a newscast together, how to operate a stopwatch, how to gauge your reading speed, how to back-time yourself so you would not have to rush your final story. Because the station was also owned by the Bryan family, management arranged to have the *Times-Dispatch (T-D)* supply WRNL with carbon copies of the stories it would be running in the morning. Late each afternoon, I would cross the street to pick the *T-D's* "dupes," as they were called. It gave us a distinct edge over the other four stations in town. I wasn't calling it the *Times-Disgrace* any longer.

The first week at WRNL I witnessed a brief drama that a newspaper reporter could rarely match. Al Reynolds, the staff announcer, was explaining the routine to me when he heard five bells ringing on the Associated Press news wire. Five bells is an alert: Stand by, a bulletin is coming. The instant the bulletin cleared, Al ripped it off and bolted across the hall and into the studio. He signaled the engineer to open his mike. Al began:

We interrupt this program to bring you the following bulletin from the Associated Press. A federal grand jury today indicted Princess Anne County Treasurer Sidney Kellam on five counts of income tax evasion. Details will follow on the next regular newscast.

For Virginians, this was a major political story. Sidney Kellam was no small fish. He was a power in the Byrd machine, controlling money and patronage in Virginia Beach and Princess Anne County. He, his brothers, and his family owned banks, motels, and real estate. The new federal district attorney, brought in by the Eisenhower Republicans, was out to bring him down.

In that brief instant, Al Reynolds, with the help of the AP, had not only broken a important story but also had instantaneously informed thousands of listeners and had beaten the competition by four minutes.

Seeing the look on Al Reynolds's face when he came out of the studio, I thought my new job could be fun.

When the announcers put together their own newscasts, I noticed they rarely did any writing. They just ripped and read. The AP made it easy for the stations by tailoring copy for a fifteen-minute roundup, complete with national, international, state, and local news. Except in the big cities, very few radio stations back then had their own professional news operation. Thanks to the AP and the United Press, radio news sounded the same all over much of the country.

WRNL had hired me to try something different. They gave me a large but portable battery-driven tape recorder and told me to get out of the office and use it. They also gave me my own ten-minute broadcast called *Virginia Headlines* each evening at 7:05. Off I went, the minute I finished doing the noon newscast, lugging my tape recorder to the state legislature, to the Hotel Jefferson to cover luncheon speeches, to the mayor's office, to the city council chambers, to the city manager's office, asking questions and recording the answers. Richmond's city manager at the time was Horace Edwards, who was well-spoken and always welcomed me. He pronounced helicopter as "hellacopatur" and arthritis as "arthur-ritis."

By five or six o'clock I was back at the station with my tapes, and for the next hour I edited and then transferred them to a big disc so an engineer could play each cut in the order I wanted, almost as a disc jockey would spin his records.

Very few Virginia politicians had ever dealt with reporters who carried tape recorders. Being recorded was new and anything new in Virginia arouses suspicions. So they were suspicious. They didn't know me and were nervous about what I would do with their words. The lieutenant governor of Virginia, A. E. S. Stephens, who presided over the state senate, summoned me to his office one morning and said "some of the members" wanted some assurance I was not distorting their speeches. I knew who "some of the members" were. He was Senator Harry F. Byrd Jr., himself the publisher of the *Winchester Star* and a director of the AP. Stephens thought it might be a good idea if he could hear my program before it was broadcast. I was outraged and told him so. I told him to tell "some of the members" to tune in to 910 on their AM dial each night at 7:05 and hear for themselves whether they were being distorted. Stephens never mentioned the subject to me again.

It took time, but the politicians learned to trust me and WRNL. Before long they were falling over one another to get on what they called my "little gray box."

Not every state agency was as happy to see me as the general assembly or the city council. The State Milk Commission refused to let me record its public hearing because I could not fit the entire six hours of testimony into my ten-minute broadcast and because my tape recorder would destroy what the chairman called the "dignity" of

41

the hearings. Guy Friddell, one of the editorial writers for the *News Leader,* heard about the contretemps and attacked the Milk Commission's decision in an editorial titled "The Right to Hear."

A month later the Milk Commission again tried to shut me down. When I refused to unplug the recorder and leave, the chairman declared a recess and left the hearing room to seek an opinion from Virginia's attorney general, Lindsay Almond. Almond later told me that his ruling, based on what he described as "a thousand years of Anglo-Saxon law," was: "Leave that boy alone."

In the wake of the U.S. Supreme Court's school desegregation opinion, Virginia's Commission on Public Education held a series of public hearings around the state. The first was to be held in Richmond on November 15, 1954. When the commission chairman, State Senator Garland Gray, announced that radio would not be admitted, I sent him a two-page memorandum of objection. The commission was not persuaded and again voted against radio, twenty to seven.

On the morning of the hearing, I hooked up my machine anyway. Senator Gray ordered me to unplug. I refused. He called a conference with his commissioners. Four minutes before the hearing was to open they reversed themselves and allowed us to record the proceedings.

I say "us," but there wasn't any "us" to it. Not a single one of my competitors — and there must have been half a dozen stations there — had said a peep about the ban or had helped to reverse it.

WRNL was an ABC affiliate in the 1950s. We had Paul Harvey each day at one o'clock in the afternoon and we had Walter Winchell on Sunday night. I came on between George Hicks at 6:45 and Bill Stern at 7:15 during the week. Richmond was still very much a radio town, with only one television station and not a very good one at that. *Virginia Headlines* was attracting a devoted audience.

One of my regular listeners was the wife of the governor, Tom Stanley. Her husband, never a particularly strong leader, had been caught in the school desegregation vise between the Supreme Court and the Commonwealth of Virginia. One evening after I had devoted most of my broadcast to the governor's predicament, the newsroom phone rang.

"Newsroom," I said.

"Mr. Mudd?" inquired the soft southern voice.

"Yes."

"This is Mrs. Tom Stanley."

The way she pronounced "Mudd" warned me she was not calling to compliment. She gave my name at least six "u's," as in "Muu-uuuudd." At about the fifth "u" Mrs. Stanley's voice went into a lower register, indicating that both my reporting and my name were basically flawed. Her complaint was vague, more about my tone than my facts. But in the end Mrs. Stanley seemed pleased when I told her she was the first governor's wife ever to call WRNL and that in itself was an honor.

"Well, thank you, Mr. Muuudd," she said, using three fewer "u's."

I was regularly out-reporting and out-hustling my main competitor, WRVA, which grandly regarded itself as the "Voice of Virginia." For the next three years, I won first place for state and local news in the annual Virginia Associated Press awards contest. In 1955, I won the first Douglas Southall Freeman Award for Public Service for a two-week series I did on the confusing and overlapping court system in Richmond.

From my series on the courts, I got interested enough in the law to enroll in the law school at the University of Richmond in the fall of 1954, taking civil procedure and torts. But it was hard, working full-time and then briefing cases until midnight and preparing for classes at 8 AM. I finished the semester but did not come back.

So life was full. After work I auditioned for a role in Robert Sherwood's play *The Petrified Forest* at the Virginia Museum Theatre. I was cast as the gangster, Duke Mantee, the role that Humphrey Bogart had played on Broadway. A week or two before, covering a big jail break at the state prison in Richmond, I made friends with the superintendent, Frank Smith. When he read about my role in the paper, he volunteered to equip me and my gang of hoodlums with three Thompson submachine guns, three Winchester riot guns, five .38-caliber revolvers, and a sawed-off shotgun, all on loan from the state police. Smith also supplied me with a prison shirt stamped with the serial number of an inmate he described as a killer and the "finest switch-blade artist in the business." Our reviews were consistently good, although I detected that the reviewers seemed more impressed by our arsenal than by our acting.

After three years in Richmond I had developed a strong reputation as an honest reporter and a talented broadcaster. I thought I had learned everything I could in Richmond, and I was itching to move on and up. A CBS news producer, David Lowe, in Richmond for a documentary on school desegregation, seemed impressed with my work and suggested I apply at CBS in New York. I actually got as far as an interview with Larry LeSueur, one of the original Ed Murrow Boys. He looked over my resumé, listened to me quietly, and suggested in so many words that I should go back to Richmond.

I went back, but not for long.

CHAPTER 4
HOME TO STAY

I had just been hired at ninety-five dollars a week by WTOP, the CBS affiliate in Washington, D.C., and my new boss, Ed Ryan, was walking me to the front door.

"Have you ever had any problems with your name?"

He asked so quietly that I barely heard him.

"I beg your pardon," I said. I knew what he'd said and I knew what he was thinking. He was thinking that I might need an "air" name, something smooth like Roger Morgan or Roger Massey.

He repeated the question.

"Just wondering if your name gave you any problems."

"Problems? What do you mean, problems? What kind of problems? I've never had any problems."

His face turned red and he started coughing. The subject never came up again, not then and not to this day.

Ed Ryan was a distinguished former correspondent for the *Washington Post,* and his sharpest skills were in reporting, not in personnel.

The *Post*'s publisher, Philip Graham, had picked Ed to run the news department at WTOP, which the *Post* had just bought from CBS. During the change of ownership, Edward R. Murrow hired Paul Niven away from the WTOP staff to work on his new series, *See It Now.* It was Niven's seat I was hired to fill, starting May 21, 1956. I said goodbye to Richmond, piled all my stuff in the 1947 Chevrolet I had bought for $475, and moved back to Washington, my hometown.

Richmond had put her mark on me: she had introduced me to one of America's great political museum pieces — the Byrd Machine; had taught me the basics of the politics of race; had given me a taste of southern civility; and had shown me first-hand the genius, the humor, and the greed of our political system.

But I was thankful to be back home. Nobody is supposed to have actually been born in Washington, D.C., but I was, in 1928. Nobody is supposed to have been raised there either, but I was. In fact, I've never left since 1956 and have never really wanted to. If you loved politics and the reporting of politics as I came to love them, Washington demanded that you stay.

No one ever being born and raised in Washington is a myth believed mostly by people far beyond the city who read their papers and watch their television and assume the place is inhabited only by presidents and politicians who come and go every two, four, or six years, by foreign diplomats who come to Washington as their last crowning assignment before retirement, and by admirals and generals who arrive only toward the end of their careers.

The local press, particularly the *Washington Post* and the late lamented *Evening Star,* reinforced the myth because their coverage tended to concentrate on the city's transient social and power elite. But when Washington became a predominantly black city, the *Post* — prodded by black protests against its earlier noncoverage — tried to compensate.

There are thousands of us — mainly white — who have never known another hometown, who didn't migrate from the South or the Midwest during World War II, but who are rarely written about in the local papers and who rarely exist on television.

I don't mean the so-called cave dwellers,

the doyennes and seigneurs of Kalorama and Georgetown, or the wealthy widows of Foxhall who worship the memory of Alice Roosevelt Longworth. I mean the sons and daughters of middle-class parents who came to Washington between the Civil War and World War I mainly to work for the expanding federal government. Reunions of my high school class of more than sixty years ago continue to draw more than a hundred men and women born and raised in Washington who have stayed and whose children have stayed.

My father, John Kostka Dominic Mudd, born in 1890 in rural southern Maryland, thirty miles south of Washington, was the son of a tobacco farmer. He graduated from the University of Maryland with a degree in civil engineering and in 1914 went to work in Washington, D.C., for the Interior Department's U.S. Geological Survey as a topographic engineer — a mapmaker.

My mother, Irma Iris Harrison, born in Colfax, Washington, the daughter of a wheat farmer, came east after graduating from Washington State College to join the Army Nursing Corps as a lieutenant in 1916. At Walter Reed Hospital in Washington, she was assigned to the physiotherapy ward, where she met my father, by then an artillery officer wounded in France.

They were married in San Francisco in 1920 and spent the next three years in Hawaii, where my father ran the federal government's first topographic mapping of the Hawaiian Islands. With their baby, John Harrison, they returned to Washington in 1924. I was born there four years later and it is there that four generations of this particular branch of the Mudd family have remained.

So I was glad to be home.

My first assignment at WTOP put me on the early shift — the 6 AM radio newscast and the local news inserts on an ill-fated morning TV show called *Potomac Panorama*. During the day, I would be out on the street with a camera crew, filming stories for the evening news or features for the next day's *Panorama*. My assignments got steadily better. In the fall of 1956 I started doing the 6 PM radio newscast — a fifteen-minute broadcast that I wrote from beginning to end, plus a weekly feature about anything that struck my fancy. It gave me the chance to develop my own style, freed from the constraints of the wire service vocabulary.

The next summer I wrote, produced, and narrated a thirty-minute television documentary on the need for a third airport for the Washington-Baltimore area. In September I suffered through my first live television studio interview. It was with Dorothy Counts, a fifteen-year-old black girl who had been assigned to an all-white high school in Charlotte, North Carolina, but had withdrawn because of the continuing racial taunts and physical abuse. The transcript of the Counts interview reveals my first-time nervousness.

I would ask Dorothy a question, she would answer, and then, like an idiot, I would repeat her answer:

"What sort of grades did you have?"

"I had a B+ average."

"B+. . . . How far was Harding High from your home?"

"Two and a half blocks."

"Two and a half. . . . Where did you go last year?"

"Northwest Junior High."

"Northwest. . . . And what grade were you in?"

"I finished the ninth."

"The ninth. . . ." Etc., etc.

It must have driven the audience nuts. I can hear them now: "She just said that, dummy!" Obviously I was fencing for time. I knew her story, but the interview was arranged so hurriedly that Sunday morning that I had not had the time to sit down and think about the questions. The station brass loved it, mostly because an AP wire photograph showing me with Dorothy and crediting WTOP with the interview was transmitted all over the country. They said I was great, but I hated it because I looked unprepared. I made sure that was the last time it happened.

Despite my growing success in Washington, I suffered that first year from Richmond withdrawal pains. Perhaps once a month I would drive back to Richmond to see my old buddies.

On one of those weekends, a friend at WRNL arranged an introduction to E. J. Spears, who had recently started work as a copywriter at the station. When I tapped on her apartment door, I did not know what to expect. My friend had told me very little about her except that the E. J. stood for Emma Jeanne. What I got when she answered the tap was a smile and a handshake. But then I said something stupid, like, "Are your hands wet?" How was I to know it was hand cream? Nice move, Rog.

E. J. was gorgeous. She had grown up in Richmond, graduated from William and Mary, joined the Foreign Service, worked in the code room at the U.S. Embassy in Rome, learned to speak Italian fluently, translated for Errol Flynn's film company, knocked around Europe for a year or so, and returned to Richmond intellectually and philosophically transformed by the experience.

It was not love at first sight but it was close. During our whirlwind courtship I learned how perceptive, observant, happily opinionated, charitable, well read, and funny she was. She was also conservative. "Realistically" conservative, she would insist. I must have come across as some hoople-headed liberal, because on one of our early dates, she took off on Franklin D. Roosevelt and the woman she called "your" Mrs. Roosevelt. After waiting a discreet hour or two, I let E. J. know I had written my master's thesis on Roosevelt. All she could do was laugh.

We met in April. I proposed to her that summer during a weekend at the beach at Nag's Head, North Carolina. She said "yes" if I promised not to come home for lunch. I promised and we were married on October 26, 1957, at the Cathedral of the Sacred Heart, in Richmond. Daniel, the first of our four children, was born in August 1958, followed roughly every other year or so by Maria, Jonathan, and Matthew.

After our honeymoon in Bermuda, I returned to my regular schedule at WTOP, finishing the day with my six o'clock radio broadcast and getting home in time for dinner. "Home" then was a tidy, two-floored, two-bedroom apartment in Silver Spring, Maryland. It was the first of the four homes we had in the Maryland suburbs until we moved across the Potomac River into Virginia. The fifth home, called "Elmwood," which we bought in 1972, is a 102-year-old Queen Anne with open porches all around, looking down on ten acres. Our children's bedrooms have long been empty, of course, but we find ourselves unable to abandon a home that has occupied for more than thirty-five years a central part of our lives.

■ ■ ■ ■

Early in 1959, I began to pick up hints that the station had become professionally embarrassed by the continued use of a staff announcer to do the news on its main late-night broadcast. The announcer, Don Richards, was stunningly good-looking, had flawless diction, and did a first-rate job reading the news on the *The 11 PM Report*. So good that President Eisenhower once told the celebrated Washington lawyer Edward Bennett Williams during a White House dinner that his favorite TV journalist was Don Richards. Don had no journalistic credentials, even though Ike might have thought so, and that worried not only Ed Ryan but also the management at the *Post*.

In March, WTOP-TV announced that I would replace Don on *The 11 PM Report*. As proud as I was of my swift rise and the promotion, I scarcely recognized what was happening to me. At age thirty, after less than two years in Washington and five years as a broadcaster, I had become the anchor of the top-ranked news program in the capital city of the nation, a program seen not only by thousands of news-obsessed viewers but also by members of the Congress, the federal bureaucracy, the diplomatic corps, the cabinet, and, unless Ike had switched channels, the president of the United States. Like it or not, I was about to become a public figure.

My new assignment meant that I got home for dinner, all right, but now I had to return to the office at night, leaving my bride of five months alone. She never complained, but a life of solitary evenings could hardly have been what she envisioned when she made me promise not to come home for lunch.

The longtime sponsor of the late news was the Standard Oil Company, and Don Richards was called "Your Esso Reporter." It was a title I declined to accept. I thought it implied an editorial connection with Standard Oil that did not exist. With the help of Ed Ryan, we also got the sign reading "Your Esso Reporter" removed from the anchor desk. A few months later, the Justice Department brought an antitrust suit against Standard Oil. That night, I insisted on reporting the full details, which brought a quiet compliment from the show's director, Jim Silman. "Thank God," he told me, "you were on duty tonight." Esso never complained, at least not to me. The ratings grew stronger and stronger and night after night we beat the opposition — Richard Harkness on the NBC station and Joseph McCaffrey on the ABC station.

My work day started in early afternoon. Whatever my schedule, I had always made a point of covering President Eisenhower's press conferences, usually on Wednesday mornings at 10:30. They were held in what was called "The Indian Treaty Room" in the Executive Office Building, next to the White House. Other than those reserved for the three wire service and the three network reporters, there were no assigned seats, so the line down the long corridor outside the Treaty Room formed early. I would fall in behind some of the mythic figures of American journalism: May Craig of the *Portland (Maine) Press Herald,* Raymond "Pete" Brandt of the *St. Louis Post-Dispatch,* Bob Donovan of the *New York Herald Tribune,* Bill Knighton of the *Baltimore Sun,* Eddie Folliard of the *Washington Post,* and James "Scotty" Reston of the *New York Times.* Reston was so respected and so powerful in Washington that no president dared ignore a question from him.

One Wednesday morning a month or two after I started doing *The 11 PM Report,* I turned to look at Reston as he got in line for the press conference. He looked at me briefly and said, "Good Morning."

I damn near died.

Getting recognized by the president for a question was a new art form for journalists. Eisenhower was the first to have regularly scheduled press conferences and the first to allow film cameras to record them. To be seen on television all over the country made it professionally important for journalists to be called on. Reporters were required to give their name and their organization. Reston would say simply: "Reston of the *Times.*" But less well-known reporters from less well-known papers clamored to let the country know who they were and who sent them there.

"Mr. President," Pat Munroe would boom out, "Pat Munroe of the *Deseret Morning News.*"

Many of us were not quite sure where the *Deseret News* was but out in Salt Lake City the publisher of the "intermountain West's oldest daily paper" must have been delighted to hear Pat spreading the word.

The six wire service and network reporters were usually recognized, plus a few of the president's favorites. But for all the others it took an exquisite sense of timing to know when to leap up at the exact moment the president was finishing an answer.

Bob Clark, who finished his career with ABC News but was with International News Service back then, once asked President Eisenhower a two-part question. Ike's answer to the first part was so long that he asked Bob: "Now what was the second part?" Bob, who'd been standing the whole time, blinked once or twice and said: "I forgot."

John McKelway of the *Evening Star,* one of my college roommates, has recalled that he used to dream about getting recognized by the president. In his dream, John would stand, clear his throat, but then be hit with a mammoth brain freeze. Helpless to remember his question, he would wind up asking the president: "Do you know what time it is?"

Cameramen were not allowed to leave the platform risers in the back of the Treaty Room during a press conference. So to get closeups and cutaway shots the cameramen would shoot pictures of the early arrivals who would more or less pose for them. The most cooperative poser was a mysterious journalist named O. C. Miller, who was always the first in line to get his seat in the front row. Almost without fail, every film report on an Eisenhower press conference would include a cutaway of O. C. Miller feverishly taking make-believe notes. After several years of seeing O. C. on the tube writing his head off, a curious reporter got in line right behind O. C. one morning so he could sit nearby and find out what kind of notes the famous scribe was taking. He watched carefully while the cameras filmed O. C.'s act. His notes consisted of page after page of "o's" looped together.

The one question I got to ask President Eisenhower came at his press conference on March 13, 1957. The instant Ike finished answering Bob Donovan of the *Herald Tribune* about Queen Elizabeth's rumored trip to the United States, I hurled myself out of my chair and heard myself saying, "Mr. President, Roger Mudd, WTOP News." My question, parochial compared with all the portentous ones, was whether Ike intended to appoint Ted Dalton, the Republican National Committeeman from Virginia, to a new federal district court vacancy in Virginia. Dalton had run a creditable but losing race for governor in 1953 against the Byrd machine's candidate, Tom Stanley, and I figured the White House might want to reward him with a federal judgeship. So I asked my question. The president looked at me as if he'd seen me somewhere before but probably was still wondering whatever happened to Don Richards. His answer was brief. It was obvious he didn't know anything about a judgeship down in Virginia for somebody named Ted Dalton. I had come up empty-handed.

But WTOP and I were so proud to have been recognized by the president of the United States that the lead that night on *The 11 PM Report* was the Dalton judgeship nonstory, complete with my dinky question and Ike's nonanswer.

Two years later, however, Ted Dalton got his judgeship.

Nikita Khrushchev's 1959 tour of the United States was for me a rare opportunity to cover a major national story, competing against virtually every leading newspaper and broadcast group in the country. It would also be a high-wire test of my ability to write and report accurately and vividly on the run, without the benefit of wire copy, studio props, and newsroom personnel. I would truly be on my own, literally and figuratively. Satellite feeds, Minicams, laptops, and palm pilots were unheard of in 1959, so the system would be very basic: I would simply write on my portable Olivetti and report by telephone four times a day — for the 8 AM, noon, and 6 PM radio broadcasts and *The 11 PM Report* on television. To cover my recorded voice on the television, the director would use a still picture of me talking into a telephone or run silent film footage of Khrushchev from one of the newsreel services. It worked flawlessly once I got used to the changing time zones.

Guy Friddell, of the *Richmond News Leader,* who had more and tighter deadlines than I had, struggled as we moved from Washington, D.C., to New York, to Los Angeles, to Coon Rapids, Iowa, to Pittsburgh. To keep from blowing his deadlines, Friddell bought four cheap watches and set them an hour apart: Eastern and Central on the left wrist; Mountain and Pacific on the right. Because the *Leader* would not spring for an Olivetti, Friddell was issued a so-called "portable" typewriter so heavy we all figured the carrying case was made of mahogany. He would store his big box in the overhead racks on the planes and trains but was forever having to haul it down to write for his next deadline, which seemed always just minutes away. One afternoon, just as he was teetering on the armrest reaching up for his machine, the train hit a curve that brought the box crashing down on the head of Friddell's seatmate, a radio reporter from KMOX in St. Louis. Both of them missed their deadlines.

"There were no cheers, no boo's, no applause and no demonstrations for Nikita Khrushchev today," I wrote on September 15, the day Khrushchev landed in Washington, ". . . only thousands of silent Americans."

September 16: "Khrushchev performed at the National Press Club as the ultimate politician — a man who charmed, amused, angered, lectured, and evaded."

September 17: "New York's official welcome to Khrushchev was performed in a maelstrom, in the baggage room of Penn Station, a dark, subterranean hole, filled with exhaust fumes, shouting photographers, scurrying Secret Service agents, and nervous police."

September 20: "On the movie set of *Can-Can*, Khrushchev was treated or subjected to a Hollywood bottom-bosom spectacular . . . a wild, raucous, half-naked, leg-shaking nightmare that threw the State Department protocol men into a fit of anguish, despair, and shock."

September 21: "Khrushchev plunged up and down the hills of San Francisco today like a runaway cable car. . . . His security agents are limp, winded, and ragged."

September 23: "Soviet Premier Khrushchev more or less escaped from Iowa this evening. . . . When he arrived yesterday, the entire press corps of the United States, Europe, and the Orient sprang out at him behind the rows of tall corn. . . . The infighting that followed was fierce."

My Khrushchev assignment was Ed Ryan's idea, and he was proud of what we had done. He was beside himself when he heard that my radio reports on the six o'clock news were required listening in the State Department's Press Office.

When it was all over I felt I had held my own. In the piece I wrote on Khrushchev's jet flight from New York to Los Angeles, I described a solitary highway snaking its way across the Great Plains as "looking like a ribbon of white toothpaste." Harrison Salisbury of the *New York Times* used those very words in his story and I got accused of stealing them. Salisbury's story, however, ran the morning after my broadcast.

I had, I thought, been faithful to the essence of the story, that Americans found out Khrushchev was no buffoon and that he found out the American proletariat was not about to revolt. But I had also had fun with the story — the volcanic moods of Khrushchev; the baiting of him by the press; the embarrassing and uncontrolled behavior of the media; the chaos of the schedule; the arrogance of Roswell "Bob" Garst, the Iowa corn millionaire whose 5,000 acre farm Khruschev visited; the flattened and fraught State Department aides; and the pure pleasure of capturing all of that in my own words.

My early thoughts about returning to graduate school for a Ph.D. in history were fading fast. The Khrushchev trip reassured me that the road I was on was the right road.

It was a road that was leading straight to CBS News.

CHAPTER 5
YOU'LL BE LOCAL
THE REST OF YOUR
LIFE

The road from WTOP to CBS was actually a flight of stairs. When CBS sold WTOP to the *Washington Post* in 1955, it retained the office space on the second floor for its Washington bureau. Because reporters from the two news departments — CBS and WTOP — shared radio engineers and recording studios, the network's editors and correspondents became aware of my work on the third floor.

But the presence of such CBS luminaries as Wells Church, Larry LeSueur, Griffin Bancroft, Bill Downs, Lou Cioffi, Howard K. Smith, and Eric Sevareid made a network job seem like a pipe dream to me. Try as I might, there was no way, I thought, that I could crack that lineup.

Then a telephone call one night from Wells Church seemed to seal my fate. Church, known to all as "Ted" (his full name was Theodore Roosevelt Wells

Church), was the CBS Radio congressional correspondent. He was a squarely built, broad-shouldered man, one quarter Chippewa, with a fine head of white hair, a quick smile, and a taste for vodka. The phone on my desk rang just after I had finished doing the 6 o'clock news. It was Ted, and Ted was angry. What had angered him was a story I had not mentioned on the broadcast, a story I thought too minor to include. But the omission was obviously something Ted regarded as a major journalistic failure.

His message to me was clear: "If you pull another boner like that, you'll be local the rest of your life."

Never had I heard words like that directed at me. I had been a reporter for fewer than six years. My rise from the rewrite desk of the *News Leader* to the anchor chair of the capital's top-ranked TV news program had been swift, smooth, and marked by praise. I had become self-satisfied, perhaps, but now I was devastated. My mouth went dry. It was surely the end of a promising career. I lurched out of the office to meet my wife and two of her friends who were visiting from Rome. During dinner I sat mute, white in the face, forehead in panic-induced furrows, vainly trying to communicate my distress to E. J., who was clueless except for knowing her husband was acting like a big baby. The dinner ended in record time and the couple from Rome departed perplexed by E. J.'s decision to marry a full-fledged, card-carrying zombie.

I survived the crisis mainly because Ted Church never mentioned his complaint again, leading me to believe he had been drinking. The incident slowly receded in my memory and came to life only recently, when I woke up in the middle of the night remembering the name of the couple from Rome.

Yet I remained fearful that Ted might have passed on his comments. Apparently he did not, because the next call I got from CBS came one evening at home in early March 1961 from none other than the Washington bureau chief himself, Howard K. Smith. The "K" stood for Kingsbury, an initial he retained because it seemed to elevate him from all the plain Howard Smiths.

Would I be interested in working at CBS? *Would* I? Oh, my God, would I? I tried to keep my voice even and deep. I kept it neither. If it didn't squeak, it wobbled.

With a release from WTOP, preliminary discussions with Smith began the next day.

Smith was one of the few Murrow Boys who had made an easy transition from radio to television. After seventeen years abroad he had come home a superstar. By 1959 he was not only the chief Washington correspondent but also the Washington bureau chief.

Telephone calls from Howard K. were regularly placed by Howard's wife, Benedicte, who was also his de facto business agent, handling everything — his network contract, his assignments, his speeches, his vacations, his perks, his travel, his accommodations, his everything. Having "Bennie," with her Danish accent, telephone in Howard's name added an air of mystery in itself, but to have her say, in her whispered, clandestine way, "Howard K. Smith calling, let me put you on the secured line," made me wonder whether I wasn't really being hired by the CIA.

The formal offer came from Blair Clark, the elegant Harvard friend of John F. Kennedy and the brand-new general manager of CBS News in New York. I was so overjoyed, I didn't even think about bargaining. Whatever Clark proposed, I accepted. During our brief telephone conversation, I remember saying only two words. The first was "yes" and the second was "sir."

My salary would be $19,000 a year.

"Yes, sir."

That meant my weekly pay would almost double.

"Yes, sir."

I would stay in Washington.

"Yes, sir."

I would start as a weekend relief man at the White House.

"Yes, sir."

I would start as a correspondent, not as a reporter.

"Yes, sir."

Though I did not know it at the time, that was a critical distinction. I thought "reporter" was an honorable title and just fine. But in the hierarchy at CBS News, being a reporter was like being someone's knave. Being a correspondent was like being knighted by King Arthur and getting your own horse, sword, and coat-of-arms.

"Yes, sire."

On May 31, 1961, I became a genuine CBS News correspondent, sword and all. On that day I also became the network's first and only "Smith Boy." As it happened, Howard would not have time to hire any others. He was fired from CBS five months later by the chairman himself, William S. Paley, because he refused to soften his closing commentary on the *CBS Reports* documentary "Who

Speaks for Birmingham?"

Paley already had had his showdowns with Murrow and Sevareid over what he considered their violations of his edict against editorializing. In 1956 he forced Sevareid to back down over a radio broadcast critical of the State Department. In 1958, he canceled the groundbreaking *See It Now* documentary series because Murrow refused to grant an obscure congressman equal time to answer an attack on him. The Murrow confrontation produced the celebrated Paley quotation: "I don't want this constant stomachache every time you do a controversial subject."

Next was Smith. When Paley heard him on the radio accusing President Kennedy of failing to live up to his promises on racial policy, he was furious. He ordered Smith's last line quoting Edmund Burke to be deleted from the upcoming television documentary on Birmingham:

All that is necessary for the triumph of evil is for good men to do nothing.[1]

Smith refused and out the door went another direct link to the venerated Murrow.

But all that was ahead of me. All I knew

was that on that Monday in May I had
entered the promised land of news broadcasting, that Ted Church's call was not only
a warning shot but also a welcoming salvo
from the old boys, and that I had been
cleared to join television's finest news
bureau — the Washington bureau of CBS
News.

CHAPTER 6
TAKE TWO, TAKE THREE

The CBS I joined in the spring of 1961 was a CBS without Edward R. Murrow. His relationship with the network and its chairman, William Paley, had frayed badly because of his growing and public disenchantment with commercial television. In January, when the newly inaugurated President Kennedy asked Murrow to run the United States Information Agency, Paley urged him to accept. In February, Murrow moved to the USIA in Washington, much to Paley's relief, and CBS lost the most renowned figure in the creation of broadcast journalism.

I had never met Murrow until 1962, when by happenstance he asked me to sit with him on a late Eastern shuttle flight to New York. The pilot, rather than following the usual routine of idling at the end of the runway to check instruments and rev each motor separately, never stopped taxiing but simply gunned the engines in one swooping, rolling takeoff.

Murrow turned to me and said, "He must be a goddamn old bomber pilot."

The Washington bureau, however, still carried Murrow's imprint. The two daily radio broadcasts that originated in Washington were both anchored by Murrow hires — Bill Shadel at 9 AM and Bill Downs at 2 PM — and half of the broadcasters in the bureau had been hired by Murrow.

Yet we were basically a field office for CBS News in New York, supplying stories for broadcasts that came out of New York. We had little independence or identity of our own. There was a weekly radio news talk show, *Capitol Cloakroom,* and there was the Sunday TV talk show, *Face the Nation,* and that was about it for Washington.

Only occasionally would a Washington correspondent be seen on the *CBS Evening News with Douglas Edwards.* Coverage of congressional hearings, press conferences, and the like was handled via voice-over almost exclusively by a reporter named Neil Strawser. But he was not seen, only heard.

Radio was the bureau's strength and we kept busy cranking out radio pieces for the *World News Roundup* at 8 AM, *The World*

Tonight at 7 PM, and the hourly newscasts originating from New York.

With the 1960s, however, came the ascendancy of television and the ascendancy of the dashing and articulate John Kennedy, who gave television its first genuine political superstar. Compared with President Eisenhower, whose press secretary did not trust him to hold a live press conference, Kennedy was an elixir for television. The cameras could not resist him, his wife, his children, or his extended family. He also brought a new cadence to life in Washington, an embrace of the power and pleasure of politics, an obvious ease with money and fashion, a demand for excellence, and a heightened appreciation of literature, art, and music.

And then everything seemed to happen at once. Scattered sit-ins in the South coalesced into a civil rights movement and a political force; Alan Shepard spent fifteen minutes in space and America was on the way to the moon; young Americans found the Peace Corps more challenging than Wall Street; and television news shrank the world with satellites and videotape.

The networks' news divisions demanded more money, more air time, more equipment, and more manpower. And they got it.

CBS began the buildup of its Washington bureau in 1963. By the end of the 1960s it had doubled the number of reporters, producers, and cameramen. Stories out of Washington began to dominate the *CBS Evening News.*

Indeed, as the torch was being passed to a new generation of American politicians, it was also being passed to a new generation of television reporters. The CBS bureau I joined in early 1961 listed nine broadcasters. Within five years, however, the demands of television, cosmetic and otherwise, were such that all of them had virtually vanished — relegated to radio, prohibited by the New York producers from appearing on the *CBS Evening News,* reluctantly retired, or moved elsewhere for more money.

The bureau chief was forty-seven-year-old Howard K. Smith. Smith was a Tulane graduate and a Rhodes Scholar. In 1940, Smith, like so many of the Murrow Boys, had been hired away from the London bureau of United Press. He was a fine writer, and his distinctive southern voice made him a natural broadcaster. But behind the soft Louisiana accent was a passionate and headstrong rebel.

The correspondents included: Bill Downs, forty-seven, University of Kansas, a Murrow Boy, gruff, mercurial, but a great laugher. Downs was so rapid-fire that he occasionally lost control of his words. Some in the bureau swear that he once began a broadcast with: "This is Bill Downs, exploding from Washington. Here are the headlights." Ted Church, fifty-nine, University of Michigan, had come to CBS from the *New York Herald Tribune* as the director of radio news in New York, and he regarded television as a circus, no place for a serious journalist. As television began to dominate, Church was pushed aside and sent to the Washington bureau. Embittered though he must have been by the demotion, he covered Capitol Hill as a professional and was a formidable presence in the bureau. Nancy Hanschman, thirty-four, University of Wisconsin, was hired by CBS in 1954 as a radio producer but rose to become the network's first female correspondent. After her marriage in 1962, she became known as Nancy Dickerson. She also became known more for her social skills than for her reporting skills. George Herman, forty-one, a Dartmouth graduate, a man of wit and learning, joined CBS in 1944 as a radio news writer. He covered the Korean War with bravery and the Eisenhower and Kennedy administrations with distinction. Paul

Niven, thirty-seven, a Bowdoin graduate, the son of a Maine newspaper publisher, and a skilled general assignment reporter, was a large man with large tastes. Bob Pierpoint, thirty-six, a University of Redlands graduate, hired by CBS in 1949 as a stringer in Finland, was assigned to cover Korea in 1951 and the White House in 1957; no correspondent proved more reliable or easier to work with. Neil Strawser, thirty-three, Oberlin College, was known to millions as a voice from Washington. He was a serious journalist and a splendid TV writer, but had a slight rodential look on the screen. Charles Von Fremd, thirty-six, a Yale man, a former sportscaster in Boston, was hired by CBS in 1951; he burned out covering eight years of Eisenhower and shifted to the Pentagon and his first love, the space program. The assignment desk was run by Jim Roper, forty-six, a quiet Tennessean, ex-UP, ex-*Evening Star,* whose story of Mussolini's death in 1945 was carried in newspapers all over the world and won him the Headliner Award.

They were all serious journalists — smart, well educated, skilled, skeptical, tenacious, curious, and, above all, ferociously competitive. Nobody at CBS had told them how to do it. There were no classes in how to put a TV piece together, how to begin, how to end, how to write to the picture. You were expected to learn it yourself, and if you couldn't learn it within three or four months, you had no business being a CBS correspondent anyway.

Ten days after I started work at CBS I blew my first television assignment. Mildred Gillars, known to thousands of World War II GIs as "Axis Sally," was to be released from the Federal Reformatory for Women in Alderson, West Virginia. Convicted in 1949 on eight counts of treason for her pro-Nazi broadcasts, she had been sentenced to thirty years in prison. She became eligible for parole in 1959 but waived her right, apparently to avoid for a few more years the derision she knew awaited her on the outside. Her parole was granted when she finally applied for it two years later.[1]

My camera crew — cameraman and soundman — and I flew to Roanoke, Virginia, rented a car, and drove the seventy-five miles through the Allegheny Mountains to White Sulphur Springs, West Virginia, and checked into the very posh Greenbrier Resort. I later had to prove to the CBS business manager that there were no suitable accommodations in or near Alderson and that the Greenbrier was the best we could do. The business manager grumped but the crew loved it. They said they thought I had the makings of a first-class network correspondent.

We didn't get to enjoy the resort for long. The prison told us to be at the prison gate no later than 6 AM. We got there at 5:30 AM and found a dozen film crews already in place.

Our assignment was simple: The crew would film Axis Sally leaving in her car. The minute the car passed through the gate, the cameraman would pan over, revealing me on camera doing my stand-up closing remarks. The event seemed so cut and dried that I wrote my closer the night before — something about Axis Sally leaves here facing an uncertain future and blah, blah, blah. Waiting for her car, I went over my copy and tried to memorize it.

About 6:30 AM the shout went up: "Here she comes. Here she comes." Indeed she came — in a darkened car that went by so fast we could not see her. But we saw the car and we filmed it as the car cleared the gate. That was my cue to begin the closer. I got halfway through it and froze. I had forgotten my lines. I yelled, "Take Two," and started again. Another freeze. "Take Three." I made it on the third try, but by this time Axis Sally and her car had vanished in the dark. My closer was now worthless. My on-camera debut would have to wait. What the *CBS Evening News* got that night was my disembodied voice behind a piece of film showing what the viewer was told was a car carrying someone thought to be a woman who was alleged to be Axis Sally.

Getting on camera for the first time is for a television reporter the equivalent of getting a first byline on a newspaper. I remembered the euphoria with my first byline at the *Richmond News Leader* in 1953. Even though it was something thin about two boys biking to Florida, it put me in the public domain. So it was with CBS. Getting on camera meant you had substance, that you were reliable, that you actually existed, and that the viewer got to see the face of the person doing all this talking and telling. To be seen vouched for your authenticity, and to be seen at the site of a story vouched for it even more. It also satisfied the primal urge of every television reporter — to be seen. In television news, not to be seen is not to exist.

So beginning on the evening of July 21, 1961, I began to exist as a television correspondent. It was my very first on-camera appearance on the *CBS Evening News,* and it came on the hundredth anniversary of the Battle of Bull Run. The assignment desk sent me and a camera crew about thirty miles west of Washington to the Bull Run battlefield near Manassas, Virginia, where a re-enactor group was staging a rerun of the battle. The scene, the uniforms, the smoke, the noise of the cannons gave us the ingredients for a cracker jack piece. We got close-ups of charge and counter-charge. We got close-ups of General Barnard Bee of South Carolina pointing to General Thomas Jackson of Virginia and proclaiming, "There stands Jackson, like a stone wall," and we got close-ups of the Union Army in a panic-stricken rout. Just a decade earlier I had been studying that very battle in Dr. Bean's Civil War & Reconstruction course in college.

I closed the piece on-camera with: "This is Roger Mudd, CBS News, in full retreat to Washington." Even though my close did not quite comport with the news division's style book, it did catch the make-believe spirit of the day. Besides, New York loved it, which, I discovered in due time, was always better than "New York hated it."

CHAPTER 7
OLD FOUR FINGERS

By the end of that first summer I was beginning to feel at home at CBS News. My assignments were general and happily varied, and there were no indications I would not become the White House correspondent, as Smith had hinted when he hired me. One day when I screwed up my courage to ask him "when" or "if," Howard's soft southern courtliness hardened. He said it was not in the works.

"But," I started, "you said. . . ."

Smith cut me off.

"That's the way it is," he said. "We're going to send you to the Hill."

The Hill and not the White House? I couldn't believe it. The White House was THE premiere assignment, with its cachet and elevated social status. But without any seniority, without a leg to stand on, I dared not object or complain.

I went to the Hill and found to my delight

there was no beat like it in the country. There were a thousand sources all eager to talk, most of them well-informed and well motivated, others hopelessly in over their heads, a few outrageously greedy, but all of them conveniently confined to seven marble buildings on about two hundred acres on a hill rising eighty-eight feet from tidewater in the Potomac River. Ted Church, nominally the network's Hill man, was consistently gracious to me even though he knew I was the one easing him out.

Hurricane Carla, which was churning through the Gulf Coast in early September 1961, delayed my new assignment. I was in New Orleans for the opening of the public schools, which were under court order to desegregate. A New Orleans woman, known to the gathering media as "Mother," promised to disrupt the opening. When she fizzled, the story fizzled. Before I could catch a flight back to Washington, however, Carla was threatening to come ashore at Grand Isle, Louisiana, about a hundred miles south in Jefferson Parish. My crew chartered a seaplane and we headed for Grand Isle, so overloaded with crew and camera equipment that we rarely flew above a hundred feet. By the time we splashed down, Carla had changed course and was heading toward the Texas coast. Back to New Orleans on the seaplane we went. I left my Atlanta-based crew and flew to Houston on the last commercial flight to leave New Orleans. It was a very rough flight on an old propeller-driven Douglas DC–3, filled with some very nervous, sweaty-palmed passengers.

For the next two days, my Chicago-based crew and I chased Hurricane Carla all over southeast Texas. On the third day, heading toward the town of Victoria on the Gulf, we spotted a lone panicky horse trapped by the water. The cameraman stuck his lens out the window and started filming. Into the microphone I described what I saw, how deep the rising water was, how remote a rescue seemed, and ending with something flip about the Texas law against horse stealing.

We knew the *CBS Evening News* would love the story. But when I described the film we were sending to New York the only question producer Don Hewitt asked was "Did you say at the end 'And now back to Doug Edwards in New York?,' " as if mentioning Edwards by name was central. I had not. Nobody had told me to. I had simply recorded, "I'm Roger Mudd, CBS News, Victoria, Texas." Hewitt ran the piece but he was not pleased.

The "Now back to . . ." line I regarded as a photographic sleight-of-hand to make the viewer think I was switching live to Doug Edwards, whereas I had actually recorded the words on film a few hours before. Somebody in management apparently thought the same thing and soon enough the closing line was officially changed to "Roger Mudd [or whoever], CBS News, Capitol Hill [or wherever]."

Nonetheless, the story provoked a lot of comment and several hundred telephone calls from viewers who said I should have broken the Texas law and somehow rescued the horse.

That fall the Washington bureau was in turmoil. Howard K. Smith had left in October, to be replaced as chief by David Schoenbrun, the longtime Paris correspondent. It was an awkward fit. In Paris he had no competition, but in the Washington bureau there were other big egos, although none quite as big as his.

He was also very greedy. Because the bureau had no full-time State Department reporter until Marvin Kalb came in 1963, Schoenbrun sent Jim Roper from the desk to cover the department. Roper was to do only radio and had to pass his copy to Schoenbrun, who would then try to sell the story as his own to the *CBS Evening News.* Schoenbrun's successor, Bill Small, called it "[a] disgrace, but that's the way it was."[1]

Schoenbrun was also very social. Malcolm "Mac" Kilduff, the assistant press secretary in the Kennedy White House, called him "Old Four Fingers," because he was missing a thumb.

"Old Four Fingers wants to get invited to dinner at the White House again," Kilduff would say. "Can't you get him to ease off?"

Soon, the bureau began to snicker behind his back at his failed attempts to crack the Kennedy social circle, at his chauffeured limousine, at his hiring of a personal publicity agent. He had Louise Remmey, the bureau's librarian, write one of his daughter's term papers at her private school. "Back then," Remmey has explained, "you couldn't say no."

Schoenbrun was short, self-consciously short, and the bureau snorted about the wooden box his camera crew hauled around for him to stand on so he would not be dwarfed when he filmed his reports in front of the Capitol dome or the White House or the State Department.

For most of us, Schoenbrun represented

the best and the worst of television journalism. A felicitous writer, totally knowledgeable about his subject, quick on his feet, a superb ad-libber, he had all the qualities that were rarely present in a single broadcaster. But with them came an outsized ego, a deep suspicion of any rival, a willingness to fawn over those in power, an eagerness to enlarge his own role as a journalist, and an unfailing belief that his presence in the story was more important than the story itself.

In little over a year, Schoenbrun was gone, gone from CBS and off to New York as a freelance news analyst for ABC-TV and WNEW. His replacement, Bill Small, came to Washington directly from the CBS station in Louisville, WHAS-TV, where he was the news director. We were delighted that he was not a broadcaster himself. No longer would we have to compete against our boss for air time. Freed of Schoenbrun's divisive presence, Small turned Washington into the network's largest, most talented, and most important news bureau.

CHAPTER 8
MISTER SMALL

In 1962 when Bill Small, aged thirty-seven, took over the Washington bureau, we all called him "Mister Small," even though the average age of his nine reporters was forty. He simply did not look, act, talk, or smile like a man of thirty-seven.

But there were other qualities that made him "Mister Small" to us. There was his absolute power in the bureau and his control over our professional lives, which he could exert, if need be, swiftly and effectively. There was also a dignity about him, a way of moving deliberately, that bespoke authority. The only time I ever saw him move with any speed was on the basketball court when the bureau team played in a men's league in the Maryland suburbs.

His father was a Chicago baker; his mother, a housewife he remembers as a "bad cook." After the Army, a master's degree at the University of Chicago, and three years at WLS Radio in Chicago, Small was hired to run the news department at WHAS-TV in Louisville. Owned by the Bingham family, publishers of the *Louisville Courier-Journal,* WHAS was a first-class news operation. As a CBS affiliate, WHAS became a stopping-off place for traveling CBS correspondents. Blair Clark, on the southern political beat, got to know Small; after he became general manager of CBS News, Clark offered Small the deputy bureau chief's job in Washington with the understanding that he would soon succeed David Schoenbrun, who was on his way out. Small's arrival in Washington coincided with Walter Cronkite's taking over the *CBS Evening News.*

It didn't take long before Cronkite, the former hard-news wire-service reporter, began lobbying with producer Don Hewitt to expand his program to thirty minutes. Fifteen minutes simply was not enough, given the explosion of news, wars, assassinations, protests, and riots of the '60s. Fifteen minutes was also not enough, given the speed and ease of videotape and the orbiting Telestar satellite, which could send pictures from Europe directly into New York for broadcast that night. The newspapers' monopoly on breaking stories was broken by videotape and by Telestar.

If anything set off the seismic shift that moved television news ahead of the newspaper as the country's main source of news, it was September 3, 1963, the night Cronkite said:

"Good evening from our CBS newsroom in New York on this, the first broadcast of network television's first daily, half-hour news program."

For Bill Small in Washington, it changed everything. No longer would he be running a service bureau, grinding out radio pieces for the hourlies or noodling over whom to invite for *Face the Nation.* His bureau would be the breadbasket of the CBS News operation. The appetite of the evening news and the morning news and the midday news and, later, the Saturday news and the Sunday news would be insatiable and Small's bureau would have to be prepared to satisfy it.

Brought in from a middling market in Kentucky and plunked down in the center of the most important news city in the world, Small was told to get ready for the biggest expansion in the news division's history. Backed by the mystique of Murrow's CBS and his own uncanny judge of talent, Small helped attract a stream of reporters, correspondents, analysts, and producers whose learning, talent, skill, and experience were without precedent in news broadcasting.

First to arrive, in 1963, was Marvin Kalb, thirty-three, after a two-year turn in Moscow, to cover the uncovered State Department. Next was David Schoumacher, twenty-nine, from Oklahoma City, where he had been the ten o'clock anchorman. Then came Dan Rather, thirty-two, after two years of covering the South, including the assassination of Kennedy, to report on his fellow Texan, Lyndon Johnson, in the White House.

Arriving in 1964 were Eric Sevareid, fifty-one, an original Murrow Boy, to begin a nightly commentary; Bruce Morton, thirty-three, a Harvard man who became the bureau's finest writer, if he wasn't already; Ike Pappas, thirty-one, a blue-collar journalist from the world of New York radio, who hit the ground running with the Johnson presidential campaign; and Martin Agronsky, fifty-two, who arrived after more than two decades at ABC and NBC to moderate *Face the Nation.*

By this time, only Herman, Pierpoint, Strawser, and I remained from the pre-Small days. Downs had left for ABC, Niven for PBS, and Dickerson for NBC. Church had retired and Von Fremd had died.

Replacements and reinforcements kept coming. To fill in for Rather, who was off to London in 1965, New York sent Harry Reasoner, forty-two, an established star and Cronkite's main stand-in; Daniel Schorr, fifty, a Murrow Cold War hire, came after a decade in Europe; Marya McLaughlin, thirty-six, arrived with a wicked sense of humor as the bureau's second female reporter; Hal Walker, thirty-five, was hired directly from the local CBS station in Washington as the network's first black reporter; David Dick, thirty-six, a self-effacing Kentuckian, came fearing he couldn't hold his own in Washington, but did; and Peter Kendall, thirty, with university degrees from Cincinnati and Illinois, fluent in German, left the *Voice of America* to be an assignment editor.

Then, in 1969, just six years after Small began the great expansion, another wave of talent rolled into the bureau: John Armstrong, thirty, a Rutgers man, and one of Cronkite's writers, as a producer for the *CBS Evening News;* Ed Fouhy, thirty-five, ex-Marine, ex-Saigon bureau chief, and ex-Los Angeles bureau chief, as the chief Cronkite producer; Tom Bettag, twenty-five, a weekend writer for WNEW in New York and one of Fred Friendly's teaching assistants at Columbia, as a desk editor; Barry Serafin, twenty-eight, from KMOX in St. Louis, who said he was "dazzled" the day he walked in, as a general-assignment reporter; Bob Schieffer, thirty-two, born in Austin, correspondent in Vietnam for the *Ft. Worth Star-Telegram,* who came to Washington hell-bent to break in with a network, also as a general-assignment reporter; and Cindy Samuels, twenty-three, a Smith girl who came straight off the Eugene McCarthy campaign to CBS as a news assistant on Capitol Hill, and within a year knew more about the Congress than most of its members.

After six years Small had put together a TV news bureau the likes of which Washington had never known. For all his gruff and glower, he was simply a sophisticated judge of journalistic horseflesh. Of the nineteen reporters, correspondents, producers, and editors Small hired to work in the Washington bureau, he lost only three to the competition, all to ABC: Bernard Shaw for a chance to cover Latin America, David Schoumacher because he suspected CBS had soured on him, and Barry Serafin to become a first-stringer, even though at a third-string network.

Small knew everything that was going on in the bureau. Producer John Armstrong remembers, "He knew everything all the time. He stayed in touch with his people. 'How you doing?' 'Everything OK.?' And he never tried to produce anything by himself. I never saw him say, 'Take that out, put that in, make that longer, make that shorter.' No sir. He was an administrator and a good one."

One of the reasons he knew so much was because of Sylvia Westerman, from Columbus, Ohio, who began as a researcher but soon became Small's eyes and ears, and such a constant presence in Small's office that some labeled her as a "sycophant." Small had no need to wire the bureau, because Westerman was trolling constantly. To most of the men in the bureau, she had no other life than being Small's stewardess, almost his adopted daughter. But her life included a variety of other interests — ballet, stage design, major league baseball, and, above all, politics. During the 1972 presidential conventions in Miami, Westerman literally pitched her tent in the Fontainebleau Hotel bar, meeting various politicians and journalists for drinks, political intelligence, and convention gossip. Correspondent Bruce Morton chatted with her at the bar one evening and when she left to go to the ladies room, the bartender leaned over and said quietly, "Just so you know, I've seen her here with a LOT of different men." Westerman loved to tell the story on herself.

The deputy bureau chief was Don Richardson, who freed Small from worrying about the technical details of running a bureau. Richardson came to Washington in 1949 fresh out of the University of Iowa as the press secretary to Republican Senator Bourke Hickenlooper. CBS hired him in 1954, and he managed the CBS Newsfilm service in Washington until Small's arrival. Unlike most CBS executives, Richardson became highly excitable even in minor crises. According to cameraman Cal Marlin, Richardson was "just nuts. I've seen him stand up on the news desk and throw phone books across the room." From time to time Richardson would fill in on the assignment desk. Bob Schieffer watched Richardson under pressure one day as he "jumped from the desk and ran back toward the film processor to check on some film and he stepped in a wastebasket with his right foot." Richardson took three steps before he realized he was wearing a wastebasket. "He had to walk over and sit down in a chair because he couldn't get his foot out of it." Everybody was watching and laughing really hard.

But Richardson's presence in the bureau gave Small time to be Eric Sevareid's regular luncheon companion and to be everyone's father. Small knew all the bureau's children. When Jonathan Mudd broke his leg skiing, Small sent him a book, *How to Ski.* During conventions and election nights, he saw to it that any Washington bureau youth sixteen and over got a job running errands, cutting copy, bringing coffee. When Tom Bettag brought his little boys to the office, Small would take them back to the copying machine and Xerox their hands. Bettag says, "He treated your kids and your wife as if they were the most important things in the world, which he believed that they were, and if you treat my family that well then you can bark at me all you want."

But there was an unpleasant, sometimes bitchy side to Small. Bruce Morton, now retired after more than forty years at CBS and CNN, says, "I still remember Small coming up to some young, nervous reporter and saying, 'Anyone tell you what a good job you've done lately?' 'Gosh, no, Mister Small,' he said, obviously expecting a compliment. 'Well, there's a reason for that,' said Mister Small."

Robert Pierpoint, one of Murrow's Korean War hires, perhaps became Small's harshest critic. He thought Small resented the special cachet that the Murrow crowd carried: "I think Small tried very hard to break my spirit . . . and my basic attitude, which was 'I'm going to tell the story my way.' "

Pierpoint's hostility seemed based largely on Small's decision to demote him to the second string behind Dan Rather at the White House during the Johnson and Nixon administrations. Small was very, very pro-Rather, according to Pierpoint. "He wanted to protect Rather."

A few days after our interview, in 2006, Small called me at home. He was obviously upset by some of my questions implying that he was a harsh and unforgiving leader.

"The only thing that concerns me," he said, "is the myth that I ruled by fear. You never experienced that, did you?"

"No," I said.

"It's all secondhand," he said, "and it will haunt me forever."

For my part, I found Small fair, considerate, editorially sound, intolerant of slipshod work, generally immovable, occasionally cranky, but quietly and inordinately proud of us in the bureau.

He rarely raised his voice and when he did speak, it was with such a directness, an economy of words, and a soft tone that you hardly knew that your head was being handed to you.

The secret to his leadership and control was his ferocious refusal to let New York run around him, through him, or above him. It did not hurt, of course, that all but a few were "Small's Boys and Girls" — men and women hired by him, loyal to him, and largely dependent on his good opinion for getting ahead.

Pierpoint, Herman, Strawser, and I — because we preceded him to Washington — were not considered to be among Small's Boys, although only Pierpoint suffered because of it. I was already established when Small came, ensconced on the Hill, and, along with Dan Rather, regarded as one of the bureau's leading correspondents. As a consequence, I was rarely the target of his impatience, his criticism, or his put-downs. But neither was I the model employee, given my stubborn refusal to jump when the assignment desk said jump.

But one night Small thought I needed to be taught again how to jump. Some buddies of mine on the Hill — newspaper reporters and a Senate aide or two — had hired a bus and bought a couple of cases of beer, for a night out at the nearby Laurel Park racetrack. I was the guest of alleged honor, and they had arranged easily enough to name the sixth race the Roger Mudd Claiming Stakes. We were to gather at the East Plaza of the Capitol about 6 PM for the bus trip to Laurel Park.

Just as I was about to leave the Senate, the desk called. It was Bill Galbraith, the assignment editor.

"Small wants you to cover the Romney speech tonight at the Governors' Conference," he said.

"You're kidding," I bellowed. "George Romney! That loser! Besides, I've got a horserace in my honor." How silly that excuse must have sounded.

I should have known. With Bill Small, neither snow, nor rain, nor heat, nor gloom of night, nor racetrack beer party, nor whatever — would keep a CBS correspondent from his appointed rounds, even if it was with George Romney.

CHAPTER 9
THE DESK

If Bill Small was the shepherd of the CBS Washington flock, then Bill Galbraith was its sheepdog — keeping everyone together and heading in the same direction, nipping at the strays, fending off the predators, and bringing the herd home on time.

Galbraith ran the assignment desk, the axle of the bureau. Without the desk and without him, the place would have been chaos. He was responsible for putting the bureau into gear and into motion each day, making sure nothing of significance was left uncovered, moving camera crews with the flow of the news, and dispatching the motorcycle couriers to bring news film back to be developed and edited faster than the competition.

The bureau's producers were in awe of him. "The best assignment editor I've ever seen in my life," they said. He never forgot anything. He never lost anything. He never missed anything. No one could leave an assignment and return to the bureau or check out for home without getting cleared by the desk.

Born in 1924, the son of a naval officer and the grandson of the political editor of the *Columbus* (Ohio) *Dispatch,* Galbraith came east in 1945 with a degree from the journalism school at the University of Washington in Seattle. Blinded in his right eye by a childhood accident, he nonetheless worked as a proofreader at a Washington, D.C., printing house and as a dictationist at United Press and moved up through the ranks of the UP to become the wire's number-two man at the State Department. In 1960, he jumped to CBS, and two years later took over the assignment desk when Jim Roper retired.

Our bureau was an architecturally nondescript, three-story brick building on a stretch of M Street in downtown Washington best described as undistinguished. Next door there was, after all, a strip club and a door or two away The Black Sheep, a run-of-the mill restaurant known in the bureau as "The Sheep Dip." CBS had bought the building in 1964 from the *Army Times* and moved downtown from the far northwest, where the distance from the White House and the Hill had put us at a competitive disadvantage.

The first floor was all studios, control rooms, and technical shops.

The second floor was all news — executive offices, film edit rooms, reporters' desks, correspondents' cubicles, a research corner with towering stacks of the *Washington Post* and the *New York Times,* shelves of the news magazines and *Facts on File,* and a row of file cabinets stuffed with news clippings.

In the center of the second floor was the assignment desk — really three desks pushed together to form what newspaper people call "the slot." Galbraith sat in the slot. To his right and left were his radio editor, his desk assistant, and occasionally a TV producer.

The third floor was office space for the newest arrivals, who hated being quarantined up there, and offices leased to the BBC and French TV.

Telephones on the desk rang constantly — Schoumacher needs a courier on the Hill, Kalb has an update on Kissinger, Pierpoint is ready with a radio spot from the White House. It did not take long for the expanding bureau to learn that Galbraith left nothing to chance. He did not accept excuses. He worked harder than anybody else on the desk. The second he put down one phone, he'd pick up another.

In the pre-cell phone, pre-e-mail, pre-BlackBerry days, reporters relied exclusively on hard-wired phones. Young news assistants may have felt silly sitting in a telephone booth holding an open line, but that's how Galbraith got a jump on the competition when a big vote was expected at an important Capitol Hill hearing.

Some of Galbraith's assignments drove cameramen up the wall — piddly jobs like shooting fresh pictures of the Capitol dome or the White House, footage called "wallpaper," which might be critical for a well-produced piece but seem stupid to a cameraman who might have shot the dome the day before. Cameraman Cal Marlin says, "None of us was a very big Galbraith fan. . . . You'd have to do some silly-ass job just to cover his butt."

In a big thick notebook, Galbraith kept a diary of upcoming events in Washington. To that he would add the daybooks from the Associated Press and the Washington City News Wire for the coming day. Then, with his list in hand, Galbraith and a handful of producers would gather in Small's office about six each evening to plan the next day's coverage.

"OK, Bill," Small would say, "how many crews have we got?"

"Five," Galbraith would say.

And then he would list the cameramen by name — Marlin, Hoertel, Santos, Craven, Bessor, Hess, Alston.

Small would then pick the stories and the crews — Marlin at the White House with Rather, Hoertel on the Hill with Mudd and the filibuster, Bessor at State with Kalb and the morning briefing, and so on.

The desk operated until 10 PM, and before Galbraith left for home after the *Evening News* was over, he would write a long memo for the night editor, laying out the next day's assignments. Big breaking stories after seven o'clock or so usually meant a telephone call to Small to reassign the crews.

Most of the bureau reporters had a love-hate relationship with Galbraith. He was the one who called you at home at five in the morning to tell you an Air National Guard plane had crashed near Richmond and to get moving — he never delegated middle-of-the-night calls to others. My wife dreaded those calls, because she knew they would end with my yelling, "goddamn it," and slamming down the phone. All of us tried weaseling out of his assignments, but in the end Galbraith wore us down with what we remember as his "whining quality."

Even those correspondents who chafed under Galbraith's tight control acknowledged his professionalism. Barry Serafin, who was in the bureau for a decade before he left for ABC News, says, "I was astonished when I walked into ABC. There were nine or ten people around the desk. And I said, 'What do all those people do?' 'Well, he's responsible for Cap Hill and she's responsible for the camera crews and he's responsible for something else.' Bill Galbraith did all that essentially by himself."

CHAPTER 10
THE FRONT ROW

Lesley Stahl said we looked like miniatures in a shadow box, maybe even mannequins in a Saks Fifth Avenue window. She was talking about her first look at five of America's most distinguished television correspondents on the first day she came to work at the CBS Washington bureau.

What Lesley saw along the south wall of the newsroom were five cubicles, each about six-feet-by-eight, their walls covered in a beige textured paper and each equipped with a desk, a chair, a typewriter, a telephone, and a television star.

When the bureau moved downtown from the WTOP building, Don Hewitt, the kinetic producer of the *CBS Evening News,* designed the cubicles so that the big floor cameras could roll right up and put us on the air from our very own desks.

Several practice runs were taped and shown to the art people and the graphic people and the design people and the management people in New York, and they all agreed that on camera we looked like — well, like five guys in the window at Saks Fifth Avenue.

The Hewitt project was quietly dropped and the five cubicles became known as the Front Row. It was a sight that wowed, if not intimidated, every new hire who walked in.

Phil Jones: "I'll never, ever forget the day. . . . You're all the people I watched as a kid and I say, 'Holy shit. . . . Am I going to succeed in this or not?' "

Ike Pappas: "I was like in seventh heaven. I'm good enough to be standing next to great reporters."

Barry Serafin: "I thought there was no place in the world that could match the sheer journalistic talent that place had."

Bob Schieffer: "I felt like I'd been playing Little League baseball and all of a sudden I'd been promoted to the Yankees."

The rookies were looking at Dan Rather, Daniel Schorr, Marvin Kalb, George Herman, and me.

Dan Rather

In the extreme right-hand cubicle was Dan Rather, who joined the bureau after running the Dallas and New Orleans bureaus for two years. During his first year in Washington, we became friends. I knew what he was going through, fearful of failing, anxious about being accepted, nervous about being beaten. We had connections to, or affinities for, the South — its courtesies, its humor, and its sense of the absurd. We were about the same age, had married the same year, and had young families. Their two (Robin, six, and Danjack, four) meshed with our four (Daniel, six, Maria, four, Jonathan, three, and Matthew, one). His wife, Jean Goebel Rather, was everybody's favorite — petite, effervescent, and ambitious. The Rathers were on our dinner list, and there were occasional family ski trips. Driving back from one happy ski weekend in Virginia's Appalachian Mountains, we parted company in our two speeding cars on the highway into Washington with the windows rolled down, the kids waving, and our horns honking out "Shave and a haircut, two bits."

Rather had a sense of humor, although not particularly an active one, which he was willing to use on himself. During a political trip to Salt Lake, he popped in at the Mormon Tabernacle and was quickly spotted by the director of the Tabernacle Choir. The hundred-voice choir greeted him with several rounds of "Helloooo, Dan Rather." When the director asked if he had a request, Rather said all he could think of was "Little Brown Jug."

But for all of that, Rather was taut, tightly wound, and not quite sure of what and who he wanted to be.

He was strikingly handsome, slightly over six feet tall, with strong, even features and a full head of black hair. Gordon Manning, a news vice president, said when he'd walk through an airport with Rather young women would stumble to get a good look at him. Though not to the manor born, he had Old South manners, which were quaint and endearing to some but struck others as excessive at a time when few men held doors or chairs for women. When Rather shook hands, he used not one hand but both — his right to shake your hand and his left to grasp your elbow. (The Rather Shake found its way into the movie *Broadcast News*.)

Both his background and his education were meager. The oldest of three children in a family living at the upper edges of the working poor, Rather grew up in a forlorn suburb of Houston. His father dug trenches and laid pipe for an oil company. His mother, Byrl, was a part-time waitress, sold encyclopedias, sewed upholstery and slip-covers, and answered phones at a construction office.[1]

Rather's writing was no better or worse than most television reporters, although his prose did tend toward the fervid. But he did write, with a coauthor, three books — *The Palace Guard, The Camera Never Blinks,* and *I Remember.*

His Depression-era childhood in Texas had naturally left him scrambling for a better and perhaps more glamorous life. He once said he had always dreamed of going to the Metropolitan Opera — not so much to see the opera as to arrive in a long, black limousine.

His ordinary education in Texas left him striving to learn and to be taken seriously. He sought advice from Eric Sevareid, who suggested he take a year off and apply for a Nieman Fellowship at Harvard. But Rather did not want to disappear from television for that long, so he asked Sevareid for a reading list instead. The list included Herodotus and Montaigne. Rather happily admitted he wasn't sure he'd "heard of Herodotus before that."

A few years later, when interviewers would ask about his favorite books, he would invariably list the Bible and at least a dozen others to cover all bases. In a Hearst magazine piece on the historical figures television journalists would most like to interview, Walter Cronkite said Hitler, Tom Brokaw said Jesus Christ, Connie Chung said Greta Garbo, I said Robert E. Lee, and Barbara Walters said Jackie Kennedy. But Rather listed not only the pope, but also Gorbachev, the Prince and Princess of Wales, Moses, Jesus Christ, Buddha, Mohammed, Jefferson, Shakespeare, Louis XIV, Queen Elizabeth, and Freud.

When CBS assigned Rather to the White House, it put him in an awkward position from the start. New York told Rather they were unhappy with the reporting from the White House — meaning, of course, the work of two of the bureau's senior correspondents, George Herman and Robert Pierpoint, who had been with CBS and Murrow since the Korean War and had put in time covering Eisenhower and Kennedy. Neither was a great broadcaster but both were intelligent, tough, loyal, and very proud of their work.

It was Pierpoint who took the hit. Suddenly, after being number one, he was the backup, the weekend guy, the fill-in guy to the young hotshot from Texas. Pierpoint never got over his demotion.

Nineteen-sixty-four, Rather's first year in Washington, was not a good year. The Johnson White House tried to isolate him, refusing to recognize him at the press conferences, assuming that his eagerness to get on the air would soften his reporting of the administration. It did not work, and Johnson's people kept him at bay. Rather struggled to be recognized. During the coverage on election eve in 1964, Johnson went out of his way to avoid him. Rather had to resort to shadowing one of the president's favorites, Nancy Dickerson, then at NBC, to be in position for an interview. That, too, failed.[2] Rather said Johnson was used to a cozy relationship with the Texas press that had come to Washington with him or had covered him in Congress, and that he must have figured, "Well, we have a Texan here and a White House full of Texans . . . and we'll get a break from him. . . . He never knew quite what to make of me."

Within a few weeks, Rather got hit by another brick — he was to be replaced at the White House by Harry Reasoner. Never was there mention or hint of his having failed at the White House. It was, instead, Fred Friendly's desire for a bigger name at the White House and more exposure for

Reasoner, who was then Cronkite's main backup. To make room for Reasoner, Friendly proposed sending Rather to London. Rather had always said he wanted to work abroad but now he wasn't so sure. He was losing face, discovering that network television was no cakewalk, and not happy to be leaving. E. J. and I knew it was not an easy time for him and Jean. We tried to lift their spirits with a good-bye party when they left for London in January 1965.

When I next saw him — after ten months in London and ten months in Vietnam — he was a different Dan Rather. He returned to Washington more aggressive, more confident, more polished, more suspicious of his colleagues, and more skeptical of the powerful. He was tough, hard-working, and he belonged in the Front Row. But no White House correspondent in CBS history attracted quite as much lightning.

As he began to challenge me on specials, during instant analysis, on the year-end wrap-ups, I discovered he had become less my friend and more my rival.

Daniel Schorr

In the cubicle to the left of Rather was Daniel Schorr. When we heard he was joining the bureau, few of us knew what he was like or what to expect. We did know that he was from the Murrow era, the post–World War II era, hired on the strength of his freelance radio work covering the devastating 1953 floods in the Netherlands.

I had first met Schorr in 1962 on the steps of the CBS News headquarters on West Fifty-seventh Street in Manhattan when he, Winston Burdett, David Schoenbrun, and our other foreign correspondents were assembling from abroad for their annual year-end show. I stuck out my hand and said, "Hi, Dan. I'm Roger Mudd." He laughed, shook my hand, and said, "I know who you are," as though it was preposterous to think that he didn't.

No one ever mistook Schorr for a matinee idol. His words tended to tumble, his voice still carried traces of his Bronx neighborhood, and there were, to my eye, at least, hints in his face of Bert Lahr, the cowardly lion in *The Wizard of Oz.*

He was a fifty-year-old bachelor when he arrived in Washington in 1966, but the house he bought in Georgetown remained a bachelor pad for only a year. He met his bride, Lisbeth Bamberger, a Berkley graduate, in the Johnson administration's War on Poverty office. He may have been a soft touch as the father of their two children,

Jonathan and Lisa, but in the bureau he was an aggressive and relentless reporter.

Schorr came to Washington without an assignment, without a beat, and he found Small's welcome less than friendly. "We're covered at the White House, we're covered at the State Department, we're covered on the Hill, we're covered at the Pentagon. So you should know those things are not available to you. So what do you want to do?" as Schorr remembers the welcome.

What Schorr carved out for himself was, in effect, a beat covering Johnson's Great Society legislative program. Nobody else in Washington — not for television, newspapers, or the magazines — had such a beat. "I must say," he told me later, "I did reasonably well. That is, I got on the air every once in a while, which Small predicted I never would. . . . I don't think Small ever really liked me very much."

If by "every once in a while" he meant two or three times a week, Schorr has arrived at a new definition of "every once in a while." For those of us who watched him operate, "every once in a while" seemed like every night.

Because the Great Society beat had no boundaries and involved almost every cabinet department and bureau in the government, Schorr seemed to always be poaching. Of course he was a great reporter, but his incursions on everybody else's beat woke me up one night in a sweat from a really bad dream. I was boarding the ten o'clock Eastern shuttle on my way to New York to do the Saturday news. The plane was almost full and everybody on it looked like Dan Schorr. One Schorr was reading the paper, another was drinking coffee, a third was writing something, a fourth was talking to a fifth, and so on to the rear of the plane. When I got back to the bureau on Monday, I told Bill Small about my dream. It was one of the rare times I heard Bill laugh out loud and really hard.

Some of the younger reporters in the bureau were amused by Schorr's push to get on the air, because his success usually came at the expense of those of us on the Front Row and not the young ones on the Back Row. From time to time, those of us in the front would turn over our stories to the rookies for the radio rewrite or the *Morning News* version. But not Schorr. According to Bob Schieffer, "He insisted on doing everything. He'd do the *Evening News* version, the *Morning News* version, the radio version, and he'd knock out a couple of radio syndication pieces. He was not getting fees. But he was like a vacuum cleaner. He just wanted to do it all."

I told Schorr in our interview years later that the feeling in the bureau was, "Oh, God, here comes Schorr. You'd better hold onto your notes or he'll steal your story."

"I may have been regarded as overly competitive within the organization," he said.

"No question about that," I said.

"Right. . . . But given my background, growing up poor, growing without much help or anything, I finally found that I had to make people pay attention to me and the way you make people pay attention is to tell them stories. They may not like you but they'll like the stories. And I'll have to admit, that was the life that I led. I didn't have a lot of people falling in love with me or get invited out to a lot of little dinners, but I said 'OK, I've worked very hard all my life to make my way and I'll do it at CBS.' "

To television journalism Schorr brought the newspaper reporter's attention to facts, details, motives, and accuracy. Producer Ed Fouhy says, "I don't remember a single story when he was wrong. . . . He was the most sophisticated about the government. He understood quite well how the government worked. He was very smart about how the news operation worked — what we needed, what we were looking for. He could turn it out. He was indefatigable."

For all the griping and carping about Schorr's appetite for air time, there was another endearing quality about him. Working with the younger reporters and producers, he was always very, very tough. But he always took time to correct them, "and always in a gruff but loving way," recalls Tom Bettag. "He cared about you."

Marvin Kalb

In the cubicle next to Schorr sat Marvin Kalb, who wanted to be on the air at least as much as Schorr. Being on the air was our oxygen, just as being in print was the newspaper reporter's elixir. Without air time, television reporters die. Print journalists can survive for weeks without a byline because readers rarely know one byline from another. But for a viewer to stop you at the grocery store with "I haven't seen you on the air lately. What are you doing now?" is probably the most deflating question a TV journalist can get. It means we've lost our touch or grown tired or fallen out of favor or just can't cut it any more.

Consequently, competition among television reporters was intense, not only against the opposition, but also against your own colleagues, most of whom were your friends. We did not bad-mouth colleagues to their face about their stories being chosen over ours, and we generally took our rejections in good grace. Having your turn-down wind up on the *CBS Morning News,* however, did not give us the air we wanted to breathe. What we wanted to breathe was the air of the Cronkite show.

And while Kalb may not have been as implacably persistent about it as Schorr, he still wanted very much to get on the air. "I certainly was unhappy," he says, "if I didn't make the show. . . . Realistically, I thought I had a story two or three times a week that deserved being put on the air. Did I get on the air two or three times a week? No. But did I fight for it? Yes. And was I unhappy when I walked out of the office having been turned down? Yes."

Kalb's rise from a graduate student in Russian history to the CBS diplomatic correspondent was what he himself called a "swift trajectory." Born in the Bronx, he was the youngest of three. Kalb's father was a tailor who learned his trade in a textile mill near Warsaw, Poland. At George Washington High School, Kalb was a very good student and helped tutor the newly arriving Puerto Rican kids. They liked him, Kalb says, and they protected him against the Catholic kids who waited for the Jewish kids after school. In the dead of winter, he said, the Irish would take chunks of frozen, snow-encrusted coal and pelt the Jewish kids. "This was my first insight into how nasty people could be. My Puerto Rican friends found out about it, and we formed our own militia."

With a master's degree from the Russian Research Center at Harvard, Kalb was drafted into the Army and taught Soviet communism at the Pentagon in the mid-fifties. Then with his Ph.D. almost in hand, he jumped at the chance to work in Moscow as the press attaché at the U.S. Embassy.

A 1957 Kalb article in the *New York Times* magazine caught Ed Murrow's eye. Kalb remembers that in Murrow's office the next day, Murrow pulled out a bottle of Johnnie Walker Black Label and began to pour. "He must have seen the look of shock on my face."

"Oh, dear. You don't drink?" he said.

"No. Does that mean there's no job?"

"No. But it's going to make it much more difficult."

The following day, says Kalb, he was offered a job, Scotch or no Scotch, starting on the overnight shift as a writer for WCBS Radio. From there it was back to Moscow in 1960 to replace Larry LeSueur. "The Murrow hand was behind all this," says Kalb.

Kalb's high opinion of his own work was clearly shared by the post-Murrow brass. In February 1963, after less than six years on the payroll, Kalb arrived in Washington as CBS's first full-time and fully qualified diplomatic correspondent. He was tall, articulate, soft-spoken, and unfailingly polite. Obvious to anyone who watched the new CBS man was how perfectly he seemed to fit in at the State Department.

In short order Kalb became television's nonpareil State Department correspondent, a man of considerable learning and intellectual pride, who spent his days parsing and noodling over the impenetrable and obfuscating language of the diplomats. One of Kalb's problems — indeed, the problem for any television reporter covering the State Department — was that so many of the stories involved a policy change or a decoding of diplomatic language or figuring out whether the department's spokesman had used a particular adjective before.

That was always the danger of having a

beat — after a few months you assumed the walk and the talk of the place. You began to wear a blue suit rather than khakis to the State Department. You learned that all exchanges were "fruitful." At the Pentagon, you tended to get your hair cut a little shorter and neater and talked about force levels and payloads. On Capitol Hill, you started yammering about the vote to suspend the vote by which the committee of the whole had voted to recommit. One night during a live broadcast from the Hill I caught myself saying, "Well, Walter, we hope to get cloture by Tuesday," as if I were the Senate majority leader or at least a committee chairman.

All of us had our sources — Rather had at least Donald Rumsfeld in the Nixon White House; Bob Schieffer had a hundred different colonels at the Pentagon; I had Richard Russell and Everett Dirksen in the Senate; and Kalb had Henry Kissinger.

No reporter got more out of a source than Kalb got out of Kissinger. "Awesome" was the word Kalb used to describe Kissinger's knowledge of public relations and the media, but he insists he did not get too close to Kissinger. "I believe at every step of the way I was perfectly aware of what Kissinger was doing and that he was perfectly aware that I was perfectly aware of what he was doing. . . . I think I knew Kissinger's mind so well that I didn't get gulled on any story."

Not everyone agreed with Kalb's general assessment. Ed Fouhy recalls that during the crash-and-burn days of Watergate "we really didn't have a lot of time to think it through. And we'd rush it on the air because we were so competitive. That was very true of Kissinger. Kissinger was forever calling Marvin ten minutes before air time. We were badly manipulated in those days as I look back on it. But that of course was a function of the fact that the *Evening News* was so important."

Beginning in 1972 Kalb got a backup at the State Department. It was Bernard, his older brother by eight years. CBS had hired him away from the *New York Times* in 1962 and immediately sent him back to Southeast Asia, where he was as well-known as Marvin was in Washington. But in Washington Bernard did not flourish as he once had. No longer was he on his own, no longer free to roam, no longer free to charter a plane from Laos to Bangkok. He was landlocked, chained to Galbraith and the desk and feeling that some of the stories the desk threw at him were beneath his experience.

He balked at interviewing the stripper

found wallowing in the Tidal Basin with Congressman Wilbur Mills in 1974 — a story I gladly took on. And he recalls, "I once got [an] assignment covering a flood in Occoquan, covering a flood. Occoquan, Virginia. Right? What I am doing on this assignment?"

Kalb had to learn like everyone else. He told me later of being sent to Albany, Georgia, with a camera crew on his first field assignment. When the mayor called on Kalb for a question, the ex-newspaperman's first instinct was to tuck his microphone under his arm to free his hands to take notes. The mayor's muffled answer, recorded but buried in Kalb's armpit, was unsalvageable.

Despite such gaffes and disputes with the desk, Bernard Kalb remains proud of his time in the Washington bureau and cites in particular the aggressive role he says he played in covering the 1971 arrival of the Communist Chinese delegation to the United Nations. NBC and ABC were content to wait for the delegate's arrival in New York, but Kalb persuaded management to take the extra step. Accompanied by Walter Cronkite, Gordon Manning, and cameraman Joe Masraff, Kalb boarded the Air France flight from Paris to New York on

November 11 and persuaded the two leaders of the Chinese delegation to be filmed. They agreed to the in-flight filming, but only if their words were not recorded. As it turned out, the coup was just being on the plane. Cronkite made the most of it — filming the opening shots of the *Evening News* from inside the plane and devoting more than five minutes to the story.

Collectively, Marvin and Bernard were known as "The Kalbs" to members of the Washington bureau, who rarely bothered to differentiate between one and the other. Bernard says that he and Marvin became "fungible": He'd give a speech somewhere out of town and it would be Marvin's glossy photo in the lobby. Despite the confusion, Marvin generally overshadowed Bernard, who to this day seems to have not a jealous bone in his body for having a lesser reputation. It is widely believed, because the story is in print, that the CBS foreign desk in New York once took a telephone call from a woman who said, "Hello, this is Marvin Kalb's mother. Can you tell me where my son, Bernie, is?"

I asked Kalb if it was true.

"Apocryphal," he said, "but I cherish the story."

Roger Mudd

My cubicle was next to Marvin Kalb's. I was never easy. My late mother-in-law, who loved me very much, once told me she wished I wouldn't make such a federal case out of everything. Don Richardson, the deputy bureau chief, made the mistake of telling me at lunch one day how to take care of rhododendrons, not knowing that I planted and cared for a dozen or so at our home. When we got back to the office, he warned everybody not ever to ask Mudd about rhododendrons. "It'll be endless," he said.

I understood his discomfort, unable as I was to let misinformation, sweeping pronouncements, or just plain mistakes go unchallenged. I simply hated being wrong. That meant for me, of course, always making sure I knew what I was talking about and being almost excessively well-informed about my assignment. That gave my reporting a high degree of accuracy and authenticity, but it also gave my editors and superiors at CBS a pain in the neck and elsewhere.

I resisted fly-in, fly-out assignments — parachute journalism, with only a couple of hours on the ground — because they would have required my pretending I really knew what was going on. I resisted leaving my

Capitol Hill assignment, preferring to become a specialist on the Congress; in 1965, when CBS was not yet sending family men to Vietnam, I refused the request of the president of CBS News, Fred Friendly, to go because I had a young family and because I was a political reporter who believed Congress needed a full-time correspondent, just as the State Department needed Marvin Kalb and the White House needed Bob Pierpoint and the Great Society needed Daniel Schorr. Years later when CBS said I was not "well-rounded" enough to succeed Walter Cronkite, it was Al Hunt of the *Wall Street Journal* who defended me. He said David Broder of the *Washington Post* had never reported from Vietnam and no one had dared call the great Broder not well-rounded.

Ad-libbing, a mandatory skill for any television anchor, was frequently a problem for me. Ask me about John Gilligan and why he lost to Bill Saxbe in Ohio in 1968 or ask me why Jesse Helms gave up the chairmanship of the Agriculture Committee to go on Foreign Relations and I would light up. But if called on to do happy talk or vamp about something outside my field, like space or the balance of trade or the Middle East, I could be a no-show. And if the film broke, heaven forbid, or a live switch to Des Moines failed to connect, the audience would be treated to a glowering and grim anchorman, unable to smooth his way through. I curdled at the thought of publicity interviews, not being in control, having to talk about myself, having to dabble in self-analysis.

Doing station promos for the CBS affiliates around the country was another dread. The copy would read something like — "This is Roger Mudd, of CBS News, urging you to watch Channel Eight in Chillicothe, where the news comes fast, straight, and complete." Was that true or not? I didn't know and I had no way to find out. I could envision thousands of viewers in Chillicothe who thought Channel 8 was a joke and wondered what the hell Mudd was doing, shilling for that schlock outfit.

And finally, I was not driven. Of course I wanted to succeed, to be seen, to be known as a reporter who could be counted on to get the facts straight, add an extra depth to the story, and bring to the tube a distinctive style that helped CBS News deserve its cachet. But I was not so driven that my happiness depended on being on the *Evening News* every night. I was proud to be working for CBS, but I tried my best to keep my home and my family first. It was a twenty-four-hour job to avoid being run over. The bureau wanted you all the time; they wanted you for everything and for nothing.

All of this added up to an independence and an aloofness that many interpreted as arrogance. Perhaps it was arrogance, because I believed that the values most journalists embraced were, in fact, superior to those of our corporate owners, whose world turned on earnings, ratings, demographics, market share, and spin.

But it also added up to an integrity and credibility that came to be admired, at least by much of the television audience and by many of my colleagues in the media, if not in the front offices of CBS. If New York thought me unbending about my job, it was because I loved my job and brought to it an obvious pleasure in what I was doing and in the story I was reporting, a delight in the use of my intellect and humor, and a joy in the use of words, a process that television has devalued. A few in the bureau claimed, half-seriously, that I would think up a closing line or two and then go out and find a story to fit.

That was not true, of course. But I do recall that the first night I reported Wilbur Mills and the Argentine stripper being fished out of the Tidal Basin, the close virtually wrote itself: "The good thing about this story, Walter, is that it can only get worse."

How all these quirks and peeves and skills and strengths produced my ambivalence toward my profession I can only hazard a guess. Doubtless much of it came from my parents — my father, from southern Maryland, a civil engineer and topographer, was the polar opposite of the glad-handing, backslapping extrovert. A quiet perfectionist, he avoided guesswork and insisted on precision. One of his favorite aphorisms was that the value of a postage stamp was "in its ability to stick to it." My mother, born and raised in the wheat country of Washington State, was a real westerner — self-reliant, independent, and skeptical of the government. The last administration that knew what it was doing, she once told me, was Herbert Hoover's. She had little use for the bombast and oversold aspects of our contemporary life.

Her sense of humor was active and robust, however. We were at breakfast one morning when she was trying to be helpful. I was out of graduate school, still unemployed, and growing desperate to find a job. She said brightly, "You've always liked dogs. Why don't you be a veterinarian?" It was such a great and funny line that I almost choked on my oatmeal.

From both of them came a devotion to the truth and to honorable behavior. When I was seven, I stole a book from our neighborhood bookstore. My mother found it in a dresser drawer, confronted me with it, and received my instant confession. My punishment was to scrub the two bathrooms in our Washington, D.C., apartment at twenty-five cents per week until I had earned the money to pay for the book. Then, she said, "I'll take you up to Brentano's, but you will go in alone and ask for the manager. And you'll tell what you did, you'll give him your money, you'll tell him that you're sorry, and you'll tell him you'll never steal again."

It took eight weeks to earn the money — a very quiet eight weeks. There was no heavy or constant lecturing from my parents. There was only the terror for a seven-year-old boy in 1935 being made, for the first time in his life, to accept full responsibility for the consequences of his behavior.

If that experience wasn't enough, my probity got further enforced years later at my alma mater, Washington and Lee University, where one of the nation's only single-sanction honor code still flourishes.

But it was in graduate school at the

University of North Carolina where I got my first graphic lesson in the written truth, the importance of primary sources, the accuracy of descriptions and quotations, and the critical need for context. The lesson came when I turned in the draft of my master's thesis. A day or two later I got a note from my adviser, J. Carlyle Sitterson: "Come see me."

I tapped on his door.

"Sit down," he said. "I gather this is your first draft?"

"No, sir. It's my final draft. I just do one draft."

"Is that so? Well, some of your 'final draft' descriptions I don't understand."

"What don't you understand, Dr. Sitterson?"

"You say the House Caucus Room looks like a 'German nightclub.' What does that mean?"

"Well, it means high ceilings and big glass chandeliers and lots of ornate gold."

"Have you ever been to a German night club?"

"No, sir."

"Then where did you get that description?"

"I read it somewhere. It's in my notes."

"You didn't footnote it."

"No, sir."

"Take it out."

"Yes, sir."

It was my first confrontation with a real editor, and I was seething. But he was right and I never forgot what he was telling me: Get it right or do not use it. Your credibility rides on getting it right, he told me. It was a tough but necessary introduction to the demands of scholarship and of journalism.

So in 1963, there I was, occupying the fourth cubicle from the right as the CBS congressional correspondent, prickly, at times sardonic, slightly self-important, unnecessarily unforgiving of others' mistakes, reliable, trustworthy, knowledgeable, and regularly infatuated with the absurdities of the Congress in particular and the government in general.

There I was at age thirty-five, married to the wonderful E. J. Spears, who had just borne the fourth of our four children and who, being southern, tried hard (and still does) to soften me around the edges.

There I was, standing six-feet-two-inches with big feet, big hands, big voice, big ego, and masquerading as the bureau's resident expert on the care and feeding of rhododendrons.

George Herman

In the last booth on the left was George Herman, the bureau's senior man and its only pipe smoker. He had grown up on East Seventy-third Street, between Madison and Fifth Avenues, a quiet and shaded block in one of Manhattan's most exclusive neighborhoods. Herman's father, Sidney, was a banker, the president of a family bank — the family being, in fact, the Herman family.

When the young Herman said he wanted to become a reporter, his father solemnly summoned him into the library, sat him down, and said, "Son, don't do it. It will only coarsen you dreadfully."

Of course, it never did coarsen him. Herman was the bureau's most erudite and educated, and its unofficial encyclopedia. He was a math major at Dartmouth, but when he won the senior writing prize, outwriting the editor of the college paper, he decided on journalism. Fresh out of Columbia with an MA in journalism, he got a job writing at WQXR in New York. But when the *New York Times* bought the radio station, Herman quit, because his first cousin, Orvil Dryfoos, was part of the paper's owning family and he wanted to avoid the trap of any potential nepotism.

By 1945 Herman was working the overnight desk at CBS. He was on duty Tuesday, August 14, the evening a staff announcer interrupted with the bulletin that Japan had surrendered. If any story qualified for major coverage it was this one — the end of World War II. But the panicky announcer returned the network to its regular dance band programming. Whereupon Herman, not even a reporter but a night radio editor, took over the microphone, ad-libbing for almost twenty minutes until the great and polished ad-libber, Robert Trout, arrived.

Herman was 4-F. His poor eyesight and flat feet kept him out of the Army but left him free to strike a deal with CBS News to travel in Asia as a freelancer. After the Korean War started, Herman returned to Korea as a full-fledged CBS correspondent, and this time was with the United Nations troops when they landed at Inchon in September 1950.

When the fighting ended, Herman was reassigned to the Washington bureau, covering the Eisenhower White House, where he quietly began dating Patty Kirwan, a secretary in the press office. Her reaction when seeing him for the first time was "cute but too short." They were married in 1955 and raised three sons, Charles, Scott, and Douglas, in their Georgetown house on O Street, which they famously had painted with a myriad of colors, mortifying the local Fine Arts Commission.

Over the next three decades, Herman had a dazzling string of assignments — from the White House to Congress to the Supreme Court to the economy and finally, in 1969, as moderator of *Face the Nation.*

He was the shop steward of our union, the American Federation of Television & Radio Artists, and had no known enemies, unless they were from the CBS labor department.

He had one detractor at the White House,

however, and he was the president. In *The Powers That Be,* David Halberstam wrote that President Kennedy complained about Herman being assigned to the White House. "He's not one of our guys, you know, the guys who covered us and rode with us during the campaign — he doesn't know us," so quoted Halberstam. The implication was of course that Herman did not measure up to the Kennedy standard — not as dashing, exciting, and in the Kennedy style as was, say, Sander Vanocur of NBC, who was thought of as one of the new president's boys. Herman shrugged it off. He knew he'd be beaten on minor stories by Vanocur and William Lawrence of ABC, another JFK favorite, in the first few months, but that in the end it would even up.[3]

It did even up when Kennedy's military aide, General Ted Clifton, leaked to Herman JFK's plans to meet Charles de Gaulle in Paris in June 1961. The leak occurred when Clifton casually asked Herman what the CBS lead story was to be that night. When Herman told him, Clifton replied, "Well, I'm not so sure I'd lead with that."

"What would you lead with, then?" asked Herman.

"I think I'd lead with the president going to Paris," said Clifton, oh so casually.

139

Robert Pierpoint

There should have been a sixth cubicle in that front row and Robert Pierpoint should have been in it. But by the time Don Hewitt designed the bureau's layout, Pierpoint had been supplanted by Rather at the White House and was no longer regarded by the Cronkites as front-row material. It was a serious mistake.

When William Faulkner went to Stockholm to accept the 1950 Nobel Prize for Literature, twenty-five-year-old Robert Pierpoint, of Redondo Beach, California, was among the glittering audience, because he was dating the daughter of the president of the Nobel Corporation. Dating her "quite closely," was the way he put it more than fifty years later.

He was in Stockholm, where he had gone to learn Swedish, working as a translator at the Swedish Broadcasting Corporation, and as a stringer for CBS News.

So when Ed Murrow cabled Pierpoint for a copy of Faulkner's memorable speech — "I believe that man will not merely endure; he will prevail" — he knew how to get a copy and get it fast. His quick response led Murrow to hire Pierpoint and send him off to cover the Korean War as "fresh blood," joining some of the older journalists from

World War II. Pierpoint, who had seen no action as a Navy radar technician in the war, said Murrow told him the veteran reporters were "going to give you a hard time. But they're not the best correspondents in the world; they're just the oldest." Pierpoint did well and came to admire Murrow immensely because of his willingness to share the *See It Now* microphone and camera with the reporters on the scene.

After the Korean War, Pierpoint replaced George Herman as the Tokyo bureau chief, but six years in the Far East was enough. He cabled New York: "Either bring me home or leave me here for the rest of my life. I'm going Asian."

He came home in 1957. His first domestic assignment was covering the Little Rock school integration story, and his second was as the CBS News White House correspondent.

It was a quick seven-year rise for the son of a small-town banker and a very conservative Baptist, a graduate of the University of Redlands in California — a good school but hardly an elite one — and a man who was not a natural broadcaster, a man not endowed with a leather-lunged, basso profundo.

He was, however, adventuresome, quick-witted, hardworking, substantive, honorable, and totally reliable.

When Ted Koop, the Washington bureau chief at the time, assigned Pierpoint to the White House, he became one of the correspondents who covered the president regularly for the three wire services, the three networks, *Time, Newsweek,* and the major newspapers — the *New York Times,* the *New York Herald Tribune,* the *Washington Post,* the *Evening Star,* the *Wall Street Journal,* the *Los Angeles Times,* the *Baltimore Sun,* and the *Chicago Tribune.* Koop advised Pierpoint to take with him on his first day a bottle of Scotch and a bottle of bourbon and to leave them in the press room. It was the expected way for the new boy to pay tribute. By early afternoon, Pierpoint says, both bottles were half gone.

At the bureau there developed a Back Row of reporters with Pierpoint as its senior man. They were very talented needlers of the Front Row. They were all very good, very anxious to break out, and very available whenever the Front Row claimed it was overburdened.

When Doug Kiker's paper, the *New York Herald Tribune,* folded in 1967, Bill Small tried to hire him at CBS. But Kiker took one look at the Back Row — Pierpoint, Pappas, Schoumacher, Morton, Serafin, Walker, and McLaughlin — and told Small, "If your entire first string was killed in a single plane crash and your second string came down with the flu and couldn't work, I still wouldn't get on the air."

CHAPTER 11
THE BACK ROW

"Lesley Stahl and I had adjoining desks in the back hall-way . . . and it was hell on wheels to try to break out of that. You were just frozen there. . . . Everybody thought I was competent to do just damn near anything, but Bill Galbraith thought I was competent to sit in the back hallway waiting to hear the bell ring."

Those are the words of Jim McManus remembering the frustrations of life in the Back Row in the Washington bureau, the Back Row being almost a storeroom where Bill Small sent the new hires or the second-string correspondents.

If the competition and rivalry between and among the five of us on the Front Row were intense but discreet, they were intense but twice as discreet on the Back Row.

"There were correspondents waiting for someone to die," says David Schoumacher, an original backbencher, "and then there were reporters waiting for correspondents who were waiting for correspondents to die to die."

In the Back Row, there was only a scattering of desks and chairs and mail trays. To type up a story, second-stringers had to scrounge to find an available typewriter in the main newsroom. The sparse accommodations would have been of no consequence if the occupants could only have gotten on the air. That was the problem. There was just so much air the Cronkite show yielded to the Washington bureau each night, and most of it got assigned to the Front Row. That left slim pickings for the dozen or so backbenchers, whose numbers grew so fast as the bureau expanded that some of them had to be housed on the third floor with the French TV bureau.

Most of them, however, found ways to break out. Take McManus. He was no kid when he joined us. He was laid back and forty-five-years old, with slightly thinning hair, a comfortable Terre Haute accent, and a quick bright smile, and was a first-class writer. He started as a newspaperman in Indiana, took a turn in local television, and in 1968 ran the press advance for Robert Kennedy's Indiana primary campaign. After Kennedy's death, he came to Washington as the White House correspondent for Westinghouse; six years later he was on the Back Row at CBS. But because the assignment desk always wanted a couple of utility men available for when the bell rang, McManus was rarely out on the street looking for stories. He did a lot of filling in and backing up at the White House and the State Department, and he did his share of stakeouts.

One of those stakeouts sent him to the Government Printing Office with a camera crew to film President Ford's first budget coming off the presses, a ho-hum assignment. But McManus remembers saying to himself that he didn't think "anybody had ever scooped the president on his own budget." He happened to catch the eye of the press boss at the GPO and told him he had run offset presses back in Indiana. "Well, that guy loved his press and he started bragging on what that press would do and then he said it would collate twenty-six pages while you're looking at it and I said I just can't believe that and he went over and he actually took a budget summary and he brought it back and he put it down on a cardboard box about elbow high in front of me." Just then someone yelled his name and he left the summary right in front of McManus. "So I rolled it up in a tight little tube and stuck it up the sleeve of my trench coat."

McManus managed to sneak out and "ran like hell back to the bureau."

That night, McManus broke onto the Cronkite show with the off-lead story. "When I got on the elevator that night Sandy [Socolow, the bureau chief] introduced me to his friend and said, 'This man is going to win the Pulitzer Prize one day.' That's just an idea of how hard you had to scratch."

In the case of Bernard Shaw, it was a matter of scrambling to match a headline in the *Washington Post* on May 23, 1976:

CLOSED SESSION ROMANCE ON THE HILL

It was an exclusive *Post* story alleging that Wayne Hays, the Democratic chairman of the House Administration Committee, had his mistress on the committee payroll as a $14,000-a-year clerk. It had the city cluck-clucking. Shaw got to work. He found the two *Post* reporters — Rudy Maxa and Marion Clark — at their home not far from the bureau, congratulated them on their story, and said he was tracking down the alleged mistress, Elizabeth Ray. "Well, she's right here," said Maxa. "But she's not in very good shape. She's been taking tranquilizers." Shaw said he promised to be gentle if he could interview her. "Well, come on over," they said.

Shaw and his cameras crew set up in Maxa's kitchen. "Elizabeth Ray came in and she really looked out of it," Shaw recalls. "She was very heavily sedated, very nervous, warily looking at me. . . . We interviewed her for about forty-five minutes or so. . . . She was making good sense. Sometimes she would go in and go out. . . . She talked about being on the payroll but not being able to type, could barely answer the phone, couldn't file. And obviously it was sex that was the glue of their relationship. So, at one point in the interview I said, 'Did dinner invariably lead to sex?' She took a deep breath and she said, 'Yes.' "With that, Shaw rushed back to the bureau, called Hays's press secretary, and guaranteed him CBS would not put Elizabeth Ray on the air without a response from Hays.

Shaw was no novice at this work. At thirty-six, he had done four years in the Marines, had graduated from the University of Illinois, had worked radio and TV in Chicago, and had come to Washington in 1968 with

Westinghouse.

His ploy worked with Hays's press secretary, who hurriedly chartered a plane to fly Hays back to Washington from Ohio. Hays arrived at the bureau on M Street disheveled, Shaw said, with minutes to spare. He denied all of Ray's charges, and Shaw went on the air with a careful and balanced story. Hays's denials did not hold up for long. He was forced to resign his committee chairmanship three weeks later and from the House itself in September.

Shaw was on the Cronkite show three nights that week. With hard work and hustle, he had skunked both ABC and NBC. He still says he is most proud of that story.

For Bob Schieffer to get out of the Back Row required a combination of luck, talent, and hard-nosed lobbying. Schieffer, a compact, outgoing man, is Texas from beginning to end. He still pronounces "yes" as "yea-us." Born in Austin in 1937, he grew up in Waco and Fort Worth, graduated from Texas Christian University, went to Vietnam for the *Fort Worth Star-Telegram,* became the anchor of the newspaper's TV station, married into a wealthy Fort Worth family, and came to Washington in 1969, convinced he was ready for the network. It didn't take him long — just four months, in fact.

He made his CBS debut on May 11, 1969, with a fluffy story on a masked costume ball at the Nixon White House.[1]

During his first months about all Schieffer did was cover the antiwar rallies. "I got terrible respiratory problems that first winter," he says, "because we got tear-gassed. It was very difficult. Everybody was tired on both sides. The cameramen — a lot of them — were very hawkish at one point and resented the war protestors, as we all did. There's a whole lot of difference in the First Amendment in the abstract and having to go out there and have somebody throw rocks at you."

After less than a year, Schieffer was sent to cover a Pentagon press conference. The regular Pentagon man, Steve Rowan, was on his way out, and Schieffer quickly saw this as an opening to join the Front Row. "I kept lobbying to go back. Small called me in and said, 'We've decided to make you a correspondent.' 'Well,' I said, 'what about the Pentagon?' I loved covering a beat. The Pentagon was like being in a little town. What I figured out about the Pentagon, it was just like a big ole courthouse. You learned quickly at the courthouse that you get the best news about the sheriff from the county commissioner and vice versa. At the Pentagon you get the best news about the Army from the Air Force and vice versa. So I had no problem with it at all."

In less than a year Schieffer had become not only a correspondent but also a correspondent assigned to one of the five most important beats in the city. His early rise to prominence did not sit well with some of his colleagues in the Back Row, who thought he did too much toadying around Bill Small. Phil Jones says he watched Schieffer every night drift by Small's office just as the Cronkite show was starting. "He'd wave and Small would call out, 'Come on in, Bob, and watch the show.' I was not that kind of personality," says Jones. "I was more reserved."

Jed Duvall, after tours on the New York desk, in Vietnam, and in the Atlanta bureau, came to Washington in 1974 and joined the Back Row. "We were the guys," he says, "who were told at five o'clock to cover something that Scheiffer wanted covered. . . . I understood Schieffer was a guy who would stay in the office and other people would go out and do the work and bring it in and hand it to him. I never liked that."

For all the carping about Schieffer from his contemporary competitors, I found him funny, easy to be with, ambitious, versatile, but in need of constant reassurance.

Whenever the Cronkite show would pass on one of his stories, we would hear him bitching and kicking wastebaskets on the Back Row. I would immediately dial his office number and in a heavily disguised southern voice tell him I was Bobby Ohmahundro calling from Pascagoula, Mississippi, and that I hadn't seen him on the air for a long time and hoped he wasn't sick or something. I got away with that one twice.

I had heard that on his trips back to Texas, Schieffer was using the word "anchor" as the "handle" on his CB radio. I conned Richard Salant, the president of CBS News, into signing a blank piece of his CBS stationery and sent Schieffer the following letter:

Dear Bob: It has come to my attention that you are calling yourself "anchor" on your two-way radio transmissions while in Texas. At CBS News, the term "anchor" is never lightly bestowed. It is earned by only a few after years of hard work, loyalty, and superior talent. Walter Cronkite is an anchor, Mike Wallace is an anchor, Harry Reasoner is an anchor, Roger Mudd is an anchor.

You are not an anchor.

If I learn that you are persisting in using this distinguished title to which you have no claim, I will expect to see you in my office within twenty-four hours. Sincerely, Richard Salant.

It took Schieffer almost six months before he tracked down the sender. When my phone rang finally, Schieffer said, "You sonofabitch," and hung up laughing.

Some years later when Schieffer became one of Cronkite's occasional substitutes, he began resisting out-of-town assignments, fearing he would not be available if the call came. One night on the *Evening News,* I did catch him on an out-of-town story, but it was just a mile or two out of town. He was doing his stand-up on Chain Bridge, which crosses the Potomac River barely beyond Washington's city limits. I sent him a telegram — this was before e-mail — congratulating him on being out in the field again and hoping CBS was paying him at *per diem* rates.

The men and women on the Back Row were a proud bunch and probably had more fun back there than we did out front. They were proud because even as second-stringers at CBS they knew they could have been first-string at any of the other bureaus.

Not everyone felt that way, however. The chief malcontent was Ed Bradley, who came to Washington in 1974 after two years in Vietnam as almost a star. And if he wasn't yet a perfect star, Bill Small had promised to make him one. Bradley, a thirty-three-year-old from Philadelphia and a graduate of Cheyney State Teachers College, began his life with CBS as a stringer in Paris, where he'd gone to write the Great American Novel but had run out of steam after just two pages. For $20,000 a year and $69.50 a day in combat pay, Bradley hauled off to Vietnam as a "contract assignment reporter." In 1974, Small, then in charge of things in New York, wanted Bradley to work in New York. Bradley refused. Anywhere but New York, he said. Washington he regarded as a "hick town," but with Small's promise of stardom, he agreed to "try" Washington. It was a bad fit from the start.

Bill Galbraith found out in a hurry that Bradley "wasn't about to take any piddly assignment." Bradley remembered his typical instructions from Galbraith as, " 'Roger needs to come back and do his piece so we need somebody up there to cover the Senate. Nothing is going to happen but in the off chance it might, we need somebody up there.' So who do you go to? You go to the low man on the totem pole. That was always me. So I got frustrated with having an assignment every day that never went anywhere. We'd go to a hearing at 9 o'clock and you'd sit there 'til 12:30. Boring hearing, nothing happened. You'd shoot 1,500 feet of film and nothing ever came of it. The hearing was over at 3:30 and they say come on back to the bureau. Your day is done. So what are going to do tomorrow? 'Ed, would you go up to the Hill and take a look at the Senate?' "

His relations with the desk became contentious. Bradley was not the appreciative backbencher, thankful to be working in the great Washington bureau. Toward the end of the day, with Galbraith looking for somebody to send to the Hill, Bradley imagined Galbraith saying to himself, "If I ask Ed to go up to the Hill I'll have to listen at all his shit about the building, which side

155

of the Hill, which senator, is there a specific congressman you want me to look at, Bill?" One day, in fact, Bradley turned to Galbraith and said, "You'd better get yourself another dude." Such a challenge to the desk was virtually unheard of, but the quote was confirmed by everybody but Bradley. Bradley did not deny the challenge, however, only the word "dude." "Not in my vocabulary," he said.

Small realized he had a problem. He put Bradley on the road during the 1976 presidential campaign, first with Senator Birch Bayh and then with Governor Jimmy Carter. Bradley loved it. "You're on the air all the time," he told me five months before he died. "You're moving around. A different place every day. A new experience. The camaraderie of being with the pack." He figured that during those fourteen months, he was home twenty-two nights.

With Carter's election, Bradley became the number two at the White House, the bureau's most prestigious beat. He thought it better than general assignment, he said, because "you had a gig every day." But Bradley didn't like the White House either. It was too confining, he said. "I was in that room every day. . . . You never went anywhere unless he went somewhere."

So what to do with this unhappy, trapped, talented, handsome black man who could write his own contract at any network? In 1978 there was an opening on the highly successful *CBS Reports*. Bradley snapped it up and was gone, his four years in Washington "less than glorious."

Finally, there was the veteran correspondent passed over by the younger and more telegenic, who was still so proud of CBS that he was determined to make the best of his time on the Back Row.

That man was Robert Pierpoint. When Rather arrived in 1965, Pierpoint had been first string at the White House for six years. Up against Rather, Pierpoint's television image suffered. Rather had intense and dark good looks. His ability to memorize enabled him to deliver smoothly two minutes of copy he had just written without a teleprompter or a note within fifty feet of him. Pierpoint wasn't *bad* looking, but he couldn't match Rather's profile or intensity. In addition, Pierpoint did not have a photographic memory, which meant that he needed his script in hand, and that meant a lot of head bobbing.

One of his ABC friends at the White House, Tom Jarriel, had a solution. After you write your story, he told Pierpoint, record it on a lightweight tape recorder, hook the recorder on your belt beneath your jacket, run the cord from the recorder inside your jacket, and then fit the earpiece snugly into your ear so that the cord doesn't show. Then, said Jarriel, when the cameraman says, "Cue," turn the recorder on and deliver to the camera in your best broadcast voice exactly what you are hearing in your ear.

It worked, and "Bob got a hell of a lot better," says Small, who acknowledges that Rather had become so "dominant" that Pierpoint remained the backup.

Jarriel apparently had picked up the technique from a local TV reporter in San Antonio, who threatened to sue when he heard that Pierpoint was using what he called his "invention." Pierpoint gave the reporter's letter to a CBS lawyer, who said the guy could not sue on the basis of recording your own words twice.

To many of the backbenchers, Pierpoint was one of CBS's great names from the past. Eric Engberg, Pierpoint's junior by at least fifteen years, remembers the day the Nixon press office summoned a uniformed Secret Service cop to move everyone back five feet to make way for a visiting congressional delegation. Engberg, who is no shrinking violet himself, was nonetheless in awe when Pierpoint objected and told the cop that there was no security issue. "We use this stakeout position all the time." When the cop insisted, Engberg says, Pierpoint "stuck his chest out and said, 'We aren't moving. To get us to move you will have to arrest me. And my crew will then shoot pictures of you arresting me. And that will make a nice story.' " The White House cop retreated and everyone held their positions.

"It is hard to explain to an outsider today," says Engberg, "how proud we all were of Pierpoint."

CHAPTER 12
THE FOUR RULES OF
SEVAREID

There was no one else like him at CBS. Nor at NBC or ABC. He was tall, imposing, intellectual, and philosophical. He walked through the bureau like a god — aloof, speaking to almost no one.

Eric Sevareid, one of broadcasting's original thinkers, did not belong in broadcasting; one of television's most honored analysts was terrified of everything about television; one of journalism's finest writers was so unsure of his own gifts that he modestly entitled two of his books *In One Ear* and *Small Sounds in the Night*.

But behind his complexities, shyness, and passing dark moods, there was a lucid intellect and an eloquence unique in a television culture that seemed to prize neither. Beginning in 1964, his analysis became a nightly fixture on the *CBS Evening News* — two minutes and fifteen seconds, or about three hundred words at most, Monday through

Friday. No one in television or print did what he did. It was simply too draining. But Sevareid wrote an analysis five nights a week for thirteen years. His audience was large and devoted.

Sevareid brought the Washington bureau a prestige that raised its esprit de corps. He was an essential player in almost everything we did. Not to have a Sevareid analysis following a presidential news conference or a major speech was unthinkable. CBS News could not have been what it was without him.

Sevareid was fifty-two when he rejoined the bureau in 1964. Murrow had hired him away from the Paris edition of the *New York Herald Tribune* in 1939. He traveled with the French Army until France capitulated, and for the next twenty years he reported from Washington, New York, and London.

By the time he returned to Washington in 1964, his personal life was a mess. He had virtually abandoned his wife, Lois, who was a manic depressive. They were divorced in 1962, after two sons, Michael and Peter, and twenty-seven years of marriage. With him on his return to Washington was his second wife, the beautiful Belén Marshall, almost twenty years younger, and their two-month-old daughter, Cristina.

161

Few of us knew any of that when he arrived. What we saw was a remote, strikingly handsome Viking. He had very little to say and most of us were in awe of him.

Perhaps most in awe was the young Peter Sturtevant, the newest editor on the assignment desk. The tall, good-looking Sturtevant, with his master's degree in journalism, was eager to get started. Just as he was settling in, he looked up and saw, walking very quietly through the news room — *Oh, good Lord,* it was Eric Sevareid. Peter had never seen the great man before, but he had worshipped him for years. Sevareid didn't say a word, not a hello or even a look. He simply dropped three pages of copy on Peter's desk without breaking stride. Peter said to himself, "My God, the man drops his copy on me and I work on the editorial desk. I guess I'd better put a pencil to this."

Peter knew what to do. He'd taken courses in writing and editing back at Iowa University. The trick in journalism was "short and tight." The trouble was that Eric Sevareid didn't write short and tight. He wrote long and loose. For almost an hour, Peter worked on those three pages, and he *cut* — there was no other word for it, he *cut* — Eric Sevareid's copy from two minutes and fifteen seconds to about a minute thirty. Peter was proud. "Boy, this is great. On my first day on the job I get to edit one of Eric's pieces."

Peter took the edited copy and walked back to Sevareid's office, knocked gently on the door, and put the copy on his desk.

"Here, what do you think?" he said.

"Who are you?" the Oracle said.

"I work on the desk. It's my first day at work. I hope you think it's OK."

Sevareid started shouting at Peter and told him to get out of his office and never to touch his copy again.

Poor Peter. He thought he was doing Sevareid a favor and instead wound up being yelled at by one of the two people in the bureau you don't want yelling at you, the other being Mister Small.

After that, there was very little in the way of conversation between Peter and Sevareid. He'd occasionally bump into him in the men's room, but Peter said he'd been told that when he stood at the urinal next to Sevareid he wasn't supposed to say anything.

Peter Sturtevant on his very first day had learned the Four Rules of Sevareid:

1. Never Talk to Eric at the Urinal.
2. Never Talk to Eric in the Hall.
3. Never Talk to Eric on the Elevator.
4. Never Talk to Eric.

Sevareid was not without considerable vanity. Lillian Brown, his makeup artist, says he took very good care of his skin. "He had those magnificent cheekbones and I always tried to make them a little deeper," she says. "He needed to be made up. He liked it."

His ritual before recording a piece began with his loosening his belt and then slowly sipping a glass of water, warm water. Radio technicians were instructed not to look at him through the control room window while he recorded. When he taped his television commentary, a woman was generally assigned to operate the teleprompter in the hope that he would be less likely to get upset in her presence. Each piece of equipment — camera, microphone, lights, teleprompter — had to be checked and rechecked and triple-checked before Severeid's taping at 5:15 PM. "But if something happened, and it sometimes did," the director has recalled, "he had a fit."

By noon each day, he had thought through his evening commentary, which he tried out on a chosen lunch companion. Those companions had to admit, however, that they could never quite hear anything Sevareid had been telling them because of his shyness, his mumbles, and the noise of the lunchtime crowd. When lunching with Eric, the word was: tuck in your tie so it doesn't drag through the soup as you lean over to listen. Either that or take an ear trumpet.

My own relationship with Sevareid was minimal, though I loved his stuff and though we were thrown together countless times on late-night specials, conventions, election nights, and inaugurations. I cannot remember a single lunch with just Sevareid or a conversation with him in which he tried out his nightly piece. The reason was, I believe, that he did not regard me as a sufficiently heavy thinker because of the way I covered politics and the Congress — that is, slightly irreverently and slightly askance. In Sevareid's eyes such an approach was flip, lacked proper respect for the politicians and their institutions, and added to decline in their public esteem. He was too refined to complain to my face, but he said as much in private conversations with management.

One of Sevareid's steady luncheon companions was the bureau chief, Bill Small. Because of his daily contact with Sevareid, Small was not in awe of him. That freedom enabled Small to do something he had never done — kill one of Sevareid's commentaries. Small had generally steered clear of monitoring Sevareid's pieces, which he said crossed his desk "only as a courtesy." But this one was particularly harsh, implying that Joseph H. Hirschhorn, the millionaire art collector and speculator, had demanded that his price for giving his art collection to the government was to have the building named for him. Small told Sevareid that Washington was full of buildings carrying donor's names and that no federal building could be named without clearance from the White House. Sevareid became petulant. When Small informed the Cronkite show there would be no Sevareid piece that night, Sevareid stomped out of Small's office. But Small forgot to tell radio, and that night Joe Hirschhorn took his lumps coast to coast on the CBS Radio Network.

Despite the honors and the praise Sevareid brought to the *CBS Evening News,* his relationship with Cronkite was standoffish. The Murrow Boys had a low opinion of Cronkite. They saw him as a journeyman wire-service reporter, with tunnel vision, with no literary style, and without much intellectual curiosity. Much of that contempt was generated by Sevareid and Charles Collingwood, both of whom had had a healthy interest in succeeding Douglas Edwards as anchor of the *CBS Evening News* and resented the selection of Cronkite. Cronkite was well aware of their disdain for him, barely concealing his impatience with the two minutes and fifteen seconds Sevareid ate up each night. The show, he figured, could easily have done without Sevareid. One night after the program was off the air, Cronkite blew his stack. "We could have gotten another item on tonight," he said, "but Eric had three swallows. Goddamn, I counted them! Without those swallows, we could have gotten another story on."[1]

Even with the swallows and the gulps, Sevareid's presence was a great bulwark for those of us who did the summaries, the running stories, and the bulletins. Having him by your side brought internal comfort, knowing that if you ran dry there was always Eric to turn to.

David Schoumacher told me the story of how Sevareid saved him just as his well ran dry. The date was March 26, 1965, toward lunch time, and the bureau was emptying out. Suddenly Small appeared at Schoumacher's desk and said, "You've got to get downstairs quick. We've just heard — the wires are carrying that the president and J. Edgar Hoover are going to make an announcement of arrests and we've got to get on the air."

The arrests, they assumed, were in connection with the murder in Alabama of Viola Liuzza, the Detroit housewife who had gone down for the Selma-to-Montgomery civil rights march.

Schoumacher ran to the assignment desk, grabbing wire copy from Galbraith as he zipped by. He went on the air and said he was standing by for an important announcement from the White House and he expected the president and the FBI director to appear any minute. Except they didn't appear and they didn't appear.

So Schoumacher began to speculate. The Liuzza rumor was in the air, of course, and "it very well could [be] that when the president comes out he will (blah blah blah). . . ."

Five minutes went by; Schoumacher had used up every speck of material he had; he started to repeat himself and nobody was helping him.

Then, in his ear, he heard Small tell him, "David, we've found Eric and Eric is over at the Provencal [Restaurant] and he's on his way."

David rejoiced. Help was coming. But he knew how far away the restaurant was, and he began to figure. "That's at least four blocks. Eric's an old man. He'll never get here."

Then Small said, "Eric's in the building. Eric has arrived. Eric is coming. Hold on, David."

But no Eric. Maybe Eric had stopped to sign autographs.

Small said, "Eric will be there any minute. He's gone to makeup."

Eric finally walked in.

At last Small said, "OK. Eric's ready. Throw it to him."

Schoumacher recalled years later that he asked something profound like, "Eric, what's your reaction to all this?"

"His mouth opened," Schoumacher said, "and the words flowed and flowed and flowed and I just looked at him and I thought, 'How the hell — 'cause he doesn't know any more than I know.' But it was sensational and I was awestruck."

By the time Schoumacher finished the story we were both laughing so hard we had to wipe away the tears.

Sevareid was also a major player in the Mudd household. Any announcement by Walter Cronkite that "Eric Sevareid has a few thoughts on that" set off a chain of events that our four children still remember. E. J. and I both tried very hard to make sure that seeing their father on the tube was nothing special, that it was just routine for him to appear out of a piece of furniture. We kept the TV set in the sun parlor, which doubled as a playroom where the children gathered before dinner. If I had a story on the news that night, one of the four might look up and say, "There's Daddy," but they'd go right back to their coloring. But the minute Cronkite said the magic words "Eric Sevareid has some thoughts . . . ," it was as if a guillotine had dropped. E. J. came swooping in, bringing with her the Sevareid Rule of Absolute Silence. No talking, no laughing, no hitting, no crying, no nothing. It was a moment of thoughtful and elucidating discourse that E. J. looked forward to all day, and she was not about to miss a word of it. I could tell her later over dinner what I had said, but she wanted Sevareid firsthand, up front, and person-to-person.

For breaking the Sevareid Rule of Absolute Silence there was a sliding scale of punishment. The worst was: "Go to your room and remain there."

CHAPTER 13
WOLVES ON THE PROWL

The first and only conversation I ever had with John Kennedy lasted a full twenty seconds. The senator had been scheduled to speak at the Women's Club of Chevy Chase, Maryland, but canceled at the last minute because of what his staff told the club women was an important announcement of some sort. My mother, a member of the club, tipped me off. Knowing Kennedy was in the midst of intense preparations for his 1960 presidential campaign, I called his Senate office. I explained who I was — WTOP News — and what I wanted. They put me on hold. Suddenly it was the senator himself on the line. I blurted out my question, a real toughie: Does your Women's Club speech cancellation have anything to do with your presidential campaign? "No, no," he said. "No connection. Nothing to it. Okay?" Click. Boy, I really nailed him on that one. He didn't lay a glove on me. I'm still convinced the two were connected, otherwise the senator would not have taken the call. But at the time I felt silly trying to morph a motherly tip into a national political scoop.

Less than two years later, John Kennedy was president and I was just starting at CBS, filling in at the White House on Saturdays and Sundays or whenever he flew to Hyannis, Newport, or Palm Beach for the weekend. On my first trip to Cape Cod, Press Secretary Pierre Salinger declared a "lid" for the afternoon. That is, a promise that there would be no news that afternoon and the press was free to play.

Tom Wicker of the *New York Times* and I headed immediately for the Hyannis golf course. Somewhere around the sixth hole, I spotted Jacqueline Kennedy wearing clam diggers and playing along on a parallel fairway. With nothing to lose, I gave her the big wave. She waved back, all right, but with so little enthusiasm that I knew the last thing in her mind was for Tom and me to join her twosome.

On one of those Cape Cod breaks in November, the president decided to fly directly to Waco, Texas, to pay his last respects to Sam Rayburn, who was dying of cancer. At the airport on our way back to

Washington, I was on the telephone in the terminal hurriedly recording a radio report to New York. The press, which was required to use the rear stairs to Air Force One, was already on board and the rear steps were up. I ran out on the tarmac in a panic. An Air Force sergeant stood at the main front cabin door, preparing to close it. Watching from the plane was an Associated Press photographer, Frank Cancellare. Frank yelled to Salinger: "Wait for the kid!" Salinger quickly ordered the portable front stairs to stay in place. Up I came, out of breath and sweating. To get to my seat in the rear I had to pass through the presidential quarters. There stood the president of the United States himself, with Salinger grinning and hovering, ready to pounce if I dared ask a question. I dared not. The president stepped aside to let me pass. He smiled ever so slightly and threw me a quick nod. As I slipped by, I noticed that there were shelves in the space usually used for coats — shelf after shelf of shirts, stacks of freshly laundered presidential shirts. There must have been four dozen of them. Only later did I learn that Kennedy put on a fresh shirt each and every time he deplaned from Air Force One for a public appearance.

The very next weekend the president was

off to Palm Beach to help Florida Democrats celebrate Senator George Smathers's
forty-eighth birthday. Smathers seemed
almost too smooth for the United States
Senate. A handsome ex-Marine, barbered
and expensively tailored, Smathers was
probably John Kennedy's best friend in the
Senate. Together or singly, they were wolves
on the prowl, always able to find or attract
gorgeous prey. On that Saturday afternoon
in Palm Beach, I was the network representative in the press pool boat that tried to
follow the Kennedy yacht. It was a joke, our
pretending to be covering the president,
bobbing around in the ocean, squinting
through binoculars to find out who was
coming and going but always having our
view blocked by a Secret Service boat just
as another long-legged Palm Beach beauty
climbed aboard. What would today be called
the "mainstream media" didn't and
wouldn't touch that story. We couldn't
identify the women and Salinger wasn't
about to check. Besides, they could have
been long-legged White House staffers or a
friend's long-legged wife. Besides, we figured, who cares? Besides, we told ourselves,
we were political reporters, not gossip columnists.

CHAPTER 14
WANTED BY THE FBI

During the early months of the Kennedy administration, Vice President Johnson was the hang-dog presence in the White House photographs, seemingly unhappy and ill-fitted for playing second banana.

My earliest impression of him dated to 1958, when I would watch him on the Senate floor, cajoling and maneuvering, whispering and squeezing, standing in the aisle by his majority leader's desk, his hands jammed in his pockets, playing what appeared to us in the galleries to be "pocket pool." One afternoon Jennings Randolph, the immaculate and rotund senator from West Virginia, approached Johnson to thank him for some legislative favor he had done for him. In his exuberance, Randolph threw his arms around Johnson's waist so he could pat him in appreciation. Johnson was a good four or five inches taller than Randolph, so that in their quick embrace Randolph's nose seemed to nestle right into Johnson's armpit. From that point on, Randolph was known in the TV Gallery as "Cuddles" or "Sniffy."

As vice president, Johnson let very little get by him, and he was particularly aggressive in protecting himself against what he viewed as a pro-Kennedy, anti-Johnson press. One of Johnson's main allies and sources of information was the director of the FBI, J. Edgar Hoover. As they each gained power over the years, the two men helped one another along, a relationship that was strengthened by their mutual distrust of the attorney general, Robert Kennedy.[1] Hoover never hesitated to keep his senior staff abreast of Johnson's myriad complaints, suspicions, and rumors. About 2 PM on June 13, 1962, Hoover dictated to his inner circle the following memorandum:

While talking to Vice President Johnson, he mentioned that he gets about ten or twelve rumors a day and finds out they all tie in with the governor's race in Texas and he mentioned specifically one that CBS had a girl doing research for a reporter, Roger Mudd (phonetic) of CBS, and this girl had played for her a tape which purported to be an interview between a newspaper man and Estes' partner in which Estes' partner said Mrs. Lyndon Johnson lent $5,000,000 to Estes, and a lot of stories.[2]

The Estes, of course, was Billie Sol Estes, the Texas millionaire, who had been charged the previous April with fifty-seven acts of fraud. The Roger Mudd (phonetic) was, of course, me.

How I got caught up in the Estes scandal remains a mystery. The specifics in Hoover's memorandum, when put to even a cursory test, wind up in smoke. I was never assigned to the Estes story. Dan Rather, then in the Houston bureau, worked on it and so did Charles Kuralt, who did a news special on the scandal.

One of Estes's partners, A. B. Foster, still living in Pecos, denied, in a conversation with me, ever telling anyone that Lady Bird Johnson had lent $5 million to Estes. Foster laughingly mentioned the rumor that Estes had paid Lyndon B. Johnson $3,000, but the L. B. Johnson, he said, "turned out to be L. Barrett Johnson."

The newspaperman who allegedly taped the interview with Estes's partner presumably was Oscar Griffin Jr., the *Pecos Enterprise's* editor. Griffin won a 1963 Pulitzer Prize for his Estes coverage and later worked for the *Houston Chronicle* as a White House correspondent.[3] But Griffin, now retired and living north of Houston, says he has no memories of "anything to do with CBS or a tape recording." He says the rumor of the Lady Bird loan to Estes was "one of a zillion stories one heard in April and May of 1962 — especially late at night when the whiskey was flowing in rooms of the state and federal investigators looking into the case. I put no credence in the loan rumor at the time and still don't. Bobby Kennedy had between seventy and eighty Justice Department investigators working the case, according to stories circulating in those smoke-filled rooms late at night. All the federal agents were trying to discredit Lyndon Johnson. As far as I know, they didn't turn up anything to give Kennedy ammunition against Johnson."[4]

According to the Hoover memo, Johnson complained to CBS and "Frank Stanton got in to it and sent the girl back and this employee of Estes said he had never been interviewed, had never heard of it [Lady Bird Johnson's $5 million loan] and he had access to Estes' books and it was not true."[5]

Frank Stanton was, of course, the president of CBS. The vice president was par-

178

ticularly jumpy about getting tied to the Estes scandal. The slightest whiff of a Lyndon Johnson connection brought the press running. Such a misstep would give Robert Kennedy the leverage to force him from the ticket in 1964. Johnson made no secret of his concern about the Lady Bird rumor, and he asked Hoover to use the full weight of the FBI to have the weekly *Enterprise* help kill the rumor:

> The vice president wondered if the bureau could talk to the editor of the weekly newspaper in Pecos. . . . I stated I would get started on it right away.[6]

The Lady Bird loan story may have died a natural death, but Johnson's vigilance did not. A tip that I look into Johnson's TV and radio holdings sent me to the Federal Communications Commission, where I found that the Brazos-Tenth Street Company was the holding company of KTBC-TV in Austin, Texas, whose principal owner was Lady Bird Johnson. In 1943 Johnson — he was a Texas congressman at the time — bought in Mrs. Johnson's name KTBC, a struggling daytime radio station, for $17,500.

With the approval of the FCC, KTBC soon began operating twenty-four hours a day at five thousand watts at a better position on the dial, and the money began rolling in.[7]

The rapidly increasing profits from KTBC formed the basis for the Johnson fortune of land, cattle, radio, and television. Until the day he died, Lyndon Johnson maintained that there was no conflict of interest with such holdings. "I don't have any interest in government regulated industries of any kind and never have had. . . . All that is owned by Mrs. Johnson," he said during one of his presidential press conferences.[8]

From the day in 1938 when Frank Stanton helped KTBC join the CBS Radio Network, the Johnson–Stanton relationship flourished to the advantage of both men and to the increasing embarrassment of CBS News. Those of us in the Washington bureau knew through osmosis that anytime we set foot on Lyndon's territory, whether innocently or not, Frank Stanton would hear about it. We also knew that Stanton had become Johnson's TV advisor.

Given all that, the fallout from my visit to the FCC should have come as no surprise. To examine the Brazos-Tenth Street file, I had to sign my name and affiliation. The clerk either recognized me or more likely spotted the CBS connection and reported it up the line. That evening Blair Clark, the general manager of CBS News, called me at home. He said he was calling to tell me that Vice President Johnson had heard I was at the FCC snooping around, that Johnson had called Frank Stanton in New York to find out what Mudd was doing, that Stanton had called him, and that he was calling me. I told Clark briefly why I had been at the FCC, but as I explained it I became so outraged that I must have hung up on him. Clark called right back and told me in a surprisingly evenhanded way never to hang up on him again. Then he said, "Stanton told Johnson he would have Mudd called. Stanton told me to call you. I have now called you. So forget about it and go to bed." There was no telling what, if anything, Clark passed on to Stanton and whether Stanton followed up with Johnson. Of course, I assumed the worst.

If there was any reassurance in Clark's deflecting the front office inquiry, it did little to relieve the anger and shock from learning firsthand that the president of CBS had a relationship with the vice president that involved doing his gumshoeing and his bidding, that the vice president had a string of informers capable of tracking reporters from one office to another, and that J. Edgar Hoover ran a sloppy, smearing, and incompetent shop. I had a lot to learn about my hometown.

CHAPTER 15
NOTHING COULD BE
FINER

Covering Congress during Kennedy's thousand days was catch-as-catch-can for television news, because TV cameras were not allowed in either the House or the Senate chamber for another fifteen to twenty years. Beyond that, the fate of Kennedy's New Frontier program was largely in the hands of a few doddering old committee chairmen, who distrusted the TV camera mainly because it revealed just how doddering they were. In addition, Kennedy's Democratic majorities in the House and the Senate were sometimes ephemeral and always deceptive. With nearly sixty southerners from his own party frequently voting against him, Kennedy rarely overpowered the numbers. Dealing with the Congress was his great frustration.[1]

But Kennedy's ratings were still high after his first year, and the congressional election in 1962 gave the Democrats a ripe opportunity to break the southern Democratic–conservative Republican coalition.

To prepare for election night I proposed traveling through the South not with a camera crew but with a notebook; if I came across a good story I would do it for radio. Much to my surprise, management approved the idea. It was a hallmark at CBS News, particularly in the Washington bureau, that we got time to prepare and that once we were assigned a beat we were not jerked around but left alone to learn it.

So off I went that October, to Richmond, Virginia; Charlotte, North Carolina; Columbia, South Carolina; Atlanta, Georgia; Chattanooga, Tennessee; and Huntsville, Alabama, and without a camera crew I was able to hang around, unnoticed, listening and watching, brain-picking the local reporters and politicians. That invisibility did not last long. By 1968, I was well enough known to cause a stir, so I learned to stay on the press bus until the candidate had started to speak. Then I could slip out and listen from the fringes. David Brinkley famously said he tried doing some reporting during the 1960 West Virginia primary but had to come home hounded and empty-handed.

North Carolina drew me back many times

over the years, not only because I'd been a student there, but also because it contained all the fascinating and contradictory characteristics of southern politics. During one southern swing I diverted my camera crew to North Carolina to put together a speculative piece on the role of the fall line on southern politics. The line, beyond which the tide does not rise, is marked by waterfalls, which provided the power to run the mills in nineteenth-century America. In North Carolina the fall line separates politics from day into night. East of the line meant sandy loam and that meant cotton and that meant slaves. Slaves meant plantations, a white oligarchy, and a long-bred conservatism mixed with racism. West of the line meant the gravelly soil of the Piedmont, small farms, a merchant middle class, and a nonslave economy that muted racism as a political issue.

Standing by the falls on the Roanoke River on the outskirts of Roanoke Rapids, I filmed that story, using pictures from both sides of the fall line to illustrate. The camera crew wondered whether such a weird piece could ever get on the *Evening News*. But thank God for Walter Cronkite. It was a slice of arcane politics that he couldn't resist.

By the third week of October I was in

Texas, checking on John Connally's run for governor. New York had sent Hughes Rudd, himself a Texan, to cover the Republican candidate, Jack Cox.

Hughes, a serious and talented writer, an ex-reporter for the *Kansas City Star* and a dedicated Cutty Sark-and-soda man, was worth every bit of trouble he caused.

We met at the Dallas airport and boarded a plane to Corpus Christi to catch up with the candidates. When the stewardess asked for our names, Hughes said "Rudd" and I said "Mudd." She looked at us without amusement. Her baleful face set something off in Hughes, so when she asked for our names again, Hughes said "Mudd" and then I said "Rudd." She gave up and stalked off not knowing which was which. We were howling with laughter, which doomed our chances of ever getting a drink from her.

After a day or two with the candidates, I caught up with Hughes on Sunday, October 21, in McAllen, in south Texas. That evening, with several other reporters, we walked over the bridge across the Rio Grande River into Mexico and the dusty, honky-tonk border town of Reynosa for margaritas and enchiladas. Late that night I wrote and recorded a Connally piece for the next morning's *World News Roundup* and went to bed. At 6 AM the assignment desk in New York woke me up, ordering me back to Washington as soon as possible. The capital city was locked down and President Kennedy was going on television that night. It was the Cuban Missile Crisis and the U.S. and the Soviet Union were heading toward a nuclear war. New York had chartered a plane to get us out of McAllen to an airport that had commercial service. We landed in Austin and barely made a flight to Dallas. Hughes headed back to Atlanta; I went to Baltimore. Out of breath and ill-informed but in time for the Cronkite news at 6:30 PM, I was standing on the steps of the Pentagon, ready to go live. A week later, a listener wrote in, accusing CBS of faking it. She said she had heard my radio piece from McAllen that morning and saw me at the Pentagon that evening. There was no way, she said, I could have gotten from that place to the other place on the same day.

CHAPTER 16
"THE HUNKIES HAVE RUN AMOK"

Less than a week after the Missile Crisis began to deflate, CBS News assembled its election-night team on the corporate campus of IBM in Poughkeepsie, New York. We — that is, Bill Stout, Charlie Kuralt, Eric Sevareid, Hughes Rudd, Harry Reasoner, and I — were there to learn an experimental method of reporting election returns. It was called Vote Profile Analysis and had been developed by Lou Harris, who had been John Kennedy's pollster. VPA isolated enough voting precincts to construct a model of each state. In each model there would be enough Protestant, Catholic, Jewish, Irish, Italian, German, black, poor, rich, Democratic, and Republican precincts to enable a correspondent to predict with some certainty the winner of a statewide race even before the polls had closed. The cost to construct fifty such models was enormous, because it required careful and nationwide field research, the computer expertise and hardware from IBM, and the stiff fees due Lou Harris.[1] But CBS management had grown tired of being whipped by NBC on every election night and was willing to pay what it had to.

For two days, we tried to learn a new political language, a new way of reading the raw vote, and a new way of talking about the voting habits of ethnic America. It was hard, uncomfortable work, because most of us felt awkward talking about the Jews in Manhattan or the blacks in Chicago or the Poles in Hamtramck. The IBM people would print out sample VPA sheets and Fred Friendly, the CBS producer, would make each of us do a mock broadcast, using Harris's data. Most of us hated it. We couldn't get it right — we were not allowed to say that someone had won — we had to say "CBS News projects that . . ." or "CBS News estimates that. . . ."

Toward the end of the first, long session, when everybody wished we could go back to the old raw-vote system, Friendly called on Hughes Rudd. Never much of a political aficionado to begin with, Hughes looked at politicians about the same as H. L. Mencken did — with comic derision. The computer spat out a VPA sheet from Cleveland with its sizeable Hungarian population. Hughes looked at the sheet for a good ten or fifteen seconds. And then he burst out: "Great God Almighty, the Hunkies have run amok!"

We collapsed in laughter. Even Friendly, who was not prepared to have his precious project made fun of, couldn't resist a smile. For all our misgivings about VPA, Election Night '62 was a great triumph for CBS News. Every VPA prediction stood up that night. NBC, without VPA, continued to rely on the raw vote and the wry wit of David Brinkley. It was not enough. The main story that night was in California, where Richard Nixon, trying to put his political life back together, was running against Governor Edmund G. Brown. Late in the evening, CBS decided it had a large enough sample of the California vote to predict that Nixon would lose. Theodore White, the chronicler of presidential politics, wrote that "At this moment, [Director Don] Hewitt struck — Cronkite announced that CBS declared Brown the winner. . . . Hewitt swiveled in his chair to watch his monitor on the chief enemy, NBC. Brinkley was on. Obviously NBC was monitoring CBS just as CBS was monitoring them. In Brinkley's ear was the tiny earpiece of all commentators. . . . Brinkley visibly winced as his earpiece told him of CBS's call. Hewitt chortled, "Wry that, you wry son of a bitch, try and wry that one."[2]

My assignment was the South, which had a scattering of close races. There were a dozen or so in the House. The tightest was in Richmond, Virginia, my old home ground, where the nine-term congressman, J. Vaughan Gary, barely made it to a tenth term. He did not run again in 1964. In Texas, John Connally had a much easier time for governor, defeating Jack Cox with room to spare. And Alabama's longtime progressive leader, Lister Hill, squeaked back into the Senate for his fifth and last term. Because of CBS's willingness to turn me loose for that ten-day southern swing, I was able to add something of substance and something of local color to my reporting that night.

Election Night '62 marked my long and welcome assignment to the South every two years. Politics in the South I found to be the most outrageous, most dramatic, most hilarious, and most fascinating of any section in the country. Turnovers in the South were much less frequent because of the Democratic Party's dominance, but when someone did turn over, it reverberated — Albert Gore Sr.'s loss to Bill Brock of Tennessee in 1970, Dale Bumpers's defeat of Arkansas senator J. William Fulbright in the 1974 Democratic primary, and Mack Mattingly's defeat of Herman Talmadge, of Georgia, in 1980. Election Night '62 was also such a success that it brought THE chairman, William S. Paley, into our studio for a congratulatory tour. When he stopped at the South desk, I was meeting him for the first time and could think of nothing meaningful or insightful to say, except something really stupid like, "Mr. Paley, would you like one of my cookies?"

But there was also to be a downside to the CBS/VPA triumph. It meant that, henceforth, election night would no longer be an evening of communal pleasure in America, of staying up until two or three o'clock in the morning waiting for the returns, of listening to H. V. Kaltenborn tell us about the critical farm-belt vote, of tracking the rise and fall of Democrats and Republicans. Henceforth, election night would also become a contest among the networks to see which would call the election first.

That ferocious contest reached its perigee on November 4, 1980, when NBC called the race for Ronald Reagan at 8:15 PM, hours before the polls had closed in the West. That was the night television took control of the country's electoral system. The networks had, in fact, penetrated the sanctity of the ballot box with VPA and an exit polling system that was breathtaking in its simplicity and startling in its accuracy. The secret ballot in America was hardly a secret anymore.

CHAPTER 17
THE USEFUL PEST

With the sacking of David Schoenbrun in February 1963, I got a major break — my first assignment as anchor, picked to replace him on his Sunday program, called *The Washington Report*. Schoenbrun had demanded that he be given his own program, commensurate with his stature as a bureau chief. But the minute he got it, he complained that 12:30 on Sunday afternoon was an insult.

With Schoenbrun gone, the network no longer was obligated to him. Whereupon, James T. Aubrey, the president of CBS-TV, announced that *The Washington Report* would be canceled in September. It was Aubrey's price for agreeing to expand the *CBS Evening News with Walter Cronkite* to thirty minutes.

But with the seven months we were given, the program did wonders to pull the bureau back together. Everybody got to do stories for it, even those like Ted Church and Neil Strawser who rarely were seen. The ratings were minimal, but we all had fun.

We would do just two or three stories in the half hour — everything from crime in Washington, D.C., to equal time for presidential candidates, the political impact of Nelson Rockefeller's divorce, the slipping halo of Defense Secretary Robert McNamara, water pollution, the nuclear test-ban treaty, and Bob Pierpoint's interview with the director of USIA, Edward R. Murrow, on the impact in Europe of America's civil rights revolution.

For Murrow, once an editorially fearsome TV commentator but now a political appointee, it must have been difficult to acknowledge that his agency was in effect censoring what it distributed about America's racial violence. Pierpoint asked Murrow if the USIA released pictures of police dogs snarling at the blacks in Birmingham.

"No, we do not," he said. "They have a way of securing their own dissemination. They are damaging, there is no question of that, Bob."[1]

For Pierpoint, the interview must also have been difficult. It was Murrow, already diagnosed with lung cancer, who gave Pierpoint his first job at CBS in 1951 and sent him off to cover the Korean War.

With each Sunday I felt more and more confident about anchoring, writing copy that had some style, and trying not to take myself too seriously. Anchoring a generally relaxed weekend program was not hard, mainly because I wrote all my own copy and did not have to worry with rewrites and possible mistakes of others, only my own. After that, you comb your hair, you put your makeup on, and you talk.

By the spring of 1963 I had about gotten my sea legs on Capitol Hill. I was covering the Congress full-time for the Cronkite show, in addition to at least one or two interviews for the Sunday report. As I did more and more interviews on the Hill, I found a genuine pleasure in asking questions that went against the grain, not provocative or confrontational questions, but questions that produced unrehearsed answers, answers that revealed something about the member's character we hadn't known before. I tried never to ask questions in which I suggested a possible answer or ones that could be answered with a yes or a no. The point was to get the subjects to do the talking with words of their own choosing. The Congress was absolutely the prime place for a political reporter to be. Everybody was a source and everybody loved to talk.

But there was at least one member of the House, Republican H. R. Gross of Iowa, who had never been interviewed on network television until I called him that spring. Television had judged him not powerful or charismatic enough. But he was known as the curmudgeon of the House, the "useful pest" who knew every bill that came to the House floor and objected to most of them. He was a tiny man with a voice that seemed bigger than he was. Gross couldn't have weighed much more than 135 pounds or been taller than five feet six inches. And his eyes were truly dog eyes, almost bloodhoundlike. Over the course of three interviews I did with Gross that year, he told me that he had never been inside a foreign embassy, never voted for a foreign aid bill, and never been on a foreign junket.

Mudd: You don't play golf or go to the beach?

Gross: No, I don't.

Mudd: What do you do on Saturday and Sunday?

Gross: Read bills and reports and hearings.

Mudd: Do you ever jump into Washington's social stream?

Gross: Very seldom. I'm not here to climb social ladders.

Mudd: Do you own a tuxedo?

Gross: No, I don't. Never have owned one.

Mudd: When was the last time you were outside the U.S.?

Gross: Well, I took a trip overseas in 1918.

Mudd: As a doughboy?

Gross: As a dogface, yes.[2]

Gross's expression never changed. It was all I could do not to laugh out loud.

Gross ran his last race in 1972. As much as Washington and its ways got under his skin, Gross — like so many others — caught Potomac Fever and never left Washington.

But there was one congressional custom that did not get under his skin. After twenty-six years of protecting the Republic against waste and venality, Mr. Gross cashed in his unused stationery allowance when he retired in 1976 and left office at least $23,611 richer. It shocked even Capitol Hill.

Toward the end of the summer, Schoenbrun's producer on *The Washington Report* was replaced by Bill Crawford, who had heroic status in the bureau because of his willingness to tangle with the New York brass, and together we produced a show they still talk about at CBS.

When John Kennedy held his first presidential press conference, he changed the rules. No longer could reporters identify themselves by name or affiliation when they stood to ask a question. Kennedy was convinced the reporters were simply using the opportunity to promote themselves and their newspapers or networks on live television. So, for the next two and a half years, the TV audience had had no idea who those men and women were who were interrogating President Kennedy.

Crawford and I decided to give the reporters a break. We got White House clearance to put our camera on the stage behind the president so we could film the reporters leaping up and down for recognition instead of the president answering.

As each reporter rose, I would give his name, age, birthplace, affiliation, and some identifying morsel, as in:

Albert Merriman Smith, fifty-three, Savannah, Georgia, "Smitty." UPI's White House correspondent since 1941. Dislocated his shoulder running for the telephone with the German surrender bulletin.

Bill Lawrence, forty-seven, Lincoln, Nebraska, ex-AP, ex-UP, ex-*New York Times,* hired by Jim Hagerty in 1961 as ABC's White House and political reporter, gregarious and voluble.

Marianne Means, twenty-eight, Sioux City, Iowa, blue-eyed, blonde, ex-model, Phi Beta Kappa from Nebraska, got her assignment as Hearst's White House reporter with Kennedy's help.

And so on through the remaining thirteen reporters who got recognized that day.[3] It had never been done before — a press conference seen through the eyes of the president.

Forty-five years later, Crawford's son found a 16-mm film of the program in the family's West Virginia farm house and had it transferred to a DVD, which is now part of the archives at the Newseum in Washington, D.C.

By the 1960s most members of Congress were camera-savvy, had sharp press people on their staff to brief them, and were eager to come to the TV Gallery for interviews. Those of us in television news gravitated to the members who were powerful or articulate or knew what they were doing, like Senate Minority Leader Everett Dirksen, or the leader of the Senate's southern bloc, Richard Russell of Georgia, or the House Democratic Whip, Hale Boggs, or the defiant and outrageous Adam Clayton Powell of Harlem.

But for one of our Sunday broadcasts on the approaching civil rights march on Washington, I tried someone different, someone who was not known to be very powerful or articulate. He was Senator A. Willis Robertson of Virginia, a splendid-looking man, with a strong profile, an erect six-foot-four-inch frame, a brisk stride, but a slightly reckless gleam in his eye. For years he had lived in the shadow of Virginia's senior senator, Harry Byrd. That shadow, coupled with his sometimes antic behavior, meant he was another who got systematically bypassed by the national press and by television.

When I interviewed him at the end of May, he was so delighted to have a real network crew in his office — probably for the first time — that he made the most of it. His first answer about the coming civil rights legislation ran 680 words and lasted three minutes and fifty-five seconds.

What about our domestic racial violence damaging our image overseas?

Well, I think that is a lot of hot air. . . . I have been overseas. I don't know of any nation in the world that has the standards of living of our colored people. The colored people in the United States have more automobiles than all the 200 million people in Russia put together. . . . You take these ignorant tribes in Africa where they say we are hurting them — nineteen of them, they are just tribes, but we call them nations. They with the communists now control the United Nations. They are the ones that talk about our image being hurt overseas. To me it is just a lot of tommy-rot.[4]

At the time I couldn't believe he had said all those things, and reading them today strains credulity. But the senator, who was the father of the evangelist Pat Robertson, was delighted with the interview, or so he told me in a thank-you note. He was a full and eager participant in the civil rights filibuster in 1964, although his speeches would occasionally wander. In floor debate, he was powerful and blustery but seemed unable to deliver a knockout blow. As the Senate's leading admirer of John Adams, he would without any apparent or logical reason ask the chair "for unanimous consent to insert at this point in the [*Congressional*] *Record*" certain of John and Abigail Adams's letters. The senator was defeated in 1966 and died in 1971. He is buried in Lexington, Virginia, in the Stonewall Jackson Memorial Cemetery, along with Jackson and 144 Confederate veterans.

The Washington Report ended on September 8. On the last broadcast I announced the show's demise with these words:

If you have been enlightened or delighted by any one of these programs, we are happy. If you have not been, we ask you to blame not us but the wonderful men and women whose names will follow in a moment.[5]

Thereupon the names of producer Bill

Crawford, director Bob Camfiord, the cameramen, the audio techs, the lighting director, and the makeup woman were scrolled across the screen. They had all been warned ahead of time and had a big laugh.

CHAPTER 18
THE MARCH ON
WASHINGTON

During the seven months I anchored *The Washington Report,* the civil rights story was all around us, and on at least one out of every four Sundays we did major takeouts on the coming crisis.

The White House had seen on television in early May pictures of young black demonstrators in Birmingham being washed down the streets by overpowering blasts from the city's fire hoses. It had seen Safety Commissioner Bull Connor's police dogs leaping and snarling at Birmingham's marchers. Over the next two months the networks could barely keep up with the spreading racial violence — more than seven hundred demonstrations in almost two hundred cities.

Kennedy's 1960 campaign promise of a civil rights bill remained an empty promise until June 11, barely a month after Bull Connor turned on the fire hoses. Kennedy is said to have given Bull Connor more credit than Abraham Lincoln in advancing the civil rights movement.

Kennedy tried his best to dissuade the country's black leaders from their March on Washington. It would jeopardize, he said, any chance his civil rights bill would have on Capitol Hill. But when the president realized he could not stop the march, he decided to join it, according to Nicholas Katzenbach, the assistant attorney general.[1]

Washington, D.C., was virtually without experience in controlling crowds, big crowds. Inaugural crowds were sizeable but respectful, bubbly, and joyful because their man had won. True, twenty-thousand unemployed veterans of World War I — calling themselves "The Bonus Expeditionary Forces" — had descended on Washington in 1932. And a panicky President Hoover barricaded himself in the White House and ordered General Douglas MacArthur, his troops, his cavalry with drawn sabers, and six midget tanks to clear Pennsylvania Avenue of the Bonus Army's ragtag remnants.[2]

Two-hundred-fifty-thousand mostly black civil rights activists and protestors on their way to Washington in August 1963 was a different story. During the spring and early summer, the capital was consumed by fear of the rising tide of black militancy.

The march brought my biggest assignment to date: to anchor CBS's live coverage. Doing live cut-ins on the *Evening News* or anchoring a live studio program was one thing — those were highly controlled, scripted, usually with a teleprompter, and isolated from external noises and distractions. But to anchor a four-hour marathon with a constantly changing timetable, with events subject to the whims of others, with great gaps of dead air to fill, with switches from one remote location to another using a jerry-rigged system, with loudspeakers and a brisk wind competing — all of that made it a totally different ball game. The videotape of that day shows me and my six colleagues using huge microphones and wearing ancient and bulky earphones like the kind the airline pilots wear — not the invisible wires that snake unseen into the ears of today's anchormen. Somehow it all worked.

Bill Small made sure I had plenty of help and a constant flow of updates. He deployed the six correspondents around the Mall: Charles Von Fremd at the Washington Monument, Paul Niven and Stan Levey in and among the crowd, Dave Dugan at Seventeenth Street and Constitution Avenue, Bob Pierpoint at the Capitol, and Hughes Rudd at the Reflecting Pool. Each was on alert to be ready with an interview or color piece if I ran dry.

The nervous administration ordered the city's bars and liquor stores closed, put the National Guard on alert, told the local police not to use dogs, persuaded the Washington Senators baseball team to postpone their night game, and drafted an executive order declaring martial law.[3]

Attorney General Robert Kennedy called in two of his assistants, John Reilly and John Douglas, and his chief marshal, James McShane, and told them, "You take care of it." Reilly said he was stationed at the Lincoln Memorial equipped with a cutoff switch on the sound system if the rhetoric got too inflammatory. "We had a turntable hooked up to play music if necessary." Reilly says, "I picked Mahalia Jackson's, *I Got the Whole World in My Hands* on a 78." Reilly says that he was going through a stack of old 78s five years later and "there was the record still sealed."

What happened was almost nothing. The march was a magnificently peaceful display of discipline, genuine love of country, and grit. It changed the face of the civil rights movement from one of isolated acts of violence and defiance into an indefatigable, determined, and respectable movement that gave notice to President Kennedy and the Congress that they had to deal with the issue.

After four hours of watching and listening, broadcasters had to resist being caught up in King's soaring rhetoric and the crowd's euphoria. During the wrap-up of our coverage I tried to inject an element of reality by listing each of the march's demands and the chances of even getting out of committee, let alone passage on the Hill. The prospects were dim from top to bottom. It would take almost a year following Kennedy's assassination to change the outlook.

For all the professional praise the bureau got for its work on August 23, 1963 — we were the only network to carry the entire March on Washington — it was for me nerve-racking, simply because I was heading into the unknown. My skill at ad-libbing had not been tested. Failure was omnipresent. My career was on the line. Early that morning when I got to my anchor spot on the steps of the Lincoln Memorial, I suddenly felt nauseated. Repeated deep breaths did not help. Sips of Coca-Cola brought no relief. I slipped down behind the huge boxwoods at the base of the Memorial and threw up.

CHAPTER 19
THE RUMORMONGER

Impressive and dignified as the March on Washington was, the right wing in America was not persuaded of the innocence of the civil rights movement. Fear that Congress would give in to black demands joined a long list of other fears that kept conservative America on edge — the United Nations, the so-called Jewish media, the women's movement, and communism.

In early March 1963, Senator Thomas Kuchel of California had begun to get letters, thousands of letters, from constituents who feared that foreign troops, some described as barefooted Africans, were about to invade Georgia as a prelude to a United Nations takeover of America.

The rumor had gotten passed around the country on the so-called Liberty Network, a patchwork of newsletters, weekly newspapers, and radio programs run by John Birchers, ex-McCarthyites, white supremacists, anti-Semites, and the other far-right groups.

What sent the Liberty Network into action was the U.S. Army's announcement of a full-scale training exercise to combat guerrilla warfare. It would take place in Georgia in early March and would involve up to three thousand troops, including about four hundred recent graduate officers from the Special Warfare School at Fort Bragg, North Carolina. More than a hundred of the four hundred would be from sixteen allied countries — Vietnam, Thailand, Indonesia, Iran, Korea, Turkey, etc. — that were vulnerable to guerrilla attack. Four of the officers would be from Liberia. The guerrillas would be Army enlisted men dressed in civilian clothes.

In New York, one of the producers for *CBS Reports,* the documentary series Fred Friendly had started with Murrow, spotted a brief news story about the uproar and proposed an hour show. Friendly gave it his OK and the producer, Gene DePoris, went to work. I was assigned to be the host and reporter. It would be my first *CBS Reports.* And it meant I would be working with the best documentary producers, researchers, and camera crews in the business. *CBS Reports* had become television's most honored documentary series — "Biography of a Missile," "Harvest of Shame," "Lippmann on Leadership." For me, at least, it was a very big deal.

A television documentary for the most part is put together almost exclusively by the producer — the producer conceives it, oversees its filming, interviews for it, writes it, and edits it. Only in the final stages of the production is a correspondent called in to do a token interview or two and record the narration. Unlike the newspapers, whose investigative reporters go underground for a month or two at a time, the networks do not have enough correspondents to go around. Besides, television reporters do not like to disappear from the screen for months at a time. And truth be told, producers have always liked it this way, free from the meddlesome and second-guessing presence of a correspondent.

Gene DePoris, who had been with Friendly since the early 1950s, was implacable and driven. He was going to get to the bottom of the rumor or else. He did, and the trail took him to Capitol Hill and the office of Republican Congressman James B. Utt of Santa Ana, California. In interview after interview, Gene had been told the source of the rumor was an Utt congressional newsletter that began:

> By the time this Washington Reports reaches you, there will be under way one of the most fantastic, and to me, frightening military maneuvers ever to be held in the United States. It is called Exercise Water Moccasin III and is just as deadly. . . . We do not know whether African troops will be involved or not, but we do know there's a large contingent of bare-footed Africans that have been moved into Cuba for training in guerrilla warfare. . . . Who brought these Africans to Cuba? Was it the United Nations? Was it Russia, or was it the United States . . . for the forth coming invasion of peaceful Angola?[1]

Jimmy Utt had been in the Congress for ten years. His reputation was that of a congressional spokesman for the far, fringe right. Utt's Thirty-ninth District has been a refuge for conservatives since it was broken off from the left-leaning, celebrity-soaked Los Angeles. Orange County not only helped Richard Nixon and Ronald Reagan carry California but also has sent to the Congress, in addition to Utt, such wackos as John Schmitz and "B–1 Bob" Dornan.

214

Given Southern California's abundance of ornate cemeteries and the political power of the death industry, Utt's denunciation of Jessica Mitford's 1963 book, *The American Way of Death,* was predictable. But Utt attacked her as a pro-communist anti-American and said that profits from her book "no doubt will find their way into the coffers of the Communist Party, U.S.A."[2] For the Orange County Republicans in the early sixties, that was standard political patois.

DePoris and Friendly both knew that unless Utt agreed to an interview they had no show. That's when I got called in. My assignment, in addition to hosting the program, was to nail down interviews with Utt and Senator Kuchel. Kuchel was no problem, but Utt knew CBS had been tracking the rumor and questioning the true believers. Utt wanted no part of us. My brief appointment with him did no good. He turned me down flat.

When I called Friendly to tell him I had struck out, he became agitated and nervous — and if you're working for Friendly, an agitated Friendly is not good news.

The next day Friendly called me with a proposal he said he had never made before to any interviewee: *CBS Reports* would give

Mr. Utt up to three minutes to explain his role in the Water Moccasin rumor; Mr. Utt could redo his statement until he was satisfied with his performance; *CBS Reports* would run his statement in its entirety; *CBS Reports* would not edit his statement. In return, Mr. Utt would answer my questions.

To our surprise and delight, Utt agreed. We sat down together during the first week of November for the interview. Because the program was scheduled to be broadcast a week later, DePoris and Friendly had left a huge hole in the end of the show for the Utt segment.

Jimmy Utt was not a firebrand in person. He was small, slightly tanned, bespectacled, with a soft voice and a generally pleasant manner. True to our word, we filmed his explanation without interruption. He said he didn't know whether there would be any African troops involved in Water Moccasin, but he said there would be troops there from Ghana. Utt said he was opposed to the U.S. training troops from communist-controlled countries like Indonesia and Yugoslavia. Beyond that he said he feared the consequences if "some irate farmer, or somebody, happened to shoot a foreign officer." He said it would require a U.S. apology.[3]

That ended his explanation. I stopped the cameras and made sure he was satisfied and did not want to do a second take. He thanked me for the chance but said he was happy with what he had done.

Then it was my turn.

MUDD: Did you think, Mr. Utt, before the Water Moccasin Operation started, that there would be barefoot African troops involved?

UTT: No, I did not at all. That part of the letter referred to something in Cuba. . . . I didn't realize that people would tie the two together. . . .

MUDD: Why did you put the two facts in the same sentence?

UTT: Well, I can't answer that. . . . The sentence should have been separated . . . but I didn't. . . .

MUDD: Do you believe, Mr. Utt, that there is a UN plot to take over part of the United States or that a UN plot was in any way involved in Operation Water Moccasin?

UTT: No, I don't think there was. . . . I think that the whole UN is a plot to take over the world. . . .

MUDD: If you had to do it over again, Mr. Utt . . . would you have issued your warning in any different way?

UTT: Well, I would not, of course, [have] included any extraneous matter. I would limit it right to the facts on the subject.[4]

Utt's answers were, to say the least, pathetic. Here was a politician, a senior member of the House Ways and Means Committee, overwhelmingly popular in his district, returned to the House year after year, drawing a generous salary with an abundance of office help and all the perks of office, using his free franking privilege to send out hysterical warnings about barefooted Africans, to keep alive the tattered UN plot theory, to claim that the U.S. Army would take over a million and half acres of Georgia without due process, to so hype the rumors that the Army was forced to curtail the operation and then, after all of that, promising that in the future he would stick to the facts. It was a pitiable performance.

"Case History of a Rumor" was broadcast at 7:30 PM on November 13, 1963. Gene, of course, had written it, but I was proud of my interviews with Utt and Kuchel.

The fallout on Capitol Hill was minimal. Utt was just being Utt, they said. McCarthyism had about run its course in the early sixties, and few on the Hill took Utt and such like-mindeds as Bruce Alger of Dallas or John Rousselot of San Marino seriously. The program, though, did help expose just how tawdry the far, hard right had become.

Looking back, I think I should have spelled out the deal that Friendly and I cut with Jimmy Utt. Perhaps Friendly did not want it known that such deals were available.

Within a week or two we were all consumed by the president's assassination and the rebirth of the communist conspiracy lobby in American politics.

By early January 1964, I was covering the Barry Goldwater campaign in New Hampshire and had forgotten all about Jimmy Utt and Exercise Water Moccasin. But on February 24, here they came again. Utt had filed in the U.S. District Court for the Southern District of New York a libel suit against CBS, Friendly, DePoris, and the three sponsors of "Case History of a Rumor," asking for $5 million in punitive damages and $250,000 in economic damages.

The court's process server found me in the Green Room off the Senate floor waiting, strangely enough, to talk with Senator Kuchel. The suit described my "gloating expression" at having successfully defamed Mr. Utt and labeled me as the "straight man" for my "yes man," Senator Kuchel. Utt claimed the defendants had "entrapped" him into giving them a television interview that turned out to be a "cross-examination" by Roger Mudd, who acted as "prosecutor, judge, and jury."

Oh, well, at least I was not named as a defendant. Utt and his attorney must have figured I was just a puppet at the end of the Friendly-DePoris strings.

Utt said the program held him up to "public contempt and ridicule," that as a consequence he had "lost many valuable supporters," that he had suffered "great mental pain and anguish," that his "reputation with the press" had been impaired, and that he had been "deprived of valuable engagements and income." He thought five and a quarter million dollars would take care of it.[5] The lawsuit was a cheap way to save face. It was, of course, dismissed.

But to give Mr. Utt his due: Over his nine terms in Congress, his average election majority was 66 percent. In 1964, however, the election the year after "Case History of a Rumor," his percentage dropped from 68.5 percent to 65 percent. A real squeaker.[6]

Jimmy Utt was reelected for the last time in 1968, a Nixon year. On a Sunday in March 1970, he suffered a stroke during church and died soon after at the Bethesda Naval Hospital. He was seventy-one years old. His successor, chosen in a special election, was John G. Schmitz, one of those right-wing radicals who leave everyone gagging. Schmitz was anti-immigrant, anti-women's lib, anti-communist, anti-black. He named his dog "Kaiser." He once said "Jews are like everybody else, except more so." He said he didn't object to President Nixon going to Communist China. He just didn't want him to come back.[7]

Just another Orange County sweetheart.

CHAPTER 20
WHERE WERE YOU
WHEN. . . . ?

Most Americans now in their seventies remember exactly where they were and what they were doing on at least three dates in their lifetime:

The bombing of Pearl Harbor on December 7, 1941 — I was thirteen and having Sunday dinner at home with my parents.

The death of Franklin D. Roosevelt on April 12, 1945 — I was seventeen and pumping gas at an Amoco filling station in Chevy Chase, Maryland.

And the assassination of John F. Kennedy on November 22, 1963 — I was thirty-five and having lunch with Warren Duffee and Bill Theis, both of United Press, at the Senate press table in the U.S. Capitol.

At 1:34 PM came the first wire-service flash of the shooting. It had been dictated by Merriman Smith of United Press in Dallas. Six minutes later, Walter Cronkite went on the air in New York, interrupting the soap opera *As the World Turns.*

Our lunch came to an abrupt halt when someone running by in the hall yelled at us that President Kennedy had been shot. Everybody at the table broke into a run for the nearest telephone. CBS told me to start rounding up senators.

Presiding over the Senate just then was the president's youngest brother, Edward M. "Teddy" Kennedy. He had been a senator barely a year. During routine sessions, the newest members took turns presiding, but always guided, and sometimes told exactly what to say and do, by a watchful parliamentarian. The chamber was deserted. Kennedy, sitting in the big chair at the top of the rostrum, was signing photographs.

David Schoumacher, who had started work at CBS News that very week, was watching from the gallery. Suddenly he saw Richard Riedel, a Senate employee, rush in and go right up to Kennedy.

"I could hear him," Schoumacher recalls, "because it was so quiet. 'Your brother's been shot.' I could hear him. I had no idea where I was in the building or where the elevators were or anything else. I saw an elevator but I figured that's too slow. So I ran down the stairs and there's Teddy running down the stairs. He's got somebody with him and they're deciding whether to walk or take the subway. He decides to take the subway and I stay right with him right into his office. I told him I was a CBS reporter. He doesn't say much. 'I don't know anything. I just heard.' "

The Senate had gone into recess, which meant that the reporters were permitted to enter the Senators' Lobby, the long corridor that runs behind the Senate chamber. The scene I came upon is still vivid. The Lobby, adorned with two huge French vases and equipped with big leather chairs, racks of out-of-town newspapers, and two wire-service ticker machines, is normally and exclusively for senators. Gathered around the AP ticker were half a dozen senators. In the center was Richard Russell of Georgia, no public admirer of John Kennedy. As the bulletins from Dallas spilled from the ticker, Russell began to read them aloud. His voice began to wobble with each devastating detail until finally tears ran down his face. I watched as one senator after another gulped, lowered his eyes, and bumped into the others, seemingly in a daze.

In the Washington bureau on M Street, Bill Small ordered remote trucks and cameras rolling to the White House, the vice president's home, and Capitol Hill. As the news spread, the bureau soon filled with off-duty couriers, editors, reporters, camera crews, and technicians, all of them asking, "How can I help? Where do you want me?"

Neil Strawser was in the office and became the studio man in the bureau, standing by with live updates and film. George Herman was at the White House. Chuck Von Fremd went to Andrews Air Force Base to await the arrival of the presidential plane. Marvin Kalb shifted from the bureau to the State Department. I was on the Hill. Bob Pierpoint, who had been in Dallas with Kennedy, returned to Washington that night on the presidential press plane. Dan Rather and Nelson Benton remained in Dallas. Paul Niven backed up Herman and Pierpoint at the White House. Reporters Dave Schoumacher and Tony Sargent were on the street, ready to move where needed.

For the next hour, waiting for what everyone knew was coming, Cronkite held the air, reporting cautiously on a growing mass of details, on the arrival of two priests at the Parkland Hospital, on the condition of Mrs. Kennedy and Governor Connally, on the whereabouts of Vice President Johnson, and was helped immeasurably by Eddie Barker, the news director of KRLD, the CBS station in Dallas.

Finally, it came at 2:38 PM. Cronkite, in shirtsleeves, said it:

From Dallas, Texas, the flash, apparently official: President Kennedy died at 1:00 PM, Central Standard Time, 2 o' clock, Eastern Standard Time, some thirty-eight minutes ago.[1]

The video of Cronkite announcing the president's death is still powerful. He paused, he gulped, he removed his eyeglasses, he paused again, and then he went on to the next story — "Vice President Lyndon Johnson has left the hospital in Dallas but we do not know where he. . . ."
Did Walter cry?
"I was far too busy covering this story for the first couple of hours," Cronkite told me recently, "until I had to say, 'The president is dead.' And when that moment came, I choked. I cried a tear or two, but I didn't boo-hoo. Tears certainly filled my eyes. I know because I felt them."[2]
Moments of poignancy and eery eloquence occasionally broke through our flat reportorial accounts:
Pierpoint quoting Nellie Connally's words to President Kennedy just before he was hit — "You can't say Dallas is not friendly to

you today."[3]

Von Fremd remembering Senator Kennedy from the 1960 campaign, cool and detached, telling him that the Secret Service was virtually powerless to stop a sharpshooter, "however mad," and that agents running alongside the presidential limousine succeeded "only in blocking the public's view."[4]

Tony Sargent, a newly arrived rookie pressed into service along Pennsylvania Avenue, describing the riderless black horse "so well selected for its spirit, seemingly imbued with all the unspent energy our president still had to share."[5]

And Herman, whose knowledge of the presidency kept us on track, trying to stay collected — "There doesn't seem to be anything more to say. The White House will remain; the city will remain."[6]

Our newest correspondent in the bureau was Stan Levey, who had just joined the bureau because his paper, the *New York Times,* was weathering a costly strike. This was his first experience with live television. Small pressed his interrupt key to tell Stan that the cortege would soon be in his view. "When you see the head of the cortege, then you can mention it," Small told Levey. "Don't answer me because your mike is open." Sure enough, Stan answered him right into his live mike, coast to coast, "Okay, Bill."[7]

Television's coverage of those four days was spare, dignified, and superb. Linking control rooms with cameras at the Capitol, the White House, St. Matthew's Cathedral, Andrews Air Force Base, Pennsylvania Avenue, and Arlington, lashing up correspondents with microphones, sometimes in a driving rain, splicing monitors with program feeds, coordinating pool coverage among the networks involved a degree of coordination, and sharing unknown in the highly competitive television world. Technically, the results were extraordinary.

Occasionally there would be small slips. Stan Levey had trouble, as we all did, with program feedback — when you hear your own voice coming back into your ear after a micro-second delay. It happens when the audio engineer forgets to squelch your own voice feeding back into your ear and you find yourself trapped in a ghastly echo chamber. You have two choices: either rip the earpiece out or kill the volume on the little switch you wear on your belt. But if you're inexperienced and the echo hits you unprepared, either you freeze vocally or you try to plow through the echo. Sadly, Stan tried talking through it. Just as he finished saying, "This is Stanley . . . ," here came the "ley . . . ley . . . ley" from "Stanley" back into his ear with such an unhinging sound that he never could get started on the "Le . . . Le . . . Le" part of "Levey."

As President Kennedy's body was moved from Andrews Field to the White House, then to the Capitol, then to St. Matthew's Cathedral, and finally to Arlington Cemetery, Bill Small shifted us like checkers, figuring how to keep each of us just ahead of the cortege. Kalb went from inside the Capitol Rotunda to St. Matthew's; Von Fremd followed Lyndon Johnson from Andrews Field to his home in Spring Valley; I went from the Capitol Plaza to the roof of the Lincoln Memorial; and Bill Leonard, then just a correspondent, brought down from New York to help, jumped from Fourth and Constitution to the Arlington grave site.

On Sunday morning, November 24, as we waited for the procession carrying the president's body from the White House to arrive at the Capitol, Lee Harvey Oswald was being transferred from the Dallas city jail to the county jail. Instead of covering the transfer, the CBS producers in New York had Harry Reasoner switch to me on the steps of the Capitol. After I laid out the schedule of events in the Rotunda — the wreath-laying, the eulogies — my mike suddenly went dead and the red lights on my camera went out. New York, monitoring NBC's coverage from Dallas, had just seen and heard NBC's Tom Pettit at the city jail shouting, "He's been shot. He's been shot. Lee Oswald has been shot." CBS cut away from me, of course, and instantly switched to Dallas. Not only was the killing of Oswald almost too much to believe but also we had been beaten on the story, forcing us to play catch-up with NBC, using a taped replay of a live homicide.

The ceremony in the Capitol Rotunda was brief. Chief Justice Earl Warren, House Speaker John McCormack, and Senate Majority Leader Mike Mansfield gave the eulogies. It was Mansfield's words I remember most clearly, because they seemed so out of place. Mansfield, the undemonstrative and subdued leader, had never been much of an orator. Even so, his phrases, his cadence, and his pitch that morning felt inappropriate, so unlike the senator I knew. With Jacqueline Kennedy listening, Mansfield's voice was near a shout when he said, "And so she took a ring from her finger and placed it in his hand. . . ." Five times Mansfield repeated the line, which seemed almost cruel. Perhaps shouting was the only way he could have gotten through the eulogy without breaking down. I never had the nerve to ask him about it. Years later, Charles Ferris, who had been the chief counsel of the Senate Democratic Policy Committee, told me Mansfield's speech had been written by Frank Valeo, the senator's administrative assistant, that the text was unfamiliar to him, that he had not had the time to edit it or practice it, and that his shouting was indeed to mask the deep emotion Mansfield felt over the loss of the man he had once looked upon as his little brother in the Senate.

When the eulogies were over, the huge bronze doors of the Capitol were opened and the first of America's grieving citizens moved into the Rotunda and passed the president's closed casket, which rested on the same catafalque on which Abraham Lincoln's body had lain. The line of mourners that had been forming since early morning seemed to be without end. I was astonished. Astonished because many of us who covered the Congress had quite a different view of the Kennedy presidency, colored by the legislative lethargy of the Hill, the dug-in opposition of the southern Democrats, and the snide cracks of the Republicans (Hugh Scott of Pennsylvania, the assistant Senate minority leader, privately referred to the three Kennedy men, John, Robert, and Edward, as "The Brothers Grimm.") Much of the Washington media, cocooned as it is, simply was not aware of how Kennedy had touched the country. So it was astonishing, almost breathtaking, to watch thousands of Americans filing by the president's coffin through the night. CBS stayed on the air until midnight. My comments were sparse, just enough to reassure the viewers that they had not lost the sound.

For the last eight hours, without surcease, mourning Americans have moved through this Rotunda. . . . The line which formed here . . . runs across the East Front of the Capitol Plaza . . . down Maryland Avenue, down Massachusetts Avenue . . . behind Lincoln Park, to the D.C. Stadium on the Anacostia River, then doubles back down East Capitol Street — forty blocks long, four abreast, estimated by police at five hundred thousand.[8]

The plan had been to close the big doors at 9 PM, but by then the line was two miles long and growing longer. The Associated Press reported that at about 2:30 AM, former heavyweight champion Jersey Joe Walcott walked by the coffin. He had been in line for nearly eight hours.[9] Small arranged with the Capitol police to admit any of the CBS people who wanted to slip into the Rotunda at the last moment to pay their respects, and scores of them did.

By mid-morning on Monday, when the line finally began to thin and they closed the bronze doors, more than a quarter of a million people had passed by the bier.

"This outpouring of affection and sympathy for the late president," I said, "is probably the most majestic and stately ceremony the American people can perform."[10]

It was a death that touched everyone instantly and directly; rare was the person who did not cry that long weekend. In our home, as my wife watched the television, her tears caused our five-year-old son, Daniel, to go quietly and switch off what he thought was the cause of his mother's weeping.

CHAPTER 21
"A SAD, SORRY MESS"

Nineteen-sixty-four began for me with a flight to Phoenix for Barry Goldwater's announcement that he was running for president. Goldwater's was the first of seven presidential campaigns I would cover, and for a television reporter who loves politics, being assigned to a presidential candidate is comparable only to being a floor reporter at the nominating conventions. I could not wait to get started.

Goldwater's announcement was a simple affair, held on the patio of his home in suburban Scottsdale. He appeared on crutches, his right foot in a cast from a recent bone-spur operation. He said he was running because no other announced Republican candidate had said anything that would give voters a clear choice.

Goldwater's early political fame grew from his reputation as a luncheon and dinner speaker before Arizona's conservative audiences. He spoke almost as a boxer would fight — short, powerful jabs to the jaw without much concern for the damage they would inflict. Arizona press coverage of his speeches was thin, and he came to believe he could say just about anything without getting in trouble.

For most reporters and the candidate himself, the Goldwater campaign was to politics what free verse was to poetry — nothing according to form. We never knew exactly where his itinerary would lead us or why his New Hampshire staff would schedule an hour with a kindergarten class where the children's feet didn't reach the floor or at schools where only the teacher was eligible to vote.

The candidate's persistent problem was what Theodore White called the "unrestrained candor of old men and little children." On the one hand, Goldwater spoke at times with unbelievable frankness; on the other, the press tried its best to make sure he meant to say what he said. The result, however, was a Goldwater furious when he saw his words quoted and analyzed in the media and a media made the enemy by accusations that it was distorting what Goldwater really meant.

Even after twelve years in the Senate

spotlight, Goldwater was inexplicably unprepared for the scrutiny he would get as a presidential candidate. The paper trail that followed him to the New Hampshire presidential primary was already fraught with political explosives: the idea that Social Security should be made voluntary; that the Tennessee Valley Authority could be sold off; that the graduated income tax might be abolished; and, most famously, that NATO commanders might use atomic weapons. It all sounded very much like one of Goldwater's rip-roaring after-dinner speeches to the Scottsdale Rotarians. Such proclamations, reported by the press and regurgitated by Nelson Rockefeller's campaign staff, destroyed any chance he had of winning New Hampshire.

Those first weeks on the Goldwater campaign were tortuous for me, because I had sworn to stop smoking. A week or so after the Phoenix trip, the surgeon general issued his edict on smoking, and even in my brief time on the Hill I had learned enough about the pressures the Public Health Service would have been under from the tobacco states — Maryland, Virginia, Kentucky, Connecticut — to know that this was no run-of-the-mill government press release.

One of those early campaign flights, my

seatmate was Republican Congressman Bob Wilson of California, who took pity on my agitated, gum-chewing, finger-drumming condition by pulling out of his briefcase autopsy pictures of the blackened lungs of deceased Navy smokers. Wilson and his grisly pictures helped me go from two packs a day to a cold-turkey stop.

Nonetheless, I went off eagerly to New Hampshire each Monday morning, flying to Boston, renting a car, and driving to Manchester, New Hampshire, to hook up with Walter Mears of the Associated Press and Charlie McDowell of the *Richmond Times-Dispatch*. Then, off we'd go, bouncing off snowbanks, careening around the state from Manchester to Antrim to Keene to Lyme to Franconia to Center Sandwich and back again, in and out of veterans' halls and community centers and Rotary lunches, chasing after the quixotic Goldwater campaign. We were all part of a band of itinerant journalists looking for a story.

Part of the looking, of course, was negotiating the highways of New Hampshire. Whether it was Mears, McDowell, or Mudd at the wheel, the minute one of us would hit a run of ice and the car would begin to fishtail, we'd all start yelling, "We're buffeting! We're buffeting," just the way the announcers at the Innsbruck Olympics sounded during the bobsled runs, just the way grown-up journalists behaved when they were away from home.

Mears, who was from New England and thought he knew his way around, took a wrong turn one dark night and we wound up in Maine. On that same trip, with Mears as the wheelman, we hit a long patch of black ice, the most treacherous element in New Hampshire's winters. There were cars askew lining both sides of the highway where they had lost control and whacked into the snowbanks. Mears obviously was struggling. He could not bring the car under control. We were careening. He didn't dare touch the brakes. Gearing down was worthless. We were on the verge of going through a series of 180-degree whirls. The three of us were absolutely mute and dry-mouthed. Not a sound, except for some very heavy breathing. It must have lasted a full minute. Finally, finally, Walter slowed it down and got control. Nobody said anything for the longest time. I thought somebody should say something. But all I could come up with was a flat-footed "Good driving, Walter."

I had known Charlie from college days at Washington and Lee and then again in Richmond, where he became the best political color man I had ever read. He was not only very funny, he was also very quick. He loved words. He allowed me to use one of his words once when we were covering Khrushchev's 1959 trip to the U.S. As the Soviet premier was coming up out of Penn Station in New York, surrounded by a million bodyguards, policemen, and government security men, Charlie whispered to me, "Khrushchev has ascended."

The first time I saw Walter Mears was at the press table in the House Dining Room. We did not speak. He actually glowered at me because I was TV. Walter had come to the AP's Washington bureau from Boston, where he covered President Kennedy's frequent weekend trips to Hyannisport. Soon after he moved down, he lost his young family in a tragic fire. Wes Gallagher, the AP's general manager, assigned Walter to the House and loaded him with work. Slowly he pulled himself out his depression and began to reconnect. But he did not much like connecting or reconnecting with TV guys. Later, when he overheard me telling a friend at the press table about throwing up in the boxwood during the March on Washington, Walter acknowledged that maybe I did not think I was such hot stuff after all. We became friends and loyal admirers. Walter, who won the Pulitzer Prize for National Reporting in 1977, became one of the AP's sacred cows, even though Republican Senator Hugh Scott went to his grave in 1994 still thinking his name was "Warren."

But Walter kept his edge about the TV guys. The elegant Howard K. Smith, by then the chief correspondent at ABC, landed at the Manchester, New Hampshire, airport with his camera crew to do a piece on the 1964 Republican primary. The crew was filming Howard as he strolled across the tarmac, preceding him in a kind of half-crouch duck waddle so their equipment would not get in his way or in the picture.

Walter took one look at the scene and said, "Here come Prince Charming and his Trained Toads."

Walter and Charlie were great, funny, informative, and helpful companions.

Barry Goldwater was the last Republican presidential candidate reporters could approach without going though five layers of handlers. Four years later, the GOP candidate was the hermetically sealed Richard Nixon, and each of his successors grew more and more isolated and unavailable. Goldwater was not much of a crowd mingler, but he had an easy relationship with the dozen or so reporters who covered him regularly.

After I was pulled off the campaign to cover a civil rights debate in the Senate, I ran into Goldwater one morning on the Senate steps during one of his rare visits to the Hill. When we paused to say hello, he said they missed me on the campaign. I said I was doing the debate full-time.

"I know," he said, "I've been watching you."

He was in fact a warm, generous, and easy man to be with but not above sticking it to those of us in what his people regarded as "the Eastern liberal press."

By September I was back with Goldwater for one of the country's last whistle-stop political campaigns. It was a twenty-two-car train that pulled out of Union Station in Washington, D.C., with dormitory cars for more than a hundred journalists and photographers, a campaign staff of twenty-seven, two VIP cars, a lounge car, and a staff car. We were headed for the cities, towns, and villages in Ohio, Indiana, and Illinois — three states Goldwater knew he had to carry if he had the remotest chance of winning. But by the next morning, when we reached Parkersburg, West Virginia, the campaign was in shambles. The Goldwater staff had discovered a twenty-two-year-old female Democratic spy who had smuggled onboard a mimeograph machine and was cranking out flyers spoofing the campaign. In the grey dawn of Parkersburg, Vic Gold, the assistant press secretary, with a dramatic flourish, escorted the spy off the train into the railroad yards, where she was abandoned. Every moment of the incident had been filmed, of course. Producer Murray Fromson and I could not wait to leave the train and speed to the nearest big city so we could send the Great Whistle-Stop Spy Caper to the Cronkite show.

By the time we reached the CBS affiliate in Cincinnati, it was after five o'clock. The local news staff, facing its own deadlines, was not glad to see us. We needed an editing room, we needed editing machines, we needed this, we needed that, and we needed a local coordinator to arrange with Ohio Bell for a telephone line for feeding the story to New York. By 6:15 PM it was obvious to Fromson that we would have to switch live to New York. For Don Hewitt, the director of the Cronkite show, going live was like a death sentence. Everything that could go wrong when we went live usually would. The risks were enormous, but given our story, Hewitt had no choice.

Cronkite began with Dan Rather, who was campaigning with President Johnson. Then Cronkite set up the spy story and said, "Here's Roger Mudd with the Goldwater campaign train." My opening stand-upper had been filmed on the train before Fromson and I jumped off in Chillicothe. Up on the screen I came, about to say something clever about a spy who went out in the cold. But the audience did not hear me say that, because Ohio Bell had patched me not into New York but into a local radio station, which happened to be playing an old Kay Kaiser tune, "Three Little Fishies."

What the audience heard when my mouth began to move was:

Boop boop dit-tem dat-tem what-tem Chu!
Boop boop dit-tem dat-tem what-tem Chu!
And they swam and they swam all over the dam.[1]

It may be funny now, but back then nobody laughed. We swore and swore and kept swearing. Hewitt was probably the best at it.

By October the campaign was making jet stops instead of whistle-stops. One of these was scheduled in Bristol, Tennessee, to help inaugurate American Airlines' new service to the Tri-Cities Airport. After the airport rally and ceremony, we reboarded Goldwater's chartered campaign plane, a 727 called the "Yai-Bi-Kin" — "House in the Sky" in Navajo — and took off for Cleveland. Suddenly the jet went into a steep curve and a deep, screaming dive toward the airport from four thousand feet. The press section froze in fear; I can still see my seatmate yelling and clawing at the wall as we came swooping down toward the runway. Walter Mears of the AP wrote that we were almost level with the control tower as we roared by. We found out later that the American pilot was asked to give Tri-Cities a celebratory buzz. When the plane leveled off, Goldwater got on the stewardesses' microphone to proclaim: "Well, that ought to separate the men from the boys." Mears wrote that most of the reporters sided with the boys.

It was not so much the regular reporters who drove Goldwater crazy as it was the columnists and the pundits. Following one of the worst beatings a presidential candidate had ever taken, Goldwater bitterly declared that the columnists "both on TV, radio, and in the papers . . . should, frankly, hang their heads in shame, because I think they have made the Fourth Estate a rather, sad, sorry mess."

After less than three months with Goldwater, my happy routine ended when Fred Friendly called with one of his off-the-wall ideas, an idea that would catapult me into TV stardom.

CHAPTER 22
"WHAT DO WE DO NOW, DICK?"

Out of the blue, which was usually where he came from, Fred Friendly proposed that I cover every day of the coming Senate filibuster of an omnibus civil rights bill not only on the *Evening News* with Walter Cronkite but also on each of the network's four other TV newscasts and on seven of the network's hourly radio newscasts. No story had ever gotten such coverage, and my initial reaction was less than enthusiastic. It sounded more like a flagpole-sitting stunt.

Friendly, the newly installed president of the news division, had become a company executive after eight years in harness with Murrow as the producer of *See It Now* and *CBS Reports.* Huge in every way, Friendly was oversized, overpowering, and overzealous. He once said he was tired of predictable documentaries through the eyes of Little Red Riding Hood. How about a show from the wolf's point of view? Murrow said of him: "Watch out for Friendly. He doesn't know a fact."[1] But Friendly repeatedly assured me that the filibuster coverage was to be a serious journalistic undertaking. I told him I could visualize the producers in New York and even Cronkite gritting their teeth at having to run a Mudd piece day-in and day-out, night-in and night-out. Friendly said he would take care of that. So I agreed and Friendly announced the plan:

> The pending civil rights debate and the anticipated filibuster in the Senate give every indication of becoming one of the most important running news stories of the decade. It warrants continuing coverage in the same manner we have dealt with the space shots and with primary elections. The fact that cameras and microphones will not be permitted access to the Senate floor does not affect our responsibility of reporting the debate and filibuster as completely as possible.[2]

Now it was up to me to produce some serious journalism. Friendly was right. This was a high-stakes story for the country, the Congress, and the administration. The legislation, unprecedented in its reach and

247

impact, would outlaw racial discrimination in public schools, public accommodations, public facilities, housing, hiring, and voting. It was understood that some but not all of the impetus for the bill was generated in the name of the martyred President Kennedy. But following his death, there was little mention made of the general lack of enthusiasm and sympathy at the Kennedy White House for the whole civil rights movement.

For the Senate itself, it was to be a watershed. Not once in the forty-seven years since the cloture rule was adopted — the rule that a filibuster can be broken only with the approval of two-thirds of those senators voting — had the Senate been able to break a civil rights filibuster, and it had tried eleven times. The cloture rule was the South's firewall against liberal attempts to change its culture. It was also used quietly by some small-state senators (Arizona, the Dakotas, Nevada, Utah, Wyoming) who looked to the South to help protect them from the power of the big, liberal, urban states. Howard Cannon of Nevada, for instance, supported the cloture rule to deflect threats against his state's legalized gambling.

The strategy of a filibuster is to use the Senate rules to control the floor so that controversial legislation cannot be brought to a vote or is amended to make it acceptable to two-thirds of the members. Controlling the floor means talking, and talking on Capitol Hill brings out the worst and the best in everybody.

Our coverage began on Monday, March 30, 1964. My initial report was for the *CBS Morning News,* which then started at 10 AM and was anchored by Mike Wallace. It was snowing and I was waiting on the Senate steps for the Capitol Police to give our mobile truck with its cameras permission to park. Someone forgot to get the truck a permit. But we made it in time and I began:

This is not what you'd call a typical Easter Monday in Washington — the snow, the cold, the frozen forsythia and the chilled cherry blossoms buds. And inside the Senate wing, we are about to embark on an historic civil rights debate. . . . The parliamentary situation is this: The civil rights bill — already approved by the House — is now formally before the Senate. It was put there last Thursday by a 67-to-17 vote after two weeks of southern opposition. Leading off today will be the generalissimo of the pro-civil rights forces, Democratic Senator Hubert Humphrey of Minnesota.[3]

The camera then widened out to show the bareheaded senator, wearing an oversized raincoat with sleeves that hung down below his fingertips. Humphrey had arrived for the interview unaware of the snowstorm and announced that he had to go back for his coat. There was no time for that, so Bill Small lent the generalissimo his size 42L. Small promised the senator he would have the camera show him in close-up.[4] I was wearing galoshes and, believe it or not, a snap-brim felt hat.

Humphrey said he thought the debate would last until June (it did). He said there would be no compromise (there was). He rebuked the Reverend Martin Luther King Jr. for threatening direct Negro action if the talking hadn't stopped by May 1. He said King was not a member of the Senate (correct) and that the Senate would act "free from any outside forces" (doubtful).[5]

On that first day, the debate didn't begin for an hour and a half, because so many senators wanted to announce their support and sympathy for the victims of an earthquake that had occurred in Alaska on Friday and because Senator Mansfield of Montana, where they mine silver, gold, lead, and zinc, demanded action to protect the silver dollar. Humphrey finally got started on his fifty-five-page speech at 1:25 PM. He refused to take questions or interruptions because, he said, "I want to keep this short."[6] Senator Tom Kuchel of California, the Republican co-manager of the bill, followed with a fifty-six-page speech.

For a debate that CBS had touted as one of the most important of the decade, the scene was one of minor, routine floor speeches: the almost empty chamber, the solitary speaker with a stack of documents on his desk and the ever-present legislative assistant at his elbow, the presiding officer signing his mail, and the dumbfounded tourists who filled and refilled the galleries every fifteen minutes hoping to hear the Senate in action. Not exactly the "breaking story" that Fred Friendly had promised, but we were off and running.

Not until word began to circulate at the end of the first week that Edward Kennedy was to make his maiden speech as a senator did the chamber draw more than the usual one or two members. Twenty stayed to listen to the thirty-two-year-old Teddy, who had assumed his late brother's Senate seat. In the gallery were his wife, Joan, his sister, Eunice

251

Shriver, and his sister-in-law, Ethel Kennedy. His voice wobbled when he said his brother's "heart and soul are in this bill."

The South took its time about answering the liberals. Sam Ervin of North Carolina gave the first major speech of opposition. He was the perfect filibusterer — tireless, voluble, and of such good humor that no one seemed to dislike him. An outstanding raconteur, Ervin said the bill was as "full of legal tricks as a mangy dog is full of fleas."

On baseball's opening day, April 13, the Senate was deserted. Most of the Senators were at D.C. Stadium, clustered around President Johnson as he threw out the first ball. But Spessard Holland of Florida, one of the few southern senators with an inactive sense of humor, ruined the ballpark party when he called for a quorum in the third inning. Mobilized by repeated announcements on the stadium's loudspeakers and a convoy of police escorts, fifty-one senators rushed back to the Capitol to answer their names. They did it in twenty-three minutes.

That evening Holland yielded to John Tower of Texas, the only Republican member of the southern army. Tower looked and dressed nothing like a Texan. He was barely 5-feet-4-inches tall, he wore double-breasted, pinstriped, English-cut clothes, and he carried his oval cigarettes in a silver case. Tower spoke in a deserted chamber. It was the dinner hour. There were no tourists in the galleries, no senators on the floor, except for Tom McIntyre of New Hampshire, and he was presiding. The place was a tomb. Tower looked at McIntyre and said, "Mr. President, may we have order?" It was a very funny line, and no one got to hear it.

On a warm day in mid-April, when Washington's beautiful spring had arrived and the cherry blossoms were in full bloom, Harry Byrd Sr., of Virginia, appeared on the Senate floor to take his turn wearing a white linen suit and his favorite funny-looking crepe-soled shoes. Byrd could rarely be heard beyond his desk, because his voice was thin and reedy and sounded like a whistle or a hissing radiator. We watched the way he used his arms for oratorical emphasis, but they flew up and down with little connection to what he said. Even though no one heard him that day, everyone knew what he was up to. Byrd was, after all, the father of Virginia's shoddy policy of "massive resistance" to the Supreme Court's school desegregation decision. But to make sure there was no misunderstanding, Byrd's administrative assistant, Peaches

Menifee, went to the press gallery to assure everyone that indeed his boss was talking against the civil rights bill.

Because everything from beyond the Capitol, every surge of critical public opinion gets filtered through the rules, procedures, and isolating security of the Congress, journalists on the Hill can be poorly attuned to the mood of the country.

No citizen can barge in; no protestor can be heard. Shouting from the gallery means arrest and detainment for "mental observation," although what is shouted sometimes makes perfect sense. The day George Smathers of Florida had the floor, opposing the bill, a young black man from Passaic, New Jersey, yelled down from the visitors' gallery: "How can you say that, senator, when there are only five senators on the floor and this bill affects 20 million people?" Not a bad question at all, but the police didn't think so and off he went to D.C. General Hospital.

Reporters moved through the day generally unaware of the big picture beyond Washington, uninterested in the moral force of the civil rights movement or the virtue of the legislation but minutely focused on whether George Aiken's amendment exempting Vermont's hundreds of bed and breakfasts would get out of subcommittee.

That first week of the filibuster set the pattern for next two months: My day began with a scene-setter on the 8 AM radio *World News Roundup* (written and recorded late the night before), followed by a TV piece for Mike Wallace at 10 AM, then radio spots every other hour, and very short reports for the 12:24 PM and the 3:24 PM TV news. Between 5 and 6 PM, I assembled a longer account for the Cronkite show and then the day's major radio piece for *The World Tonight* at 7 PM, followed by an update for the 9 PM radio and a final pretaped TV piece for the 11 o'clock news for the CBS stations in Washington and New York.

My schedule sounded backbreaking and in a way it was. But, in fact, I was learning so much about the Senate, the senators, and their peculiar ways that I was enjoying myself enormously. Besides, covering a story that moved at such an excruciatingly slow pace meant that very little happened each day. As it developed, each story I wrote was more or less a rewrite of the one I had done just before, perhaps with a new lead if I had been able to pick up something fresh along the way. In between radio and TV spots, I shifted from my perch overlooking the Senate floor to the Press Gallery behind the chamber, where senators came from time to time for an informal press conference, to the Green Room just off the floor to ask Senator Russell about tomorrow's schedule, to the Senate Democratic Policy Committee to gather up bits and pieces of news and gossip, to the TV Gallery again to write the next spot, and then to the Senate steps to pretape my piece for Cronkite.

Three weeks of reporting the filibuster morning, noon, and night had attracted a sufficient enough following on television that my spot on the Senate steps became an unofficial, not-in-the-guide-books stop for the occasional tourist. Some of the southern senators began to sense that the constant coverage of their delaying tactics would backfire. Whereupon, Senate authorities informed Bill Small that we were beginning to block senatorial access to the steps. He was ordered to move me and our cameras across the street to the sidewalk.

After a week or two, Fred Friendly told Bill Small how delighted he and New York were with the coverage, particularly having a clock clicking off the hours consumed by the filibuster. "I've got a suggestion," said the exuberant Friendly, hoping to top Small's idea for the clock. "Mudd doesn't shave," boomed Friendly. "He grows a beard."

Small, who knew instantly how the critics would ridicule such a stunt, quietly told Friendly, "No, Fred, we're not going to do that."

Early on, the *Evening News* asked me to profile the southern filibusterers — quick, almost breezy sketches. The technique became a favorite with the Cronkite show and I used it frequently over the next few years — no more than six or seven lines of totally inside biographical detail. Even so, a collection of these sketches would run more than three-and-a-half minutes, a TV news eternity compared with today's one-minute, thirty-second so-called in-depth reports. These were the filibuster thumbnails:

Richard Brevard Russell, of Winder, Georgia. Bachelor. Baseball fan. Roman bearing. Tends toward hypochondria. Almost impossible to anger but a devastating debater. Absolute master of the Senate rules. Modest. His *Congressional Directory* biography totals seven words.

Joseph Lister Hill of Montgomery,

Alabama. From a long line of preachers and doctors. A southern liberal. Helped write TVA, the GI bill, the Hill-Burton Hospital Act. The father of NIH. Gracious, colorless, dependable. Instead of "uh" he says "ah-wa."

James Strom Thurmond of Aiken, South Carolina. "Strom" is his mother's maiden name. Hair transplant. Possesses a bone-crushing handshake. Army Reserve major general. Fellow southerners find him hard to live with. Critics say he can never be a great senator because he is without humor and lifts barbells.

Absalom Willis Robertson of Lexington, Virginia. Given to occasional legislative wildness. When he talks, he walks — two desks left, three desks right. Without apparent reason will insert the entire Declaration of Independence in the *Congressional Record.*

James Oliver Eastland of Doddsville, Mississippi. A sweetheart compared to his predecessors, Theodore Bilbo and John K. Vardaman. Delights in jabbing Jacob Javits and Kenneth Keating, New York's senators, about what he calls the "Poe-toe Ricans" in "Noo Yoke City." His fearsome visage caused the press gallery to nickname him "Sunny Jim."

Allen Joseph Ellender of Houma, Louisiana. Five-feet-four and fiery. Because Uganda and Tanganyika have banned him he will not realize his dream of visiting every country on earth. Known for his shrimp gumbo press lunches, prepared in his Capitol hideaway.

The Robertson sketch drew one complaint. Willis Robertson's press secretary, an old friend from the *News Leader* days in Richmond, called to tell me he thought using the Senator's full name, as in "Absalom" Willis Robertson, was "kind of a cheap shot," although he didn't deny that was his name. The senator hated "Absalom" and had been trying to bury it all these years.

To help brighten up and illustrate my Cronkite pieces, CBS hired a wonderful artist to sketch the scene on the Senate floor. He was Howard Brodie, the World War II combat artist for *Yank.* Each morning at the Senate I gave Howard a rough idea of what I'd need that night — sketches of, say, Humphrey and Kuchel, and a generic one of the floor. Our cameras were not allowed in the Senate chamber and neither were our sketchpads. A reporter could take notes but an artist could not draw. Howard's technique would be to sit with his eyes laser-beaming the senator I wanted, his open hands extending outward from his temples, serving almost as horse blinders so nothing could break his concentration. Howard would then hurry from the chamber to his sketchpad in the gallery, transferring in charcoal the images he had just burned into his brain. In fifteen or twenty minutes, he'd be back again to memorize the finer details of hands, hair, or chin. He did three, maybe four sketches in an afternoon, and nobody worked harder at his craft or more accurately caught both the languid pace and the chaotic tension of the later debate than Howard. After a week or two, his sketches were in great demand, and the greatest demand came from the senators themselves. CBS owned the sketches, however, which saved Howard from the embarrassment of saying "no" to the filibusterers.

One request Howard never got was from the office of Strom Thurmond. Howard was a Californian and a liberal one at that. Early in the debate he found himself unable to finish a good likeness of Thurmond, the man West Coast liberals regarded as a political piranha. Howard denied that his politics got in the way of his art, but in every Thurmond sketch he did there was always a noticeable flaw. He did acknowledge that he found Thurmond always sliding in and out of focus.

By its second month, the civil rights filibuster story was becoming old hat for the press and a drag for much of the Senate. Washington's news bureaus, which started their coverage with a splash, heard that their editors back home were getting bored with the story. I overheard my NBC competition, Robert McCormick, one morning sniffing that "our listeners aren't much interested." Nonetheless, there were five reporters who did nothing but cover the filibuster. We called ourselves "The Cloture Club": John Averill of the *Los Angeles Times,* Peter Kumpa of the *Baltimore Sun,* Ned Kenworthy of the *New York Times,* Andy Glass of the *New York Herald Tribune,* and me from CBS News. We did not share exclusives but we tended to travel in a pack to cover caucuses, press conferences, and what was called "dugout chatter" — those few minutes just before the Senate convened when the press was allowed on the floor to pick up from Mansfield, Humphrey, or Russell some sense of negotiation, movement, compromise, defections.

Thirty-three days after the filibuster began, Russell of Georgia, threatened by growing pressure toward cloture, agreed to a vote on a softening amendment to the jury-trial section of the bill, which allowed the accused to request a jury trial in criminal contempt cases. This promised to be a big deal — the first real test of how the two sides lined up. When the roll call was over, the Senate had adopted the amendment, 45-to-44. Immediately, the pro-civil rights leadership went into a stall, waiting for the absentees to show up. Finally, Gale McGee of Wyoming, who was always late, strode into the chamber. A Democratic aide whispered to him, "Leadership is voting 'no.' " McGee, in his booming voice, voted "no," not knowing precisely why. That made the count 45-to-45 and the amendment finally died in a tie. The press, which had looked forward to a real story for a change, felt let down.

In early May, Martin Luther King Jr. quietly slipped into the VIP gallery overlooking the Senate chamber, with two of his aides. One of them pointed me out to the Reverend King, as I listened to the debate from the TV Gallery. King looked over, gave me a quick nod, which I returned, trying to hide my pleasure that he recognized me or at least did a good job pretending that he did.

A day or two later, Harry Truman entered the chamber to applause for his eightieth birthday. As a former member, he was entitled to be on the floor. He sat in Mansfield's chair and told the Senate that his ambition "has always been to displace the majority leader." Everybody went ha, ha, ha.

In the early sixties, CBS correspondents were paid a basic salary plus what was called a "talent fee" for every broadcast they were part of — $25 for a radio spot and $50 for television. With five TV spots and eight radio spots each day, five days a week, my weekly salary jumped from about $400 to nearly $2,500. The fee bonanza never figured into my agreement to do the filibuster, but E. J. had just had our fourth child and we were in the midst of enlarging our home in Kensington. We laughed about how the fees enabled us to tell our contractor to switch from luan mahogany to cherry paneling in our new library wing. *Newsweek*, toward the end of the debate, did a brief piece on my coverage, called "Mudd into Gold." The piece was complimentary about my reporting and my fairness, but the first three paragraphs said my assignment had "spawned this flow of wealth," calling it

Mudd's "lucrative patrol."[7] It was accurate in its details but I was privately irritated by its tone and because the reporter, David Burnham, never asked me about it or indicated he was interested in the fee system or my salary. Very quickly I learned to be suspicious of reporters I didn't know using methods I knew how to use myself. My skin was not as thick as I thought.

With May came hordes of tourists. In addition to wanting to see the House and the Senate in "action," they also wanted to see me in "action." Becoming a tourist attraction took me by surprise, and when it happened I hated it. On a Monday morning in early May when I rushed out at 9:57 to do my piece for Mike Wallace, there stood a crowd of thirty or forty waiting for me. I was unprepared to be looked at, gawked at, pointed at, and though I was not rude to them, I was grim. How naïve I was to think I could be seen on television five times a day coast to coast and continue to insist that I was an unsullied, high-minded journalist and not some show biz performer doing his on-camera shtick. But there was nothing I could do about it. We couldn't dodge them; we couldn't change our location each day to fool them; we couldn't ask the Capitol Police to declare my spot off-limits to them, and we couldn't move inside to the TV Gallery and lose the point of being in front of the Senate. So I got used to it and to them. They meant me no harm. They were simply curious. After I warmed up a bit, I found them invariably polite and attentive, always responding quickly when I would tell them "thirty seconds to air" and ask for quiet. Not once did a tourist challenge my reporting, start an argument, become belligerent, or hold up a "Hi, Mom" sign. It was more like, "Roger, we watch you every night at home. Could you sign my guidebook?"

On the thirty-ninth day of the filibuster, May 13, the Big Three — Attorney General Robert Kennedy, bill manager Hubert Humphrey, and Senate Republican Leader Everett Dirksen — announced their grand compromise bill. Involved were seventy changes, some perfecting, some substantial, which had to be mimeographed, annotated, and interlined with the House version of the bill and circulated to the members, a process that took another two weeks. The compromise was praised by the leadership as "practical, equitable, acceptable, and enforceable" and denounced by Russell as legislation that would build a "wall around the South that will make the Wall of China look like a toadstool."

Humphrey said he hoped the filibuster would be broken by June 15.

The network management in New York was delighted with the favorable publicity the filibuster coverage was attracting to CBS and to me. TV writers around the country were taking notice. John Horn of the *New York Herald Tribune* thrilled New York when he wrote, "Mudd has been faithful as a postman. . . . His continued presence at the scene of inaction has personalized and dramatized the halting processes of our government to the average viewer in a way no amount of words or secondary reports could have. A viewer could identify with Mudd. . . ."[8] Management's response was to send a CBS business agent down to Washington to negotiate a new contract for me. The two of us did it sitting on the retaining wall just behind our camera spot. The next time my contract came up for renewal, CBS had to deal with a newly hired agent.

During the long Memorial Day weekend most of the members got home and got an earful. Republican Karl Mundt of South Dakota and Democrat Mike Monroney of Oklahoma told the press they were switching from "no comment" to favoring a vote for cloture.

The most open and craven response to home-state pressures I observed was on the day an irate group of New Jersey constituents gathered in the Senate Reception Room and asked to see their senator, Harrison Williams. Williams, who was facing a right-wing Republican in his reelection campaign, wanted no part of these particular citizens. He tried to give them the slip, but one of the women spotted him and gave chase, followed by her suddenly enraged delegation. Williams actually ran — ran down the corridor, turned the corner, and ducked into the majority leader's office, where he sought and received political asylum in one of Mansfield's inner rooms.

On Tuesday, June 9, Mansfield announced that the Senate would vote on ending the filibuster beginning at 11 o'clock the next morning. During the day on Tuesday, the remaining amendments were disposed of and the decks cleared for the cloture vote. The author of one of the rejected amendments, Republican Norris Cotton of New Hampshire, was ungracious to the last. Cotton, who punctuated his speeches with a strange honking sound, said, "The so-called minority race would have more latitude under my amendment [honk, honk] than the majority race, and I'm beginning to wonder [honk] which is which."

The Senate on this last day of debate tried to recess early, but Robert Byrd of West Virginia would not cooperate, launching into a one-man filibuster. Byrd said if he were a businessman he would cut his payroll to fewer than twenty-five employees "rather than have a federal army of agents and lawyers running barefoot through the files of my business." "Barefoot" is one of those code words for "Negro" like "welfare queens." The racism of Byrd, an old Ku Klux Klansman, though subdued, still was visible. He was chairman of the District of Columbia subcommittee of the Senate Appropriations Committee, and the city's black officials did not have an easy time at his hearings.

The next morning, June 10, CBS was on the air live for the cloture vote. I was outside in my regular stand-up sidewalk spot, rather than in the gallery. We had jury-rigged a system to relay the vote to me outside: A gallery employee in the chamber would whisper into his telephone the vote as it proceeded, as in "Aiken, aye, Bible, no"; in the TV Gallery another employee at the other end of the phone would call out the vote, which my producer, Sylvia Westerman, then would repeat into her telephone, which was connected to me through my headset. We tested a dozen times and it worked every time. I lagged behind the vote not more than seven or eight seconds.

Tracking a roll call can be almost impossible for the unpracticed. Some members whose names are toward the end of the alphabet are too impatient to wait, so they quietly cast their vote with the recording clerk and then slip out. Unless your eyesight is perfect from the gallery above and you can actually read the clerk's check mark, you have to wait until the vote is over and the clerk has read the names aloud. Other members have a system of mysterious hand signals, like a third-base coach, which the clerks have learned to interpret.

This was the twelfth time the Senate had tried to break a civil rights filibuster. And even though the southerners had seemingly thrown in the towel on this one, a roll call demands attention and respect, because it is the only occasion when a member is limited to a simple "aye" or "nay." He can do all the explaining later in a floor speech, a newsletter, or a press conference, but when he hears his name during a roll call, he cannot hedge, fence, dodge, or wiggle. He can say either "aye" or "nay." Of course he can take a walk, but ducking is usually more politically damaging than voting against home-state interests. So the moment had come.

Every senator was in his seat. The visitors' galleries, the members' galleries, the diplomatic gallery, the press and radio-TV galleries were overflowing. All of governmental Washington seemed frozen in place.

Lee Metcalf of Montana, the acting president pro tem, presided. The chamber had become so packed that he ordered the clerks and Senate staffers who had crowded in to leave the chamber, saying that under the rules they did not have floor privileges. A few moments after 11 o'clock, Metcalf said: "Is it the sense of the Senate that the debate shall be brought to a close? The secretary will call the roll."[9]

"Mr. Aiken."

"Aye."

"Mr. Allott."

"Aye."

Outside near our cameras, the CBS Art Department installed a huge Senate roll call board, resting on an easel, and as I called out each vote as either an "aye" or a "nay," a check appeared next to the name.

"Mr. Ellender."

"No."

As Ellender was voting "no," two Navy corpsmen wheeled down the center aisle Democrat Clair Engle of California, who was dying of a brain tumor. His presence meant that all one hundred would be voting and sixty-seven would be needed to break the filibuster. Engle tried to vote "aye," but he could not be heard. Engle then pointed to his eye and the clerk called out, "Mr. Engle votes 'aye.' "

By the time Abraham Ribicoff of Connecticut voted "aye," the Senate was within five votes of breaking the filibuster. But just ahead was what I inaptly referred to on the air as "Murderer's Row" — the southern phalanx of Robertson, Russell, Smathers, Sparkman, and Stennis, all voting "nay," of course. It was an attempt to liken the power of those southerners to the bats of Combs, Gehrig, Lazzeri, Ruth, and Sisler of the New York Yankees. The connection did not go down well with certain southern viewers and they let CBS know about it.

Stuart Symington of Missouri cast the sixty-sixth vote for cloture — just one vote short.

But the next four votes were all "nays" — Talmadge, Thurmond, Tower, and Walters of Tennessee.

The vote stood at sixty-six to twenty-seven.

The Senate became very, very quiet.

Then the clerk called the name of John Williams of Delaware — the ninety-sixth senator on the roll. His nickname in the press gallery was "Whispering Willie" because he was a great mumbler. But this time everyone heard him.

"Aye."

With Williams's "aye," the Senate broke the filibuster — sixty-seven to twenty-seven.

Everyone slumped. All in the chamber — senators, clerks, doorkeepers, aides, attachés, reporters, VIPs, the public galleries — all of us at that moment realized we were the only ones in history who had ever witnessed the breaking of a civil rights filibuster. We knew that when they asked at some future time, "Do you remember where you were when they broke the '64 filibuster?" we could say, "We were there."

But with that vote the filibuster began to lose its mystique, and without its mystique it slowly became just another run-of-the-mill legislative tactic of delay, no longer the exclusive weapon of the South.

The clerk finished the roll call. Waiting in the cloakroom, in case a single vote would tip it one way or the other, were two Democrats — the ancient Carl Hayden of Arizona and Howard Cannon of Nevada. Hayden, who had come to Congress when Arizona was admitted to the Union in 1912, had never voted for cloture. When it was apparent that neither man's vote would make a difference, the two emerged from the cloakroom, Hayden to vote "no" and Cannon "yes." Cannon was in an extremely tight race against Republican Paul Laxalt that year, so tight that he won by only forty-eight votes.[10]

So it was finally over. The final count, seventy-one to twenty-nine, was exactly as Dirksen had predicted.

In a blink Russell of Georgia was on his feet with a parliamentary inquiry, asking the chair to explain what life under cloture meant.

It meant that each senator was limited to one hour to offer and explain any amendments that he had submitted before the vote on cloture. With stop watches, the clerks would keep running times on each member until his sixty minutes were up. Over the next ten days, the Senate rejected scores of amendments, accepting only two.

After one session, when the Senate had rejected twelve southern amendments by margins of up to fifty-two votes, Ellender of Louisiana walked over to Russell's desk and said, "What do we do now, Dick?" Russell said, "I don't care what you do."

On June 18, the last day before the final vote on the bill, Russell was making his last appeal when his time ran out. The clerk signaled to Edward Kennedy, the presiding officer once again, who said quietly, "The time of the senator from Georgia has expired." Russell paused for a second or two before he realized what had happened. Then, with obvious bitterness, he said, "I am being gagged in more ways than one." He asked for unanimous consent to insert the balance of his speech in the *Congressional Record* and sat down.

Next up was John Stennis, his powerful voice reaching every nook and cranny of the chamber. From the gallery, a visitor yelled down, "You have betrayed the white majority. Only Rockwell can save us now." He was a white eighteen-year-old follower of neo-Nazi George Lincoln Rockwell. He, too, was hustled out by the Capitol police for "mental observation."

Late on Friday, June 19, the Senate passed what was the most sweeping civil rights bill since Reconstruction. The final vote was seventy-three to twenty-seven. The clock read 12 weeks, 67 days, 607 hours, and 4 minutes.

On the Senate steps just after the final vote an admiring crowd closed in on Hubert Humphrey, grabbing his hand and pounding his back. It was Humphrey who brought discipline, shrewd leadership, enthusiasm, and humor to the Senate's easily discouraged liberals. But it was Dirksen — courted by President Johnson, Humphrey, and Mansfield, much to the irritation of many Democrats — who emerged as the indispensable man. It was a Democratic bill, fashioned and promoted by two Democratic presidents and steered through a Democratic Congress all right, but without the Republican senator from Pekin, Illinois, there would have been no bill at all. When Johnson signed the legislation on July 2 he used seventy-five pens. The first one he handed to Dirksen.[11]

For the reporters who covered the story, Dirksen was the indispensable source. Time and again, when no one knew or even had a guess when something would happen or how it would happen, it was Dirksen who set us straight. And he did it with his uncanny knowledge of the pressures on his fellow senators and with a florid sense of humor that lifted even the grimmest day.

On that last night after the vote, Dirksen went out of his way to thank the CBS artist, Howard Brodie. "Keep them coming," he told Brodie. "I'll have that wall of mine plastered and the first thing you know I'll be able to look only at me and Lincoln."

On the Sunday after final passage, CBS took out a full-page ad in the *New York Times* picking up on John Horn's quote from the postman's motto, "Neither snow, nor rain, nor heat, nor gloom of night. . . ." Filling the page was a square of pictures of me wearing galoshes, under an umbrella, squinting in the sun, and huddled in the darkness. For a CBS reporter of three years, that ad was a big deal, and for several days I could not take my eyes off it. I could feel my head swelling.

Those sixty-seven days were for me a political education that otherwise would have taken years to absorb. For the CBS News division it must have again demonstrated the wisdom of leaving its reporters in place and not jerking them about so frequently that their understanding and knowledge of the story was thin, thirdhand, and probably inaccurate. Because each day demanded an hourly hunt for something fresh, some new angle, some overlooked speech, I found myself peeling back the layers of the Senate's skin and discovering that the legislative process was really not so much a process as it was a changing mixture of tradition, arcane rules, bruised egos, hardened public opinion, soaring vanities, senatorial ignorance, genuine patriotism, posturing, knee-jerk reactions, low motives, and high principles. How ill-informed and uninterested some senators were depressed me; how heavily some depended on their staffs to do the heavy work surprised me. All of them had to be aware of the political consequences of every move they made; not every member was admirable or likable; some were so ordinary that it was a mystery why they were elected; but a few, perhaps not more than eighteen or twenty, had something unique in their character that generated the voters' trust and brought them to Washington. Despite its self-love, I genuinely admired the Senate, because it was capable from time to time of protecting the country against a panicked public, hot-blooded House members, and misguided presidents.

Southerners attracted me from the beginning, because I thought of myself as semi-southern: my Army time was in the South, my education was southern, and my first serious jobs were in the South. Southerners were also more fun to cover, to drink with, to laugh with, and to share preposterous stories from the political South. But because I was reporting on civil rights, an issue they had owned for almost a hundred years, and because most of them knew such intense coverage, however evenhanded, would not help them in the end, I had the toughest time earning the trust of the southerners. The liberals mistakenly took my reportorial sympathies for granted because I worked for CBS. But most of the southerners, though they never said it in so many words, believed that my big eastern, liberal network employer was run by Jews who wanted nothing so much as to put the South in its place with a tough civil rights bill. So that first night on the Cronkite show, March 30, when I began with Hubert Humphrey, I made sure to mention that the next night I'd be talking to Senator Russell.

Bureau chief Bill Small recounts that a "leading and powerful southern Senator" summoned him to his office and demanded to know why the Senate should not stop my reports. "They were, after all," he wrote, "being televised on Senate property." Small said he had checked beforehand my list of interviews and the senator I had interviewed more than any other was none other that Richard Russell. "My southern friend," wrote Small, "ended our discussion with a mild plea that 'you all continue to be fair to us, you heah?' "[12]

The year I became chairman of the Radio-Television Correspondent's Association, CBS held a party in my honor following the annual black-tie dinner. Russell was invited but could not come. In his letter of regret to the party's host, Ted Koop, he wrote that he had known [Roger] since "he first broke in to the broadcasting business and have watched him grow into an international figure. While comparisons are always invidious, he is one of the fairest of all the commentators covering the news. I have never seen him color it to the slightest degree."[13]

The last filibuster story I did was on Saturday, June 20. It consisted mainly of second-day quotes from some of the principals:

President Johnson: "A major step toward equal opportunity for all Americans."

Attorney General Kennedy: "My brother would have been pleased."

Senator Hickenlooper: "A further erosion of the inherent rights of all of people."

Senator Thurmond: "It will make a czar of the president and a Rasputin of the at-

279

torney general."[14]

Good ol' Strom.

Chapter 23
"Will You Wave, Sir?"

Between the end of the Senate's filibuster and the start of the Republican convention on July 13 in San Francisco, there was hardly time to prepare for my next assignment — as a floor reporter along with Harry Reasoner, Martin Agronsky, and Mike Wallace. To be a convention floor reporter on the network's premiere showcase is like being named to the starting lineup at the Pro Bowl, or at least it used to be. Once again, I got the southern delegations and, given Goldwater's strength in the South, it was a plummy assignment.

The San Francisco convention, however, was a near-disaster for CBS News. We were a new team, and we were up against Huntley, Brinkley, and three extraordinarily sharp NBC floor reporters, John Chancellor, Frank McGee, and Sander Vanocur. Cronkite, our anchorman, was, by his own admission, not at his best. For starters, he resented the presence of Eric Sevareid in the anchor booth as the political analyst. He began swallowing up great chunks of air time for himself, even refusing one order to switch to the floor for a piece of real news. For those of us on the floor, he was probably at his worst. Nothing destroyed floor morale quicker than having director Don Hewitt tell you in your ear that "Walter is going to pass," after you've arranged a hard-to-get interview.

When Chairman Paley read our poor ratings, he summoned both Friendly and Bill Leonard, who had moved into management as head of our political coverage, and demanded to know what had happened. Why had CBS been beaten again by NBC? Friendly and Leonard suggested that one of the problems in San Francisco might have been Cronkite's mike hogging. Paley pounced. He ordered that Cronkite be dumped from the upcoming Democratic convention in Atlantic City and replaced by a new team, a coanchor team: the polished veteran radio man, Robert Trout, and the young man from the Washington bureau, Roger Mudd.[1]

Friendly and Leonard were stunned and have said they both resisted. They met with Ernest Leiser, the producer of the *CBS*

Evening News, who was outraged, and they agreed that Friendly should tell Paley it was the unanimous recommendation of the News Division management that Cronkite should not be removed. Leonard said he was certain Paley would accept their recommendation. Leonard said he was "astonished" when Paley refused to retain Cronkite.[2]

Friendly has called his acquiescence his "worst blunder," even though he said he feared that defying Paley would "jeopardize" his own authority and the future of the news division.[3] Whatever Friendly's motives, he and Leonard were on the next plane to Los Angeles to inform the vacationing Cronkite that he was out. I was aware of none of this until Friendly phoned me from Los Angeles. Could I come to New York? Friendly sounded more urgent than he usually sounded, which was highly urgent. "What's up?" I asked. Friendly said he had to tell me in person.

What Friendly and Leonard told me in person I had a hard time believing. We all knew San Francisco had been a loser, but dumping Cronkite sounded like panic. Friendly said the decision had been made and I would refuse the assignment at my own peril. Here, in less than five months, I had been given three of the network's choicest assignments — the filibuster marathon, the floor at San Francisco, and now coanchor at Atlantic City. It was all too much.

What I said next to Friendly and Leonard still leaves me aghast after forty years.

"Fred, I've got a problem."

"What's the problem?"

"I've rented a beach house for all of August."

"So?"

"Well, I was going to have three weeks with my family before Atlantic City, but now I won't even get a week with them."

"Not a problem," said Leonard. "We'll rent you another house after the convention."

Rather than thanking them, promising that I would justify their confidence in me, and volunteering to start immediately, there I was, difficult and ungrateful, haggling with management over a beach house. If Leonard didn't know it before, he must have got a feeling for my family priorities that day. I have no doubt that he remembered our exchange when sixteen years later he picked Dan Rather to be Cronkite's replacement.

The dumping of Cronkite brought CBS a heavy and negative reaction from the press and the public. Friendly's announcement on July 30 was loaded with weasel words: "We have concluded that . . . a dual anchor arrangement provides more flexibility, mobility, and diversity of coverage than does a single anchor correspondent. . . . Walter's coverage of the Republican convention was superb. . . . No single news correspondent has been able to equal his news judgment. . . ." During the first week of August, CBS got eleven thousand letters protesting the decision.[4]

My new assignment necessarily involved what I disliked most — endless publicity interviews with TV writers and columnists. I tried my best, actually agreeing to a CBS press agent's idea to pose with Bob in one of those Atlantic City boardwalk rickshaws. But in sit-down interviews with the press, I wasn't fooling anybody. Rex Reed of the *New York Times* saw right through me: "He is tough, suspicious of other reporters, hates publicity, and refuses to talk about his personal life, family, or three-story brick house in the Washington suburbs. Trout, on the other hand, seems a perfect on camera counterpart: gracious, friendly . . . one of the few genuine old-guard gentlemen left on TV."[5] I was still struggling to convince myself that I was no longer an ink-stained wretch but a highly paid, merchandisable personage.

Robert Trout and I were from the same world, but we were twenty years apart. We both grew up in Washington, D.C.; he lived in northeast D.C., where his father owned a shoe store;[6] I lived in northwest D.C. and my father worked for the government. It was the twenty-year difference that made us strangers, and we more or less stayed strangers throughout the August convention. Bob was from the glory days of radio. He was FDR's favorite announcer, and his unequaled ability to ad-lib almost without end earned him the title of "The Iron Man of Radio." He was a man of exquisite manners and dignity, but his appearance and his clothes seemed directly out of the thirties. Bob refused to fly, no matter what, and his contract guaranteed that he be given enough notice to get there by train, ship, or car. A Trout arrival by Pullman was like a scene out of a Dick Powell movie. My looks were nothing to brag about, and Bob's thick mustache and hair parted down the middle made him look more like Chief Inspector Clouseau than a TV anchorman. Bob's knowledge about past conventions — he had anchored them on radio since 1936 — was encyclopedic. Mine was strictly contemporary and highly political. I would make some comment about how the convention keynoter, Senator John Pastore of Rhode Island, made up for his size with his powerful tongue; Bob would counter with a nugget about the 1936 keynoter, Alben Barkley of Kentucky, being the last vice president to be born in a log cabin.

It was a misalliance from the start, even though the television critics were charitable. Jack Gould of the *New York Times* said we had "stylish punch,"[7] and the *Newsday* critic said our "fresh appeal . . . spread to the overall operation."[8] The audience thought otherwise. The overnight Arbitron Ratings Service gave NBC 52 percent (Huntley-Brinkley) of those watching, CBS 39 percent (Trout-Mudd), and ABC 9 percent (Smith-Morgan).[9] The next morning I knew Walter would have his old job back in '68.

The lowest point for us at the convention had nothing to do with either Bob or me. It came when Vanocur of NBC scored the big beat of the convention by hoisting himself up to the presidential box for an extensive and exclusive interview with LBJ. The CBS control room and Bill Leonard went nuts. Leonard had lost his temper so many times during those four days, swearing and slamming down his phone, that producer Bill Crawford and I went shopping to buy him a rubber call directory. When Leonard saw Vanocur come up on the screen with LBJ, he grabbed a pair of headphones and went chasing after the president. Johnson was apparently unaware of the pursuing Leonard until Vanocur touched the president's arm and gave Leonard his blessing: "He's a good man, Mr. President." Leonard lamely asked Johnson, "You don't have any doubts about your vice presidential selection, do you, sir?" even though Johnson had just finished telling the convention that his choice was Hubert Humphrey. Then, in an apparent panic to detain the president, Leonard said: "Will you wave up to Mr. Trout and Mr. Mudd, sir? You've waved to everybody else." The leader of the free world then graciously waved to Bob and me. We were mortified, embarrassed, and humiliated. CBS went quickly to a commercial to give Bob and me time to recompose ourselves.

The high point in a series of lows for me began with a piece of haberdashery advice given me by Herbert Mitgang, whom Friendly had hired away from the editorial page of the *New York Times* to be his adviser. None of us knew exactly what sort of advice he was doling out until one day, as Bob and

I were practicing in our convention booth, Mitgang said he noticed that my jacket collar kept riding up on my neck, making me look truly ill-suited. He suggested that I try tucking the tail of my jacket under my own tail. But each time I would swivel or shift, the collar would creep up again. I figured that, coming from an ex-*New York Times* man, this was serious advice. So I called the men's store in Washington where I bought my clothes and explained the problem. The tailor got on the line and said he could install what he called a belt loop on the inside of the back of the jacket. He would pick out a light-wool jacket, with a nubby finish that wouldn't reflect the light, put in a belt loop, and send it off to my hotel in Atlantic City. When I threaded my trouser belt through the loop, the system worked perfectly. Since the belt loop was sewn in and could not be moved from one jacket to another, I had to wear the same jacket all four days. Nobody said a word about my unchanging wardrobe, including Mitgang. But over at NBC, that's all they talked about. Shad Northshield, an outrageously funny and inventive man and one of the NBC producers, said my belt loop gave him more grief than fending off his correspondents' constant pressure for more air time.

He said his so-called "Gang of Four" — Chancellor, McGee, Newman, and Tom Pettit — were demanding that their contracts be rewritten to include a "tailoring allowance for belt loop installation."

After the painful defeat of CBS news in Atlantic City, there was no question in any office at the network, including mine, that Cronkite should be back as the main anchor for the elections. Election-night assignments, however, sidestepped the word "anchor." Walter was the overall "national editor," Reasoner and I split the presidential returns, Trout handled the congressional races, Mike Wallace covered the governors, and Sevareid did the analysis. Our reporting was crisp, well-informed, and considerably ahead of NBC. Jack Gould's gushing review in the *New York Times* and others like it helped take some of the sting out of Atlantic City.

For Bob Trout and me, the fallout was punishing. Bob had been passed over in 1952 when Cronkite was picked to anchor the network's first convention. Twelve years later, Bob was hoping Atlantic City would make him the kind of star in television that he had been in radio for so long. It did not, and by the late 1960s Bob had moved to

Spain and did only piecemeal work for CBS. The Cronkite loyalists did not blame Bob for the unhorsing of Walter. They took it out on me. I went back on the road as the network's principal correspondent covering Goldwater. But after the elections, I regularly ran into a general lack of interest from the *Evening News* staff, particularly its producer, Ernest Leiser, in my stories from Capitol Hill. Weeks went by that fall when I disappeared from the Cronkite show altogether. In case I hadn't figured it out, Leiser was telling me I had come too far too fast and at the expense of HIS anchorman and HIS bread and butter. My morale dropped. I began to wonder if I ought to return to teaching. E. J. had to ask one night why I kept thumbing through *The Guide Book to American Prep Schools.* But with a new Congress and an inauguration scheduled for January 1965, Leiser was finally forced to lift his gag rule, leaving me happy to be back on the air but forever suspicious of New York.

Nineteen-sixty-four did end on a rising note. Each year since 1932 the *New Yorker* humorist Frank Sullivan had been writing his Christmas poem, "Greeting, Friends," in which he sent his kind regards in rhyme to everybody and anybody who had been in the news that year. When the December 26 issue arrived in the mail, I discovered the following lines in Sullivan's poem:

Mix proper Yuletide lubricators
For our Olympic gladiators,
Stir up a toddy for John Slade,
Clarence Dane, and Paul Schrade.
A toast to thee, Charles Bracelen Flood!
Mud in thine eye, good Roger Mudd!

Ned Calmer, the only broadcaster at CBS with a Ph.D. in literature, told me my inclusion in Sullivan's Christmas poem would be the high point of my career. Nothing could ever compare, he said. Ned took me to lunch at the Players in New York to celebrate.

CHAPTER 24
THE MINNESOTA
TWINS

Nineteen-sixty-four would be hard for me to equal — the filibuster marathon, floor reporting in San Francisco, coanchoring in Atlantic City, and then two weeks with my family in the prepaid house on the ocean at Virginia Beach.

The news division itself, after the highs and lows of 1964, needed a year to settle down and get its act together.

Nineteen-sixty-five opened with Ernest Leiser in tight control of the *Evening News.* Never a success as a correspondent, he now had veto power over every correspondent's appearance on the Cronkite show. Friendly elevated Bill Leonard to vice president of public affairs, or what everybody called "soft news" — documentaries, conventions, and election night. To run the "hard news" side of the operation, Friendly hired the forty-eight-year-old executive editor of *Newsweek,* Gordon Manning, a former reporter for United Press and a staff writer for *Collier's* before it closed in 1956. Manning brought with him no knowledge of broadcasting, but he percolated with ideas for stories, for follow-ups, for interviews. His memos, most of them written on empty sugar envelopes, fluttered about the CBS offices on West Fifty-seventh Street.

The Washington bureau was getting stronger by the day. Dan Rather had left for London but in his place came none other than Harry Reasoner. His only regular assignment was the 11 PM Sunday news, which not all of the affiliates carried, and Friendly thought the White House would give him more action and more exposure.

Reasoner moved to Washington with his wife, Kay, and their seven children, whose full names and dates of birth he could recite perfectly no matter his condition or what time of night. They bought a big house in the Maryland suburbs, not far from where I had grown up.

Reasoner and I and our wives made the best of their time in Washington. They were easy, funny, bright, and interesting to be with, and we shared a steady devotion to our families and children. They had a life well beyond the world of television; rarely would we talk about or gossip about CBS or our colleagues, but when we did Reasoner was the best at it. A Reasoner party would include a minimum of TV people but a maximum of people from the arts, like the *New Yorker* writer Peter De Vries, the songwriter Richard Rodgers, and the jazz violinist Ray Nance. One Sunday after brunch at the Rodgers' home in Fairfield, Connecticut, Dorothy Rodgers gave E. J. and me a tour of the house, which she had designed and written about in her book, *The House in My Head.* What I remember about the tour every time I descend into my own dank and malorganized cellar was the Rodgers' basement. Not only was it spotless, but also every overhead pipe and valve and vent was painted in bright colors — red for steam, blue for cold water, black for sewage, green for electrical, orange for gas. It wasn't a basement; it was an art gallery.

By the summer of 1966, however, Reasoner was gone, back to New York, bored by the White House beat and frustrated by the airtight clamps Johnson put on the flow of news. His return to New York paved the way for his eventual departure from CBS. He had not done well on election night in 1966. He sometimes lacked due diligence in boning up, figuring his quick wit and skill at vamping would see him through. But on the night of November 4, he was unprepared, and it showed. Reasoner's punishment, meted out by an angry Bill Leonard, was to be frozen out altogether from election night in 1968. When his contract came up for renewal in 1969 CBS offered him only a modest raise and he jumped to ABC to coanchor their evening news with Howard K. Smith. The show's puny ratings rose almost immediately, making the ABC news division truly competitive for the first time.[1]

Along with Hughes and Ann Rudd, our friendship continued even after Reasoner went to ABC. One of his perks at ABC was a driver for his daily trip from Westport to and from Manhattan. When the Reasoners invited E. J. and me up one weekend, we rendezvoused at the ABC studios on West Sixty-sixth Street to watch him as the solo anchor on *ABC Evening News.* I also watched him whip out of his bottom desk drawer a bottle of booze and take a long pull just before the camera's red lights came on. Given what appeared to be a nightly circumstance, I concluded that Reasoner's driver was more a necessity than a perk.

Reasoner had no equal as a literary writer who could broadcast or as an engaging broadcaster who could write. He had studied journalism at the University of Minnesota, reported for the *Minneapolis Times* and then for KEYD-TV in Minneapolis, and migrated to New York and CBS in 1956. He had one prominent failing, which we all heard every time he reported on the cost of Lyndon Johnson's Great Society. He could not pronounce the word "million." Every time, it came out "mee-yun." Of course, Cronkite couldn't say "oil." It always came out "awe-yul."

Because Reasoner covered the White House and I covered the Congress, we wound up sharing an interview with Vice President Hubert Humphrey, on the grounds that Humphrey belonged at the White House but as the official presiding officer of the Senate he belonged on the Hill. During the civil rights filibuster I had gotten to know and like Humphrey, Minnesota's so-called "Happy Warrior," and had interviewed him a hundred different ways during those sixty-four days — on the record, off the record, on background, on deep background, and not for attribution. The interview with Reasoner and me, on March 12, 1965, was his first serious sit-down session as vice president, so my relationship with him was quite different from the last time we had talked.

The interview was filmed in Humphrey's

vice presidential office just off the Senate floor. Reasoner began, and we alternated questions — questions about his power, his duties, his travels, his concept of the office, his views on succession, his desire for a vice presidential mansion, the Great Society. Without any prior agreement or strategy, Reasoner's questions tended to take the long historical view and mine the short, current, and political angle. It was a rich interview, but it was Humphrey at his most long-winded. When Reasoner asked him whether he thought a vice president should "constitutionally have more duties than he does," it took Humphrey four-and-a-half typed pages — 101 lines, 1,312 words — to say, "I believe that the way it is is most likely all right."

Not until the interview was winding down were there any sparks. Humphrey was proudly checking off all the duties and responsibilities he had been given by the president when I asked why he had not been sent to represent the United States at the funeral of Winston Churchill on January 30. He said he "respected" Johnson's decision. "I wasn't unhappy about it," he claimed, although his words revealed that he was. "I do not want to become the official attender of funerals for the United States government." And then Humphrey added this whopper: "I was in close touch with the president all week long and he was a pretty sick man with a very serious cold. I thought maybe it would have been a little better that I stayed here and didn't catch cold myself," — figuring, I suppose, that two bad head colds at the top of the ticket would shut down the Great Society. His answer, I thought, needed challenging. "But Sir Winston," I said, "was a very special man who enjoyed a very special relationship with this country." Humphrey did not like the question, and he threw my words right back at me. "And the chief justice is a very special man, and the delegation that went there was very special. The secretary of state is a very special man, and there were a number of senators there who are very fine and special people."[2]

How about that for a little mud in your eye?

After his loss to Nixon in 1968, Humphrey claimed he was retiring from public life, but that claim evaporated in 1970 when Eugene McCarthy decided not to run for reelection to the Senate from Minnesota. Humphrey jumped at the chance, easily defeating Republican Clark MacGregor. He was back in the Senate and within a year

Hubert Horatio Humphrey was running for the presidency again.

Humphrey was difficult to dislike. A rare specimen, Humphrey was a liberal who was also tenacious, who did not go wobbly, who could give as good as he got, even though there seemed not to be a mean bone in his body. What did bother me about him were the union cockroaches that seemed to gather either in or near every hotel suite Humphrey occupied. One or two of them were always scurrying about, eager to drive, fetch, summon, call, or pour. A Humphrey campaign without organized labor was a Cadillac trying to run on four cylinders.

Even though he failed to stop George McGovern at the '72 convention in Miami, Humphrey was at it again in August 1976, when he considered challenging Jimmy Carter. But he decided against it and instead challenged Robert Byrd as Senate majority leader after the election. He lost. His health was already in a slow, undisclosed decline. In August 1977, after surgery, he announced that he had terminal cancer. Despite his bonhomie and humor, the pallor of death was about him when he made his brave return from the hospital to the Senate.

When he entered the chamber all the senators and all the visitors in the overflowing galleries were on their feet, applauding without slack for more than five minutes. As he made his way to his seat, he shook the hand of every Democrat and of most of the Republicans. By turns the leadership praised him, and then Humphrey spoke.

"Drugs and radiation and doctors and nurses are very, very helpful," he said, "but the greatest therapy of all is love and friendship." He said he was "old enough to know that not everything that has been said about me squared with the truth," but that he was "sufficiently weak to want to believe every word of it."[3]

It was a rare, moving, and affectionate thirty minutes, and when it was over the Senate rose again, almost dissolved by the tenderness of the moment. The Senate really loved him.

Humphrey died on January 13, 1978, at his home in Waverly, Minnesota.

Two weeks later, Governor Rudy Perpich appointed Humphrey's widow, Muriel, to fill the vacancy. The night Mrs. Humphrey was sworn in, I did a piece for the Cronkite show about Minnesota's embarrassing political situation, in which four of the state's five top officeholders were now un-elected.

It was not easy figuring it out: Perpich,

elected lieutenant governor, became governor when Governor Wendell Anderson resigned; Perpich was succeeded as lieutenant governor by Alec Olson, who had been elected as a state senator; Wendell Anderson appointed himself to succeed Senator Walter Mondale, who had resigned from the Senate to run with Jimmy Carter; Mondale was appointed to the Senate in 1964 to succeed Hubert Humphrey, who had resigned to run with Lyndon Johnson; and finally, Muriel Humphrey, appointed senator by the governor who'd been elected lieutenant governor but became governor when the old governor appointed himself senator.

I concluded the piece with, "Everyone in Minnesota assumes Muriel Humphrey will be a caretaker senator. She could, of course, break new ground in Minnesota by actually running for office."[4]

Watching the Cronkite show that night was Phil Geyelin, an editor of the *Washington Post*. He called CBS the next day for a transcript of my Minnesota piece and ran it on the op-ed page the next morning, February 9. It was a nice surprise. It was also my fiftieth birthday.

CHAPTER 25
MISTER EV, THE TALKING HORSE

Unlike the Hubert Humphrey of the 1964 filibustering days, when he was a free spirit, bursting with enthusiasm, Humphrey as vice president had seemingly become Lyndon Johnson's political valet, if not his house slave. Now, in 1965, he was out of the daily legislative swirl; his only official connection to the Congress was through Article I of the Constitution, which made him president of the Senate, without a vote except in case of a tie. But, like most vice presidents, he rarely presided.

The once invincible southern bloc, which Humphrey had so skillfully outmaneuvered, was in tatters. Strom Thurmond had become a Republican, further alienating him from his southern colleagues; Russell Long had joined the Senate leadership as whip; Richard Russell, suffering from emphysema, had been absent for months; Harry Byrd at seventy-eight had neither the stamina nor the skill; and Lister Hill of Alabama, the most capable of the old gang, had lost his enthusiasm and wanted to make only a token fight against the 1965 voting rights bill.

The new southern leader, almost by default, was Allen Ellender of Louisiana. Even among southerners, he was not completely admired. One of them went so far as to tell me that having Ellender in charge was the "worst thing that's happened to us since Appomattox."

The depleted southern bloc now faced, for the second time in less than a year, the insurmountable challenge of defeating a civil rights bill. A voting rights bill had been in the works at the Johnson White House since early February, but when Alabama state troopers began cracking skulls on the Edmund Pettus Bridge in Selma on March 7, the legislation began moving at flank speed. Johnson delivered what was probably the finest speech of his career — the "We shall overcome" speech — to a joint session on March 15, interrupted forty times by applause and twice by standing, roaring ovations.[1]

With the southerners in disarray, with Humphrey elevated to the vice presidency, with Majority Leader Mike Mansfield remaining low key, with the Republicans sharply split, standing astride it all was the Senate's dominant figure — Everett McKinley Dirksen.

Dirksen and I were no strangers. To have gone through a twelve-week filibuster as a reporter, watching him day in and day out maneuver, wheedle, dissemble, cajole, bargain, beg, and borrow, had resulted in an intimacy that at times came very close to crossing the line that ought to separate the press from the politician.

Along with dozens of reporters, I would be in the crowd that gathered in the Senate press gallery every Tuesday afternoon after the GOP's policy luncheon to hear Dirksen expound. He would bum cigarettes from us without shame, we would call him "Ev" without shame, and all but a few would laugh at his endless flow of Claghorn verbiage.

One afternoon Sam Schaffer of *Newsweek* asked Dirksen if he thought a certain controversial piece of legislation would get through by the first of the year.

Dirksen paused for a moment and then rumbled, "Well, Sam, what's today?" Sam said, "The twenty-fourth of September."

"Well, Sam," he said, "that's nearly October, which reminds me that's apple-picking time. Once you begin picking apples, almost before you know it, Sam, you are into Thanksgiving and soon everybody will be singing 'Hark, the Herald Angels Sing,' and downtown, Sam, they'll be hanging up wreaths. Before you know it, Sam, it's the first of the year. Now, Sam, where were we?"[2]

The press gallery roared with laughter and we all left smiling and happily uninformed.

Jack Germond, then with the Gannett News Service, once said those Dirksen sessions were like "casting imitation pearls before the real swine."[3]

Fortuitously for CBS, Dirksen had agreed to do a documentary profile, and on March 31 we sat down in his minority leader's office near the Senate chamber for an interview and a filmed tour of the Capitol that took up most of the day. Once the senator and I got through the endless repeats of walking together through Statuary Hall so the cameras could film us coming and going and coming and going, we sat down to get started. Dirksen seemed to enjoy our give-and-take as much as I did.

MUDD: You've been described by some writers as a chameleon. You've moved from mixed support of the New Deal, to full support of Bob Taft, to full support of Eisenhower, to a defense of McCarthy, back to a defense of Eisenhower, to a defense of civil rights. And now back to a defense of Goldwater. . . .

DIRKSEN: Why, Roger, the only people who don't change their minds have either been adjudged incompetent and sent to asylums, or they're out in the cemeteries of the country. Pray God the time will never come when under given circumstances I won't change my mind.

MUDD: Are you aware, senator, that many people who hear this style that you have, and hear you on television, think that you are a buffoon and a gasbag, if I may use an inelegant phrase?

DIRKSEN: Oh, you may be candid with me. I don't know what they think. I judge from the mails that they give approval to the way I undertake to express myself on the issues of our time.

MUDD: Your vocabulary and your general oratorical style causes, I'm sure you're aware, a great of deal of comment. Why, for instance, do you say, instead of, "I think there's going to be quite a fight tomorrow," you would say, "I apprehend there will be a substantial fulmination." Why do you put it that way?

DIRKSEN: Well, it invests it of a certain finality, knowing that it might not quite turn out that way, so you adopt slightly flexible ground. Suppose I stated to you I'm as positive as we're sitting here, that it's going to rain tomorrow? Well, how do I know it's going to rain tomorrow? I haven't seen a forecast. I may very well put that another way around and say, in your language, "I apprehend from a certain feeling in my bones, that there is a possibility of precipitation tomorrow." You see, you can't come back at me later and say that just shows what a bum forecaster you are.[4]

The program ran on a Sunday afternoon in early June and drew a fine review from Gould of the *New York Times,* who called it an "engrossing and lively visit . . . a particularly effective revelation of character."[5] The next day a delivery truck brought to our house a tree peony, raised by Dirksen in his garden at his home in Leesburg. At some point along the way, Dirksen referred to me in a semipublic meeting as "my main TV man on the Hill." I do not think he meant to embarrass me, but he did and I told him so. His apologies were effusive.

The presidents he served with — Eisenhower, Kennedy, and Johnson — found him to be a soft touch when they appealed to his patriotism, provided, of course, he got to name the next appointee to the Food and Drug Administration. After 1965, Dirksen's power began a very gradual, almost imperceptible decline, some of it traceable to Republican resentment over his tight relationship with President Johnson. His influence remained critical for the passage of the 1965 Voting Rights Act, but he had lost the support of four midwestern Republicans who had helped him break the '64 filibuster. The cloakroom gossip was that Bourke Hickenlooper, his nose out of joint with all the publicity Dirksen was getting, was also fed up with the way Dirksen had taken over as the Senate spokesman for everything Republican. Hickenlooper, as chairman of the Republican Policy Committee, figured he, not Dirksen, was the one to talk policy.[6] But he was not a particularly attractive spokesman on TV. His voice was hard and flat, befitting a native of southwest Iowa, and his face told you he did not like the way the world was going. When I first introduced myself to him, he said, "Mudd. Mudd or Hickenlooper. I don't know which is worse." He was, I believe, trying to be funny.

The congressional elections of 1966 brought four new Republicans to the Senate who were not prepared to fall in behind Dirksen: Robert Griffin from Michigan, Mark Hatfield from Oregon, Charles Percy from Illinois, and Dirksen's own son-in-law, Howard Baker from Tennessee. Faced with a changing dynamic in the Republican ranks, Dirksen began to lose here and there on a variety of issues and votes: a Vietnam peace conference resolution, a U.S.-Soviet consulate treaty, money for school aid, and the nomination of Abe Fortas as chief justice. Behind many of these setbacks for Dirksen was a very skilled political strategist, Senator Thruston Morton of Kentucky, who had become the unofficial leader of his party's so-called progressives in the Senate. Morton was talked about as Dirksen's logical successor, but Morton said he was too lazy to handle the drudgery involved.[7] In a moment of sober candor, Morton confessed that but for the Senate's steam baths, he'd be back in Kentucky.

Dirksen's likes and dislikes were apparent. He had little use for his ingratiatingly ambitious junior colleague from Illinois, Chuck Percy, whose voice was almost as deep as his. His special target was Democrat Thomas Dodd of Connecticut, who unwisely chose to criticize Mansfield's leadership during a floor speech. In a blink, Dirksen was on his feet, excoriating Dodd for his "cerebral incoherence" and "emotional inconsistency," which was Dirksen-speak for "drunk."[8] Dirksen invariably referred to Dodd as the "distinguished senator from the Nutmeg State." He also liked to tease Winston Prouty of Vermont because he had lost the thumb on his right hand from an accident. Once, when Dirksen happened to be presiding, Prouty was nearing the end of his allotted time to speak. He raised his right hand, with his four fingers quite visible, and asked "unanimous consent for five additional minutes." Dirksen granted him only four additional minutes. Finally Prouty got the joke and held up his digitally complete left hand.

Dirksen's health declined almost as steadily as his power. At age seventy in 1966, he suffered from chronic emphysema and yet remained a heavy smoker; his heart developed a leaky valve; "extreme fatigue" and "acute exhaustion" had him in and out of Walter Reed Hospital; and on one visit he slipped from his bed and broke his thigh bone. Doctors at Walter Reed discovered during a routine checkup in 1969 a small shadow on his right lung. They operated successfully on September 2. His recovery seemed surprisingly swift, but five days later he turned pale, collapsed, and died when his heart stopped.[9]

His body lay in state for twenty-four hours in the Capitol Rotunda, the fifth senator to be so honored. The formal funeral service at the National Presbyterian Church was packed. I was in the back row by the aisle with a number of other Hill reporters. As the senators made their way out, Senator James Eastland of Mississippi spotted me. There was probably no senator at the time with as bad a press as Eastland. His hunched shoulders, his long cigar, and his surface orneriness did little to dispel his formidable racist image. For most of us, he was an untouchable. And yet he was scrupulously polite and soft-spoken. He must have known I liked Dirksen. As he passed by me, he simply reached out and squeezed my hand. That gesture, so unlike Eastland, baffled me. Years later I heard a possible explanation, related to me by Brad Dye of Jackson, Mississippi, who had been one of Eastland's staff lawyers. After adjournment each day the senator and his staff would gather in the back room for drinks and gossip. The Cronkite show was on and in the middle of one of my Hill reports, Eastland turned to Dye and said, "Roger Mudd is all right. He's the only one who plays fair."[10] "Fair" about what I don't know, but I've chosen to believe it was a compliment.

Less than twelve hours after Dirksen's death on September 7, Bill Small and the Washington bureau produced a special report that I anchored with commentary from Sevareid and interviews with Gerald Ford, Hugh Scott, Carl Curtis, Gordon Allott, and Dirksen's son-in-law, Howard Baker. Marya McLaughlin asked Baker if Dirksen had ever been one-upped. Baker said his three-year-old daughter, sitting on Dirksen's lap, once said, "Grandpa, do you know what you sound like?" Dirksen said, "No, what do I sound like?" She said, "You sound like Mr. Ed, the talking horse."[11]

I closed the program with this commentary:

The key phrase for understanding and

appreciating Everett Dirksen was always "slightly flexible," for he learned after thirty-six years in the Congress that nothing in political life is bound to happen until it happens. This required an enormous capacity for disappointment, a willingness to take criticism, and the constant maintenance of room for maneuver. . . . [There was] in Dirksen a sense of humor rare in American political life. For he had become a living caricature of the politician, deliberately making fun of those colleagues in the Senate who would not admit to being flexible, or would not admit to abandoning principle, or would not admit to being wordy, ponderous, or vapid. For it was when Dirksen was the windiest that he was enjoying the joke the most. That was what most of us never understood about him.[12]

CHAPTER 26
"NOT WHILE I'M AROUND"

For the first ten years I was on the Hill, television coverage of the Congress was almost impossible on the House side and barely acceptable on the Senate side. Until 1970, TV cameras were not allowed to record any House committee hearings. That prohibition — known as the Rayburn Rule — was proclaimed by Speaker Sam Rayburn, who swore he would never allow a repeat of the tumultuous 1952 hearings of the House Un-American Activities Committee, which were televised before Rayburn clamped. The Rayburn Rule forced the TV crews to set up shop in the corridors outside the hearing rooms and bag the members as they emerged. Some of them wouldn't be bagged and others were dying to be bagged. That meant the television reporters had to re-create the essence of the hearing with their questions. It was TV news's version of stagecraft, in which the politicians were the

315

actors giving sanitized offstage versions of the drama.

We tried our best to question the principal players, but many of them were the senior, conservative members — the old mules, who were not camera-savvy in the first place and did not trust us in the second.

During the 1963 civil rights hearings before the House Judiciary Committee, one of the key Republicans was William McCulloch of Ohio. He was the ranking Republican on the committee, so his endorsement of the bill had been critical. He was, however, a milquetoast kind of man, with the look of a fussy department store floorwalker, who rarely figured in the news. So we rarely asked him before the cameras. But on this particular day, the day the committee reported out the bill, McCulloch found out we had asked almost everybody but him. Just as the networks had finished interviewing everybody but him and were about to break down, he stormed out, furious at the unintended slight, accusing me of deliberately freezing him out and demanding that he be given proper credit for the important role he had played. It was a first for him and a first for us. The honorable gentleman, needless to say, made the evening news that night.

Cameras in the House chamber were also forbidden because of Rayburn. Asked about televising the House itself, Rayburn said, "Hell, no. Not while I'm around here." Rayburn died in 1961 and thus ceased to be around. Within a year the Congress began steps that finally opened House committee sessions to television in 1970. During the hearings on the legislation, I was asked to testify in my role as chairman of the Executive Committee of the Radio and Television Galleries, even though as credentialed members of the media we were prohibited from lobbying. No one raised the issue, but I still felt out of place and nervous about being a witness and questioned by the very men with whom I normally did the questioning. Excluding TV cameras, I said, worked to the detriment of the House and the public, because television had gravitated to the Senate, which from the beginning had allowed TV coverage of its committees.

"Until you have stood outside a House hearing," I said, "and tried to re-create on film what went on inside, you cannot understand the frustration of covering the House with television. Re-creating is not the function of television journalism. It is unfair to us, unfair to you, and most of all unfair to the public."[1] The questioning came mainly from Del Latta of Bowling Green, Ohio, a conservative Republican, who was in a perpetual grouch because he thought the networks spent all their time covering J. William Fulbright and his intellectual toadies on the Senate Foreign Relations Committee. He seemed unable to understand the difference between live coverage and filmed coverage. When I told him he was confusing the two, he did not like it. But he didn't hold a grudge. Ten years later when he was retiring, I asked for an interview to be part of a series I was doing for the *CBS Evening News* on little-known but influential members. He was delighted to be asked.

Even after TV got a foothold in the House, most of the coverage was generally limited to the smaller networks like Westinghouse or Corinthian or local stations wealthy enough to open a Washington bureau to cover, say, the Texas, Illinois, or New York City delegations. Television reporters still tended to favor the Senate, because after twenty years of welcoming the cameras at its committee hearings, senators were better known to the public and to our producers in New York, were allegedly more powerful, and were presumably more articulate. It took a flamboyant representative like Adam Clayton Powell of Harlem or the fuming, foaming Jim Traficant of Youngstown to trump a steady, intelligent senator like Richard Lugar of Indiana or Bob Graham of Florida.

Delighted as we were with the expanding coverage, it became impossible for the bureau to cover every hearing of every committee. One we missed was what the desk thought would be a routine hearing of the House Education Committee. But the chairman, Adam Clayton Powell, that morning tore into the helpless witness, an undersecretary of education in the Johnson administration, and his scorching quotes began burning up the wires. Immediately the Cronkite show in New York told Washington it wanted the story for that night. Small, the bureau chief, knew better than to tell New York that Washington had not covered it. So he called in Dave Schoumacher and told him to get the story. He said it didn't matter that the hearing was over.

"Go to Powell and see what you can do," he told Schoumacher.

"I went to Powell on bended knee," Schoumacher said. "Mr. Chairman, I've got a problem. We missed your hearing and the Cronkite show wants a story. Could you help me?"

Not a problem, said the chairman. While

Schoumacher and his camera crew set up, Powell not only reassembled a few stray committee members but also summoned the witness back to the hearing room. Thus properly staged, Powell repeated his excoriating quotes word for word for the CBS camera.

"Did I do 'em all?" he asked Schoumacher.

"Yes, sir, and thank you very much."

Small says he had no memory of the incident but that "it may well have happened. I would have sent David up there, assuming he would just interview Powell. I didn't know Powell would go the extra mile. I can live with that."

Schoumacher's story is vivid proof of how far a politician would go to get on the *CBS Evening News* and how far Washington would stretch its staging rules in fear of having New York cut Small's bureau down to size.

Not until July 24, 1974, did the nation fully realize there was such a place as the House of Representatives. On that evening the House Judiciary Committee began televised hearings on the impeachment of President Nixon. To the TV audience, the thirty-eight members of the Judiciary Committee were mostly no-namers, obscure backbenchers, and supposed second-raters. Who outside of Washington or their home districts had ever heard of Wayne Owens of Panguitch, Utah, or Jerome Waldie of Antioch, California, or Ray Thornton of Conway, Arkansas? Even the committee chairman, Peter Rodino of New Jersey, was best known not for his jurisprudence but for his resolution making Columbus Day a national holiday. But once the networks descended on the committee, their electronic cameras hidden behind black curtains, and began live gavel-to-gavel coverage, the nation sat transfixed by what it saw: one unknown representative after another rising to the solemnity of the occasion, each no longer an unknown but becoming a distinct personality — the booming cadences of Barbara Jordan from Texas, the tightened midwestern vowels of Robert McClory from Illinois, the snarl of Charles Sandman of New Jersey, the soft, rounded consonants of Caldwell Butler of Virginia — and all thirty-eight alive with the portent of their assignment.

The TV networks had worked out a pool system in which PBS carried the morning and afternoon sessions and the commercial networks rotated the evening meetings. The committee itself specified that there could be no commercial breaks during the hearings. Bruce Morton and I were there for CBS, one of us always inside the hearing room and the other standing by in the crowded hallway in case the committee suddenly called a recess and we had to fill the time. Each night during that week, CBS did a late special from the Washington bureau, in addition, of course, to the enlarged coverage of the *CBS Evening News.*

On the fourth evening the committee voted on the first article of impeachment — that President Nixon had obstructed justice. As the clerk called their names, each member seemed to wear a mask and the masks revealed nothing — no pleasure, no rejoicing, no defiance. The final vote came from Chairman Rodino himself — a hoarse, almost whispered "aye."

If anything persuaded the leadership of the House to expand TV coverage it was the impressive, dignified, and reassuring performance of the Judiciary Committee. One of the first actions Tip O'Neill took after he became speaker in January 1977 was to announce a ninety-day test of televising live the House itself. Two years later — it took that long to work out control of the cameras themselves — the system became permanent on March 19, 1979, and for once the House began to feel it was no longer the "lower body."

The Senate — or the "other body," as the House calls it — took seven more years before it could overcome the opposition of Russell Long of Louisiana, Claiborne Pell of Rhode Island, and a few others to having TV cameras in the Senate. Live coverage began June 2, 1986.

Despite the grim predictions, there is no evidence that the cameras altered legislative procedure or resulted in excessive grand-standing — self-policing has seen to that — but they have sharpened the members' rhetoric, perhaps improved their haberdash-ery, and inspired them to bring charts and graphs onto the Senate floor to help the TV audience decipher their words. Although the public's esteem for the Congress has not improved appreciably, the presence of cameras has helped restore some rough bal-ance between the Congress and the White House, where presidents have traditionally dominated the air waves.

It was during 1963 — my first full year on the Hill — that I began to get acquainted with the members and their staffs, and they with me. CBS News and Walter Cronkite regarded Congress as being as important as the White House. My steady appearances as a full-time congressional correspondent on the *Evening News* was a signal to House and Senate that CBS took the Hill seriously. ABC News, with a minuscule budget, was a weak sister during the 1960s. NBC News used David Brinkley in his Washington studio to do whatever congressional stories made the show. NBC had a Hill reporter, Robert McCormick, but he was nearing the end of his career and was confined to radio and seemed to lack energy, if not interest. With weak competition and regular coverage, it did not take long before CBS became the dominant television presence on the Hill. All of that made easier CBS's access to the members, their staff members, and the officers of the Congress.

As heavily as most members leaned on television to promote themselves, protocol discouraged them from coming to the TV Gallery without being asked by a reporter. It was simply not done. But it was done once in my time. A month or so after the new class of freshmen senators had been sworn in January 1967, there appeared uninvited in the Senate TV Gallery, lo and behold, Charles Percy, the new man from Illinois. He was a small, personable man with the voice of a basso profundo. As former industrialist and president of Bell & Howell, he must have figured that as a corporate giant he needed no invitation. The gallery staffers, who are on the Senate payroll, were not about to offend Senator Percy by telling him to go away. They begged us to interview him. We refused. What followed was a fifteen-minute stand-off, with Percy wondering why no one wanted to talk to him and TV reporters deserting the gallery for a quick coffee. Finally, one of the nervous staffers whispered to the senator's press secretary what was what.

To film on the steps of the Capitol required police permission, and the request for a permit had to come from a senator or a representative. One of my best Hill friends was the executive secretary to Republican Senator Tom Kuchel of California, Margie Whelen. Any time I needed the steps to film something on-camera, Margie would call the Capitol Police to tell them Roger Mudd wanted to interview the senator on the steps. Instantly permission would be granted. With the camera in place and a policeman looking on, I would film my stand-up, mentioning to the officer that Kuchel was due out any minute. Of course, he never came, because he knew nothing about the interview. I would pretend to check with his office and then tell the policeman that Kuchel had to cancel because of a roll call vote. It worked for at least a year before the police caught on.

Kuchel was the Republican whip and as such was rewarded with a hideaway office just off the Senate floor and directly above the old Supreme Court chamber. The walk-in coat closet in Kuchel's hideaway had once housed the shaft for the elevator that raised and lowered the three-hundred-pound chief justice, William Howard Taft. After the Court moved to its own building in 1935, the old chamber got used for party caucuses and the like. Any time the Democrats caucused, Margie would let me slip into the coat closet and eavesdrop through a very thin drywall partition. But never with the Republicans.

Except for late-night specials, rarely did I have need to go into the CBS bureau. My radio reports and television voice-overs I recorded from our soundproof booth in the Senate Gallery. Motorcycle couriers picked up our film and took it to the film lab in Georgetown to be developed. The booth was not more than three feet wide and six feet long. In it was a telephone, a microphone, a typewriter, a shelf desk, and room for two people in a squeeze. It was generally understood that when one of us was working in the booth, the other would use the telephones and typewriters in the main TV gallery. Lesley Stahl, new on the job and perhaps not aware of the custom, says she came into the booth one day while I was working and after a few minutes was ordered out because I said she was wearing "too much perfume."[2] Her story sounds about right. It's bad enough sitting next to a *l'Air du Temps*–doused woman at the theater, but to be trapped in a three-by-six-foot cubicle with one can be unhinging. I never understood why Lesley wore perfume to work anyway. She was too good a reporter to need it.

CHAPTER 27
"OF COURSE, IT'S A GREAT BODY"

For the better part of fifteen years, the Congress was my professional home. Figuring out and reporting what went on there was what I did for a living. There were interruptions — summers I'd be in New York to substitute for Walter Cronkite, every other fall I'd be on the road doing political stories, and once or twice a year I'd be detached to work on a documentary. But when I was back in the bureau in Washington, it was to the Hill I went. I went happily and eagerly, because CBS's keeping me on the Hill gave me time to develop sources and to write with perhaps more sophistication, authority, and even humor.

In the mornings I would drive directly from home to the Hill and park on the East Front Plaza, where each network had a reserved slot. I would duck into the Senate restaurant for a quick and very cheap cup of coffee, take the "staff only" elevator, whose operator knew my name, to the gallery level, put together a radio spot on the upcoming day, and then a few minutes before noon stride into the Senate chamber as if I belonged there. At least half a dozen reporters would gather in the well of the Senate — that open area just in front of the reading clerks — awaiting the arrival of the leaders, Mansfield, Byrd, Dirksen, and Kuchel, so we could extract a few quotes from them to update our stories. We called those mini press conferences "dugout chatter."

Few of us regarded our special treatment as perks. They were, we thought, designed simply to facilitate the flow of news. It never occurred to us, or to me at least, that we were being seduced into becoming part of the congressional apparatus. Regarding myself as clean as a hound's tooth, I did a piece for the Cronkite show on congressional perks, which was picked up and reprinted in *Reader's Digest*. A day or two later, the inestimable David Obey of Wisconsin cut me down to size when he rose on the House floor to list all the perks I was provided by the taxpayers.

Whether reporters worked on the Senate side or the House side, the Congress made sure we got everything we needed, except perhaps access. In almost no time a reporter would begin to identify with the Congress, even feel a part of it. Everything was free: gallery space, desks, typewriters, paper, telephones, file cabinets, leather couches, and soundproof studios. The Congress provided full-time staffs in the press, TV, and periodical galleries to answer telephones, handle messages, track the debates, and distribute press releases, bills, and committee reports.

In a showdown between reporters and the Congress over space or access, however, the staff would invariably side with the people who paid them. During the 1960s, Robert Hough, the superintendent of the Senate TV Gallery, was notorious for his refusal to push our requests for more camera space or hallway stakeouts. He once told me, "I work for the Senate, not for you."

Free desks, free paper, and free parking on the Capitol Plaza were not our only perks. We could get our hair cut in the congressional barbershops for $5.00, and in both the House and Senate dining rooms reporters had a reserved table with an assigned staff of waiters and waitresses. A lunch of Senate bean soup, a club sandwich, a double scoop of chocolate and vanilla ice cream, and iced tea cost, thanks to the taxpayers' subsidy, about $4.50. At the Senate table, the waiter was King and the waitress was Ruth. After your third or fourth visit, both King and Ruth knew by heart what you regularly ordered. When King died in the 1970s, a delegation from the congressional press walked over to the funeral at his Capitol Hill church. We were the only whites in the church, and when the minister asked if one of us would like to come forward to say a few words about King, the newspapermen all nudged me with their elbows, on the dubious ground that the TV guys knew how to ad-lib and they didn't. I stepped up on the altar with a blank brain and sweaty palms. Somehow the words came out, and behind me before long I could hear the church elders calling out "Amen. Amen."

The Senate and House press tables were exclusively and aggressively reserved for the press. No lobbyist, no congressional staffer dared sit there. A stray remark or a piece of inside intelligence carried back to the member might enhance the staffer's reputation in the eyes of the boss but could seriously embarrass the reporter. The senior wire-service men were the enforcers. F. Lee Bailey, the renowned and flamboyant defense lawyer, sat down at the Senate press table by himself one day. The chatter suddenly stopped. Forks and spoons were suspended in midarc. Warren Duffee of the United Press then cleared his throat and briefly but firmly told Mr. Bailey why he had to leave. He did, without a word.

Slowly and surely through the early 1960s I began to widen my circle of sources. They helped me learn the intricacies of Congress: the relationship between committee chairmen and the full membership, between chairmen and speaker, between majority and minority, between House and Senate, between the House and the Committee of the whole House; the power of a motion to strike the enacting clause; and the meaning of a motion to reconsider the vote by which the vote was taken to recommit the bill. Some of it was so arcane that few in the bureau knew or cared what I was talking about when I'd call in. A bore I must have been to those producers who had to suffer through one of my explanations about why a vote had been put off until Monday when I had promised the vote would come today. But I was simply unwilling to not be prepared or to be unable to answer my producer's questions.

The Congress was absolutely the prime

place for a political reporter to work. The White House media were subject to the whims of the presidential protectorate, and the State Department media to the layered language of the diplomats. But on the Hill it was open hunting season. Reporters had no trouble finding out what back-home pressures made the members vote the way they did or break the promises they had made. Because television could not easily handle the fine print of legislation, I gravitated toward learning about the members' personalities and idiosyncrasies. I also thought a member's religion could be critical in explaining a vote.

One of the early congressional pieces I did was on a procedural vote involving school prayer. In the aftermath of the Supreme Court decision outlawing prayer in public schools, the House Judiciary Committee in 1964 held eighteen days of hearings on a stack of amendments aimed at overturning the decision. Because the vote was not scheduled until nearly Cronkite's air time, I was standing by in the studio at the bureau, ready to go live. Figuring that the committee members' religion would be a legitimate part of the story, I had prepared a run-down of their religious affiliations. So when the vote came in, I reported that the majority was basically conservative and mainly Protestant, but that the minority included such and such and such and the committee chairman, Emanuel Celler of New York, "a Jew." When I came upstairs from the studio, Schoenbrun and the desk were yelling at me, because New York was yelling at them. I was ordered to rewrite the piece for the 7 PM update, eliminating all references to religion. I was not told whether my journalistic sin had been mentioning religion or had been in using "Jew" instead of "Jewish." A colleague told me later that the order to rewrite was no surprise given the number of CBS news executives and producers who were Jews, or Jewish.

With deadlines for radio and television every two to three hours, there was rarely time to reflect on the impact of the legislation, whether it was the Trade Expansion Act of 1962 or the Area Redevelopment Act. Jack Germond, the former political columnist for the *Baltimore Sun,* believes that "in the end, it is far wiser to focus attention on the kind of people who are running rather than which one seems to have the best plan for providing drug coverage for old folks."[1]

The Congress is probably the nearest thing

America has to a government-subsidized plantation. For 535 men and women, not to mention the 200 or so journalists who spend their days there, it is a homestead with an isolated, independent, and almost self-sustaining economy. It has its own subway system, restaurant, cafeteria and catering service, barber and beauty shops, furniture warehouse, gift shops, interior decorators, police department, print shop, daily paper, gardeners and greenhouses, ministers, chapels, world-class library, professional research staff, picture-framing shop, school for the pages, physicians and nurses, carpentry shops, post offices, gymnasiums, pools, fitness rooms, and reserved underground parking, all paid for by the taxpayer from an annual appropriation of almost $4 billion to run the Congress. Thruston Morton, the Kentucky Republican, once acknowledged he would have retired long ago had it not been for the Senate's steam baths.

With a comfortable rollaway stowed in the closet, a bachelor member could do worse than living in his office. It would eliminate rent, mortgage payments, commuting, gasoline, car insurance, and grocery shopping. Except to fly back to the district six times a year at government expense, the member would never have to leave the plantation except to do laundry and dry-cleaning. But an indentured servant (aka intern) would take care of that.

Even the social structure mirrors plantation life. In the Senate are the grandees, the nobility, the select few, representing the great acreage of their state's economic interests and identifying characteristics. Where else but Massachusetts could Leverett Saltonstall have come from, or where else could Bob Kerr have come from but Oklahoma? In the House of Representatives is quartered the gentry of 435, not to the manor born but generally well-bred. Occasionally undisciplined and feverish, House members are linked politically to the nation's small businesses, law firms, and farms. They sometimes seem interchangeable and not precisely tied to their districts. Except for his Arkansas accent, Wilbur Mills could just as well have been an accountant from Albany or Dubuque and Jim Wright of Weatherford, Texas, a chamber of commerce booster from Phoenix or Billings.

In the offices of the clerks, the sergeants-at-arms, the doorkeepers, the committee counsels are the overseers, imported and hired by the owners to run the plantation and enforce the rules. Beneath all are the slaves — freed slaves, of course — who serve everyone above them in the shops, in the restaurants, in the men's rooms and the ladies' powder rooms, at the cafeteria steam tables, and on the cleaning crews.

Indeed, the Congress has been graced over the years by a rich assembly of aristocrats, political aristocrats to be sure: the Adamses and the Lodges of Massachusetts, the Bayards of Delaware, the Frelinghuysens of New Jersey, the Roosevelts and the Livingstons of New York, the Muhlenbergs of Pennsylvania, and the Tylers, Harrisons, and Byrds of Virginia.

Harry Flood Byrd Jr. was one of the Senate's true aristrocrats. A direct descendant of William Byrd of Westover, Harry Byrd was forever being confused with Robert C. Byrd of West Virginia, who is not and never was mistaken for an aristocrat.

The West Virginia Byrd probably has the least distinguished origins of any member of the Senate. He was born Robert Sale in Wilkesboro, North Carolina, orphaned before he was a year old, and raised by his aunt and uncle, Mr. and Mrs. Titus Dalton Byrd, of Stotesbury, West Virginia. Titus Byrd was an itinerant coal miner. Robert Byrd became a butcher in Crab Orchard, West Virginia, until he entered politics after

World War II.

Despite these striking differences, the media, the public, and the *Congressional Record* are forever mixing them up. A transplanted West Virginian now living in Florida once wrote a letter of complaint to NBC's Floyd Kalber, who wrote back:

> Dear Madam: Apparently you are not aware that there are two Byrds in the Senate. Senator Robert Byrd represents the state of Virginia; his father, Harry Byrd, represents the state of West Virginia. I appreciate your trying to help."[2]

In 1971, Robert Byrd was elected assistant majority leader, defeating Edward Kennedy, who in two years as whip had never quite got his act together. Byrd won largely because of his technical proficiencies. Within a month, he took over from Mansfield, the majority leader, all the trivial and fussy details of scheduling, recesses, and, believe it or not, senatorial deportment. He posted in the *Congressional Record* a list of ten Bobby Byrd Helpful Hints for his colleagues, some of which follow:

- Please use your microphone.
- Always refer to fellow colleagues in the

third person — that is, never "you" but always the "senator from" such and such.

- Do not introduce anyone sitting in the galleries.
- Remember to call extension 53735 to arrange a long floor speech.

Snickers, guffaws, and whoops of laughter were inevitable. Byrd had become a sort of senatorial concierge, even a persnickety librarian, shushing everybody.

A humor columnist for the *Washington Star,* John McKelway, took a crack at writing an extension of Byrd's list:

- Rule Eleven: Brush your teeth before and after every meal.
- Rule Thirteen: Do not ride the subway just for fun.
- Rule Fifteen: Never wear perforated shoes or iridescent suits onto the Senate floor. You will be tagged for what you are — a small-town lawyer who served four years in the state legislature.[3]

The Senate chamber is not very large or particularly ornate considering the importance its members attach to the Senate itself. Many of them proudly embrace de Tocqueville's 1831 observation that the Senate is composed of "eloquent advocates, distinguished generals, wise magistrates, and statesmen of note," whereas the House is "vulgar . . . mostly village lawyers, men in trade . . . even persons [of] the lower classes. . . ."[4] The chamber measures eighty-by-forty-eight feet, with ceilings forty-two feet high. Flat marble columns punctuate the walls, the lighting is indirect, the one hundred desks all look the same, and the big leather sofas in the southeast and southwest corners are identical, government-issue.

Empty, the Senate chamber does not look real. It gives off the feel of a Hollywood set. But in session with most of the desks occupied, the Senate is rarely without movement and vitality. It becomes still only during times of unbearable suspense, as during a close roll call or when the fraud of a senator's argument is exposed and his colleagues suddenly fall silent, waiting for his reply.

Usually, the chamber is the scene of dozens of conversations, huddles, lingering exits, and booming entrances. Senators seem to be taught, from the first day they arrive, to enter the chamber as if leading a parade, as if everyone else were in train.

After a decade of watching down from the gallery, I took notes on what I saw early one afternoon in the fall of 1971:

Ralph Yarborough of Texas bursts into the chamber, looking like a young heifer released into a bull ring. He glances quickly from left to right, as he always does, fearful that the right wing in Texas has laid a trap for him.

John Pastore, the diminutive Rhode Island rooster, sits at his desk, as if at the breakfast table, his face totally obscured not by the *Providence Journal* but by the *Congressional Record.*

Strom Thurmond of South Carolina lifts his desk top to reveal the neatest desk in town. In one corner is a stack of copies of the paperback book he wrote, *The Faith We Have Not Kept.* Rarely in anyone's avant garde, Thurmond has strangely become the Senate's style-setter. Today he is wearing a blue-black Edwardian suit.

James Pearson, the laconic Virginian who now comes from Kansas, talks with Edward Brooke of Massachusetts, the Senate's first popularly elected black. Pearson is shining an apple. When he realizes the press gallery is watching, he goes through the motions of flinging it at the grinning reporters.

On his feet, hands jammed into his pockets, is J. William Fulbright of Arkansas, the great dissenter. He is again dissenting, arguing against a House bill giving more foreign aid to Korea and Taiwan. He finishes, sits down, and flips his dark glasses — the kind outfielders wear — back down over his spectacles.

Fred Harris, the ambitious Oklahoman, listens quietly and alone. He's probably thinking about running for president. He is wearing a matching shirt and tie.

Eugene McCarthy of Minnesota, the witty dazzler of the press, spots the apple in Pearson's hand and can be heard from the gallery telling Pearson to put the apple in his mouth for effect. Pearson guffaws, and the two talk about various wind-ups and side-arm deliveries.

Mike Mansfield of Montana, the respected majority leader, rises to urge passage of the Fulbright foreign-aid amendment as a "matter of principle." The voting bells ring and the amendment carries, sixty-two to twenty-eight.

The members begin drifting out of the

chamber for lunch. Clifford Case, the ramrod straight Republican from New Jersey, is seen leaving. In his cupped hand is Pearson's shiny red apple.[5]

Red apple clowning aside, the senators take the Senate so seriously as a place of dignity, as a place of contemplative and studied debate, and as "The World's Greatest Deliberative Body" that they set themselves up for being spoofed. The wags have had a field day with that last claim: "The World's Greatest so-called Deliberative Body" and "The World's Greatest Deliberative so-called Body."

Visitors to the Senate are regularly amused, and sometimes turned off, by the inordinate amount of deferring, complimenting, and praising that goes on between and among members during floor debate. Why did John Glenn refer to Howard Metzenbaum as "the distinguished senior senator from Ohio" when everybody on the floor knew the two men detested each other? Why all this puffing up and preening? It sounds so archaic and out of touch when the world just beyond the Congress is full of "guys." But the exaggerated courtesies have a purpose — protecting an absent member from attack, promoting the Congress as a civilized and rational branch of government, and enabling it to function with a minimum of rancor and harangue.

Because the Senate welcomed television to its committee hearings years before the House did, TV and its reporters naturally gravitated to the Senate side. At CBS News, I was the chief congressional correspondent, but eight out of ten of my pieces were from the Senate. With such attention lavished on the Senate, the House suffered from an institutional inferiority complex. Even the wire services and the nation's big metropolitan newspapers used to maintain separate staffs for covering the House and the Senate, with cooperation and communication between the two sometimes at a minimum.

The late Warren Weaver Jr. of the *New York Times* said that one of his paper's Senate correspondents, reporting on a debate in the Senate chamber, began a new paragraph with: "Meanwhile, there were reports from the House that" — as if they were "unverified rumors from an unreachable land."[6]

The best line of all came from C. P. "Peck" Trussell, who for years covered the House for the *New York Times* and therefore had only minimum high regard for the Senate.

"Of course, it's a great body," said Peck. "It's just been in the water too long."

CHAPTER 28
"WHO THE HELL IS ALEXANDER KENDRICK?"

Both 1963 and 1964 were rich and tumultuous years for the Washington bureau — from the Kennedy assassination, the Kennedy funeral, the Johnson presidency, the March on Washington, the civil rights filibuster, the Republican primaries, the nominating conventions, the presidential campaign, and election night, to the inaugural in January 1965.

The fifteen months stretching from Kennedy's death to Johnson's swearing-in was an unbroken string of stories fraught with drama, importance, and emotion. For journalists, never had there been a bucket brigade of such compelling stories. In each of them, the bureau and its ten reporters were at their best and playing fundamental roles — from the bureau's senior man, George Herman at the White House, to the newest arrival, Ike Pappas, who covered the Johnson campaign for CBS Radio.

Robert Trout, Roger Mudd
and Eric Sevareid

Roger Mudd at the
Lincoln Memorial

Bruce Morton and
Roger Mudd (Susan
Zirinsky in the
white blouse)

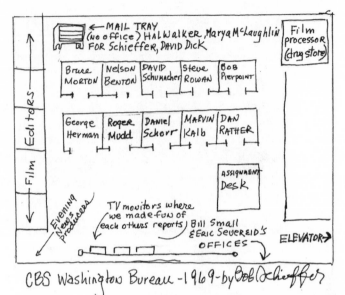

Floor Plan (credit: Bob Schieffer)

President Ford outrunning Phil Jones's questions (credit: CORBIS)

Roger Mudd and
Edward Kennedy

Robert Kennedy and Roger
Mudd at Hickory Hill

Roger Mudd, Hubert Humphrey,
and Harry Reasoner

Roger Mudd interviewing Speaker Carl Albert (l to r: Bob Clark of ABC, Sen. Wendell Ford, Albert, Robert Strauss, Rep. Tip O'Neill, Sen. Mike Mansfield, Rep. John McFall, and Sen. Robert Byrd)

Everett
Dirksen and
Roger Mudd

Ed Bradley

Bill
Plante

George Herman (credit:
CBS Photo Archive)

David Schoumacher

Bernard
Kalb

Marvin
Kalb

Marya McLaughlin

Lesley Stahl with
Chicago Mayor
Richard Daley

Fred Graham

Bernard Shaw (Credit: Bradford Bachrach)

Dan Rather (credit: CBS Photo Archive)

Bill Galbraith

David Dick

Ike Pappas

Rita Braver

Bob Pierpoint

L to R: Walter
Cronkite, Barry
Serafin, Bob
Schieffer, and
Nelson Benton

Connie Chung with
George McGovern

Daniel Schorr (credit:
Diana Walker)

Sandy Socolaw (Credit: CBS Photo Archive)

Bob Vitarelli (Credit: CBS Photo Archive)

Ed Fouhy

Jim McManus (Credit: Diana Walker)

Bill Small and Roger Mudd

Truth be told, though, most of us in the bureau were looking forward to a little less tumult. Passage of the Civil Rights Act of 1964 was assumed to have quieted America's racial discord. But with the unprovoked and televised violence on the Edmund Pettus Bridge, President Johnson knew he had to act. On March 15, he sent to Congress the Voting Rights Act of 1965, which put me back in the civil rights saddle again. Now, however, the southern bloc was not up to mounting a serious challenge.

Without the tension, the story lost much of its appeal for television. I reported on it regularly, but this time there was no Cloture Club of reporters and this time CBS did not spring for around-the-clock coverage or for Howard Brodie's sketches. In less than two months the Senate broke a pro forma southern filibuster and cleared the bill; in less than five months the bill was law. It has been renewed repeatedly since then and stands as the most successful and effective piece of civil rights legislation ever enacted.

As 1965 closed down, my career took another dramatic turn. Gordon Manning, always pushing to put his stamp on the hard news operation, got clearance to extend the *CBS Evening News* to a sixth night —

Saturday. Would I be interested in being its anchor? Would I? You bet I would. It was the perfect assignment. Not only did it put me in the exalted company of the three men who anchored major, regularly scheduled broadcasts — Cronkite on the weeknights, Harry Reasoner on Sunday nights, and Mike Wallace in the morning — but also it kept me on the Hill and doing politics during the week. With Paul Greenberg as the producer and Heywood Hale Broun as the sports essayist, we went on the air in January 1966, but not before I had another showdown with New York, a head-to-head with Ernest Leiser, the Cronkite producer.

Leiser insisted that the sixth night be called the *CBS Saturday Evening News with Roger Mudd* rather than the *CBS Evening News with Roger Mudd,* suggesting that the Monday-to-Friday *Evening News* was the exclusive and not-to-be-messed-with property of Walter Cronkite, which was not to be contaminated by being linked with a mere weekend show and the likes of the upstart Roger Mudd. My answer was that unless it was the *CBS Evening News with Roger Mudd* it would not be with Roger Mudd. If I hadn't learned by then to "hate up," in Bill Leonard's memorable phrase, then Leiser's continued petty power plays sure got me started.

For the next seven years I anchored the Saturday broadcast, taking the 10 AM Eastern shuttle to LaGuardia and returning on the 8 PM. Most of official Washington must have ridden my shuttles at one time or another during those seven years — from Evangeline Bruce with her little carry-on, crustless sandwich to the man who told me he had been my camp counselor in 1936 and had taught me to swim. He was President Johnson's special assistant for national security, Walt Whitman Rostow.[1]

The Saturday broadcast began in first place, rolling over both Robert MacNeil and Ray Scherer on NBC, and remained in first place through my two successors, Dan Rather and Bob Schieffer.

In addition, the Cronkite show was about to overtake Huntley-Brinkley on NBC after five years of chasing. The broadcast had locked in on the hard news under Cronkite, rather than the relaxed, wry, and featurey approach of NBC. *Time* magazine put Cronkite on its October 14, 1966, cover, calling him the "single most convincing and authoritative figure in TV news."

But without the professionalism and strength of the Washington bureau, the

Huntley-Brinkley chase might have taken another year or two. No other network could match the ability and aggressiveness of its lineup — Rather and Pierpoint at the White House, Kalb at the State Department, Charles Von Fremd at the Pentagon, Bruce Morton and me on the Hill, Schorr on the Great Society, Martin Agronsky at *Face the Nation,* and George Herman at the Supreme Court.

If we had a weakness it was at the Pentagon in the years right after Von Fremd's sudden death in 1966. Not until Bob Schieffer took over in 1970 did the Pentagon get the steady coverage it deserved.

Whatever holes needing plugging got plugged by a second tier of reporters who could, and did, run rings around most of the first-stringers at NBC and ABC: David Schoumacher, Ike Pappas, David Dick, Bruce Morton, and John Hart.[2]

The bureau had never had an ex-SAC pilot until Schoumacher arrived in late 1963. He was another Chicago man, who worked for Small at WLS as a summer intern from Northwestern. But his college ROTC commitment meant five years of active duty, which Schoumacher spent flying tankers around the country. Then, after a brief turn in Illinois with the *Rockford Morn-*

ing Star, he landed in Oklahoma City, anchoring the 10 o'clock TV news at $125 a week.

When Small offered him a job in Washington, he was not sure he wanted to come. Oklahoma City was too good a deal and he wasn't much in awe of CBS or Sevareid or even Murrow. But he came, and when he got put on the weekend radio shift along with old pros Paul Niven and George Herman, Schoumacher began to see the light.

"These guys would murder you when you'd come off the air about how bad the newscast was," he says. "They weren't talking about your delivery; they were talking about the content and the writing. And even Alexander Kendrick called. I mean, who the hell is Alexander Kendrick? I really didn't know who he was. He called to criticize one of my newscasts — something I had said. It was a combination of hazing and setting certain professional standards. 'Why the hell did you say that? You've got no right to say that.' But it was in good fun. And the other thing — they'd sit around and tell stories. In a sense, that's when I became a CBS person and began to develop that pride which I think we all had about being a CBS reporter."

■ ■ ■ ■

Ike Pappas was one of the few new arrivals who had not been handpicked by Small. Pappas was what Peter Boyer called a "bluecollar journalist."[3] The son of a first-generation Greek father who ran a deli in Queens, Pappas went to Long Island University, where he was a college stringer for UPI. He learned the radio ropes working for Lee Hanna at WNEW, where everybody carried a tape recorder so the listeners could "actually hear the mayor say something." CBS in New York had hired Pappas based on his superlative work for WNEW in Dallas when Jack Ruby shot Lee Harvey Oswald.

But at CBS, none of the correspondents carried a tape recorder — we were too lofty for that; we had a union to carry our machinery. Lee Hanna's boys, we sniffed, were sharpies, too fast and fancy and not above cheapening the news. They were known as "the Metromedia Mafia."

Pappas's first day at the bureau must have flattened him. As he went from desk to desk, not everybody shook his hand. We all felt we were so untouchably pure, all so conscious of being Murrow's heirs apparent. Dan Rather stiffed him and I refused to shake his extended hand. Pappas remembered the only thing I said to him was, "So, you're Lee Hanna's fink."

Pappas said he felt "destroyed. . . . I was livid. I turned my back and I walked out. . . . I went back to my hotel and I said, 'Screw 'em. I'm going to cover this damn story [the Johnson campaign] the way I want to.' And I started cutting and editing in the back of the bus and I was ready with stories and when we hit another stop I would feed through those alligator clips — I fed radio day and night and they loved it. We were beating the crap out of everybody."

It took a while for us so-called Murrow descendants to soften, but we all came to admire Pappas's grit and refusal to fold. John Armstrong, the producer who went through a rough patch or two with Pappas, has recalled, "If you could have one Ike Pappas you could beat anybody in the world, because he always hit the ground running, always had the story, and he could always get it on the air."

David Dick, hired by Small, who knew him from their time in Louisville, arrived in the Washington bureau in 1966. At thirty-six, he'd been around — raised in a foster home in Paris, Kentucky, four years in the Navy on a light cruiser, schooled at the University of Kentucky, and seven years as a writer and anchor at WHAS. Dick says he was honored to be network "cannon fodder" at $195 a week.

On his very first day, Small sent him to cover a House Un-American Activities Committee hearing, a routine assignment, because the committee was in decline. But that day the witness list included the Chicago Seven — Jerry Rubin, Abbie Hoffman, and the boys. Even before Dick could get his notebook out, all hell broke loose. The Seven went wild and started throwing chairs.

"All of a sudden," Dick says, "police were collaring people and dragging them out. . . . And surprise, surprise, I was getting on the air on every newscast there was. And making all kinds of money."

With a talent fee of $25 for radio and $50 for TV, his paycheck that first week was $600. The rookie was not only making a mint but he was also crowding everybody else off the air on his very first day. "But bingo," says Dick. "I'm on the HUAC hearing and I'm describing it and I remember Marvin Kalb wondering, 'WHO is David Dick?' "

What delighted the rookie the most,

however, was when Small called him in to tell him about bureau policy: The story is yours and all yours, he said. I will not let New York shunt you off to the *Morning News* so Mudd can take it away from you for Cronkite.

With the advent of a sixth night of the *Evening News,* Saturday became a work day for me. I began to take Mondays off, and Bruce Morton quickly became the number two man on the Hill.

Morton was another Small hire, through his reporting from London for a radio news syndication to which Small's Louisville station subscribed. A Chicago native, Morton was drafted soon after Harvard, learned Russian at the Army's language school in California, and spent the next winter on an island in the Bering Sea eavesdropping on the Russians.

The bureau found out soon enough that nobody could write as quickly and clearly as Morton. The producers — Ed Fouhy and John Armstrong — were in awe of his ability to turn a cluttered story into an understandable TV piece.

"You'd ask Morton for a script," says Armstrong, "and no sooner had you turned around than he would hand you a finished story."

As his reputation as a writer spread, however, he became prickly at times when New York passed on one of his stories or an editor suggested a change.

"You couldn't change 'and' to 'the,' " says producer Susan Zirinsky. "Then he'd just rip up the script and say, 'Give it to syndication.' "

Despite his dour demeanor, Morton loved politics.

"I just liked the players. I liked the handlers," he says. "The candidates were good fun. Even George Wallace was fascinating to talk to."

The bureau's political expertise generated growing respect, particularly from newspaper reporters.

Morton remembers Rowland Evans telling him, "Most TV reporters don't understand politics but you guys do." Morton soon became one of TV's most sophisticated, knowledgeable, and perceptive political observers.

Nineteen-sixty-six was, of course, a political year, with a dozen close and intriguing elections, which put me and dozens of other reporters on the road during September and

October.

So off I went:

- To Texas, where John Tower campaigned for a second term but refused to do it Texas-style. Not being a cowboy either in height or outlook, he rode not on a horse but in an open convertible, his jacket off, his tie on. The joke at the Brazoria County Fair parade was that Tower's cufflinks were so heavy he was unable to raise his arms to wave.
- To Michigan, where Governor George Romney — the man the press nicknamed Dudley Do-Right — got a huge win for a second term as a prelude to what he hoped would be a presidential campaign in '68. He crushed his opponent, whose unlikely name was Zoltan Ferency.
- To Cincinnati, where Democrat John Gilligan found out what it was like to run against a Taft when every building in town — from the library, theater, and museum, to the high school — is named after a Taft. He lost.
- To Alabama, where Republican James Martin found out what it was like running for governor against a woman. The woman, of course, was Lurleen

Burns Wallace, wife and stand-in for the great white nonesuch, George Wallace, who could not succeed himself. Martin also lost, and lost badly.

- And to Georgia, where the vote for governor was so close it had to be decided by the state legislature. The winner was Lester Maddox, the man who had used a gun to keep three blacks from entering his Pickrick Restaurant in Atlanta.

Looking back, those races in which the war in Southeast Asia was rarely an issue seemed almost beside the point, because everything — racial turbulence, social upheaval, campus teach-ins, protest marches, presidential dissembling — pointed to a divisive and corrosive presidential campaign in 1968.

By the spring of '66, the dump-Johnson movement was beginning to coalesce around Senator Robert Kennedy of New York, who had become the leader of the Democratic Party's disaffected and disillusioned. As the pressure built up for him to take on President Johnson, Kennedy gave no public indications that he was willing, although every speech he gave that year revealed the depth of his break with the White House.

CHAPTER 29
"HOW ABOUT BOBBSIE?"

Late in 1966, Richard Salant, the president of CBS News, said we should do a documentary on Robert Kennedy, believing that he was about to become the closest thing the country had ever had to an unnominated, nonelected president. Salant asked Philip Scheffler, one of the brightest and most talented producers at *CBS Reports,* to take it on. Scheffler did not want the assignment. He said he had gotten to know Kennedy "too well" from covering his trip around the world in 1962. Their friendship was so close that Kennedy invited both Scheffler and cameraman Walt Dumbrow to go with him on his 1964 trip to Indonesia, not as journalists but as merry pranksters. Such a relationship, Scheffler told Salant, involved "just too many conflicts." But Salant insisted that Scheffler was too good a producer not to be able to avoid them.

So Scheffler agreed and I agreed, and

when the Senator agreed, this was a clear signal to Phil and me that it was an early but tentative move toward running in 1968, figuring that an hour of prime time on CBS wasn't going to hurt.

What journalistic linkage I had with Kennedy began routinely enough in 1957 when WTOP assigned me to handle our live televised hearings of the Senate Rackets Committee. The chief target of the committee was the president of the Teamsters Union, Jimmy Hoffa, and his chief interrogator was Kennedy, the committee's chief counsel. Faithfully present each day in the reserved section of the Senate Caucus Room was Kennedy's wife, Ethel. This was her husband's debut on live television and she was his ambassador of good will. During one of the committee recesses for a roll call vote, Mrs. Kennedy introduced herself. She was direct, candid, complimentary, and funny.

Occasionally I covered Kennedy after he became attorney general, because until Fred Graham was hired from the *New York Times* in 1972, CBS had no correspondent assigned full-time to the Justice Department or the Supreme Court. What to call an attorney general was always a problem. "Mr. Attorney General" or "Attorney General

Kennedy" was cumbersome; "General" was correct but sounded inaccurate and misleading. So, before I started our first interview, I asked the attorney general what I should call him. He said, "How about Bobbsie?"

Sometime in the summer of 1963, E. J. answered the phone at home to hear Ethel Kennedy calling to invite us to dinner at Hickory Hill. E. J. said, "But I'm pregnant," meaning "I don't have anything to wear." Ethel's response was "That's wonderful!" Of course we went. But this was our first of many invitations to Hickory Hill, and driving from Maryland over to Virginia, it took us four or five passes before we found the right Beltway exit to McLean. Ethel was at the door, making sure we met those of her children who were old enough to be up. When she introduced me to Bobby Jr., then nine years old, he exclaimed: "Roger Maris!" "No, no," I said. "Roger Mudd." "Oh," he said.

After that, the invitations to Hickory Hill kept coming and we kept going and having the time of our lives. Whenever someone came to town, there would be a dinner party — Andy Williams, El Cordobés, David Ormsby-Gore, John Lennon and Yoko Ono, Don Meredith. Most of the regulars — Sue and John Reilly, Judith and David Hackett,

Mary and John Douglas, Joan and John Nolan (those men were all in Bobby's Justice Department), Ann and Art Buchwald, Kay and Rowland Evans, Nancy and Ray Schoenke (the Redskin football pro), and the sisters, Eunice Shriver, Pat Lawford, and Jean Smith — learned the main rule early: Never, never allow yourself to be goaded into making a standing toast, because once you rose you were fair game for the toast bullies of Hickory Hill. The first-timers had to learn for themselves. The only time I succumbed was the result of unrelenting pressure from Sergeant Shriver, who had somehow heard about the night on the radio I called the Pontiff "Pipe Poeus." Shriver started chanting, "Pope joke, Pope joke" until the guests joined the chant and would not stop until I stood and told the story.

On spring and summer weekends, the Hickory Hill tennis court and pool were in constant use, and regularly Ethel would call for us to join the crowd. But there were Saturdays when the Mudd family had its own schedule. As a cover story, the children were instructed to tell Ethel when she called that "Daddy is at the hardware." Ethel caught on very quickly and learned to start with, "When Roger gets back from the hardware tell him that. . . ."

Covering the Kennedys became a regular Washington beat, not only for the political press but also for the social and party press. Hickory Hill habitués loved to talk to the gossip columnists about who was there, including themselves, of course, and what they wore and what they ate and who said what to whom. Everybody in town knew who was on which guest list, whether at the White House or Hickory Hill or the Shrivers in suburban Maryland or the Steve Smiths in Georgetown. It did not take long before E. J. and I got tagged in the social columns as "Kennedy family friends," there not being space to explain we were friends of only one branch of the Kennedy family, the one headed by Robert and Ethel. But the tag stuck, even though Robert, after seeing some of my TV reports during his 1968 presidential campaign, told me he wondered how I ever got that tag.

For me Kennedy's campaign began March 13, 1967, on Braniff Flight 103, New York to Oklahoma City. To prepare for our coming documentary interview I got his OK to travel with him on his next trip out and to be a fly on his Senate office wall. For the next week I scribbled on page after page in my blue 4 × 6 spiral notebook[1]:

- Waiting for K to arrive, the Braniff stew tells me I'm in for a big surprise. She says, "He's the one who wants us to give up, just give up. I've got somebody over there." She means Vietnam and his bombing halt speech.
- At 2:10 PM K arrives with Adam Walinsky, his speech writer. Jacket comes off, sleeves go up, tie gets loosened. K flips quickly thru *Life, New Republic, Time, World Journal Trib, SatEvePost.* He offers me the mags. "Want to catch up on me? You'd better pick a winner."
- Walinsky moves in the seat behind to work on K's farm speech. I slip in beside K. Does he know why I'm along? He says no. I explain CBS show — his great polarity, his wealth, and youth attract & repel. He agrees about the polarity. He asks about Fred Friendly. What kind of man? I say he's undisciplined, uncollected but volcanic and exciting and has restored esprit at CBS.
- Why are you going to Oklahoma City? K: "I don't know how we got mixed up in this one. Well, the Farmers Union

was always good to us back in '60. Fred Harris is a good fellow and his wife heads that Indian job corps in Norman."

- K picks up the new *Time* and points to the sentence "Bobby is said to have called the president an s.o.b." "That's the trouble with the press and the magazines. They print that and there's no catching up." He confirms general accuracy of the piece but says LBJ did not use the phrase "blood on your hands" and that he did not swear. I ask if the meeting was horrible. "No, it wasn't horrible. I've been through worse experience. But the president of the United States ought not to behave that way."

- During the flight, K ate nothing and drank only Coke and 2 cups of tea. He works steadily on the farm speech, reading it over, his lips moving as he reads, making notations with felt-tip pen, telling Adam to rewrite this, add that.

- During a stop in Tulsa, the nervous Braniff station manager comes aboard to ask K if he wants to talk to the press. K makes no move to get up. I take a look out the door and overhear

366

a photographer saying Bobby is still mad over not carrying Tulsa in '60. I tell K what I heard and his face reveals he was expecting exactly that. When I suggest he land only at those cities JFK carried in '60, he laughs and says he can't remember them anymore.

- A Braniff stew goes by carrying K's bag, thinking a Tulsa passenger left it. "Miss, miss, where are you going?" She comes back with the bag — a red, tweedy, overnight zipper case monogrammed with "PLK." The bag belongs to Pat Kennedy Lawford.

- On the ground in Oklahoma City, K is greeted by mostly young crowd of maybe 300. Signs: "Bobby in '72" and "Welcome Bobby." Nine-car motorcade to Norman. OU Field House at capacity of 7,000 explodes when K enters. OU president gives a gracious and funny introduction. K calls him "one of the friendliest presidents I've seen in a long time." K's speech is brief and amusing. Says the first thing LBJ asked at their recent meeting: "When are you going to get a haircut?"

- During the Q & A, K says he's opposed to college deferments. A rumbling dissent. "I was not overwhelmed by that applause." Student asks if he favors lowering voting age to 18. "I favor lowering it to 12 (big laugh). When they get above 25, I lose them very rapidly" (roar).

- K's farmers' speech not well delivered. He misreads lines, mispronounces a few words, and makes countless false starts. Walinsky says K was anxious about it because farmers are tough audience and has never identified with them. Pat Furgurson writes in the *Baltimore Sun* that the farmers weren't sure who was their friend — Bobby or his speechwriter.

- During dinner in the Harris suite, K sits stiffly in the corner, coat on, surrounded by young Oklahoma City matrons. After they leave, the coat comes off, the sleeves go up and the tie gets loosened. Remembers how Oklahoma clobbered them. "It was horrible." [60/40 for Nixon.]

- March 14. Breakfast meeting with several dozen Democrats, a few were early JFK supporters. A question on civil rights produces a long, rambling answer: "Martin Luther King would have a very hard time walking thru Harlem today. . . . No white politician can talk to the young Negro. . . . Our poor people are quiet because we pay them off each week."

• Back to Norman for Oklahomans for Indian Opportunity, a project of La-Donna Harris, who is Comanche. At his best again with young audience. "I'd like to be an Indian, but it's too late. . . . Don't drop out of school. . . . The only award I got in school was voted the boy with [fifth] best sense of humor. . . . Don't take prejudice from white classmates. I mean, when did you arrive?"

• Flying back to Washington, K picks up the new *Vanity Fair* with the Gore Vidal article on the Family. K: "I guess it's too late to suppress this one." He says Vidal is a "vicious" man who traded on his family connection with Jackie. "He got drunk one night at the White House and was never invited back." He said Vidal told people it was because "I was such a bastard." Charles Bartlett of the *Chattanooga Times* told me he remembered Bobby telling Vidal that night at the White House, "Get your hands off my sister-in-law," meaning Jackie, not Joan. He hands me the magazine and I can tell he is looking

369

at me as I read.

- Talk turns to the Senate. He says it's not intellectually very stimulating. No interest in art or poetry. No communications between & among members. K asks which members I think are capable. I suggest McGovern, Javits, Ribicoff, Harris. He says "Gale McGee?" I say I don't think so. "Herman Talmadge?" "Yes." "Richard Russell?" I say he's more an institution who watches over the Senate. K says, "You like Dirksen, don't you?" "Yes." "Why?" "He can make fun of himself." K says that's a rare quality. K says Russell Long is not ever seen anymore and has been backsliding (I assume drinking) since elected whip. K: "Can you imagine [Mansfield] having Russell Long and Bob Byrd as your chief assistants?"

- At Page Terminal at National Airport, two network crews run toward the plane and trap him. I hear K tell Tony Sergeant of CBS the *Time* piece was "generally inaccurate." I ask if the reporters had picked him on what parts were generally "accurate." No, he says, "I was lucky."

- In the NSOB, Teddy arrives about 2

PM and stays until 3:15 PM. Frank Mank [Mankiewicz] says, "After all, they haven't seen each other in at least 24 hours." It turns out they were talking about moving JFK's vault at Arlington.

- I go into K's office with two reporters from *Financial Times* who want to question him about his European trip. This time K calls the *Time* piece "wholly inaccurate." Another call causes K to ask us to step outside. As we do, K says, "Hello, Bob." This is McNamara calling about Arlington.

- Returning from a roll call vote, Dan Blackburn of Metromedia and John Chambers of UPI Audio are lurking behind the columns at the top of Senate steps. K agrees to answer one question on Vietnam. He's back to "generally inaccurate." Blackburn, talking very fast, says: "So you completely repudiate the story?" K breaks away, saying that was the one question. Out of earshot, K tells me Blackburn is so "cloying" and such a "leech" that it's hard to be civil. K says Blackburn's office has heard he's mad at Blackburn and they fire him. K says he has to call

371

Metromedia to tell them Blackburn is really ok.[2]

- Teddy White is waiting for K on return and is still there at 5:45 PM when I leave.
- March 15: At 9:40 AM K and I walk toward Caucus Room for Joe Clark's poverty hearings. I show him the *Baltimore Sun,* which is playing the *Time* story above the fold. K: "You just can't win. Even if I did try to deny the whole thing, even if it were absolutely false, the people want to believe the worst." After the poverty hearings, I read him the UPI's day lead: "Senator Robert F. Kennedy today joined one of America's leading mayors to attack the Johnson Poverty program for raising false hopes and contributing to racial violence." He stops dead in the middle of the sidewalk: "Oh, this is awful. I can't do anything. I'll have to crawl down in some cellar."
- At the office, Dick Schaap, on leave from the *WJT* [*World Journal Tribune*] to write a Bobby bio, is waiting. Off to Muskie hearings on establishing a Senate Select Committee on Science and Technology. K says Muskie hearings

are "dull & musty." Concedes Muskie is a "good man, a hardworking senator." Agrees that Prouty is a "mean, little man."

- Back at the office, Frank Mank shows K a letter draft to LBJ. K says better make it just "inaccurate." Frank insists it read "almost wholly inaccurate." K agrees. Frank says *NYT* wants to know about Arlington, the arrangements, how it was done, who invited the president. K answers only the last question. "Mrs. Kennedy and I invited him." Frank says "that's a good story." K says "it's not a good story." Frank says "Well, it is from their standpoint."
- K dials Hickory Hill. "Oh, Mrs. Kennedy, please. . . . Ethel? Hi, hi." Lays out travel plans. New York tomorrow, Albany Saturday night. Talk of taking Bobby Junior to Groton and Putney to look at schools. "I could get the Caroline, I suppose." Jerry Bruno calls in from Syracuse. "What should I do about Saturday? When could I leave NYC? Is it good to go there? The only thing I get into now is Vietnam. It's the only thing people ask about and the only thing people write about. It looks like I'm trying to prolong it."

- Frank M asks if K wants to see the Women's Strike for Peace. K says he doesn't want them "screaming at me." Frank says, "They won't scream at you. You could see 50 of them in your office."
- Angie Novello brings K a cup of chicken rice soup. Someone calls in that LBJ is on TV. All hands crowd into Frank's cubicle. K spoons in soup, sleeves rolled up, watching with staff. A call for Joe Dolan. The girl says he'll call back. "He's watching the president." K says, "Ask him why he isn't." Big laugh. LBJ says, "We've just lived through another flurry of peace rumors." K and staff laugh lightly.
- Cecil Stoughton arrives with pix from Arlington. He tells me Jackie showed up in a miniskirt and every time she genuflected, the skirt climbed higher and higher. Cecil says, "I guess they're screening them pretty carefully."
- Angie reminds K he is to preside over the Senate from 2 to 3:50. She calls for a page to carry his briefcase over. K asks for another apple and "that book of poetry." Angie can find only Emily Dickinson's Love Poems and a paperback of American verse. She

reminds K, in bad French, to comb his hair. "Combez les chevaux." K: "Oh, yes."

- Spong of Va. relieves K at 3:50.
- On the walk back, K says Johnson's speech was "powerful and hard to resist," whereas his position is "complicated and unsimple." Says he was prepared for the beating he took on his Vietnam speech. Except for Sorensen, all his advisers warned against giving it. K says it was his "personal" decision to give it. "I'm glad I gave it."
- Another roll call vote sends him back to the Senate.
- Returns to office about 4:30. John Nolan, ex-Justice Dept., now Steptoe & Johnson, is waiting. Also waiting are Charlie Bartlett, George Lodge of the Harvard Business School, and Tom Ottenad of the *St. Louis Post-Dispatch.* Bob Healy and Jimmy Doyle, of the *Boston Globe,* get put off until tomorrow.
- Before leaving, K agrees to do our interview in early April. [It gets put off until May 18]. In hopes of getting him to unbend we are doing it at Hickory Hill.

CHAPTER 30
"I DON'T KNOW. I DON'T KNOW"

Over the next few weeks, preparing for my interview with Kennedy, I talked with his critics — Gore Vidal, John Tower, and Sam Yorty — but also his worshipful Senate staff, vacuuming up as many bits and pieces as would come loose.

Ed Guthman, his former Senate press secretary, said he had discovered the time and place where the adulation switched from John to Robert. It was, he claimed, in Scranton on March 17, 1965, a cold day, a snowing day, with no reason to watch an attorney general drive by, and yet, he said, the crowds were large and enthusiastic, just like those in a campaign.[1]

Joe Dolan, his administrative assistant, described him as the "best compartmentalized man I know. He works kind of like he's in a campaign, seeing through all that smoke and figuring out where to move next."

Adam Walinsky, his speechwriter, said after our on-camera interview, "What I should have said instead of all that ponderous crap was, 'Well, it's just fun to work here.' "

Peter Edelman, his legislative assistant, said, "I should have mentioned how he zeroes in on something. How he goes into California and comes out wound up on migratory workers and won't stop until he knows everything about it."

Then came a string of off-the-record interviews with Kennedy's senatorial friends and foes, all now deceased. These are my notes:

- Karl Mundt, South Dakota Republican: He hasn't been involved in the Senate much. Not much clout. Getting better as a debater. Pretty resourceful. Thinks pretty fast. His Vietnam speech hurt him. He'll bear the stigma of our first military defeat in history. I can't imagine any U.S. senator walking in a peace parade. He's out of touch with the majority of young Americans. His aura is simply from Jack's voters but they are getting to be fewer and fewer.
- Everett Dirksen, minority leader: Our

fellows don't know him very well. He's seldom discussed. We watch with a slightly baleful eye as he barges off. I'm beginning to doubt him in '72. He's had his day as far as the campus kids.

- Carl Curtis, Republican of Nebraska: He's ruthless. He'll never forget. You just don't know how long he will hound you. I doubt he has clout. He's only fair, not above average. Sure he'll make a drive for '72 but he's not qualified. Has no expert body of knowledge that would cause respect.

- Senator Tom Kuchel, Republican of California: He's bright, ruthless, and has lots of guts. We don't treat him differently. He doesn't invite it.

- Mike Mansfield, majority leader: He's a loner. An individualist. I don't expect Johnson to drop out. I do expect K [Kennedy] to be a candidate in '72. LBJ-RFK are at arm's length, watching each other. In a second Kennedy administration, he would try to emulate his brother but by then the legend would have faded and he would have to be president in his own style, which he would have developed from the great differences with Johnson in foreign policy and to some extent in domestic. He is not ruthless, quite the contrary. He is very cooperative and considerate. The Kennedy clique is small. Just Joe Tydings and Birch Bayh. To a lesser extent, George McGovern.

- Russell Long, majority whip: I've not made a judgment on whether he's ruthless. He's pleasant, well met. I like him, sure, but I'm not wild about him. He's talented but he spends a lot of time outside the Senate. He's shooting for the White House for sure. He'll try when the time is appropriate — no later than '72, and '68 if LBJ drops out. Doesn't pull as many votes as Teddy. Maybe he'll get Muskie, McIntire, Pete Williams, Tydings, and Bayh. Distinctively his own man.

It was on May 18 that I got to put all this Bobby-gleaning to use. I did indeed wear a sports jacket, as Phil Scheffler had suggested, but the senator wore a dark-blue pinstripe suit. He was not stiff and he was not loose. He was wary. He knew why we were at Hickory Hill with our cameras. It was because CBS and Phil and I believed that he was the odds-on favorite to be the next Democratic presidential nominee in

1968, if not the next president. And yet this was not 1968 and he could ill afford to deepen any further his alienation from the Johnson wing of the Democratic party with an untoward remark or a slip of the tongue. He also knew, given the time I had spent with him, his staff, and the politicians, that I would be well prepared. He had never been an easy interview, mainly because he wanted to set the ground rules, because he did not like surprises, and because he needed to control the political consequences of what he said. Beyond all that, he was uncomfortable talking about himself or answering questions about his public image. Self-analysis he dismissed as a waste of time. My suspicions were that as an Irish Catholic he also thought self-analysis was unmanly, weak, and too loosely associated with the babbling world of psychiatry.

During one of the breaks in the interview, while the camera crew changed reels, I noticed that Ethel Kennedy had been listening from an upstairs bedroom where she was recovering from a bite inflicted by one of the small, uncaged animals that twelve-year-old Bobby Kennedy let run loose in the house.

After we finished, she came downstairs and asked me in a voice that revealed some irritation why I had asked her husband all those "couch questions." It was her way of complaining that I had, in effect, played the psychiatrist and put Kennedy on the couch. Indeed, he was at his most inarticulate with the couch questions:

MUDD: Can't you do anything to stop the [ruthless] public image that you have?

KENNEDY: I don't know.

MUDD: How did it get started?

KENNEDY: I don't know. I don't know. I don't know. I don't know. . . . I suppose I have been in positions in which — but I don't know exactly. I don't know.[2]

Rereading my notes and the transcript of the program I was genuinely surprised at how little of the Hickory Hill interview we used and how barely we touched on Vietnam. It was more about the glamour, the atmospherics, the excitement, the burden, the adventure of being a Kennedy, and the mass-production press operation with publishers, editors, reporters, and TV crews shuttling in and out of his office as if on a conveyor belt.

In my initial draft, I had written: "He is, first of all, an avatar of his slain brother. He is the closest any American politician will ever get to John F. Kennedy." When we screened the first cut for Bill Leonard, who was then in charge of documentaries, the only comment I remembered him making was about the word "avatar." Leonard perhaps did not know the word but claimed it was "not a television word." I shot back, that it was a perfectly good word, that it was in the dictionary, and that it meant an "embodiment." He was not pleased by my cocky reply. The final draft read: "He is, first of all, an avatar — a reincarnation — of his slain brother."

Buried in the unedited transcript were some gems we did not use, revealing Kennedy not perhaps at his most eloquent but at his most passionate and perceptive. One of my questions was: "What do you think of television?"

I don't think it's very good. I think some of the news broadcasts and public-service broadcasts are interesting, but I think the entertainment programs are just terrible. . . . Very rarely there's one that's worthwhile, but I think, by and large, it's really a terrible, terrible waste of time. . . . The wavelengths belong to the American people, not to CBS or NBC or ABC . . . but I think it's used frequently as a private corporation to make money. . . . The programs that come in the morning when mothers are off babysitting, off washing dishes, and making the breakfast, children usually are sitting in front of the television set, and what are they seeing, just sort of cartoons. Not improving their minds at all, not teaching them, and again, with a little effort, you could teach them in an entertaining way about our own country and about the rest of the world, about history — really, very, very little of that is done. And I think it's a — I think it's most, you know, terribly, terribly unfortunate.[3]

The last question I asked was about the constant theme in every speech he gave — that the world is capable of change and that one individual can change it.

There are a lot of riots and the disorder and the lawlessness that occurs in the United States focus attention on ourselves as an individual because so much here in the United States, we think that we're losing our individuality, we can't affect the future of government, you can't affect what's happening in business, you can't affect what's going on in the course of events around the rest of the world, whether you approve or disapprove of Vietnam. And if everybody gives up and everybody decides they can't have an affect, what are [we] going to do in the most powerful nation in the world, when it's just left to a few, just left to those perhaps whose motivations won't be the same? So if everybody makes an effort and decides that they're going to make an effort and make their views heard, and all the rest of it, I think that's worthwhile and I think, my judgment, there's nothing else that's worthwhile.[4]

In early June while the program was being edited, E. J. suggested we give a dinner party for the Kennedys at our home in Kensington, Maryland. The timing was perfect, because the senator hadn't yet seen the program to complain about. But the challenge for E. J. and me to put on such a dinner — this was our first really big power dinner — was daunting. Who else would we invite? How many tables? How would I seat them? Of course we would have it catered, but what would we serve? All E. J. remembers about the dinner is that she made so much watercress soup (to hold down the cost a bit) that we had it for the next two weeks. I think the entrée was veal.

We didn't think to rent tables from the caterers so we used what we had, and each one E. J. covered with a beautiful linen tablecloth from Italy. From somewhere in her overstuffed files, E. J. miraculously plucked a piece of yellow paper showing about six different seating arrangements. That night, this is what it looked like: At the walnut table, E. J., Sergeant Shriver, Mary McGrory, Phil Scheffler, Lucy Keker (a prominent Maryland Democrat and family friend), and Charlie Ferris (the chief counsel for the Senate Democratic Policy Committee); at the Formica table, Senator Fred Harris of Oklahoma, Mrs. Ferris, Dan Rather, and Mrs. Jimmy Doyle; at the Salterini table, Eunice Shriver, Sam Keker (of *U.S. News & World Report*), Jean Rather, and Fred Vinson (a Washington lawyer, the son of the late chief justice, and a college friend); at the round end table, Senator Kennedy, Linda Scheffler, Jimmy Doyle (of the *Boston Globe*), and LaDonna Harris; and at the cherry gate–leg table, Ethel Kennedy, a distinguished cleric from Catholic University, Nell Vinson, and me.

At some point in the dinner, Doyle, who had been in the *Globe*'s Washington bureau for less than a year or two, took on Kennedy. He said that LaDonna Harris's Oklahomans for Indian Opportunity was better run and far superior to President Kennedy's Alianza para el Progreso. Doyle remembers also goading Kennedy about zeroing in on Jimmy Hoffa to such an extent that as attorney general he neglected everything else.

Kennedy apparently blew his stack. In the midst of the argument, Ann Doyle, not feeling well, whispered in Jimmy's ear that she had to go home. Jimmy whispered back: "We cannot go. I am about to go head-to-head with the attorney general of the United States. Go sit down." Doyle's wife has yet to forgive him after nearly forty years.

The priest, God rest his soul, remains nameless because as the dinner was ending, he excused himself and vanished, the long cocktail hour and dinner wine having taken their toll. We could not find him until his driver arrived. The driver knew exactly where to look, based obviously on past pickups. The driver asked directions to our attic and there found our collared guest in a prayerful but prone repose.

The broadcast went on the air on June 20, but WTOP-TV, the local CBS station, chose not to carry it that night so we — that is, Senator and Mrs. Kennedy, Andy Williams, who was in town for a concert, E. J., and I — watched the network feed at the CBS bureau and then went off to dinner at the Jockey Club, the five of us crammed in my Volkswagen with Andy, in the backseat, singing "Moon River" upon Ethel's demand. They all thought the show was great, although Ethel quietly and firmly said I was wrong to say, "Certainly the name Kennedy and the money it represents are important in the life of Robert Kennedy. . . ." The senator wrote that he enjoyed the program "immensely," and although it did not generate much press coverage, the *South Bend Tribune* did review it. "Roger Mudd," the reviewer wrote, "obviously not a Kennedy fan, was the reporter." The clipping, with that sentence highlighted, arrived by page at my office in the TV Gallery a day or two later with the senator's scrawled note: "Roger. See — I overcame these odds."

CHAPTER 31
TOO DEEP A HOLE

Before 1967 shifted to a total preoccupation with a Kennedy candidacy, two other political stories got traction, and they both ended badly for the central figures — one a Democratic senator from Connecticut, the other a Republican governor of Michigan. But forty years later their political sons, Christopher Dodd and Mitt Romney, were both hip-deep in the race for the presidency.

For much of June 1967, the Senate deliberated the fate of Thomas Dodd, accused by the Senate's Ethics Committee of diverting more than $100,000 in political funds to his personal use. The committee, headed by the estimable John Stennis of Mississippi, wanted Dodd censured for bringing the Senate into "dishonor and disrepute." Dodd's defense counsel was a volunteer — none other than the exuberant, flamboyant, and exasperating Russell Long of Louisiana. Dodd was in no position to decline Long's services, so he and the Senate had sit through Long's stories day after day about his "dear ol' daddy" Huey and his uncle, Earl, with his white linen suits and diamond stickpins. He likened Dodd to Jesus being crucified and to Daniel Webster receiving a Cadillac from the grateful voters of Massachusetts. The Cronkite show could not get enough of the Dodd story. Every night on TV and two or three times a day on radio, I reported the story with its irresistible cast of characters — the arm-waving, wang-doodle Russell Long, playing to the press gallery and infuriating his colleagues; John Stennis, held in awe for his sense of decorum and probity, his voice bouncing against the Senate marble, overpowering everything and everybody; and Tom Dodd, white-maned, wedgeshaped, a Uriah Heep who blamed everything on his bookkeeper. But beyond those compelling three, there was the spectacle of the Senate passing judgment on one of its own, something a senator abhors doing for fear that one day the Senate might turn on him. And never is the Senate more ponderous or more consumed with self-love than when it talks about itself, its honor, its respect, and its traditions.

Each day in the Senate as I watched

Russell Long fulminate, I also watched in the Family Gallery Dodd's wife, Grace. If she struggled to keep a straight face during Long's pyrotechnics, it must have been even harder to control her emotions during her husband's mawkish defense. "How many times do you want to hang me?" he cried. "If you want to brand me a thief, do it today, do it before the sun goes down and let me skulk away."[1] On the eighth day of debate they branded Dodd a thief. The vote was ninety-three to five against him. Dodd later thanked Long for his help. Said the antic Long, "Anytime, Tom. Anytime."[2]

Tom Dodd could not help himself and neither could George Romney. He was just too righteous for the American people. As a Republican politician and a Mormon, he said he believed that the Declaration of Independence was divinely inspired, the Creator put Americans on earth for a special purpose, and that this purpose was to spread democracy around the world. He told his audiences that a decline in religion had helped break down moral courage, individual responsibility, and family life. Only the Republican Party, he said, could reverse the trend.

In his third term as governor of Michigan,

Romney said he was ready for the presidency. In October 1967, using a small chartered jet, he began a ten-state swing to try out his message. The accompanying press contingent was small — Walter Mears of the AP, the Michigan papers, Mudd of CBS, and a few other reporters from Washington.

CBS was not interested in sending a full-blown TV crew on the trip until we got to Denver, so all my pieces were for radio. In many ways, radio is ideal for political reporting on the road. With radio, there are no TV picture crutches — the reporter must make the pictures with his own words out of his own head. With radio there is no worrying about film or whether the camera was running when the candidate said something dumb or having to leave the campaign to feed the film to New York — the reporter simply calls New York and records his story on the telephone.

Bruce Morton has recalled how hard it used to be with film, before the days of videotape and satellite dishes and instantaneous feeds from virtually any place in the world. In 1972 with the McGovern campaign, he said, they "were all staying in a little town called Custer in the one motel" in the heart of the South Dakota Black

Hills. "And to do the evening news piece — it's film — you drove at an illegal speed to the Rapid City airport. You flew to Denver on the charter. You got on the motorcycle that was waiting for you at the Denver Airport. You put the film in the processor and you had one shot probably at feeding it to New York. You fed around 6:20 because you didn't have it before then. And people did all that routinely. Yeah, that's what I did every day."

Our first stop with Romney was in Bismarck, North Dakota, where a high school band played six different versions of "Stout-Hearted Men." He told his small airport crowd that "the people don't know whether the Johnson White House is telling the truth or not." As a campaigner, Romney came across as earnest, seemingly in personal possession of the truth, always in charge, but occasionally hectoring.

John Swainson, the Democrat Romney had defeated for governor in 1962 and one of my classmates from the University of North Carolina, told me to watch Romney's technique when the cameras were around. "Immediately," Swainson said, "George will start gesticulating with his pointed finger so that everybody else in the picture seems to be listening to George. When I finally caught on," Swainson said, "I would raise my pointed finger the minute he raised his."[3]

But Romney's presidential campaign had died more than a month before he ever set foot in Bismarck. In an interview with a Detroit TV station, the reporter asked Romney why he had reversed his support for the war in Vietnam. The governor's answer was that during his 1965 visit to Vietnam, "I'd just had the greatest brainwashing that anybody can get." No one in the TV studio thought the brainwashing line significant, but when it showed up in the *New York Times* a few days later, Romney's campaign engine conked out.

As we tracked him through the west, Romney could not shake the quote. From Bismarck and Fargo, North Dakota, to Rapid City, South Dakota, to Phoenix, to Denver, the quote followed him like a little snapping dog. He tried turning the quote against Lyndon Johnson, saying it was the president himself who had been doing some brainwashing. "Apparently, there were a lot of brainwashed voters in 1964," he said, not figuring on there being a fallout from the 43 million brainwashed Americans who had voted for Johnson in '64.[4]

When Romney got to New England, he

was hit by a devastating comment, from a fellow Republican, Congressman Robert Stafford of Vermont: "If you're running for the presidency, you are supposed to have too much on the ball to be brainwashed."[5]

Two weeks before the New Hampshire primary, Romney folded his campaign. At the Republican convention he finished a feeble sixth with fifty votes — forty-four from Michigan and six from Utah.[6] The brainwashing line got quick admission to the Foot-in-Mouth Hall of Fame, alongside Tom Dewey's "What's the matter with the idiot engineer?" Roman Hruska's "Aren't the mediocre people entitled to a little representation?" George Bush's "Read my lips," Bill Clinton's "It depends on what the meaning of 'is' is," and John Kerry's "I actually did vote for the $87 billion bill before I voted against it."

Chapter 32
"Ma'am, I've Been Hit, Too"

For the entire Kennedy political apparatus, the balance of 1967 and early 1968 revolved around the single question: Should the senator challenge President Johnson for the presidency in '68 or wait until '72? Senator Eugene McCarthy had already announced in late November, and George Wallace became a third-party candidate early in 1968.

On January 30, Kennedy opened the door a crack after a background breakfast with reporters when he agreed to be quoted as saying he had no plans to oppose Johnson "under any foreseeable circumstances."[1] The press logically interpreted "foreseeable" as meaning "unless something not anticipated happened," such as the Tet Offensive or President Johnson's dropping out. On March 12, McCarthy came close to defeating Johnson in the New Hampshire primary; the next day Kennedy said he was "reassessing"[2]; and on March 16 in the Senate Caucus Room, Kennedy announced. His decision to wait for McCarthy to test the waters against Johnson before pulling the plug on McCarthy only reinforced Kennedy's "ruthless" reputation and added to the bitterness between the two candidates and their followers.

Years later that bitterness was still near the surface. At a big springtime square dance at our home with a guest list that included politicians, lawyers, judges, diplomats, and journalists, I had to step between Eugene McCarthy and David Hackett, one of Kennedy's most intense loyalists, who was in the midst of a tirade against the senator.

By the end of March, it was apparent that President Johnson had become almost irrelevant. Having barely survived in New Hampshire, he was now on the verge of losing to McCarthy in Wisconsin, where his campaign headquarters resembled a funeral home. Even worse, the American people no longer trusted him. They doubted his word.

Nonetheless, Johnson's twenty words, uttered March 31 on prime-time network television — *I shall not seek and I will not accept the nomination of my party for another term as your president* — left me shocked, disbelieving, and babbling.

Walter Cronkite, anchoring our coverage from New York, asked me for my reaction. I said, "Walter, I want to go home and come back tomorrow."

Four days later Martin Luther King Jr. was murdered in Memphis, and that night Washington's Fourteenth Street became a war zone. In May, the Poor People's Campaign arrived in Washington, and for the next six weeks the plywood shanties and tents of canvas and plastic of Resurrection City in West Potomac Park became a regular beat for the Washington bureau. It was an assignment nobody liked. Overbearing young black marshals pushed and shoved the press and cameras to prevent interviews with what were called the "homeless." Bruce Morton with his camera crew had been staked out there all one day. "We all had got tear gassed once or twice — it was your basic demonstration day," he says, and tempers were short and frayed. About 5:15 PM Dan Schorr showed to do his stand-up for the Cronkite show and, according to Morton, one of the crew looked at him and said in fury, "I won't do it. You should have been here for the tear gas. Goddamn it, go home."

■ ■ ■ ■

The Kennedy campaign was a blur. I joined on April 16 in Fargo, and until June 5 my life was one city, one courthouse rally, one Indian reservation, one airport welcome, one logging site, one labor hall, one community college after another. It was Fargo, to Portland, to Eugene, to Indianapolis, to Vincennes, to Valparaiso, to Richmond, to Omaha, to Redondo Beach, to Portland, to Stockton, to Eureka, and finally, fatally, to Los Angeles.

In Portland I put together a long piece for the Cronkite show on Kennedy's traveling staff — baggage chief, bodyguard, secretaries, speech writers, TV ad men, press secretary, and his dog, Freckles. One of my sentences read: "On the road, the traveling cadre is jammed into a chartered plane with a press corps of thirty and a covey of stewardesses who seem to spend most of their time as barmaids." When I rejoined the campaign in Indianapolis two days later, Ethel presented me with a gift of appreciation for my reporting. Somehow she had acquired one of those red-and-black waiter's jackets with the piping and the epaulets from the hotel bartender. On the back of the jacket in white adhesive tape she had written: "Personally I Never Touch the Stuff."

Each Friday I would break off from the campaign to do the Saturday news, and on one of those flights from Indianapolis, Ethel, a notoriously hyper flier, was my seatmate. The smallest bump or pilot warning about "a little turbulence up ahead" would turn her rigid. On our final approach into Washington, the pilot without warning yanked the plane up to avoid another jet still on our runway. Ethel lunged at my arm and hand and dug in with her nails. The woman who was potentially the nation's first lady not only broke my skin. She also drew blood.

Covering McCarthy from the start was David Schoumacher, who after a turn in Vietnam had returned to Washington hating the war and became convinced that a McCarthy presidency had the best chance of ending it. Imbedding himself in the McCarthy apparatus, Schoumacher set out to own the story "physically, intellectually, and energetically," as he put it. "The truth is I went too far," Schoumacher says. "Nobody was going to know more about McCarthy and his campaign than I was. And the result of that was that probably from the outside that looked favorable."

Schoumacher says two incidents convinced the Kennedy campaign that he had become too close to McCarthy. The first occurred during our coverage of the May 7 Indiana primary, when Schoumacher spontaneously arranged with the New York producers to stage a McCarthy-Kennedy debate by showing both men on a split screen with Cronkite as the moderator. Kennedy was furious with CBS for trapping him into a debate that he had been trying to avoid.

The second came later, in Wisconsin, when Schoumacher and his cameraman, John Smith, caught Teddy Kennedy using the freight elevator in McCarthy's hotel on a secret mission to talk McCarthy into dropping out of the race. The Kennedy people were convinced McCarthy had tipped off Schoumacher. He says he was able to nail Teddy because he hung around McCarthy's hotel, refusing to stay with the press at a different hotel some distance away. It was the work of a tenacious and indefatigable reporter.

Following primary victories in Indiana and Nebraska, Kennedy flew into California, stopping in Redondo Beach, Sacramento, and Davis. At every stop he fell further and further behind, so that when he reached Eureka, in Humboldt County in the northwest corner of the state, he was almost two hours late. At the airport he told the crowd of almost a thousand that the main reason he decided to run was that he would get to come to Eureka. Then in a cloud of dust the twelve-car motorcade drove the eighteen miles to the Eureka Inn, where he gave Humboldt Democrats the same speech he had given the night before. He also invited a delegation from the local Hoopa Indian tribe to his suite for a twenty-minute session. The poverty-stricken Indian had become as strong a symbol for Robert as the poor white of West Virginia was for John.

At 10:15 PM we were back at the Eureka airport and once more Kennedy worked the crowd along the fence, grabbing hands in a sort of Australian-crawl overhand stroke. I had decided not to follow along but instead took a position near the podium in case he spoke again. I stood there — racked and very hungry, typewriter and briefcase at my feet on the tarmac — probably looking a little like Willy Loman, the exhausted and dying salesman.

Over my shoulder I saw a flying phalanx

of cameras, lights, bodyguards, policemen, and teenyboppers bearing down on me. Barely in time did I drag my typewriter and case out of the way as the phalanx — with Kennedy in the vortex — went roaring by. Suddenly, the human wedge stopped. Kennedy broke out and jogged back to where I was standing. He looked me right in the eye and said, "Roger, half the trick is to look like you're having fun."

The last time he looked me right in the eye he was laughing again. It was on June 4 just before midnight in Los Angeles at the Ambassador Hotel, and Kennedy appeared to be on his way to defeating McCarthy in the California primary. Before going down to greet the crowd in the Embassy Room, he made the round of interviews with the networks. First, with Sander Vanocur of NBC, then with me, next with Bob Clark of ABC, and finally Dan Blackburn of Metromedia.

Our interview, seen on the full network, was genuinely funny, playful, and relaxed. Jules Witcover, in his account of the campaign, wrote: "Thanks to Roger Mudd's phrasing of questions, the interview soon became one of the most authentic appearances Kennedy ever made on television — capturing his wry sense of humor as it seldom had been seen in public."[3] Jack Newfield, who called it "one of the most appealing and natural [interviews] Kennedy ever gave on television," reprinted the entire transcript of the interview in his book *Robert Kennedy: A Memoir.* Newfield, a man not lacking in hubris, told me at one of his book parties, "I made you famous."

The chaos, the shrieking, and the madness that followed the shooting of the senator that night at the Ambassador Hotel have almost been whited out in my memory. I do recall that once I got into the pantry beyond the stage I saw Mrs. Kennedy standing all alone. She'd been abandoned for the moment. I put my arm around her waist. She turned and recognized me. She hugged me as if I were an oak tree — just something to cling to. She was teetering there on the edge — not knowing whether the senator was dead or alive. Then she bumped into a young man sitting behind her and he said something about Senator Kennedy. Mrs. Kennedy turned and snapped at him, "How dare you say anything about my husband." The young man said, "Ma'am, I've been hit, too." She suddenly realized what an awkward moment it was for both of them. She leaned down and kissed him on the face. I recall forcing some screaming, bellowing men to give way so that Ethel could reach her dying husband. Six years later, Ethel told a luncheon in the senator's honor that "it was Roger who led me through the crowd so that Bobby and I could say goodbye to each other." There was a pause and then she added, "So, I'll always love him for that."

I recall the deathwatch outside the Good Samaritan Hospital and scrambling down a grassy bank in front when the final bulletin was issued, falling and tearing my trousers. I recall flying from Los Angeles to New York to anchor a special broadcast on the senator and not saying a word to anybody about anything — not my seatmate, not the stewardesses, not the taxi driver. I recall the outrage I felt as I watched thousands of New Yorkers going about their business as if it were just another Thursday in June — and he was *their* senator.

Did they not know what had happened in Los Angeles? The world knew it. How could they be laughing? How could they not know it? How could they not be enraged? How could they not be devastated?

The next night at 7:30 I anchored a program from the CBS studios on West Fifty-seventh Street, called "Some Friends of Robert F. Kennedy" — Douglas Dillon, former Treasury secretary; Charles Evers, field secretary of the NAACP; Peter Edelman, the senator's legislative assistant; Frank Mankiewicz, the senator's press secretary; and William Walton, artist, family friend, and head of Citizens for Kennedy in New York.

For an hour they talked and talked and talked about him. They talked about his "perpetual sense of outrage"; his total identity with children; his gentle sense of humor. Not one of the five had ever heard him tell a joke — a man-went-into-a-bar kind of joke. His wit, they said, was always situational and mostly directed at himself. He was ruthless, they thought, but ruthless toward the unjust and cruel.

In the end we all agreed that what made so many Americans admire him and oppose him was that he meant what he said.[4] Though I barely uttered a word, it was as cathartic for me as it was for them.

Nineteen-sixty-eight was a terrible year, full of violence, social upheaval, and racial chaos. It was a year we all could have done without.

CHAPTER 33
"NIXON'S THE ONE WHAT?"

The death of Robert Kennedy caused some of us to lose our appetites for politics and the intense coverage and commitment that the coming conventions would demand. His campaign — as brief and intense as it was — was pure pleasure, and most of the reporters had looked forward to an epochal Kennedy-Nixon campaign in the fall, even though Kennedy was no better than fifty-fifty to get the nomination.

Had he lived he would have become the only alternative to Vice President Hubert Humphrey for the Democratic nomination. But when Eugene McCarthy became the alternative, he proved too much the romantic and began to show signs of being bored with the nitty-gritty of presidential politics. Repeatedly he declined to take charge of an organization that needed a chief of staff. Humphrey, without running in a single primary, arrived in Chicago with the nomination virtually locked up, handed to him by the unions, the Democratic governors and mayors, and the Johnson White House. Humphrey left Chicago, however, staggered by the angry clashes between the antiwar demonstrators and Mayor Daley's police, and by a still-divided Democratic Party.

Most of that I was spared, because CBS had a problem with my assignment. Four years earlier in Atlantic City, I had coanchored the Democratic convention with Bob Trout, and to have put me out on the convention floor as one of four or five reporters would have been seen, they feared, as a demotion. So the producers teamed me up with the humorist Art Buchwald in a small amphitheater studio to do commentary. It was fun to work with Buchwald but, given what was happening in the streets and on the floor, we were out of the loop. I did not earn my pay in Chicago.

The Republican convention in Miami had been a yawn. Nixon's nomination was inevitable. During the 1968 campaign I saw Nixon only twice — he was regularly in the hands of our White House reporters, Rather and Pierpoint. The first time was in North Carolina at a meticulously organized Greensboro Coliseum rally and the second in Indianapolis, and both times he seemed hermetically sealed off from the public and the press. Covering Kennedy during the Indiana primary, we'd gotten used to marathon motorcades, with crowds lining the streets, kids running or riding their bikes alongside, women grabbing and pawing at him in his open convertible. Late one afternoon, we heard police sirens in the distance, and within minutes came the Nixon motorcade — six or seven long, black limousines, their closed and darkened windows making Nixon and his entourage invisible — nosing through downtown Indianapolis without slowing or stopping, on its way to the local country club for dinner and a fundraiser. The comparison between the chaotic and jubilant Kennedy motorcade and the cocooned and joyless Nixon motorcade set us all to laughing — howling, actually, some even chanting the Republican campaign slogan, "Nixon's the One."

Every time Kennedy saw someone in the crowd holding one of those "Nixon's the One" posters, he would stop what he was saying to ask, "Nixon's the One What?" It always got a big laugh.

What suspense there was in Miami revolved around Nixon's choice of a running mate. Half a dozen names buzzed about the hall — George Romney, Dan Evans, Howard Baker, John Tower, Rogers Morton, John Volpe, and Spiro Agnew.

I had met Agnew early in the sixties through my brother, who was an active Republican in Baltimore. Subsequently I covered him when he defeated Democrat George P. Mahoney for governor of Maryland in 1966. Two years later, Agnew had switched his allegiance from Nelson Rockefeller to Richard Nixon and at the 1968 Miami Beach convention was sweating out Nixon's choice for vice president. On the convention floor, I would float by the Maryland delegation from time to time, and each time found Agnew, Maryland's favorite son, sitting with his twenty-six-vote delegation in his aisle seat, immaculately erect and available. Annapolis reporters said Agnew confided to them that he kept his jacket and trousers crisply creased and unwrinkled by never crossing his legs or letting his coat touch the back of the chair.[1] With the first-ballot nomination of Nixon a virtual lock, the only remaining story was his running mate. On one of my floats by the Maryland delegation, I knelt down in the aisle next to Agnew's chair, and before I could get a word out, he turned to me and whispered,

"Whaddya hear?" If anybody wanted to be vice president so much he could taste it, Spiro Agnew was the man.

Within a year or so, Vice President Agnew had become, in Jules Witcover's phrase, the Nixon administration's "dragon slayer." In a series of half a dozen speeches that began in New Orleans and ended in Montgomery, Agnew's rhetoric became increasingly inflammatory, reaching its white-hot stage in the Grand Ballroom of the Hotel Fort Des Moines.

The afternoon of Agnew's speech, copies of it were released in Washington. The networks took one look and knew they had to carry it live, wanting to be fair but, more than that, afraid that not carrying it would be less than helpful in their relations with the new administration.

Agnew did not mince words. He said that in Nixon's "silent majority" speech of November 3, the president gave "one of the most important [speeches] of our decade," only to have a "small band of network commentators and self-appointed analysts" subject it to "instant analysis and querulous criticism." Ten times Agnew zeroed in on "this little group of men," "a small group of men," "a handful of men," and "these men of the media." "What do Americans know of the men who wield this power?" he asked. "Practically nothing," he answered.[2] Our post-speech analysis and comment were held to a minimum on orders from above. The CBS formal reply came ten days later, when Frank Stanton said that not since the 1798 Alien and Sedition Acts forbade criticism of the government had there been a more "serious episode" in government-press relationships.[3]

A more informal answer to Agnew came in a speech I gave that winter as president of the Radio-Television Correspondents Association at its annual black-tie dinner in Washington. The dinner attracts the entire world of television news — correspondents and their sources, anchors, editors, photographers, the network management, the stations, the chain owners, the regional bureaus, and the freelancers.

That night the Hilton Hotel ballroom was packed, because word had gone out early that Nixon was coming, his first visit to the dinner as president. He had sent Vice President Agnew the year before. The ballroom was also overflowing with men and women who knew by heart and hated virtually every word of Agnew's scathing denunciation of them from Des Moines.

So when I began, "Mr. President, we are honored to have you with us and we welcome you to the twenty-sixth annual dinner of the Tiny, Closed Fraternity of Privileged Men," there followed a howl of laughter. I said television's troubles with the administration began not in Des Moines but in this very ballroom a year ago. As my predecessor, Robert McCormick of NBC, finished his speech that night, "one network, the one with studios at the White House, trotted out Spiro Agnew," who subjected McCormick's words to "instant analysis and querulous criticism." More howls. How does the White House network determine the news? I asked. "A small group of men, most of them Germans" — a huge roar went up at this reference to Herb Klein, Ron Ziegler, John Ehrlichman, Bob Haldeman, Henry Kissinger, Alvin Snyder, and Clark Mollenhoff — "settles upon the thirty minutes of news that is to reach the public. This selection is made from the eight or nine minutes of actual news."

The afternoon of the dinner I had showed my speech to Charlie McDowell, my old friend from college and a splendid wordsmith. In the Senate Reception Room just off the Senate floor amid the Brumidi frescoes, we sat together and went over what

I had written. He loved it. He suggested the opening line about the "Closed Fraternity of Privileged Men," and then he remembered how prickly the ever prickly Chief Justice Warren Burger had again been with the press the week before. So Charlie added these lines: "And just last weekend, the White House sent its chief legal correspondent to Atlanta, but he refused to work when he discovered the rest of the press corps were not also chief justices."[4]

So there I stood at the podium, sticking it to the president of the United States in person. I could not see his face, but my guests right down front — Charlie, Walter Mears of the Associated Press, Steve Gerstel of United Press International, and Charles Ferris, chief counsel of the Senate Democratic Policy Committee — told me later he tried to laugh when the crowd laughed but he was always a second or two late.

When I sat down, everyone in the hall stood up, applauding and cheering. Nixon and I shook hands, but he said nothing about my speech. It was the first time I had ever been with a president at anything other than a press conference, and I found him socially geeky and, unlike Ronald Reagan or Bill Clinton, an awkward dinner companion, unable to banter.

The entertainment that night was George Carlin, who paid me a great compliment when he said, "How come I get to follow *him?*" The singer was Diana Ross and, believe it or not, the president turned to me during one of her songs and said, "They really do have a sense of rhythm, don't they?"

CHAPTER 34
HITTING OUR STRIDE

The triumph of Richard Nixon over Humphrey and the Democrats roughly coincided with the triumph of the *CBS Evening News with Walter Cronkite* over *The Huntley-Brinkley Report* on NBC.

President Nixon couldn't have hated it more. For the next six years his administration had to deal every day with something new — a hard-driving, no-nonsense TV news network that was for the first time producing first-class, unblinking coverage not only from Europe and Vietnam but also from the White House, the State Department, Capitol Hill, and the Justice Department.

It was no wonder that Nixon attended the Radio-TV Correspondents Dinner only once in his six years in the White House.

By 1969, the Washington bureau was hitting its stride. Over the next four to five years, dozens more talented reporters and producers swelled the bureau, but it was the staff Bill Small had first assembled that set it apart from all the others.

We had a first-class library and research department, initiated by Howard K. Smith and run by Louise Remmey. Against the north wall of the bureau were ten or twelve file cabinets of newspaper clippings — our so-called morgue — and on the shelves were the *Encyclopedia Britannica, Facts on File,* and various *Who's Who*s. Remmey was a gracious, selfless, and soft-spoken helpmate who never failed to respond to the most challenging demands. One of her classmates at Bucknell University was Philip Roth, who has yet to forgive her because she got a Fulbright and he did not.

It was in Remmey's corner that I would spend Friday and Saturday poring over the folders she assembled for me, preparing questions for *Face the Nation* on Sunday.

What helped make the bureau the envy of the competition was the beefing up of the production staff. Until 1969, Washington had only one producer assigned to the Cronkite show — Jim Snyder. How the towering Snyder did what he did is still a professional mystery. Everything between Snyder and the Cronkite show and everything between Snyder and the correspondents was done by phone, and everything that the Washington bureau fed to the Cronkite show — sometimes 65 percent to 70 percent of the broadcast — not only went through Snyder but was also produced by him and his film editors.

Clearing the newsroom floor of all obstacles between the edit room and the back steps to make way for Jim Snyder became a nightly 6:27 ritual in the bureau. He'd go roaring by with his huge stride, clutching the reel of film on his pell-mell dash to the projection room to rack up the film less than thirty seconds before Walter said, "Good Evening."

Running a solo shop for the Cronkite show was a prescription for burnout, and when Snyder got an offer to run the entire news operation at the local CBS station, WTOP, he took it.

In his place came not one but three producers. The first, already in Washington on the assignment desk, was Bob Mead, an Indiana boy, who produced for Rather on many of Nixon's overseas trips and in 1974 left CBS to be President Ford's TV adviser.

In the spring came John Armstrong, thirty-five, a graduate of Rutgers whose father, an electrical engineer, had helped develop radar. Armstrong had been working for CBS in New York, writing mostly for radio. Swift, hardworking, totally organized, impatient, hip, goateed, brusque at times, he quickly became a first-class TV producer. The goatee that Armstrong cultivated gave him a slight Charlie Chan look.

Soon after Armstrong, Ed Fouhy arrived to become the senior Washington producer for Cronkite. He was an ex-Marine with a trace of the godfather in him. When New York decided the Saigon bureau needed straightening out, they sent Fouhy. Saigon, he said, was "missing stories, nightly specials weren't going well, and there was some playing with the currency in the black market." With Saigon straightened out, New York rewarded Fouhy with the Los Angeles bureau, but the traveling proved onerous with his young family.

Born in Boston, Fouhy grew up in Milton and worked his way through UMass. His father was a timekeeper at the Bethlehem shipyards at Quincy, and his mother was the secretary to Dr. Karl Compton, the president of MIT. After his discharge from the Marines in 1959, he tried the *Boston Globe* but was told, "Well, we've got the Harvard boys here for the summer." But WBZ-TV had no problem with a UMass graduate. By 1965, Fouhy had a master's degree from Boston University, and quickly rose to be WBZ's news director. CBS hired him in 1966 as a producer on the *CBS Morning News.*

In Washington, the thirty-five-year-old Fouhy made things happen. He was determined to show New York how good the bureau could be. "We were just crazy about what we were doing," Armstrong recalls. "We just blew the doors off the place."

The mission that drove Fouhy was to "cover the news and beat NBC," and beginning in the seventies, beating NBC, which was without Chet Huntley, was getting easier. There was in NBC's Washington bureau a "lassitude" — Fouhy's word — brought on by David Brinkley's dominance of the Washington scene. Being first for more than a decade generated a smugness that left NBC unprepared for the swarming competition CBS threw at it. Brinkley's wit and sophistication had propelled the *Huntley-Brinkley Report* into first place, but at the expense of NBC's Washington staff.

Richard Valeriani at the State Department, Carl Stern at the Supreme Court, Tom Brokaw at the White House, and Doug Kiker anywhere he went were all very strong and accomplished reporters, but they had a hard time getting on the air because David Brinkley did their stories for them. An NBC correspondent could spend the entire day at a lively and important congressional hearing only to be told that "David wants to tell that." Brinkley's rendering of the hearing more than likely would be slightly flip, if not cynical, reinforcing the image of a Congress full of preening blowhards and Washington as a not very serious place. In 1967, NBC hired Carl Stern, a man with a law degree, to be its law specialist but then it lost its nerve, deciding that the Supreme Court and the law were not exciting enough for TV. Rarely was Stern seen on the screen. NBC's anchor-first policy was a gift to CBS. Because Cronkite believed reporters should do the reporting and that Washington was the news capital of the world, we became better known not only to the audience but also to news sources.

"Air time is like oxygen," says Eric Engberg, a long-time CBS correspondent. "I think that Brinkley helped create a whole generation of 'name' CBS correspondents by sucking up so much oxygen himself."

In 1974 Fouhy left CBS to become NBC's Washington producer for John Chancellor in New York. He found NBC's lassitude very difficult to deal with. The bureau, he says, "was really not very competitive. . . . It didn't have the all-consuming sense that you had as you walked into CBS that this place was about the news." Lassitude is the last thing an ex-Marine can put up with. Three years later, Fouhy was back at CBS.

Not until 1977 did NBC realize that its Washington bureau needed an overhaul. It hired Sid Davis from Westinghouse News to replace Don Meaney as bureau chief. Washington was not as aggressive as New York wanted, they told Davis. "Go down there and make it tougher," they said.

What Davis found was a "wonderful culture that [news] was a gentlemanly thing. They were proud of the fact that some of the old-time correspondents said, 'Look, we may not be there first but once we get on the story we do a better job on the follow-through and the aftermath than anybody.' "

Davis also found NBC's beat system had been allowed to atrophy; he lacked the manpower to run a seven-day-a-week operation; the consistency of assignments for producers was helter-skelter and Hill coverage was in shambles. Nominally, it was in the hands of sixty-five-year-old Robert Mc-Cormick, who, according to Davis, "held court in the Radio-TV Gallery on the House side," where the game of Hearts was a favorite time-killer.

McCormick's highly publicized replacement was to be Jessica Savitch, "the Golden Girl" NBC was grooming to be a *Nightly News* anchor. She was initially assigned to the Senate because NBC News president Richard Wald said the Senate was "not a pivotal job. If she didn't do it right, we didn't suffer."[1]

The day Savitch made her first appearance at the nonpivotal Senate, we all turned to watch her entrance. She was, of course, accompanied by her own producer and guide, who pointed out, "And this is the Senate TV Gallery where you'll be working. . . ."

But the Senate, with its arcane ways, its layers of history, precedence, and political nuance, was her undoing. She was in over her head, and her career went into a dive from which she never pulled out.

Sid Davis did toughen up his bureau somewhat, and recently he praised Chris Wallace, Bob Hager, and Andrea Mitchell as reporters "who would kill for a story." Asked for the "one clear victory over CBS" during his time, Davis cited White House correspondent John Palmer's exclusive on the 1979 mission to rescue the fifty-three American hostages in Teheran. "It was the cleanest beat I've ever seen," said Davis.

As clean as Palmer's beat was, it did little to close the gap with CBS. John Armstrong, wondering why CBS so consistently beat NBC and ABC, finally realized that no one in those bureaus "read past the front page." None of us, however, took NBC for granted. Each evening, a minute or two before 6:30 PM, we would gather in the bureau in front of the three newsroom monitors to watch the competition, mostly NBC.

Rita Braver, who was just getting started in the early seventies, recalls that evening gathering as "one of the great things, because you got to know each other; you got to know what people who were good thought was good. If you thought they were tough on our bureau, think of how tough they were on people from the other bureaus. . . . If somebody who covered your beat was up, you'd run up and turn up the monitor to make sure they didn't have something that you had."

After a year or two of producing stories in the field and watching the competition, Braver came up with some similes to describe the networks:

CBS was like the Marines — we thought

we were tougher, stronger; we were a tight-knit band. NBC was the Navy, because in the old days they'd used to kind of like sail in. ABC was the Air Force — they had all the fancy graphics and they were chartering planes all around. In later years when CNN was invented, they became the Army, because there were so many of them. And Fox, of course, was the Coast Guard. . . .

CBS News was driven by a simple dictum — that excellence produced excellence. Jim McManus, who came to CBS after Westinghouse folded, says that the excellence went all the way back to the 1930s, when William Paley hired Ed Klauber from the *New York Times* and Paul White from United Press to run radio news. The "sheer weight" of the CBS reputation "got you in the door," McManus says.

But most of us had only read about Klauber and White. What we knew about firsthand was our network president, Frank Stanton, who felt that the news division was the first among equals; our division president, Dick Salant, who set a standard for decency and fairness few of us ever matched; and Walter Cronkite, our anchor, whose sticklerlike devotion to unadorned hard news kept us in his thrall.

Ike Pappas says that after he had a piece on the air he would sit at his desk and "wait for a call" from Cronkite. Sometimes Cronkite would call if he "didn't like a line in your script or he wasn't sure you were right, and if he wasn't convinced he'd throw out the story." If you didn't get the call, Pappas says, "then you felt pretty good."

Eric Engberg, who began his career on his grammar school newspaper in Highland Park, Illinois, realized after twenty-seven years at CBS that he never worried about criticism that his writing might have lacked style or elegance. What he worried about endlessly was being beaten by the opposition on simple facts and pictures. Jim McManus recalls, "The idea of screwing up a story was just an anathema. You'd want to go out and shoot yourself."

Nothing gave us more pleasure — quiet pleasure — than to stick it to the opposition. It meant we were special and were maintaining standards that others did not or could not. There were times when we deliberately lorded it over the other guy. Barry Serafin, a young Oregonian, recruited from KMOX-TV in St. Louis, had been in the D.C. bureau less than six months when he became our specialist in the politics of the United Mine Workers. His assignment followed the 1969 murder of Jock Yablonski by the hired hit men of union president Tony Boyle. Wired into union politics, Serafin was covering a closed-door meeting in Washington on the 1974 UMW strike with his film crew. Covering a closed meeting mainly involves sitting and sitting, waiting for a spokesman to come out and announce that the negotiators are making progress. Serafin's competition that day was a network rookie, Charles Gibson of ABC. But Gibson was not, Serafin knew, as wired as he was, and he saw his chance to show Gibson what he was up against. It was also a chance to break the tedium. Serafin, equipped with a huge voice box, was quiet and thoughtful. But he loved to laugh, and his rumbling laugh seemed to come from somewhere below his knees. Quietly, Serafin told his crew, "Don't say a word. Just break down your equipment and follow me." They left the stake-out position and began circling around the building. Sure enough, in less than a minute or two, here came Gibson and his crew, hauling it as fast as they could, convinced Serafin was on to something, huffing and puffing to catch up.

"It was one of those things you did," said Serafin recently, "because you could." Just telling the story made Serafin laugh. At twenty-eight, the young man from Roseburg, Oregon, had picked up the CBS swagger without being told.

Many of the Washington bureau's breaks came from just being there, watching, listening, and asking questions.

Soon after the Nixon inaugural, Small assigned a young woman to help me on the Hill. I was beginning to work both Saturday and Sunday in New York, and I needed someone to keep track of legislation and politics on my days off. The someone was Cindy Samuels, a whip-smart 1968 graduate of Smith College, the daughter of a Republican lawyer from Pittsburgh and one of the Gene McCarthy kids, who had made friends with almost everybody on his press plane.

Within a couple of months on the Hill, she was so informed and informative that repeatedly I had to ask her to slow down so I could take it all in.

In 1970, the year after Clement Haynsworth's appointment to the Supreme Court crashed on the Senate floor, Samuels began picking up signals that the nomination of Harrold Carswell to the Court was also in deep trouble. Watching from the TV Gallery in the Senate chamber one day, she spotted a clutch of senators talking together. She sensed they were talking about mounting a filibuster against Carswell. One of the senators confirmed her hunch and that night CBS broke the story.

The next morning a furious Bob Clark of ABC and Bob McCormick of NBC accused Charles Ferris, the chief counsel of the Senate Democratic Policy Committee, of playing favorites. They were really mad and were yelling at Ferris. Ferris told them, "Well, she figured it out. You could have figured it out."

Later, Ferris said to her, "I told them you did it all by yourself and they should shut up." Samuels still glows at the thought of her small triumph. "That was a very thrilling thing for me. I just loved helping."

At twenty-four, Cindy Samuels had taught two old pros how to work the territory.

The Samuels story illustrates just how collaborative TV journalism could be, despite the internal competition between and among the correspondents and producers, despite its appearance of being a totally personal form of communication. A first-class newspaper story can be turned out by one first-class reporter. But as Ed Fouhy laid it out for television, "If Galbraith on the desk hadn't been so good, if camera-men like Bruce Hoertel hadn't been such fine craftsmen, if John Lesner, the courier, hadn't been willing to ride as though his hair was on fire, if Don LeBlanc, the film editor, hadn't been not only so talented but also so fast, none of the fine stories you, Schorr, Kalb, Morton, Rather, Pierpoint, Herman, and Schieffer did would have made it to people's living rooms."

When Bruce Morton arrived in '64 he had done nothing but radio. So he began hang-ing out in the film-editing rooms, where everyone was always under the gun. But far from telling the new guy they didn't have the time, they took him in. "Sure, you want to learn? Sure, stand there. I'll show you how we do this." Morton learned what a good transition shot was because he'd heard the editors liking one, hating the other. "I owe those guys a lot. Don LeBlanc, Ray Kramer, Lee Shepp, Charlie Ryan, Phil Gillespie, Carol Hamedy — they were really helpful."

Competition within the bureau on M Street was intense yet controlled. Ed Brad-ley, whose four unhappy years in the bureau he called "less than glorious," said the competition was "cutthroat."

If it was cutthroat, the blood was rarely

visible. On occasion the competition broke into the open, as when Rather at the White House and Kalb at the State Department sparred over who would cover Henry Kissinger at a time he was actually running the State Department out of the White House.

Generally, though, the competition and the personal dislikes were submerged — Phil Jones and Barry Serafin were thought not to trust Bob Schieffer, who had moved ahead of them in the pecking order; Rita Braver and Bill Headline, the assistant bureau chief, it was said, found Fred Graham to be less than energetic; everybody knew that Rather and Pierpoint operated under a negotiated truce at the White House; many resented my arrogance in thinking I owned Capitol Hill; and even the superaggressive Daniel Schorr had to admit that he "didn't have a lot of people falling in love with" him. But a bureau without Schorr, Rather, Kalb, and Pierpoint would have been unthinkable. The tension, the competitiveness, the happy cynicism were essential ingredients in our success.

If anybody knew how to play on those qualities it was Bill Small, the bureau chief. After a long flight from Moscow with Nixon in late May of '72, Rather and Pierpoint landed at Andrews Air Force in the afternoon and checked in with the desk. Rather said there was to be a routine White House briefing but they were both exhausted and wanted Small's OK to go home. Tom Bettag, the desk editor, put Rather on hold to tell Small. Small replied, "Tell Dan that's just fine. I'll send Schorr over to the White House." Rather said, "Tell Small I'll be at the White House in half an hour." That was Small the godfather at his very best. "The way Small delivered the message," says Bettag, "was very much like, 'Just tell him there'll be a horse's head in his bed in the morning.'"

The opposition was never quite able to figure out why CBS Washington was the way it was. At NBC, they believed we would walk *over* our own grandmother to get a story. At NBC they would walk *around* her, says Valeriani.[2] Charles Gibson at ABC once asked Phil Jones, "What is it about CBS? You all think you're so great. Is it this Murrow thing? I look at some of the pieces and I think we're as good or better than you on some of them. But none of us feel as good about ourselves as you feel."

They were both right, of course.

CHAPTER 35
THE HAND THAT
FEEDS YOU

Like so many others who get hired at CBS News, Susan Spencer looked up at those letters on the front of 2020 M Street — "C" and "B" and "S" — on her first day of work and went "wobbly." And like so many other young men and women who were so dazzled and astonished at being at such a power-house, she never planned to leave, and has not.

Indeed, until the 1980s, when switching networks became as common as pro ball-players switching teams, voluntary defections from CBS News were so rare that the list contained only three big names — Ed Murrow, Harry Reasoner, and Fred Friendly. Murrow left in disgust to work for President Kennedy, Reasoner went to ABC for money and fame, and Friendly quit to protest the network's refusal to broadcast the Senate's 1966 Vietnam hearings. We understood Reasoner's defection — Cronkite was blocking his ascension — but we still didn't like it. Besides, ABC was barely a network. We thought anchoring five nights at ABC couldn't hold a candle to just Sunday night at CBS plus filling in for Cronkite and documentaries and late-night specials. But Reasoner wanted his own show. When ABC gave it to him in October 1970, he was gone.

That seemingly put me next in line as Cronkite's principal substitute. A month later, however, I gave a speech that almost put me on the list of involuntary defectors.

Giving a speech was the easy part; it was the writing of them that took the time. After almost ten years on the network, my face and reputation were known well enough to generate half a dozen invitations a year to speak. At first I tried to put together a fresh talk for each occasion, but that took more time than I usually had. I solved the problem by developing several basic speeches on national politics, on television, and on the Congress but always preceded by very specific and current references to the audience, the city, the college, or the buzz about the local politicians and their foibles. I signed up with a lecture agent, who negotiated fees, travel, and hotels and took 15 percent of my fee, which ranged anywhere from $10,000 to $15,000. It was quick, easy money and did not involve much heavy lifting.

But an invitation to speak at Washington and Lee University was different. Because it would be the first at my alma mater and at a highly prestigious event — the annual tapping ceremony of the Omicron Delta Kappa, the student leadership fraternity — I decided to write a brand-new speech, top to bottom. The ceremony would be the perfect occasion for talking about some issues that had been troubling me for some time — the Nixon administration's attacks on the media, the media's isolation from the so-called silent majority, and television news's failure to live up to its responsibilities.

So on December 7, 1970, before a full house in Lee Chapel — the marble statue of Robert E. Lee in recumbent glory on the stage behind me — I gave my speech. After some preliminary fluff about Washington and Lee's president, Bob Huntley, who was also my college roommate, I laid out what I thought about television and TV news:

It is now my belief . . . that broadcasting in sound or vision will not prove to have contributed to the advancement of ideas

434

or the education of man as much as the printed word. The inherent limitations of our media make it a powerful means of communication but also a crude one which tends to strike at the emotions, rather than the intellect. For television journalists this means a dangerous and increasing concentration on action which is usually violent and bloody rather than on thought. . . . The bright hopes that we all had for television forever elude us. . . . The industry somehow still is unable or unwilling now to move beyond its preoccupation with razzle dazzle. . . . Our broadcasts have not improved. If anything, the quality has declined. The tube has become a trip, a national opiate, a babysitter who charges nothing, something to iron by, to shave to and to doze over, and in the news departments of the networks the first question a producer asks a reporter is not "what's in it?" but "how long is it?"[1]

The timing of those words could not have been worse. Vice President Agnew's denunciation of the media was still ringing in the ears of CBS management, and to them I had seemingly joined the enemy with my public denunciation of the profession that was paying me so handsomely.

I thought my criticism was within the bounds of fair comment and that CBS was a grown-up company and could handle it. How wrong, how naïve, I was.

Word of the speech reached the management of CBS in New York two weeks later, when a story about it appeared in *Editor and Publisher.* The story was a reprint from a small Missouri paper owned and edited by a Washington and Lee graduate who had received a copy of my talk from the alumni newsletter. An interoffice memo from West Fifty-seventh Street, to me, read:

I would very much like to have the text of your December 7 Washington and Lee speech which is quoted at some length in the December 19 issue of *Editor and Publisher.* I hope against hope that Mr. Brown took you out of context. If he didn't, I would be glad to discuss with you when next you are in New York the issues which you raise and how both you and I can contribute to better television journalism as well as to a Mudd who is not publicly ashamed of the hand that feeds him.[2]

"Ooomph" — right to the solar plexus. I felt sick reading those words — "ashamed," "the hand that feeds him," and "*a* Mudd," not "Mudd" or "Roger Mudd" or "Mr. Mudd" but "*a* Mudd," as if I were some exotic spider from the zoology lab.

This was no routine memo from New York. This memo was from Richard S. Salant, the president of CBS News and one of the industry's most pungent and persistent memo writers. Correspondents were used to being coddled and mollified and nursed but never spoken to harshly. The Salant memo broke the mold. I had thought that CBS was mature enough and respected dissent and criticism enough that my critique, which I felt deeply about, would be taken seriously. On January 5, 1971, when I replied to Salant, I still thought a meeting with him would take care of it:

The *Editor and Publisher* excerpts from my Washington and Lee speech are accurate and in context. The omissions are minor or have no bearing on my comments about television. I would be delighted to meet with you when I am next in New York. I hope your conclusion that I am "publicly ashamed of the hand that feeds" me is tentative, not final. I am sometimes depressed by it and frequently disappointed by it but never ashamed of it.[3]

Salant's response revealed how little I knew about the corporate politics of TV journalism. The minute Salant got my reply, he summoned me to New York for a luncheon. The luncheon, it turned out, was a Salant set-up. He had passed the word about the speech and had assembled the news division's executives and ranking producers to do some kneecapping. The attack was led by the former executive producer of the *Evening News,* Ernest Leiser, the same Leiser who had mothballed me in the months following the 1964 convention in Atlantic City, when Bob Trout and I had unhorsed Cronkite. But for Paul Greenberg, not a single voice was raised in my defense or about the validity of my speech. Paul's support salvaged a modicum of my self-respect, but our colleagues all knew that Paul and I were partners on the Saturday news and that our careers were editorially linked. Nonetheless, I was thankful Paul was there for a very uncomfortable confrontation during which I ate little or none of my food.

Salant's scourging of me was not over. The

minute the luncheon broke up, Salant took me in his waiting limousine across town to the CBS corporate headquarters at Fifty-second Street and Sixth Avenue, the building known as "Black Rock." Salant and I did not speak during the ride over. The trip was for another dressing-down, this one administered by Richard Jencks, a vice president who was fourth in the corporate lineup. I did not know it then but Jencks, who later told me confidentially he agreed with my critique, was clearly speaking for Jack Schneider, the aggressive president of the CBS Television Network. According to Gary Gates, the biographer of CBS News, Schneider had for some time been lumping me in with Gordon Manning and a few others as news division "purists," rigid in their contempt for the company's preoccupation with ratings and profits. The Washington and Lee speech gave Schneider the perfect chance to knock loose some of my arrogance.[4]

Tail between my legs, I slunk back to Washington, only to be taken out for another lunch. My host this time was my esteemed and admirable bureau chief, Bill Small, carrying out the last of Jack Schneider's orders. Because of the speech, I would not be substituting for Cronkite during the coming summer. I would return to work on Capitol Hill and try to prove myself worthy. It was handled very discreetly by Small. Not until John Hart, the anchor of the *Morning News,* appeared on the *Evening News* filling in during Cronkite's August vacation did anyone realize I had been iced.

On the bureau bulletin board outside the edit rooms, someone posted a clipping about my speech. As I walked by, Ed Fouhy stood reading the clip and the quote, "In the news departments of the networks the first question a producer asks a reporter is not 'what's in it?' but 'how long is it?' " Fouhy did not like what he had read. He turned to me and said, "That's pretty rough." That was all he ever said about the speech.

The Schneider-Salant reaction, was, I thought, way out of proportion to the damage I had done, if any. Not until David Halberstam expounded his theory at lunch one day did it dawn on me what had pushed the corporation into such a frenzy. His theory found its way into his book on the media:

The response at the higher level of CBS went far beyond anything Mudd had said, and the reason was simple: he had

440

recalled all too clearly the vision of Murrow, and a man who thought he was a little better than broadcasting, and those critical assessments, so admired when they were turned to other subjects, were not [at] all admired when they were turned to the home industry.[5]

After that pillorying it was no wonder that New York, sustained and energized by the daily power plays and schemes, was the last place on earth I wanted to work.

Not until the summer of 1973 had I proved worthy enough to be reinstalled as Cronkite's primary substitute. CBS had given Cronkite a new contract that guaranteed three months' vacation. Viewers began to worry about his long absences. I knew where he was — he was sailing — but I couldn't say that each night. As an inside joke, we wired Walter and told him to change the name of his boat from "Wyntie" to "Assignment," so I could say each evening at 6:30 PM that Walter was "on Assignment." The phrase, of course, never made air.

The summer before Jack Schneider was booted upstairs, we sat together by happenstance on a Washington-to-New York shuttle flight. Despite our prickly relationship, we began laughing when we discovered we were both wearing blazers, golf shirts, khakis, loafers, and no socks. It was the no-socks part that was the clincher — not what you'd call the solid foundation for a lasting friendship, but it was a start.

CHAPTER 36
YES, NO, AND JUST A
LITTLE BIT

Even as Richard Salant was excoriating me
with his memos, I was busy working on
another, but quite different, memo from
him. It was the memo that led to one of
CBS News's most explosive and controversial documentaries, "The Selling of the Pentagon."

The program began as an exposé of the
Pentagon's bloated public relations budget
and it ended with a defiant CBS refusing to
bend to a congressional attempt to bring it
to heel. In between there were five months
of acrimony, full-bore attacks on the editing
of the program by the Pentagon, accusations of shoddy journalism by the political
friends of the Pentagon, congressional
subpoenas and hearings, a series of defen-
sive responses by CBS News, and a dramatic
denouement that saved Frank Stanton from
facing charges of contempt.

Salant had seen a film made by the Atomic

Energy Commission that got him wondering about how much the federal government was spending to persuade, rather than inform.[1] Salant's memo went to a quick, thoughtful, and talented thirty-four-year-old documentary producer, Peter Davis, a Harvard cum laude, the son of California screenwriters, and a writer and associate producer at CBS since 1965. Davis spent a stretch in Washington looking at the State, Justice, and Interior Departments, but finally settled on the Department of Defense.

Davis called me about being the narrator/reporter but I resisted. I told him I preferred doing my own research and reporting, whereas the network's documentary system put that almost exclusively in the hands of producers, with correspondents brought in only during the final stages of production for a high-profile interview or to record narration that had been researched and written by others. Rarely was a correspondent involved in the editing of the film and rarely did a correspondent get a writing credit on a documentary, because rarely did they do any. Big-name correspondents were too much in demand doing other assignments — anchoring, getting ready for elections, covering their own beats. Out of necessity, correspondents learned to put their faith in their producers. (This was precisely the system that blew up in Dan Rather's face and caused him such grief over the George Bush Air National Guard story in 2004.) I told Davis I would do a few interviews for him but until I saw a rough cut of his program I would not sign on as the narrator.

That fall I did do two interviews — the first with Assistant Secretary of Defense for Public Affairs Daniel Z. Henkin, a well-liked former newspaperman, and the second with Jack Tolbert, a former Air Force public information officer, who delighted in telling me how he had conned CBS News into putting out a favorable report on the U.S. bombing campaign against North Vietnam.

In early December, Davis came to Washington to show me his rough draft. For whatever reasons — and I have forgotten them now — I said no. Not until after Christmas, when Davis had eliminated many of what he called his "conclusory" remarks from his draft, did I agree. Davis was approaching the final stages of production without an assigned correspondent, so he was greatly relieved when I said yes.[2] So much for my insistence on doing my own reporting. Faced with the choice between reading what was written for me and not getting on the air in prime time, I caved, just as most network correspondents would have caved.

Actually I did more than just narrate, but after twenty-five years I sometimes wish I had also helped with a bit of the film editing.

During January of 1971 I was busy on the Hill — Robert Byrd had ousted Ted Kennedy as Senate whip, the appropriation bill for the development of a supersonic transport plane was headed toward defeat on the Senate floor, and the Senate Foreign Relations Committee was in the vortex of the Vietnam debate.

In New York, Davis was editing and bringing the second rough draft into final form, dealing with a series of obstacles and spending more time than usual with Salant and Bill Leonard, the vice president for "soft" news. Davis said his two bosses, "who generally saw our documentaries only once before air time, must have seen the Pentagon film a dozen times."[3] What was bothering Salant and Leonard was Davis's inclusion in the program of a 1952 Pentagon propaganda film, *The Eagle's Talon,* which dealt with America's response to communism. The film's narrator intoned: "To meet immediate threats on any front we must build up our land forces at home and overseas. This soldier, guarding one of Asia's gateways against Soviet aggression, symbolizes the determination of free men everywhere to resist communist expansion by force of arms."[4]

What bothered Salant and Leonard was not so much those lines; what bothered them was that they were uttered by none other than the trusted star of CBS News and TV journalism's new icon, Walter Cronkite. They were worried, said Davis, "how to tell [Cronkite] about it, how to get him not to complain." The job of telling Cronkite was given to Salant's "hard" news deputy, Gordon Manning, who was scheduled to accompany Walter on a trip to the Middle East in early 1971. Salant told Manning he should tell Cronkite in an "Oh, by the way" tone that the Pentagon show would be using a clip from a Pentagon film he narrated during the Cold War. It was no big deal, Manning was to say. Manning decided to wait until after Walter had interviewed Egypt's President Nasser. But the flight from Cairo to Tel Aviv was so short that Manning put it off again. And when they flew back to New York, Cronkite was so exhausted that Manning thought he'd better wait a little longer. So Manning, hardly anxious to confront Cronkite generally, never told Cronkite and the job got bounced back to Salant. When Salant broke the news, Walter said, and said reasonably, "Let me see the piece." Perry Wolf, the executive producer, and Davis screened the entire film for him. When it was over, Cronkite turned to Davis and said, "Fine job." But on the long walk down the narrow corridor from the screening room to the front office of the CBS News building, Cronkite turned to Salant and said, "All right, get that piece out of there." Salant told Walter his clip would have to stay in because it had been furnished by the Pentagon and without it the Pentagon would beat CBS over the head with the omission and trash the entire broadcast.

Our insistence on keeping the Cronkite segment put another chill on my relations with the anchorman. My speech a month earlier at Washington and Lee University had put me in general disfavor with the New York office. Added to that, Cronkite had heard — and heard accurately — that I had complained about his plug for Pan American Airways in a radio commentary from the Caribbean.

To add to Davis's problems, the CBS

lawyers were vetting the program repeatedly, looking for anything they thought might be "actionable." (The actor Robert Stack and John A. MacNeill, one of the Pentagon's so-called traveling colonels who lectured around the country on foreign policy, both brought multi-million-dollar suits against CBS after the broadcast.)[5]

"The Selling of the Pentagon" ran on Tuesday, February 23, 1971, at 10 PM, an exposition of how the Pentagon spent an estimated $30 million a year to win the public's approval for its weapons of war. Denunciations started before the program was over. *Newsweek* reported that at 10:14 PM an outraged viewer called the CBS Washington bureau to flail me as "an agent of a foreign power." Next came the Air Force colonel who promised to remove the nose from my face. By 11 PM the switchboard at CBS in New York had logged five hundred calls, at least half of them berating me and CBS.[6]

We were prepared for criticism but not for its unrelenting ferocity over the next five months. Democrats F. Edward Hébert of New Orleans, the ex-newspaper editor and chairman of the House Armed Services Committee, and Harley Staggers, former

449

West Virginia sheriff and chairman of the House Interstate and Foreign Commerce Committee, led the attack, backed up by both the Pentagon and the country's military industrial complex.

Neither man attacked the accuracy of the documentary; neither man denied that the Pentagon had a bloated public-affairs budget that was used to propagandize; neither man denied that the Pentagon promoted military solutions to international problems; and neither man denied that the Pentagon tried to persuade the big industrialists to support an ever-larger military budget.

What they attacked was the editing of the film, and in particular the editing of my interview with Dan Henkin, a strategy that Salant called a sham to avoid dealing with the issues the program raised. Peter Davis said the charges were "political, not journalistic. No one ever produced a scintilla of evidence that anything in the broadcast was trumped up, distorted, or unfair."[7]

Film editing is difficult to explain, its terms arcane and its techniques mysterious. But Dan Henkin's bald accusation that CBS had not played straight with him was uncomplicated, easy to believe, and very effective.

In his letter to Chairman Hébert, this was

Henkin's charge:

> Needless to say, as a person who has spent his life in the news profession, I could not be pleased by the fact that the program's producer chose to rearrange my words as given during an interview of more than one hour with the CBS narrator. In one instance, CBS censored the first sentence of a reply I made, and then put in two sentences which were lifted from my answer to a different question.[8]

Henkin was dead wrong to accuse us of censoring the first sentence of one of his answers (a line-by-line comparison of the broadcast transcript with the interview transcript proves him wrong), but he was right in accusing us of rearranging his words. The CBS explanation was that the rearrangement of his words was benign and did not distort Henkin, only tightened and improved his argument.

In the world of television documentary editing, Davis's "rearrangement" would be viewed as standard in technique, minor in substance, and virtually harmless in effect. Our honest acknowledgment, however, that we moved sentences around, rearranged them out of order, and took an answer from one question and attached it to another left us seriously vulnerable.

All the Pentagon and the politicians had to do was utter the dread phrase, "they took us out of context," then sit back and enjoy the show.

Hébert, who had succeeded Mendel Rivers as chairman of Armed Services only a month earlier, led the way with almost daily press releases and TV blasts, calling the program "un-American," "Goebbels-like," and filled with "false innuendoes." Hébert knew how to play the press game. As the political editor of the New Orleans *Times-Picayune*, he had helped send a Louisiana governor and LSU's president to prison. He was also, according to Dan Rapoport of UPI, "unbending in his rightist ideology, shrewd in combat, flamboyant in style, and comfortable with power."[9] CBS found him to be all of the above. Salant claimed it was Hébert who was "so instrumental in persuading" Harley Staggers to open an investigation of CBS.[10] A day or two later, *Air Force Magazine* weighed in, saying Davis was "less interested in responsive answers that made sense than he was in portraying Mr. Henkin as a bureaucratic buffoon."[11] Meg Greenfield, in a series of editorials in the *Washington Post,* thought the Pentagon had a point about the CBS editing. And on St. Patrick's Day in Boston, Vice President Agnew, whose 1969 speech attacking TV's "small band of self-appointed analysts" set network teeth on edge, kicked in with his review of the program: "A subtle but vicious broadside against the nation's defense establishment."[12]

The intense political heat was almost too much for Salant. On March 23 he ordered "The Selling of the Pentagon" to be rerun, partly as a rationale for broadcasting the comments of the critics — in this case, Agnew, Defense Secretary Melvin Laird, and Hébert. Salant tried to answer them but, alas, his twenty-two-minute rejoinder seemed to drift off course and never came to grips with the "rearrangement" issue. He did say "the validity of the broadcast stands unscathed. . . . We are proud of 'The Selling of the Pentagon' and CBS News stands behind it. We are confident that when passions die down, it will be recognized as a vital contribution to the people's right to know."[13] Not for another fifteen years did Salant reveal what he thought about the "rearrangement." In his memoir, written in the late 1980s, Salant wrote, "Of all the criticisms of this broadcast, the editing of

Henkin, I believe, raised the most legitimate questions; the issue was ambiguous. While I am convinced that the editing was not intentionally mischievous and that it fairly reflected Henkin's statements, it is possible that the editors misunderstood him."[14] For a lawyer with Salant's skill, that last sentence is not only mushy but also baffling. If the edited version "fairly reflected" Henkin's statement, then the editors could not have "misunderstood him." The boss, I fear, was wiggling and waffling.

As much as Salant hoped that the passions would die down after his March commentary, they did not. They grew even more inflamed. On April 7, and by a unanimous vote, Harley Staggers and his five-member Special Subcommittee on Investigations issued a subpoena to CBS for all tapes, films, outtakes, and script material that had been issued in the production of "The Selling of the Pentagon." A week later CBS lawyers gave the Staggers subcommittee a copy of the film and a complete script of the program but refused to turn over outtakes, telephone records, draft notes, payments to those who were interviewed, and anything else that had been subpoenaed. On July 1, the day the full Commerce Committee was scheduled to vote on the contempt citation, Chairman Staggers asked Frank Stanton, president of CBS, to come to his office. According to Stanton, Staggers told him if he would only show him just "some" of the outtakes so that he "could tell the committee we haven't cheated, so to speak," he would forget about the whole thing. When Stanton refused, the white-haired, cherub-faced Staggers said, "You need divine guidance and I want you to pray." Staggers then knelt down "behind his desk and wanted me to join him. And I declined and this so infuriated him that he dismissed me."[15]

The full committee voted that day twenty-five to thirteen to cite Stanton for contempt. When Staggers opened debate on the floor on July 13 he was still confused about the issues. He insisted the First Amendment was not at stake because the committee was not asking for notes from me as the reporter but only film shot by a cameraman "and not somebody who was asking the questions. But the cameraman," said Staggers, "he is the man who actually did the work, acted in good faith." In other words because the cameraman's work was mechanical and did not involve "any man's thoughts, any man's notes or concepts, or anything that he had in his mind," there had been no invasion of the First Amendment. From there, Staggers went on to accuse CBS of "deception" and "fabrication." In his speech, Staggers imagined for the House what went on at CBS News after the Henkin interview:

They took eleven months to take this into some darkroom somewhere and to say, "All right, this man said something that we did not want him to say. So we are going to take an answer from another question over here, and make him say something he did not say." And he did not say it. We know this because we have the testimony, the sworn testimony of the Assistant Secretary of Defense that he did not make them in this sequence; he did not say these things.[16]

Henkin never testified or implied or suggested that he had not said those things, only that they were not in sequence. But Staggers knew he had no case if it rested solely on our "rearrangement," so he equated "rearrangement" with "fabrication."

The galleries were packed the day the debate started, but I was not at my usual spot in the TV section overlooking the floor. I was in the visitors' gallery just behind, because CBS News had taken me off the story, as it should have, and assigned it to George Herman. In fact, during that spring and summer CBS made my role in "The Selling of the Pentagon" invisible. I was the nameless narrator. My name was never heard or mentioned in testimony or in floor speeches or in press releases. It was as if I didn't exist. The CBS strategy, drawn up by Kidder Meade, the corporate public relations chief, was to have Frank Stanton "to be out front as the symbol, the ideal. Frank stood for the First Amendment," said Meade. "He was a pure person. People couldn't say he was up to hanky-panky or part of the jet set."[17] Not until the day of the vote did my name crop up, when Democrat Robert Eckhardt of Texas asked for unanimous consent to "revise and extend [my] remarks in the manner of Roger Mudd."[18] Eckhardt had seen me in the gallery and looked up with a laugh when he made his request.

To sit in the gallery and listen to the House debating your own broadcast and its veracity is an out-of-body experience, as if your life belongs to someone else. Customarily, congressional reporters cover appropriation bills for HEW or the Justice Department, amendments to the Voting

457

Rights Act, leadership negotiations on the pending business or an adjournment, partisan outbursts about the economy or the president's appointments, and so forth, but almost never themselves. Reporters tend to work at unemotional remove from what they're covering. They're not so much interested in the rightness or the morality of the legislation as they are in the politics of the bill — when will the bill get out of committee, is the chairman powerful enough to convince a majority on the floor, and will the Senate go along? So it was with the debate on "The Selling of the Pentagon."

I was only vaguely aware of the stakes involved for CBS and TV news. Not until much later did I read what I had been a part of and witnessing — "a milestone in the development of the television documentary" and a "clear statement that the networks could not be made to bend to government control." I found that I was less worried about whether Frank Stanton went to jail than I was itching to see whether Staggers could pull enough moderates along with him to approve the contempt citation.

In the end, it was a few conservatives who denied Staggers and his committee their victory. Looking back to that day, I now realize that if I had a hero from the debate, he was Jack Edwards, an ex-Marine, a lawyer, and a Goldwater Republican from Mobile, Alabama. It was Edwards who turned Staggers on his head:

It would be ever so easy to vote "yes" today. CBS has maligned the South, colored the news, handled the coverage of the war in a biased manner, played up the bad, and played down the good — all of this and more. But I would not exchange all this, as bad as it may be, for the evil that would infect this nation from a controlled press. Oh, there are times when I get so exasperated with them I would like to ban all TV, but that exasperation is nothing compared to what it would be if we had a press that had to answer for its editorial judgment, however bad, to a committee of the Congress.[19]

Just before the vote, Staggers pointed to the frieze above the Speaker's podium. "In God We Trust," quoted Staggers. "Are we going to change it to 'In the Networks We Trust'?"
But when they called the roll, Staggers went down in flames, a rare rebuke to a powerful, twelve-term committee chairman.

The vote was 226 to 181.[20] It was the first time in its history that the House had rejected a recommendation for contempt. Staggers told reporters, "Lord, I'm disappointed. The networks now control the Congress."[21]

Why Staggers lost is up for grabs. Fred Friendly, a former president of CBS News, thought it wasn't so much that the Congress believed in the First Amendment as that it was vulnerable to the pressure applied by the sympathetic CBS affiliates to their local representatives.[22] Salant credited the last-minute lobbying by two committee chairmen perhaps more powerful than Staggers — Wilbur Mills and Emanuel Celler — in persuading their fellow chairmen to break ranks.[23] Corydon Dunham, for many years general counsel at NBC, credits in his account Republican James T. Broyhill of North Carolina and columnist James J. Kilpatrick with persuading sixteen conservative Republicans to reject the citation.[24] And *Variety* magazine reported that President Nixon's special counsel, Charles Colson, claimed he had made a deal with CBS to influence the GOP House members in return for softer coverage of the White House.[25]

Stanton instantly became a media hero. He regarded his decision to defy the Congress as one of the high points of his public life, thankful that his contempt case never got to court, where the outcome would have turned on whether radio and television are protected by the First Amendment. A court of law was the last place the networks wanted to argue the issue, so fearful were they of losing that no decision was better than a bad one. Salant, who claimed ultimate responsibility for the Pentagon documentary, felt he was risking Stanton's freedom and at one point briefly considered resigning to save his boss.[26] But in truth, Stanton was never really in much danger of going to jail. Had the House held him in contempt, the citation would have gone to the Justice Department for possible prosecution. Stanton has said that while President Nixon was probably delighted to "see me get my sleeves caught in the gear box," he thought it highly unlikely that Nixon would have given Attorney General John Mitchell a green light to prosecute,[27] given the political danger in having a Republican attorney general prosecuting a distinguished American media executive for contempt against a Democratic Congress.

During the weeks following the broadcast

and the House vote, Peter Davis was tied up writing memos and dealing with what the CBS lawyers called "interlocutories" pertaining to the Stack and MacNeill lawsuits — suits that were thrown out in the end. Davis did go on the lecture circuit briefly, but CBS stopped him after his third speech. "So, in a sense," Davis recalls, "I was muzzled. But CBS had a lot more at stake than just the defense of one television program. The conglomerate's entire relationship with the government was on the line, which involved a great deal of commercial interest well beyond the simple accreditations from the FCC, besides access for their Washington journalists. . . ."[28]

Frank Stanton recalled later that he sent Chairman Staggers a four-page, handwritten letter after the vote, trying once again to explain his refusal to submit and, not incidentally, hoping to repair a severely damaged relationship with the chairman of the legislative committee that had life-and-death power over the networks. But, said Stanton, Staggers "never forgave me."[29]

After the turmoil died down, Davis was offered a plum — a documentary on the Rockefeller family. Before he could get started, he got an offer from a California film production company, an offer that led to his leaving CBS News to make his Vietnam film, *Hearts and Minds*, which won him an Oscar in 1974.[30]

But the turmoil over the editing of the Pentagon film continues to erupt from time to time. Thirty years later some conservatives were still fuming. In *The Weekly Standard*, John Podhoretz wrote one of my exchanges with Dan Henkin was "concocted" and that Davis and I had filmed a question after the interview so as to fit Henkin's answer and then "edited it in."[31]

In a letter to Podhoretz, dated April 19, 2005, I explained that because the Henkin interview was shot with two cameras, there was no need to reshoot anything. Podhoretz never answered my repeated requests over a period of two years for the source of his accusation.

So that still leaves the questions: Was the editing of "The Selling of the Pentagon" within the bounds of fair journalism? Was there distortion? Was Henkin taken out of context?

My answers are "Yes," "No," and "Just a little bit."

Putting together a documentary, stitching together its disparate parts, and weaving in a narrative involves working under the constant pressure of balance, pace, length, the need for pictures, the search for revealing sound bites, and the choice of significant detail. Thus, the need to condense is great, to eliminate the extraneous and to jettison whole chunks of interviews because of defective questions, nonresponsive answers, and worthless meanderings off the subject.

But to be in public life is to be edited. Some understand why it's necessary and how the system works. Others regard their words as too portentous to be edited. Henry Kissinger, after he left government, where he could not control the media's editing of his public remarks, decided as a private citizen not to go on television unless live, thereby eliminating what he regarded as the evils of being edited. That meant, of course, his appearances became generally limited to the morning news shows, the Sunday talk shows, *Charlie Rose,* and PBS's *NewsHour with Jim Lehrer,* a restriction that has done no apparent damage to either his celebrity or his consulting fees.

Newspaper reporters are constant rearrangers of words, eliminators of spoken waste, and inflators of telling quotes, but I cannot recall a single newspaper or newspaper reporter being hauled before the Interstate Commerce Committees of the

Congress and ordered to cough up note-books or recordings from their interviews. The explanation is, I think, threefold: First, the press is truly protected by the First Amendment, whereas television's constitutional protection is unsettled and the industry remains vulnerable to government edict; second, rarely does the interviewee, unless a high-ranking government or corporate executive, have his own and complete recording of the interview with which to charge "rearrangement" or "fabrication" or "deception"; and third, the same quote seen in print can be ten times more damaging when seen on the tube, thus inviting political retribution against TV. The contrast between the black-and-white printed word and the televised word is stark and dramatic. In the one case, the words are flat, inanimate, and attached to nothing but a name. But in the other, the words can be heard and almost watched coming from the mouth of a face that has expression and in a voice that has tone, inflection, accent, feeling, even innuendo. The senator or the CEO or the assistant secretary can accuse the newspaper reporter of "misquoting" him, but it becomes virtually impossible for them to deny having said what millions of viewers heard and watched them say. Only when those words have been "rearranged" do the interviewees have a chance to lessen the damage of the words by attacking the motives and integrity of the "rearrangers."

The fallout from "The Selling of the Pentagon" left CBS News with considerable scar tissue. Stanton's celebrity did not sit well with Bill Paley, the founder, owner, and chairman of CBS. In fact, it stuck in his craw. So determined was Paley to reenter the swirl that he went to Washington to lobby Speaker Carl Albert, not knowing that Albert's political clout had lost its punch. "Even worse," wrote Paley's biographer, "Paley had in his back pocket a compromise ready to offer Albert." If Stanton feared that Paley had been trying to deal behind his back, Stanton himself had also tried to cut a deal without actually dealing or cutting. In late June, a week before the Staggers committee vote, Speaker Albert was informed that Stanton had issued a new set of CBS News operating standards: that combining answers in an interview or moving answers out of their chronological order had to be revealed in the lead-in narration or in the internal narration or in a "crawl" across the bottom of the screen, and that copies of unedited transcripts from interviews were to be available to the inter-viewees upon request. Such changes, which went straight to the heart of the Staggers-Hébert complaints, were presented in a let-ter from Stanton to Albert on July 7, a week before the House vote.[32] Whether the re-vised standards were ever enforced or remained on paper still is in question.

Despite CBS's victory in the House, Paley remained irritated for weeks, complaining about the film editing in "The Selling of the Pentagon" and telling a group of CBS executives that Stanton made a "mistake" in defending a defective program. A dis-heartened Stanton must have seen what was coming. Late that year, Paley forced him out as president, demoting him to vice chairman even as Paley was rewriting the terms of his own contract so he could continue leading CBS as long as he wished.[33]

CHAPTER 37
THE STAKEOUT
QUEENS

Whatever complaints Bill Paley had about "The Selling of the Pentagon," the program got the Best Documentary Emmy that year. And regardless of his carping about the program, it did mark the first time a TV network, this one in the person of Frank Stanton, refused to bend a knee to government control.

The turmoil in the executive offices of CBS in New York — three corporate presidents in less than a year — had little immediate effect on the Washington bureau. We were caught up in covering one of the country's fattest news years of all: the shooting of George Wallace, the presidential primaries, Nixon's trip to China and the Soviet Union, the Watergate break-in, the presidential conventions, the Nixon-McGovern campaign, the reelection of Nixon, and the final troop withdrawal from Vietnam. And as each new story piled on top of the others, the news division management responded with a fresh injection of reportorial and production talent.

In 1961, the year I started with CBS, the Washington bureau had nine reporters; three years later we totaled eleven; five years later we were up to seventeen. But between 1971 and 1972 we reached twenty-four correspondents and reporters with the addition of Nelson Benton, a transfer from the Atlanta bureau; Phil Jones, back to the States from Vietnam and Hong Kong; Fred Graham, hired away from the *New York Times;* Bernard Shaw from the Westinghouse D.C. bureau; and Connie Chung, John Meyer, Tony Sargent, and Lesley Stahl, all plucked out of local television.

Until Chung and Stahl arrived, CBS Washington had one woman reporter, Marya McLaughlin, and until Shaw arrived one black reporter — Hal Walker.

McLaughlin, born and raised in Baltimore and a graduate of Marymount College in Tarrytown, New York, had come over from NBC in 1963 as an associate producer but soon enough became a reporter and then a correspondent. Her mind was sharp, her wit was sharp, but her elbows were not. During those crowded hallway press conferences on Capitol Hill the camera's cutaway shots showed her in the crowd but rarely up front, never body-slamming her way past a competitor, and only when the press conference was winding down would you hear McLaughlin asking her question, the question she been waiting to ask until all the others had had their turn at playing "Gotcha." The late Eugene McCarthy, with whom McLaughlin lived during the last decade of her life, told me he often warned her she would need steel fingernails to survive, but she just wouldn't wear them.

It was her sense of the absurd that got her through, I think. She worked on the Hill irregularly but still had nicknames for the more portentous members. Carl Curtis of Nebraska was "Piglet." Charles Percy of Illinois was "Furry Feet."

She and the other second- and third-stringers didn't have desks and didn't have offices. One day McLaughlin brought in some miniature doll furniture and arranged it in her mail tray so that it looked like a dwarfed office. It became the talk of the bureau because it was funny and because Mr. Small did not think it was funny.

In a bureau where all the other women were secretaries and worked for men, McLaughlin felt the natural restraint of being the only one who didn't. She decided she would not be a threat to anyone.

But with the coming of Chung and Stahl there were now three women reporters who were routinely assigned the bureau's grunt work — the predawn stakeouts, the minor congressional hearings, press conferences of little consequence — which threw them into the all-male rough-and-tumble world of camera crews and courier corps.

Most of the men got along with Chung, because she had a robust sense of humor and was not afraid to play their game. Chung says she played the game because "I was trying to get rid of them so I could just do my job. They were always chasing me." But she was also easy to work with. She was smart enough to say, "I need help," and in asking for help, says Tom Bettag, "she got a lot of help."

But the ink-stained wretches still love to tell stories about Chung, stories that they enlarge upon with every telling. Everybody's favorite occurred during the 1972 presidential campaign, according to Jim Naughton of the *New York Times.* Chung was up earlier and stayed at it longer than anyone else, says Naughton, "always nosing about the campaign's edges." One evening he spotted her in a phone booth in the lobby of the old Biltmore Hotel in Manhattan working on what was obviously a major story. In an attempt to tease Chung about her intense work habits, Naughton says he and Jules Witcover of the *Baltimore Sun* "sauntered over to the glassed-in phone booth and pressed our noses against the door, mugging for Connie's benefit." Chung never missed a beat. She cupped the receiver between her neck and shoulder, opened the booth, and "without any pause in her phone conversation . . . reached out both hands and simultaneously unzipped both of our flies. I didn't miss any deadline, nor did Connie. But I got the hell out of there as fast as possible."[1]

Asked years later whether that had actually happened, Chung said at first she had no memory of it "but it's such a great story I think you should use it." Later she said, "I think I remember it. It sounds like something I would have done back then." Naughton acknowledges that his memory has loosened up a bit but is sure his fellow prankster was Witcover, "although it might have been Walter Mears." Witcover says he has "absolutely no memory of the incident" and Mears says it couldn't have been him because "back then there were buttons on my fly."

Chung was not known so much for her

writing as she was for her happy persistence; she would go anywhere and do anything she was told to do. When President Nixon made a critical remark about George Meany, Chung was sent in pursuit of Meany at the AFL-CIO building. She found him getting on an elevator. As the doors were closing, she hopped on, microphone in hand but leaving her camera crew behind. As the elevator descended, soundman Tommy Novak fed out the mike cable as fast as he could so she could at least conduct a sound-only interview with the trapped Meany. The interview ended when the mike suddenly popped out of Chung's hand.

In May 1972, when Richard Kleindienst was undergoing a grilling during his confirmation hearings to be attorney general, Chung and her camera crew were staked out on the sidewalk, waiting for him to emerge. CBS had sent her after him for an exclusive interview. When he did emerge he jumped into his government limousine without speaking and drove off but was chased by Chung and her crew. They chased him all the way into the Maryland suburbs to the all-male Burning Tree Club. Unaware of the males-only rule, Chung charged after him into the club, where, she said, she was "unceremoniously kicked out." When Kleindienst heard about her expulsion he gave her "as a reward" a brief interview the next day. Chung said she always thought him a "lecherous soul."

Bill Small hired Chung from one of the local TV stations after watching her barge into *Le Provençal* restaurant with her camera crew for a story on health violations. Small says that he was so impressed he gave her his card in case she wanted to talk about a job at CBS. "Yeah, yeah, yeah," she said, and stuck the card in her pocket. "An hour later," Small says, "she called."

A local girl, a graduate of the University of Maryland, and the daughter of an official in Chiang Kai-shek's Nationalist Chinese government, Chung recalls that she tried to preempt the ethnic jokes about her by using them herself. She insisted that the only reason Small had hired her was because he "loved the way I did his shirts."

But Chung's brass was not always admired. On the McGovern campaign, David Schoumacher was told to take Chung around with him "supposedly to train her," but instead, he says, "I found her on the phone behind my back selling stories to the *Evening News*."

Lesley Stahl had a rougher time, especially with Bill Galbraith on the assignment desk.

"She could be a bitch," he says. "She was unhappy because I made her stand in the rain on a stakeout for John Dean, Nixon's chief counsel. I don't think she's ever forgotten that." Stahl denies any bad feelings toward Galbraith, although she has written that he had "little use for women and minorities."[2] Stahl's great dread in the beginning was dealing with the camera crews. They would humiliate her in public, she says. "I would say, 'Could you get me that shot?' and they would mimic me, 'Could you get me that shot?' in front of everyone. I was dreading just being with them." But Stahl learned quickly that if she knew everything there was to know about a story, the crews would come around. "Not, 'What does *she* know?' " The crews, she says, could see right through a bluff. "If you don't know what you're doing, they can smell it."

Thirty years old when she joined the bureau, Stahl had twice the experience of most of the new hires. The daughter of a wealthy Massachusetts businessman — "Stahl Finish" and "Stahl Polyvinyl" — and a cum laude graduate of Wheaton College, she moved from the speechwriting shop of New York mayor John Lindsay to NBC's political unit to NBC's London bureau to reporting for the CBS station in Boston, WDHD.

When she arrived in Washington she was apprenticed to Daniel Schorr and the Watergate story. She complained about the system and the "degrading" assignments, but she made her early name as the "stakeout queen."

The third 1972 affirmative-action baby was Bernard Shaw, CBS's second black reporter. He was also not quite a fledging just out of the nest. Right out of high school in Chicago, Shaw joined the Marine Corps for a four-year stretch, started at the University of Illinois the day after he was discharged, worked his way through college by moonlighting at three different Chicago radio stations, and in 1968 came to Washington as part of the Westinghouse bureau.

The son of a Chicago house painter and a mother he called a domestic — "she scrubbed floors" — Shaw was an even-tempered, deliberate, and seemingly imperturbable thirty-one-year-old when Small offered him a job at CBS. "I was virtually numb," he says. "Since I was thirteen all I wanted to be was a CBS correspondent."

His first days in the bureau could not have been what he had dreamed about — covering four and five stories in one day and never getting on the air with one of them. Shaw remembers one day in which his first story ended up in my piece, another in another piece, and because of "Walter's magic number," a third one as a voice-over with a sound bite.[3] Despite his anger at the system, Shaw concedes that it was "great training."

CHAPTER 38
"I THINK I GOT IT — I HOPE I GOT IT"

During the great influx of talent in the early seventies, not only reporters were being hired but also desk assistants and associate producers. Rita Braver had just moved to town from New Orleans with her husband, who was starting a Supreme Court clerkship with Associate Justice Byron White. Braver's job was to take in radio spots and help move the camera crews from one spot to another. Braver had worked at WWL in New Orleans as a copygirl, writer, and producer, so she knew the score. Her first day at CBS was Monday, May 15, 1972. "I was just a kid," she says, "and I felt like I was watching giants and was so lucky to be breathing the same air."

Her first day at CBS was also the day George Wallace was shot at a shopping mall in Laurel, Maryland. David Dick, who was on his second Wallace presidential campaign, had just been cleared to leave the

Laurel rally and head toward the bureau to put together a piece for the Cronkite show on Wallace's day in Maryland. Dick's cameraman, the absolutely fearless Laurens Pierce of Montgomery, Alabama, said he wanted to stay behind for a few more shots he needed and waded into the crowd with Wallace.

Dick and Pierce had decided before the campaign they would not do what they called the standard New York treatment of Wallace's state troopers and "his goon friends. We were going to get to know them," Dick says. "We were going to be good ol' boys with 'em and because the Secret Service knew us and liked us, Pierce and I were able to move with Wallace inside the SS circle."

Indeed, Pierce was the only TV cameraman inside the circle that afternoon when Arthur Bremer, another of America's misfits, fired four or five shots into Wallace. Dick was nearing the bureau on M Street when he heard the announcer break into WTOP radio with a bulletin on the shooting. Pierce was on his way to the bureau with his precious film. He had commandeered a Singer Sewing Machine delivery truck and, waving a crisp fifty-dollar bill as a token of encouragement, told the driver to ride the sidewalks if he had to.[1]

The minute Pierce arrived at the bureau I went on the air live to interview him as a rare firsthand witness. As we all waited in the editing room for the film to emerge from the developing chemicals, Pierce paced back and forth, sweating out what we knew was the only film of the shooting. This was film, not video, so nobody knew what they had until they actually saw it. David Dick was also worried, because "almost always there was a hair in the gate of any film Pierce shot." A "hair in the gate" is what the film editors call a piece of dirt on the film, like a floater in the eye and usually enough to keep a piece of film off the air. In addition, Dick says, "Pierce was forever fiddling with his camera with Scotch tape and chewing gum and anything else he could get his hands on to hold it together." So Pierce was really sweating and pacing. Bruce Morton remembered Pierce saying over and over, "I think I got it. I mean, I hope I got it. I feel like I got it."

Not only did Pierce have it, he had it clean. His film was graphic, revealing, and totally exclusive, and it helped convict Bremer. Seven years earlier it had been Pierce's film of the police brutality at the Edmund Pettus Bridge in Selma, Alabama,

480

that outraged the nation and led to the Voting Rights Act of 1965. (Our coverage of the Wallace shooting won CBS five Emmys — for Pierce, of course, but also for Dick, Cronkite, Rather, and me.)

Dick was distraught at the time, because he hadn't stayed behind with Pierce. On the way to Holy Cross Hospital in Silver Spring, Maryland, Dick kept pounding on the dashboard "because my guy had gone down and I wasn't there to report it."[2]

But Dick regrouped and recouped nicely. He and Pierce, known at the hospital as "friends of the family," were consistently beating the opposition on the Wallace story, which drove correspondent Cassie Mackin of NBC News to distraction.

And when Dick heard Barbara Walters promoting her coming exclusive with Cornelia Wallace, he and Pierce simply knocked on Cornelia's door at the Holiday Inn near the hospital and talked her into their own exclusive. Walters threw what Dick called a "sizeable fit" that night when she saw Cornelia on the Cronkite show. When an editor on the assignment desk congratulated Dick, she told him, "It's not every day you get to screw Barbara Walters."

CHAPTER 39
"STAND BY FOR A RAM"

The contest was of minor consequence, but it was ferocious. During every presidential news conference the three network Washington bureaus raced to see which would be the first to identify and flash on the screen the names of the reporters who stood to question the president. The CBS control room would be jammed with everybody trying to help, yelling out the names of those they knew. We would watch NBC and ABC on the monitors and hoot every time we got a name up before they did. It was one of those esoteric forms of competition between the three bureaus that meant little to the viewer but drove the bureau chiefs crazy if they lost.

CBS won most of the early races, but not until 1974 did we take the trophy every time. Sandy Socolow, the new bureau chief, says he sat down with his number two, Bill Headline, and "we decided — goddamn it

— we were going to super the identification of every reporter. This had never been done before. Headline and I worked out a scheme — just the two of us — the first time it had happened and we were scared if it didn't happen, but it succeeded beyond our wildest dreams."

It succeeded because of a young, self-starting, and very bright technician named Carol Hamedy. "CBS brought down a machine," she recalled recently — "a title machine, the Vidifont — and it had a keyboard and the guys all looked at it and said let the girl do it. And in the CBS tradition, they never taught anybody how to run anything or how it operated. You had to figure it out yourself. So I was putting up titles and punching them in and I needed to recognize people at the press conferences." Supplied with the names of all the White House reporters, Hamedy simply loaded them into the Vidifont, giving each a number. Then, when she heard a name called out, she punched the reporter's number on the keyboard and up came his or her name on the screen. With Joan Barone, from the *Face the Nation* staff — who seemed to know the name of every reporter who had ever been born — standing at Hamedy's side, CBS won every time.

Hamedy, from a Lebanese family in Flint, Michigan, came to the bureau in the middle of Watergate, hired as a union technician, and for the first few months she hauled TV cables with the men at the White House. Television was then gradually converting from film to videotape, and with her degree in communications from American University, she learned fast. She became the bureau's second videotape editor and was soon teaching the film editors, Ray Cramer, Lee Shepp, Charlie Ryan, and Don Le-Blanc, how to work with videotape. In turn, they taught her the rules of editing — never put two shots together if both are zooming in or zooming out and never combine a shot that is zooming in with one that is zooming out.

Switching from film to videotape was relatively seamless, although the early video cameras did not produce high-quality pictures. It was the ease of editing videotape that was the leap forward, allowing the electronic transfer of pictures and sound from the camera's tape cassette to a larger so-called show reel. Roughly comparable to the copy-and-paste combination in computer editing, the use of videotape saved time, money, and nerves. Hamedy estimated that videotape gave the editors an additional hour of editing time. It also meant the videotape could hit the bureau an hour later than film.

What Cramer, Shepp, Ryan, and LeBlanc left behind was a complicated, stressful, high-wire act that could produce beautiful pictures but burned-out editors. It was, however, the creative skill of the camera crews who shot the pictures and the editors who shaped them that made television news unique. For all the money and publicity lavished on the correspondents, they would have been reduced to mere talking heads without the realism and the punch that film and video gave their reporting.

But even with videotape there was always the photo finish. Not more than fifty yards from the bureau was a small triangular park formed by the intersections of M Street, New Hampshire Avenue, and Twentieth Street. It became an easy and favorite spot for the correspondents to do their last-minute, on-camera stand-uppers. The triangle, however, was also a favorite spot for drunks and vagrants. Ike Pappas was only minutes from air one evening, his copy memorized, the crew in place, and his producer standing by at the front door of the bureau. As Pappas started to record, he noticed out of the corner of his eye "this guy coming toward me. . . . He had no shirt on. He comes up to me, 'You an American?' "

"Oh, God," Pappas said to himself.

"Yes, I am," he said. "Would you please give me a minute? I've got to get on the air. Would you please stand over there?"

Just then another guy appeared, who blathered, "You 'merican flerb in that TV gluff over at the nabshru?"

Pappas was desperate. Quietly he said, "Yes, I'm an American. You are an American. We are all Americans. But I must do this. You understand that? So if you go over there and just wait for thirty seconds, I'll be done. I'll talk to you and I may even buy you a beer. But get out of my life."

The men moved off. Pappas finished his close, dodged the traffic on M Street, and handed the cassette to his waiting producer, who dashed into the control room, where a technician slapped it on the machine just in time.

The triangle is still in use and was named in honor of the bureau chief who followed Bill Small in 1974. It is called "Socolow Park."

Along the east wall of our newsroom was a line of four edit rooms, each equipped with a hand-cranked Moviola for viewing film fast-forward and backward, a hot-glue splicer, and a three-foot-high barrel. Attached to and rigged two or three feet above each barrel was a metal crossbar that held a row of short, thin, stiff wires from which the editor hung strands of film into the barrel in the precise order they were to appear in the story. If the editors were pushing a deadline, heading for what they feared might be a "crash and burn" ending, they would double up on the story. As the first editor went through the film on the Moviola, locating the required scenes and hanging them up over the barrel, the second editor worked just behind the first, lining up the sprockets, scraping off a frame or two of film emulsion, and hot splicing as he went.

The scene sequence was dictated by the narration, which the correspondent wrote and recorded in the field or wrote in the bureau after watching the film. With a stopwatch the producer timed each paragraph of the narration so the editor knew exactly how long each length of film had to be and in what order. Twenty-four frames equaled a second.

Whether the correspondents had learned to write with precision and write to the pictures was critical for the producers and editors who handled our copy each evening. Their opinion of each correspondent, therefore, came from a different angle.

Bruce Morton was their favorite, because he never wrote without seeing the film first. Ike Pappas was difficult to edit, because Pentagon policy stories lacked pictures. Fred Graham was easy to work with, but it took him six or eight tries to do his stand-ups. I was slow but was regarded as the bureau's best writer, next to Morton. Marvin Kalb was very fast, very neat. Not a terrific writer but he got it all in. Dan Rather's writing was just OK. Dan Schorr could turn it out and was very accurate.

As 6:30 PM got closer and closer, everyone in the edit rooms began to get nervous, but quietly nervous. Rarely was there any yelling. At 6:28, an assistant director, known as an "A.D.," would stick his head in and call out, "Two minutes. You've got two minutes." The editors would calculate how many more edits they could make and still get the film downstairs to the control room, cued up and ready to roll in two minutes.

"It was nerve-wracking but it was silent nerve-wracking," says Hamedy. "Except for Vitarelli, who you thought was going to have a heart attack right before your eyes." Vitarelli was Bob Vitarelli, the Pittsburgh boy who always wanted to be a TV director, and there he was, at age thirty-three, running the Washington control room, directing the live switches on the Cronkite show, and directing *Face the Nation* on Sunday.

"All that responsibility was on my back," Vitarelli says, "and believe me, New York was watching." Vitarelli started with CBS in the New York mailroom in 1953, right out of the University of Pittsburgh. He worked his way up and in 1963 came to Washington as the bureau's first full-time director.

"There was a time when I really thought I was going to die and that was during Watergate," he says. "For a year and a half, we'd have the whole damn show and then an hour special right after that. And we had Howard Brodie sketches which we'd do live because we didn't have time to package them. I used two easels and two cameras so I could dissolve and a floor director who would pull the sketches. Sometimes he'd pull them too soon and you'd see it on the air."

Night after night during Watergate, Vitarelli got red flags from the upstairs edit rooms that they were "crashing." With that, he immediately warned his control-room technicians, "We're going to crash — stand by for a ram," meaning the kind of ram when two ships collide. The techs understood it meant that the film editors were bringing the story down in pieces and they would have to put it together on the air. The moment the editor burst into the control room with the first reel of film, a tech would grab it, thread it up, and cue it up. Exactly seven seconds from the end of Cronkite's lead-in to Marvin Kalb at the State Department, for instance, Vitarelli would call out, "Roll it." The switcher would hit the button and seven seconds later Kalb's face would appear. While the first part of Kalb was running, a second editor arrived and the tech cued up part two. To make switching from reel to reel smoother the film editors put a very small scratch on the first reel as a cue for Vitarelli to cross over to the second reel.

In the control room, Vitarelli was forced to listen to many different sounds — chatter and commands at the same time, not all of them helpful. An audiologist once told him after a hearing test that he had selective hearing. He had developed it after years in the control room to block the sounds he didn't want to hear. Vitarelli says his wife had known that for years.

■ ■ ■ ■

None of the editing and crashing could start, of course, until the developed film reached the bureau. In the early 1960s there was only one conveniently located film lab in Washington — Byron's in Georgetown. It was first come, first served at Byron's, and after a hot hearing on Capitol Hill, the network's motorcycle boys — they were called couriers — would roar down Pennsylvania Avenue, carrying their precious film, and then go bombing through the narrow streets of Georgetown to reach Byron's first.

Losing the race a time or two forced CBS to install in a corner closet in the bureau a small film processor that could handle up to a four-hundred-foot magazine, the equivalent of ten or eleven minutes of film. It was called the "drugstore," as in "I'll take this to the drugstore to be developed." Andy Paddock ran the processor, but when it wasn't running, Andy read Shakespeare.

Correspondents were urged to give the cameramen some guidance about turning the camera on and off to avoid wasting film. At one congressional hearing, Martin Agronsky, who never bothered much with the mechanics of television, didn't say a

491

word to his cameraman. Late in the day, when the courier delivered twelve hundred feet of film from the hearing to the bureau, the producer asked Agronsky where the good stuff was. Agronsky said, "There isn't any."

The couriers were a breed apart. They wore the black-leather jackets all right, but they all had different interests. One of them grew azaleas. "Always take your cuttings on the Fourth of July," he told me. "Dip 'em in Root Tone and stick 'em in wet sand." They were also semireporters. It was a courier who spotted former Attorney General John Mitchell sneaking into the White House the day Bernard Shaw trailed him to New York. If they saw something they knew was news, they would call the desk with a tip. Bob Schieffer says, "If they knew what you were working on, they'd say, 'Listen, you'd better check on this or that.' "

The couriers could also be a rowdy bunch. Before the 2000 block of M Street became gentrified, there was next to the bureau a small parking lot, and at the corner of Twentieth and M Street a go-go joint. "These couriers would go over to the go-go joint," says Schieffer, "and pick up these dancers and take them to their cars, and if you came back from a late assignment and you'd walk through there you'd see the cars bouncing up and down and people hollering and drunk. It was quite a colorful sight."

The cameramen were not so much a different breed as they were a proud breed. The pride grew out of their professional and artistic skills, which were essential parts of television news. But their pride could turn prickly, even belligerent at times, because many of the correspondents treated them as less than equals. For a correspondent a Washington assignment was the ultimate; for a cameraman it was deadly and uncreative.

Four times out of five a camera crew's assignment would involve the following steps: Unload camera, tripod, lights, microphone, audio equipment, batteries, and cables; load the equipment onto a dolly and take the freight elevator to the interviewee's office; set up the tripod, the camera, and the film magazine, and hook up the mike and the audio thingy; set up the lights, film the interview, shoot cutaways, and reset the lights so the correspondent can re-ask his questions from a reverse angle; fill out a film dope sheet, hand the film to a waiting courier, and knock down the equipment; go sit in the truck and wait until the desk calls

493

and assigns you to do the same thing at another office.

"That was the story of our life," says Cal Marlin, a cameraman who joined the bureau in 1965. A graduate of the University of Miami with a degree in radio and TV, Marlin broke in with a group of Florida stations. The correspondents and the crews in Florida were like a team, he says, but "when I came to Washington there was a definite difference. . . . I think the correspondents figured they were different from us. . . . If you went out on the road, like on the campaign or something, all of a sudden you were buddies again. The minute you got back into Washington, they were the stars and we were the beasts of burden." What the camera crews longed for were out-of-town assignments, White House trips, campaigns, feature stories that played to their ability to shoot beautiful pictures. Out of town, says Marlin, "There was lots of moving around. There wasn't any sitting around."

Bruce Morton learned early never to tell a cameraman what to shoot. You made suggestions. He says he'd begin with, "What if we. . . ."

Cindy Samuels, our Capitol Hill producer, never ate until the crew got a meal break. "I was very solicitous," she says. Nonetheless, life was rough for women dealing with the crusty crews. Samuels remembers Jerry Adams, a first-class cameraman, being "cranky." You could tell, she says, "there was a lot grating on him." He had been in Vietnam in the midsixties, and "if you've been in Vietnam and done that kind of shooting and all you're doing is shooting talking heads all day — I just think they were bitter. They were bored, they were bitter."

One noontime on the Hill, Samuels caught up with cameraman Bruce Hoertel eating lunch in the Senate dining room. She told him he had to come to the TV Gallery right away, because some senator was on his way. In everybody's hearing Hoertel snapped at her: "I don't have to go anywhere." But when he wanted to, Hoertel could out-film anybody. He began as a still photographer with the *New York Times,* moved to Washington, and in 1950 with his Speed Graphic captured a famous series of images of a D.C. policeman shooting at a Puerto Rican nationalist in front of Blair House. With CBS, he was one of our best. He filmed Richard Nixon's 1959 "kitchen debate" with Nikita Khrushchev and also John Kennedy's Berlin speech in 1963.

For all his professionalism and ability, he

was a difficult case. Marya McLaughlin, not one to be disrespected, ran into one of Hoertel's foul moods and said to his face: "On the outside you may be pretty but on the inside you are rotten, selfish, and full of worms."

CHAPTER 40
"WE COULD HAVE DONE BETTER"

George Herman had already left his Georgetown home for work that Saturday morning, June 17, 1972, when his neighbor,
Louis Hausman, rang the doorbell at 3115
O Street. Hausman's wife had sent him
down to borrow the Hermans' rose sprayer.
Hausman, an official at the Democratic
National Headquarters, wondered what
George thought about the predawn break-in
at the DNC in the Watergate Hotel. Patty
Herman didn't know what her husband
thought, because neither one of them had
heard about it. Hausman said his secretary
had just called him. He told Patty he
couldn't imagine what anybody would want
in the DNC. "You could take every piece of
paper," he told her, "turn it face up, and lay
it down all the way to Pennsylvania Avenue
and they wouldn't learn a thing."

But Patty, who had worked in the Eisenhower press office, knew a tip on a good

story when she heard one. She immediately called her husband at the CBS bureau and he immediately called the Metropolitan Police. Herman nailed down the details and within the hour was on CBS radio breaking the story that ultimately ruined Richard Nixon's presidency.

On duty with Herman that Saturday was Barry Serafin, although he was not due in until later. But the Washington producer for the *Evening News,* Elizabeth Midgley, was there. She had been in the bureau less than two years, but she knew her way around Washington from turns at the State Department, the Kennedy campaign in 1960, and as a producer with PBS. She was not about to let this story get away.

With Herman tied down in the bureau with hourly radio assignments and no other reporter yet available, Midgley herself took off for the Watergate complex. On a Saturday morning in downtown Washington, however, the streets are without taxis. So she started *running* from M Street to the Watergate — *running* south on New Hampshire Avenue toward the Potomac River, ten or twelve long city blocks, almost a mile. Midgley knows she ran because she "remembers the shoes I had on." They were pigskin lace-up oxfords like men wear, she says, which meant she never tripped or stumbled on her dash to the Watergate. In the late sixties Midgley had been Walter Lippmann's subeditor and "leg woman," never dreaming she would someday be running anchor leg for CBS.

At the Watergate was a *Post* reporter and someone Midgely took to be an intern from the *New York Times.* "This green guy was sitting there and not really saying very much. I said to him finally — it was the only time I've done that — both because he was green and he was black and I thought I should say it to him as a kid, 'Tell them this is a big story and you need help.' The *Times* had zero. NBC had nothing, and ABC wasn't around."

Serafin, now in the bureau and saddled up, says they didn't know quite what to make of the story other than that it was bizarre. That afternoon at the arraignment of the five Watergate burglars, Serafin says, there was only one other reporter in the courtroom, a "young guy" who had been used to "covering school board meetings." He didn't have important stories to cover like Serafin felt he did — the upcoming conventions and campaigns — so he "just stayed with Watergate and became rich and famous and renowned and the ultimate insider in Washington, and Serafin went on blithely in his own ignorant way." The young guy was, of course, Bob Woodward.

Both Serafin and Herman had strong pieces on the *Evening News* that Saturday night — Herman on the break-in itself, the five burglars hiding behind desks with their sophisticated electronic bugging gear, and Serafin from the courthouse on the arraignment, the burglars' names, the bail, the CIA connection, and the Cuban connection. For almost twenty-four hours CBS owned the Watergate story outright, because the *Post*'s story did not appear until the next morning, June 18. Midgley says, "We were all over the story that night. . . . We went live to the jail. We had George Herman on live. We were great. We were all over it."

On Monday night the Cronkite show had a second Watergate story, reported by Serafin, that ran almost four and a half minutes. But his piece was mainly a recap, plus the predictable and outraged reaction from the DNC chairman, Lawrence O'Brien, and the three leading Democratic presidential candidates, Hubert Humphrey, George McGovern, and Edmund Muskie. The GOP's national chairman, Robert Dole, always ready with a zinger, said he thought the only thing the burglars would find was a "bunch of unpaid bills."

ABC, with Howard K. Smith, did well on Monday and Tuesday night after the break-in, devoting big chunks of time to the story. NBC, however, never quite caught up. On Monday night, June 19, it was a twenty-second "tell" story read by the anchor, John Chancellor. Two nights later, NBC's coverage consisted entirely of a David Brinkley commentary about the Democrats finding a novel way to raise money by filing a million-dollar lawsuit against the Republicans. On the third night reporter Don Oliver got on a sidetrack about the evidence tying the burglary to the Free Cuba Movement.[1]

Over the next ten days, nonetheless, CBS did only one Watergate story — Lesley Stahl reporting on the bail hearing for the five burglars. "We dropped the ball," says Midgley. "We failed to assign anybody to the story, day-by-day. It didn't seem that important afterward. We didn't know it was part of the dirty tricks and that it was just part of the 'vast right-wing conspiracy' to poison that election."

Most of the bureau's political reporters who would have picked up on the story were either on the road with the presidential candidates or preparing for the Democratic convention in Miami, which was to open in early July. Producers, editors, and vice presidents were all preoccupied with Miami. Nixon's press secretary, Ron Ziegler, dismissed the break-in as a "third-rate burglary"; the New York Times handled it as a fourth-rater; in late July, Bob Woodward and Carl Bernstein feared the Watergate story was dying.

The nation's political press, massed in Miami, watched the Democrats wrestle with new rules, quotas, liberal activists, contentious debates on abortion and gay rights. On the final day — in a school's-out atmosphere — many of the younger delegates, on a lark, turned the vice presidential roll call into a joke, nominating among many others Mao Tse Tung, Mickey Mouse, Martha Mitchell, and Jerry Rubin.

When Wisconsin's chairman stood up, he cast a big vote for Thomas Eagleton and then rattled off a long list of other names, including at the very end, "two votes for Roger Mudd." There were major yuks in the convention hall. My votes, I found out later, had come from two young women from Prairie du Chien who were fans of the Evening News on Saturday.

I was not on the convention floor at the time, but the CBS control room had me come out for an interview with Cronkite. With a deadpan face, I told Walter I would have no comment until I had assembled my campaign staff and put the finishing touches on my farm plank.

The roll call took so long it became almost hilarious. When Eagleton finally made his predawn appearance at the podium, he began by asking, "Didn't I give Roger Mudd one hell of a beating?"

Not until after we had gotten back from Miami and the GOP convention in late August did CBS create a Watergate beat. Bill Small called Daniel Schorr into his office and told him, "You've been talking Watergate all this time. Congratulations. You are now our Watergate correspondent. Just drop whatever you're doing and go see whatever you can find out." CBS News did not like playing second fiddle to anybody, including newspapers, but our late start meant the *Post* would always be ahead of us. Schorr says, "I did what I could. It was nothing like Woodward and Bernstein, but I came up with things here and there."

His voracious appetite for getting on the air strong as ever, Schorr had his first Watergate story on the Cronkite broadcast on Tuesday, August 29, two more stories in

August, and then nine in September and eight in October.[2] None of his early stories was a true exclusive, but Schorr kept us in the game.

He did not do it alone, however. Lesley Stahl was assigned to be his backup. Stahl preferred the terms "His slave. His apprentice. His handmaiden." Stahl worked the beat just as hard as Schorr did, but everything she learned she had to turn over to Schorr for his TV reports. That left the radio for her, although Schorr, she says, "often insisted that radio was part of his franchise as well." But when one of her exclusives got folded into a Schorr piece without any air credit or even an office "Way to go, Lesley," Stahl exploded. In her fury she announced to no one in particular, "I will never give him a story again." Her explosion got results. Small anointed her as the official *Morning News* correspondent on Watergate — "now that you've showed me a little spine," she says he told her — and stories she got on her own were eligible for the *Evening News*.[3] Schorr himself says, "I remember nothing of this. I should have read her book. . . . My only recollection was saying to her that I enjoyed working with her and she was very good and enormous help."

■ ■ ■ ■

In late September Carl Bernstein tracked down former Attorney General John Mitchell in New York to tell him the *Post* was running a story about his control of secret funds from the Nixon campaign to finance espionage against the Democrats. Bernstein quoted Mitchell as follows:

All that crap, you're putting in the paper? It's all been denied. Katie Graham's gonna get her tit caught in a big fat wringer if that's published.[4]

The *Post* ran not only the story but also Mitchell's quote about Graham, though without the word "tit." The full quote was all over town, of course. The next day I told Ben Bradlee, the *Post*'s editor, that the *Post* should change the call letters of its TV and radio station from WTOP to WTIT.

For the most of the summer the *Washington Post* was almost alone on Watergate, nervous and fearful the story would blow up in its face. For television, with its dependency on pictures and sound bites, Watergate was difficult to cover. But CBS hung in with the story even though it meant playing catch-up with the *Post* night after night. It also meant not being afraid to modify the "No Talking Heads" rule to show Schorr and Rather and Stahl at length on camera telling the story, rather than passing it up for want of pictures or sound bites.

By fall Watergate had become more than just a botched burglary; it was now a story of political espionage. Cronkite and the New York news managers decided they could no longer cover such a scandal in fits and starts. They would lay out the story in two full-bore reports. The first was broadcast on Friday, October 27, just ten days before the presidential election. Although it contained very little that was new, the report had a force of its own; it had Cronkite's imprimatur, and it had a length almost unprecedented — fourteen minutes in a broadcast whose news hole was twenty-two minutes.

The second part, broadcast the following Tuesday, had been sharply cut back on orders from above, the above in this case being William S. Paley, who had received a telephone call from an outraged Charles Colson in the White House.

Whatever their shortcomings, the two CBS reports helped get the *Washington Post* off the hook. Katherine Graham told Richard Salant, "You turned our local story into a national story"[5] and Bill Small quoted Ben Bradlee as saying, "That story never left the Beltway until CBS started doing it."

For more than two years no other story consumed the press and the politicians of Washington like Watergate. Through the years, the capital witnessed the usual string of scandals, most of them minor; it reveled in the campaign tricks of Dick Tuck, the Merry Prankster; but never had there been anything to equal Watergate — burglars, dirty tricks, political slush funds, forged letters, enemy lists, a plumbers unit to plug media leaks, the involvement of the attorney general and the White House itself. Every morning all of Washington lunged for the *Post* to read what new "holy shit" story Woodward and Bernstein had dug up about Nixon aides Bob Haldeman, John Ehrlichman, or Chuck Colson, and every morning Galbraith on the desk would order another predawn camera stakeout on the front lawns of the usual suspects.

Precious little reporting accompanied those stakeouts. It was mostly yelling at the president's men for a comment and coming back to the bureau with fresh pictures. Stahl called the assignments "degrading," but none of them seemed to hurt her career.

When it became apparent that John Dean's Senate testimony was going to be huge, Stahl camped at his house every day. One afternoon she rang his doorbell. "He had a front door with a mail slot and two windows on each side of the door that were kind of opaque. 'I know you're in there. I know you're in there.' I can see him moving around. I opened the mail slot. 'It's Lesley Stahl with CBS. Talk to me. I want to ask you a few questions about your testimony.' But instead of opening the door, he knelt down to the mail slot and the only thing I remember he said was that he was going to wear his glasses when he testified. I made a whole story of it."

Missing from the story, of course, was the president, who had effectively been hiding. Each day and each new Watergate story drove him deeper and deeper into trouble and depression. Rumors of his heavy drinking were easy to hear. One day reporters lounging in the West Wing press room were flabbergasted to see through the window the president himself walking on the North Lawn with none other than Connie Chung. John Herbers of the *New York Times* said no one had ever seen or heard of Nixon setting foot on the North Lawn. But there he was with Chung. Returning from lunch, walking down the driveway from the Northwest Gate, she had spotted him wandering about. He recognized her and steered her away from the press, which had come spilling out of the press room, clamoring to listen, only to be held back by Nixon's Secret Service detail. "All I wanted to talk about was Watergate," Chung says, but instead he smothered her with questions about how much money she was making at CBS. "I told him about $25,000 but with fees for radio and fees for the Cronkite show I might get up to $26,000, and if I had a really good run it might get up to $28,000. All he wanted to talk about was the money, and he kept asking about the money and then he said he thought I should try to make more money." She never got a Watergate question in edgewise. As weird as the conversation was, as exclusive as it was, the bureau agreed Chung really didn't have a story. They figured that any story that began with, "President Nixon told me exclusively today that I should be making more money," somehow didn't measure up. But it did deserve to be squirreled away.

Rankled as he was by having to follow in the *Washington Post*'s wake, Small says the bureau's coverage of Watergate was "one of the most important things we ever did." But Galbraith thinks we did only "pretty well. Our biggest failure," he says, "was a lack of really honest-to-god first-rate original reporting. We were extremely good at jumping on stories that others broke — the Watergates, the Pentagon Papers — and developing all kinds of angles from those leads. But we didn't seem to come up with the big ones first."

Fred Graham, our first full-time legal correspondent, praises CBS for being "willing to go with the story. . . . We assumed we were going to have a Watergate story every day." What bothered Graham, a product of the *New York Times* culture, was the failure of TV news to weigh the importance of new information. Each fresh nugget meant "we'd do a story every time there was a new fact floating around. . . . And I felt there was just not enough weighing of the importance of these things." Graham was able, however, to persuade CBS to broadcast his weekly summing-up of the evidence and the growing legal case against Nixon. For that initiative, Graham got a prized Peabody Award.

Stahl says, "We could have done better. We could have done what Woodward did — shoe leather, calling everybody in sight, getting a good source." Not that Stahl didn't try. Once the Senate Watergate Committee opened hearings in March 1973, she was on the Hill every day, learning which senators and which staffers would leak. Her most reliable source was "golden," she says, so accurate that his tips always resulted in Galbraith's moving crews and shifting assignments. "Lesley's guy," as he was known in the bureau, called her late one afternoon with a major tip — a group of U.S. marshals were about to surround the White House to serve a subpoena on Nixon's secretary, Rose Mary Woods, who had been deliberately dodging the marshals. The story was to be the lead on the Cronkite show. About 5:30 Bob Pierpoint, posted at the White House gates waiting for the marshals, called Stahl to tell her the marshals were a no-show. Stahl called her guy. "They should be there," he assured her. By 6:15 Stahl was beginning to panic. She called the committee's chief investigator, Terry Lenzner, and pleaded with him to confirm the story or deny it. He said he would call back. At 6:25 Lenzner called, so late that Stahl had already had to kill the story, to tell her, "There are no marshals. We were trying to catch your source . . . and now we have."[6] Stahl says her source is still anonymous. "He never set me free. I never asked him to." She did acknowledge that he worked for Republican Senator Lowell Weicker, who was no admirer of Richard Nixon or the men around him.

Being assigned to cover Watergate meant joining a reportorial club that had its own camaraderie, its own patois, its own sense of humor. John Mitchell, the former attorney general, was the "big enchilada"; documents that were destroyed got "deep-sixed," meaning burial at sea in at least six fathoms. The Watergate world was also intensely competitive at the same time that it was filled with bonhomie. At CBS, virtually everybody in the bureau felt the excitement of being part of a critical turn in history. Even for those of us who did not do Watergate every hour of every day, there was a shared pleasure and pride in our colleagues who did. Elizabeth Midgley says we had such good people that "any one of them could have taken on another role." Our film editors could have easily produced an entire piece; producers could have doubled as correspondents; and, as Midgley says, "the motorcycle couriers were semireporters." But even as semis, they were invaluable to the desk.

The September Saturday in 1972 when Bernard Shaw spotted John Mitchell trying to slip in and out of the White House, the desk posted a courier at the Northwest Gate to the White House to report on exactly who was going and coming. After half an hour or so, the courier radioed in that Mitchell had just left, heading east on Pennsylvania Avenue, with the courier following. Fifteen minutes later, the courier was at the airport and radioed in that Mitchell was boarding the four o'clock shuttle to New York. Shaw, Dan Schorr, and a film crew, dispatched by the desk, plowed onto the plane to find Mitchell in one of the front seats reading his paper. Schorr promised Mitchell an uninterrupted flight to New York provided he agreed to an interview when they landed. He gave them the interview, denying all knowledge of, or participation in, the Nixon campaign's secret slush fund. Shaw grabbed the film magazine and roared off in a cab to CBS News headquarters on West Fifty-seventh Street. When Shaw told Paul Greenberg, the Saturday producer, and me what he had, we were elated. The *Post* had broken the story the previous morning. This was Mitchell's first flat denial and it was ours. Not often on a Saturday night did we get a newsy, hard lead like this one.

Shaw says he has not forgotten what happened just as we went on the air. As the announcer was clicking off the names of the broadcast's reporters, "you reached over and hit the intercom and said, 'Wait 'til those fuckers at NBC and ABC see this.' " I am in no position to deny those words. It was a small but exquisite moment.

CHAPTER 41
NATTERING NABOBS

Nobody could recall a heavier news flow than during the spring of 1973: Two of the Watergate burglars, Gordon Liddy and John McCord had already been convicted of conspiracy, burglary, and wiretapping. In April, Nixon's two closest aides, John Erhlichman and Bob Haldeman, and his attorney general, Richard Kleindienst, resigned. On the same day Nixon fired his chief counsel, John Dean. On the last day of April Nixon released more than twelve hundred pages of Oval Office transcripts. In mid-May, the Senate's Watergate Committee began live televised hearings. In late June an unmuzzled John Dean went public. It was almost more than the bureau could handle — morning news, evening news, live hearings, specials, late-night wrap-ups, radio hourlies. The edit room, run by Ed Fouhy, was cranking out anywhere from four to seven pieces a night, plus a daily Sevareid analysis. John Armstrong, the deputy producer, said it "was crash and burn all the time."

In the middle of this maelstrom, the chairman of CBS, William S. Paley, dropped a bomb. Henceforth all CBS News correspondents were forbidden from engaging in what Vice President Agnew had disparagingly called "instant analysis." Paley acted against the advice of the president of his company, Arthur Taylor, and the president of his news division, Richard Salant. He had bought into the argument of the Washington bureau's most distinguished journalist, Eric Sevareid, who thought it not fair for us to jump on a president before we and the public had had time to digest his remarks. He believed a president was entitled to a twenty-four-hour fire-free zone. Perhaps it had slipped Sevareid's mind that we were daily journalists, not quarterly scholars. Perhaps it was Sevareid who carried the day with Paley, but no one in the bureau had forgotten the Agnew diatribe of 1969 against the "nattering nabobs of negativism," or Paley's interference with the editing of our two-part Watergate report following complaints from the White House, or the constant carping about our instant analysis from Bob Haldeman, with whom Paley had met at the White House in late spring.

For most of us, it was another craven corporate capitulation to political pressure. Paley's edict was also a blow to the solar plexus. To be assigned to put the president on and off the air, to engage your colleagues in a lively and informative give-and-take was a treasured assignment for me. It was serious work that we all took seriously, an opportunity to put to good use the knowledge, insight, and perceptions we had spent years acquiring in Washington. More than likely, I would anchor those programs, whether a press conference, a speech from the White House, or the State of the Union address, and at my request, Bill Small, the bureau chief, would clear my other assignments for the day. Our cast would normally include the reluctant but always invaluable Eric Sevareid; Daniel Schorr, who was ready, willing, and quite able to analyze on an instant's notice; Dan Rather, who had the unenviable role of being a straight White House reporter during the day but a critic at night; and Marvin Kalb, whose superlative grip on foreign affairs and the State Department was the envy of every TV bureau in town.

If Kalb ever demonstrated his chops as an instant analyst, it was on November 3,

1969, the night of Nixon's "silent majority" speech. Kalb's claim that Nixon had misread Ho Chi Minh's latest peace proposal so enraged the White House that it led directly to Vice President Agnew's scorching attack ten days later on "this small and unelected elite" of anchormen, commentators, and executive producers. In the months that followed, Kalb's telephone was tapped, his tax returns audited, and his office broken into. Kalb said he had a "creepy feeling" he had been shadowed at the Paris Peace Talks.

Another of our regular nabobs, Daniel Schorr, thought our instant analysis was a "terrific success." Watergate was a very big, complicated story but "here you have these guys who seem to understand what's going on."

Excluding Sevareid, the five of us who did most of the postspeech work — Kalb, Rather, Schorr, George Herman, and I — put together a letter of protest to the management, the basic drafting done by Herman. Various accounts have credited me with toughening the language, but my memory is of no help. What I do remember, and quite vividly, was that Rather thought the letter too tough and told us he wanted to write his own. But when we were told

518

that Dick Salant in New York heard about the letter and approved it, Rather figured the letter wasn't quite as tough as he first thought and asked if he could sign it after all. The four of us sent word that there was no way we would let him sign the letter, that we were the ones who had taken the risk and we weren't about to have him riding in on our coattails. In the bureau, we had learned to be on guard working with Rather, because of his transparent aggressiveness and his practiced, almost manufactured way of taking issue with each of us during our instant analysis. So we were particularly angered by what we saw as his attempt to have it both ways. I was angered the most because Rather and I were professional rivals not only in the bureau but also for Cronkite's chair, and Herman, Kalb, and Schorr were not. Rather was quoted at the time as saying, "It was not one of my heroic moments."

Rather made no excuses about the letter when we spoke in September 2006, and he asked me not to portray his explanation as an excuse. He was, he said, "under increasing pressure about our White House coverage." Not just from the White House but also from within CBS. They were asking, he said, " 'What is Dan doing?' 'Has he got us too far out on a limb?' 'Where is this going?' I was feeling pressure." Rather said that Bill Small had reservations about sending such a letter and suggested he talk to Sevareid. His advice, of course, was "Do not sign." Given Sevareid's role as what Rather calls his "mentor," and given Small's stout support against White House attempts to move Rather out, he decided not to sign. Rather insisted that "the decision was mine, the final decision was mine."

According to Sanford Socolow, who was filling in as bureau chief while Small was on vacation, the protest letter did not originate in the Washington bureau but was Salant's idea from the very beginning. Always the crafty lawyer looking for a way to outflank Paley, Salant suggested *soto voce* to Socolow that he get a letter drawn up. Without knowing where the suggestion had come from, Herman set to work on the letter, we added a bit here and a bit there, and Socolow sent it off for Salant's approval. Salant loved it, of course. When I told Rather about the Socolow version, he said, with no little irritation, "First time I heard that. I wish the hell he'd told us that before."

Through that summer and into the fall, Nixon rarely appeared in prime time. His four press conferences were daytime events.

After five months of complaints from Taylor and Salant that CBS News was suffering from a "lack of spice," and after hearing that his friend, Averell Harriman, no longer watched CBS because it didn't do analysis, Paley did an embarrassing about-face. He restored instant analysis. Just in time for Nixon to tell the nation that he was "not a crook."[1]

Schorr remembers the night I asked him about Nixon's claim of innocence. Schorr's answer was "But he is a crook," and he thereupon cited the details of Nixon's taking a charitable deduction of $576,000 for the vice presidential papers he gave to the National Archives and the backdating to qualify for a tax loophole that had closed — all points that were appropriate, accurate, relevant, and available only through instant analysis.

CHAPTER 42
THE LEGAL EAGLES

When the Watergate burglars pleaded guilty to conspiracy on January 15, 1973, just a few days before Richard Nixon was sworn in for a second term, the White House figured the guilty pleas would send the Watergate scandal into a fade. Not only did Watergate not fade but three months later, Nixon was hit with another scandal — the charge that his own vice president, Spiro Agnew, had taken bribes from Maryland's construction companies while he was governor of Maryland and that those bribes continued even after he became vice president. During that summer and early fall, negotiations between the White House, the Justice Department, the U.S. attorney in Baltimore, and the vice president moved inexorably toward a plea bargain, although Agnew himself remained publicly and defiantly on the offensive. He accused the Justice Department of using him as the "big trophy" to recoup its reputation, which he charged had been damaged by its "ineptness" during Watergate.

One of the new reporters in our bureau, Phil Jones, who had cut his TV teeth in Minneapolis, got a tip from a newly arrived friend from Minnesota that the Justice Department had enough evidence to indict the vice president. Jones's friend was Richard Moe, a Minneapolis lawyer who had just come to Washington as Senator Walter Mondale's administrative assistant.

Jones said the tip was that one of Moe's lawyer friends, at the Justice Department for a meeting, had overheard Henry Petersen, the chief of the criminal division, talking about the Agnew investigation on the telephone. The visiting lawyer quoted Petersen as saying that Agnew "was not getting off the hook." The visitor was then told by another Justice official who had also heard Petersen, "You know what that's all about — Agnew is trying to plea bargain and it's not going to happen. They've got him cold."

Moe's account differs in the details. He recalls that it was Jones who had dropped by his office and that he casually passed on the tip, as in "Phil, you won't believe what I heard." Moe says his friend had overheard in a Justice Department corridor someone of "high authority" — Petersen's name was never mentioned — say that Agnew "was going to cop a plea." Whatever the quotes were and whoever said them, Jones took the tip to his bureau chief, Bill Small, who had him turn it over to Fred Graham, the bureau's legal correspondent assigned to the Agnew story. Graham was also a practicing attorney and a member of the D.C. Bar.

What unfolded next revealed as much about the two men as it did about the bureau's competitive tensions in a very competitive culture.

Like many others through the years, Jones had come to the network from one of CBS's Triple-A farm teams, WCCO in Minneapolis. He was an Indiana farm boy, typically self-sufficient and independent. At Indiana University, he was the color man on the university's sports network alongside Dick Engberg. CBS hired him in 1961, sent him to Atlanta, then to Vietnam and Hong Kong. At age thirty-six, he joined the Washington bureau in late 1972. A compact man, with a high forehead and thinning hair, he was hardworking, feisty, and taut. There was on his shoulder a frequently visible chip. Jones did not like to share stories or assignments. As he phrased it, "it did not sit well." So when Small told him to give Fred Graham his own exclusive story on Agnew, it did not sit well. Nor did it sit well when CBS assigned Susan Spencer to be Jones's backup on the Kennedy campaign and then told the two to rotate between the evening news and the morning news. Jones blew up, says Spencer. "He made a big stink about it and left the campaign." Simply put, Jones was prickly.

Fred Graham, on the other hand, was a laid-back southern boy, born in Little Rock and raised in Texarkana, Arkansas, and Nashville, the son of a Presbyterian minister. Finely educated at Yale, at Vanderbilt's law school, and as a Fulbright Scholar at Oxford, Graham was unique in the Washington bureau because he had come directly to television from a successful career on the *New York Times*.

Many of us had worked for newspapers before, but only in short bursts and mostly for the wire services or rinky-dink papers. Graham's conversion to television took time and took help. His southern accent provoked mail, critical mail. Small gave him a tape recorder to practice his diction on and to knock off the edges of his drawl. A voice professor from NYU corrected his pronunciations, his dropped "g's." The word "affluent," the professor scolded, was pronounced "AF-loo-ent" and not "a-FLOO-ent." At the *Times,* Graham said, he could write "as long as I wanted to." At CBS, he had one hundred forty seconds and rarely more. Graham tried his best, he learned the system, he got better, he knew his stuff, but he never quite fit in the bureau. There was a certain air of detachment about him that he attributed to being off "in my own world of the law and the courts" but that others who had worked with him attributed to laziness and a tendency to avoid the nitty-gritty work required to produce a piece. Susan Zirinsky, the bureau researcher, says, "There were the workhorses and then there was Fred Graham. Fred was always like, 'Where's Fred?' " Graham says he was "mystified" by such criticism and believed that his gentler southern tempo might have been misunderstood by those who thought television required "a more frenetic style."

Whatever Graham's shortcomings, his knowledge of the law and his sources in the capital's legal, judicial, and law-enforcement circles were not among them. His sources, built up over the years with the *Times,* were extensive. So it was with a seemingly detectable pleasure that Phil Jones recounted

526

years later how Graham was unable to confirm his Agnew tip and had to pass on the story; how the New York desk called Graham in the middle of the night to tell him the *Washington Post* was reporting that Agnew had started to plea bargain; how Graham hurriedly telephoned a story from his home for the 8 AM *World News Roundup* on radio "with the very stuff I had given him but nothing new."

In his 1990 memoir, Graham said he had worked on the Jones tip for several days but could not confirm the story with a second "more traditional source. . . . I chose not to do a story and went home for the weekend." But when the New York desk called him at home, telling him "the *Washington Post* has confirmed your story — it's all over tomorrow's front page, 'Agnew Plea Bargaining' " — Graham apparently decided to use the *Post* as his second source and recorded his story over the telephone for radio.[1] Graham's current recollection is slightly different. "I got a story that Henry Petersen, who was head of the criminal division in the Justice Department, that he had told someone that they had the evidence. . . . I was able to confirm that they did have the evidence. . . . I was able to confirm that Petersen had said, 'We've got the evidence here. We've got it cold.' So I went with the story."[2]

But in Graham's account to me he made no mention that Jones was his source or that he failed to match Jones's story or that the New York desk had roused him before dawn or that the *Washington Post* served as his second source. When presented with Jones's version of the sequence, however, Graham confirmed its accuracy.

During those early days in October, breaking the Agnew story had the highest priority. Rita Braver, a desk assistant, was occasionally posted at the Justice Department, which repeatedly denied that Agnew was resigning. In the press room one day, with reporters marking time, waiting for handouts or playing cards, the NBC correspondent walked in and said to no one in particular that Justice was saying "No comment" about an Agnew resignation. And he went back to playing cards. Braver said to herself, "Oh, my God," and immediately called Fred. "You know as well as I do that when people change from 'no' to 'no comment' it bears investigating." It was another case of what Ed Fouhy called NBC "lassitude."

Graham's reporting, along with that from

the *Washington Post,* the *New York Times,* the *Baltimore Sun, Time,* and *Newsweek,* was cited by Agnew's lawyers in their subpoena as proof the Justice Department and Henry Petersen in particular were deliberately trying to deprive the vice president of a fair hearing. Graham was reasonably fearful that his standing with the bar might be damaged if he were to be questioned by Judge Walter Hoffman or deposed by Agnew's lawyers about his sources. According to Jones, Graham asked him for his source but he refused, because Graham never assured him he would not disclose Moe's name to the judge. "So I told Fred to tell the judge that Phil Jones told him and I would worry about that later." On October 10, Graham and eight other reporters and their lawyers showed up in Hoffman's Baltimore courtroom. Graham wrote later that he had packed his briefcase "with a toothbrush, a razor, and a long racy novel and prepared to do some time in a Baltimore jail."[3] But before the reporters' hearing began, Attorney General Eliot Richardson and his legal team suddenly appeared, the courtroom doors were locked, and in walked Vice President Agnew to "cop his plea." With Agnew's resignation that day, the threat of contempt of court against Graham and the other Agnew reporters had vanished.

Two days after Agnew went down, President Nixon nominated the House minority leader, Gerald Ford, to be his vice president. His nomination zipped through the Senate Rules Committee, and on November 27 I was standing by in the bureau for the vote in the full Senate, which was expected to break during the Cronkite show. The outcome was never in doubt; it was only a matter of when and how many "no" votes. Still, this was a major story, given the unprecedented scandal that had created the vacancy and an administration that was beginning to "wallow in Watergate." I had written and pretaped a story, complete with artist sketches from the afternoon debate. All we needed to break into the Cronkite show was the vote itself, a figure I would tack on live at the end of the piece.

Sweating out the vote with me was Susan Zirinsky, a twenty-year-old product of the New York public schools and of American University — a woman so diminutive and petite that she joked about filling in her wardrobe with doll's clothes, and a researcher who became a producer of formidable skill and energy, the model for the Holly Hunter role in the 1987 movie *Broad-*

Minutes after the Cronkite show started, the Ford story did break and I took off for the studio downstairs. Zirinsky says, "These kids around here have no idea what it was like," meaning the kids of the twenty-first century. "Roger Mudd running down the stairs to a live studio switch for Cronkite, yelling at me, 'How many no votes did Ford get?' There were no computers, no Palm Pilots, no wireless. We had to check everything twice." Checking was done strictly by telephone.

At 6:49:50 PM the Cronkite show switched to the Washington studio for my Ford story. The Senate vote was ninety-two to three, and the three "no" votes were Democrats Thomas Eagleton, William Hathaway, and Gaylord Nelson. On both ABC and NBC the vote was handled by the anchormen, Reasoner and Chancellor, and not by their reporters, one of those minor journalistic distinctions that set CBS apart. Zirinsky still says that "being in the bureau was the greatest thing that ever happened to me."

Despite Zirinsky's criticisms, Fred Graham's law reporting dominated the opposition for at least fifteen years. Between 1973 and 1986 he was on the *Evening News* an average of once a week, covering the Supreme Court, the Watergate trial and the lingering legal fallout from Watergate, the Billy Carter scandal, the bribery trial of John Connally, and the confirmation hearings of Justice Sandra Day O'Connor and Attorney General Griffin Bell.

Where Graham excelled was in putting a face on the Supreme Court's cases. The standard technique had been to use a courtroom artist; interviews with the lawyers, who had to squint in the blinding light that bounced off the Court's marble walls; and a stand-up close from the reporter. No wonder the producers groaned at the thought of another piece from "SCOTUS," the acronym for Supreme Court of the United States.

What Graham and his producers did was develop a fresh way to cover the Court — leaving Washington and visiting the scene, talking to the defendants and the plaintiffs and their lawyers and the special interests and the lobbies involved. Graham picked a dozen or so cases from the Court's docket each year, cases he thought would be newsworthy. By the time the cases were heard by the Court, all that was needed for a completed piece was Graham's on-camera close.

Much of the prebroadcast work was done by one of the three or four producers who worked with him through the years. Rita Braver became his producer in 1976, and the word around the bureau was that "Rita had to carry Fred," a phrase not entirely fair to Graham, who undoubtedly suffered from culture shock.

Graham joined us thinking, as he said, that the bureau was full of a lot of "hotshot TV people" who put on makeup, cleared their throats, and recorded whatever was handed them. He arrived unaware of how much harder TV reporters had to work than newspaper reporters — watching over the filming, checking the facts, doing the interviews, assembling the film, writing the copy to fit the film, and recording a close against a deadline that was unforgiving. "It was much more businesslike in the sense that each of the correspondents was a highly driven person," Graham says.

"They didn't drink during the day. We had two-martini lunches at the *New York Times,* and it was a pretty casual attitude. But each of those individuals . . . at CBS was a comer. . . . There wasn't a lot of socializing — sometimes at lunch. . . . A lot of them were very hard working. There was no nonsense and they were sober when 6:30 came."

One of those "comers" was Rita Braver. Her interest in the law came naturally — she was the daughter of a Justice Department research analyst, a graduate of the University of Wisconsin, and the wife of Washington lawyer Robert B. Barnett, her college boyfriend. Brought up in a Chevy Chase, Maryland, family that watched Huntley-Brinkley, she became a news junkie as a kid and with a friend once did a teeny bopper stakeout at Eric Sevareid's nearby home. "I was hoping to get a glimpse of him but I never did because he went home quite a bit earlier than I thought." Years later, as a CBS producer, Braver spotted a mistake in one of Sevareid's scripts after he had recorded it. He had written "the war in Indonesia" instead of "Indochina." Braver went to Sevareid's secretary, who said, "You found it. You tell him." He was "grateful to me but he was furious that the evening news people had not caught it."

After six years as Graham's producer, Braver began to think she could do it as well as Graham. ABC offered her a reporter-producer job, but CBS quickly countered, and in 1983 Braver became the bureau's junior law correspondent covering, she says, "sex, drugs, violence, and rock-and-roll, and leaving the important issues to Fred."

In looking back over his fifteen years in the bureau recently, Graham singled out, on first thought, Watergate and the John Connally trial as the stories he enjoyed covering the most. But on second thought, he cited two others. The first was his coverage of the declining health of Justice William O. Douglas, his inability to do the Court's work, and his stubborn refusal to retire. Graham tracked Douglas down to a New York hospital and with cameras rolling interviewed the justice as he was wheeled out. Graham said it was obvious from "his weak, slurred speech and his halting, disjointed comments that he was in no condition to function as a Justice of the Supreme Court." Douglas finally retired in November 1975.

The second of Graham's favorites was his story marking the tenth anniversary of the Court's Pentagon Papers case. Graham somehow got a copy of the audiotape of the Court's oral arguments in June 1971, tapes that had been routinely made but were under seal at the National Archives. This was the first time the justices' voices had been broadcast, and Graham's story ran on the evening news and the morning news and on radio. As expected, Chief Justice Burger went ballistic and ordered an investigation of the leak, that, of course, got nowhere. Today the Court regularly makes public audiotapes of its important cases.

There was one story Graham regretted — the Nixon so-called "Jew boy" story. He'd gotten a tip from someone on the Watergate prosecution staff that Nixon on the Oval Office tapes had used the phrase "Jew boy" and called Judge John Sirica a "wop." Graham, however, lacked a second source, just as he had lacked a second source in the Agnew "cop a plea" story. Finally he did get Albert Jenner, the chief Republican counsel on the House Judiciary Committee, to say, in that inside-out and backwards language reporters use with their off-the-record sources, that Graham "would not be in trouble" if he went with the story. So Graham went with it, leading the Cronkite show on Friday, May 10, 1974. Six minutes later, an enraged White House chief of staff, Al Haig, called Bill Small and denounced the story as a lie. Graham called Jenner back and Jenner said, "Well, I didn't say Nixon said that. I said you wouldn't get into trouble." Jenner turned out to be a second source you could do without. Small told Graham it was his call. "If you don't feel comfortable, Fred, we'll pull it." Graham pulled it in less than five minutes. On the 7 PM repeat, Graham's story was quickly replaced by one of his standby Watergate pieces, and Cronkite himself reported that the White House denied reports that the president had used such racial slurs and that the denial was backed up by Judge Sirica himself.

The problem came from errors at the White House in transcribing the tapes. In the corrected versions, the "Jew boy" phrase was changed to "Jewish boys" and attributed to John Dean; the "goddamn wop" line was misheard on the scratchy tape by the stenographer as "that's the kind I want," referring to Sirica's tough reputation.[4]

If ever Fred Graham and Phil Jones learned that just because they believe something is true doesn't mean they can broadcast it, they sure learned it during Watergate.

When the Watergate trial opened in January 1973, CBS News swarmed the federal courthouse at Sixth and Indiana. Schorr was the lead reporter but there was also Lesley Stahl, Barry Serafin, and Howard Brodie, the great news artist I had so admired during the filibuster of 1964. And when the Watergate grand jury more than a year later named Nixon as an "unindicted co-conspirator," the courthouse was again swarming with CBS staffers, but this time they were Fred Graham, Robert Schackne, Jed Duvall, Daniel Schorr, artist Angie Whelan, and our old friend Phil Jones.

Small told Jones he wanted him to learn everything he could about the grand jury. This is Jones's account: "Late one afternoon there was nobody left in the courthouse halls but me. I was about ready to head back to the bureau when I saw this guy walking toward me coming from where I knew the grand jury was meeting. . . . As he neared me I said something to the effect [of], 'Been a long day, huh?' . . . He indicated it sure had been a long one, and he then volunteered the information that the prosecutor had asked them if they wanted to indict Nixon and that all the jurors 'had held up their hands.' "

Instantly, Jones had visions of a national scoop dancing in his head. He could not wait to get back to the bureau with his career-launching, world-beating exclusive. Before he left, though, Jones fashioned a system to stay in touch with the grand juror, an offset platemaker who worked at the nearby Government Printing Office: When Jones wanted to talk with him he would go to the GPO and take a freight elevator up to the sixth floor, where the juror worked. When the juror saw Jones standing there, it was a signal to call Jones at the CBS bureau in thirty minutes. Jones still thinks his clandestine system ranks right up there with Woodward and Bernstein's Deep Throat caper.

But there was a problem at CBS. They wouldn't touch Jones's story. He kept at it, however, using the freight elevator drop twice more as the grand juror fed him "little nuggets here and there," including the nugget that "some of the jurors raised both hands." After three or four nights of rejections, Jones got a call from Sandy Socolow, the Cronkite producer: "Are you sure you want to do this? You'll get hauled before Judge Sirica. You'd better check with a lawyer before you do this."

A frustrated Jones never did consult a lawyer, but he did consult first Dan Rather and then me. Our advice was so different that it left Jones in a journalistic limbo. Late one afternoon in the bureau Jones spotted Rather in his cubicle on the Front Row. He closed the door and told Rather everything. "What should I do?" Jones asked. Rather told him to go with it. "It's the biggest story of your life. It will make your career. Even if you go to prison, it will be a badge of honor. What a scoop."

Jones then walked down the line of cubicles and stopped at mine. He did not close my door but he laid it all out. I said, "Phil, what are you doing? Why are you doing this? It's not right. It's illegal. It's unethical. This is not what reporters are supposed to be doing. If you can't have people on the grand jury who can keep a secret, it will foul the whole system."

Jones stopped seeing his source and years later one of my bureau colleagues said, "That's what got Dan in trouble — that approach. Get it on. Go with it. The biggest scoop. It'll make your career."

Jones did not need that story to make his career. The day Spiro Agnew resigned, Jones became our full-time man on the new vice president designate, Gerald Ford. For the next ten months, Jones spent more time with Ford than with his own family, traveling 250,000 miles on a Convair turbojet — that's all Nixon would give Ford — that the pressies called "Slingshot Airlines." With Ford's defeat in 1976, Jones came to the Hill to replace me as CBS's chief congressional correspondent. He had lost none of his Indiana feistiness.

CHAPTER 43
"VOICES FROM HELL"

Late on Tuesday afternoon, April 30, 1974, the White House dumped in the lap of every news bureau in Washington a blue telephone-book-size soft volume containing about twelve hundred pages of the transcripts of the Oval Office tapes President Nixon had been withholding from the House Judiciary Committee. Actually the book was available only at the Government Printing Office at $12.25 each, and its official title was *Submission of Recorded Presidential Conversations to the Committee on the Judiciary of the House of Representatives by President Richard Nixon.*

What followed was a frantic scramble unlike Washington had ever seen, as a hungry media began tearing the meat from the bone. The *Post* turned Woodward and Bernstein loose on the story; the *New York Times* made plans to publish the twelve hundred pages; the Associated Press brought editors down from New York to handle the traffic. The morning-paper deadlines were pushed back until near dawn the next day. Bureaus worked through the night.

But at the networks deadlines are immovable — 6:30 PM for the evening news and 7 AM for the morning news. That meant the CBS bureau had less than three hours to digest twelve hundred pages in time for the Cronkite show. Rather than trying to make sense out of the entire transcript, Daniel Schorr and Fred Graham concentrated on just four critical meetings Nixon had with his counsel, John Dean. At 6:30, Cronkite turned over the first ten and half minutes to Schorr and Graham and to Phil Jones, who reported on the cleansing and the editing of the transcript.

As proud as the bureau was of the pressurized work that night on the Cronkite show, nothing excited the bureau quite so much as the way the *CBS Morning News* handled the twelve hundred pages the next morning. The morning news program had been for years the stepchild of the news division. Bill Plante, our long-time White House correspondent, once said, "If it ain't on Cronkite, it ain't on." CBS had had a morning program since 1954, but not until 1963, when Mike Wallace took over, did it become a serious and popular news broadcast. A shift from the 9 AM to the 7 AM time slot, up against the *Today* show, however, cost it much of its audience, and there followed a revolving door of anchors. By 1974 the co-anchors were Hughes Rudd and the glamorous recruit from the *Washington Post,* Sally Quinn. On a publicity tour to promote the program, Rudd told the TV press that at his age he had to get up every morning around four to go to the bathroom and figured he might as well stay up and do the show.

For the Washington morning news staff the question on the evening of April 30 was how to handle the Nixon transcripts the next day. There were two choices — reporters could do their standard stand-uppers, by paraphrasing the words and getting reaction from the politicians, or they could quote long passages from the transcript as the Oval Office words crawled across the screen.

But in 1974 there were no special effects and running fonts on the air was a slow, cumbersome, and sometimes dicey process. Everything had to be typed in, and unless the background was dark, the white letters would fade. The alternative was the standard report opening with something like, "Here at the House Judiciary Committee they are poring over the transcript," or "The White House says this morning the telegrams are running two to one in the president's favor."

But the Washington producer of the morning news, Bill Crawford, suddenly said, "No, no, no. We're not going to do either one. We'll have Serafin, and his rumbly voice, do Nixon, and Schieffer, who's kind of compact, do John Dean, and they'll read from the transcript." Crawford dubbed them "the 20/20 Players." He then called New York and said, "We need the whole hour to do this," and New York gave it to him. It was an absolutely original idea, and the men and women who worked on that broadcast still talk about it with awe. Rita Braver says, "People loved it. It was so great. It was really fun just to be there for that." Nothing had raised the morale of the morning news staff as quickly as the Crawford scheme. Even *Time* magazine took note of it under the headline "VOICES FROM HELL."

At forty-five, Bill Crawford had run the course. He started as a writer for CBS in New York, moved up into middle management, but was purged by Ernest Leiser, who correctly believed Crawford lacked sufficient respect. Shunted off to Washington, he had no trouble reviving his career, because he was a quick, smart, inventive, tough producer. New reporters in the bureau would be assigned to Crawford by Bill Small with instructions to "polish them up." His biggest assignment "to make it work" was with Sally Quinn. He tried but failed. In his diary, Crawford rarely passed judgment on the quality of the correspondents, but the January 10, 1974, entry read: "She is not a good writer and is only fair at handling a story," and the January 17 entry (in capital letters) was: "SALLY QUINN QUITS. . . . Whew!"[1]

Never reluctant to speak his mind, Crawford spoke it the night Leiser and Cronkite and their news staff came down to Washington for a major meeting and dinner. Leiser wanted to impress the Washington bureau with his importance and the importance of working for the first network news show that had expanded to thirty minutes. Leiser said grandly that a thirty-minute broadcast involved creating "a new art form."

Not only was there a burst of laughter from the Washington end of the table, but then Crawford chose to remind Leiser that there were only three ways that a TV report could be done: the correspondent was seen at the top of the report and the bottom; the correspondent was seen from the top all the

545

way to the bottom; and the correspondent was never seen. Leiser was furious; the meeting almost became a rumble. Cronkite and Leiser flew back to New York so mad they did not tell their staff, which then had to scramble the next morning for a hurried return to Manhattan.

Crawford had become, in Gary Gates's phrase, "something of a cult figure."[2] His idea of using correspondents to read the words of Nixon and Dean not only elevated his standing in the bureau but also proved such an effective way of handling the story that the network repeated the concept that night in a one-hour special, anchored by Cronkite and Rather. It was so simple it was dazzling. Serafin and Schieffer each stood behind a podium, and on the studio wall behind their right shoulder hung enlarged pictures of Dean and Nixon. Nelson Benton was added for the prime-time special as the voice of Bob Haldeman. Schieffer says they "protested that they weren't actors and they would look silly trying to act the parts, but Small told us, 'Don't act, just read them.' "[3] But Schieffer conceded that, cast as John Dean, he was "ever the ham. I wore a tan suit like his. He also wore a little tie pin and so did I."

So they read, resisting as best they could

the temptation to be dramatic or to take journalistic pleasure in the self-incriminating words. Lack of inflection or expression or emphasis did not seem to matter, because the unadorned words were so devastating. Their impact did not hit Serafin until he got off the air. "I suddenly realized that everything had changed," he says. "I realized at that moment that Richard Nixon was gone. I didn't know whether it would be a month or six months, but he was gone. It was over. It was just this extraordinary stunning moment." In his personal diary, Crawford wrote, "Nixon seems to have been a major conspirator. . . . How can he hope to escape now?"[4]

One of the bureau's major Watergate reporters who never got on the air during those fraught forty-eight hours was Lesley Stahl. Already a star after only two years on the network, Stahl was giving a speech at Bowling Green University in Ohio the night of Nixon's speech on the transcripts. I asked her recently if she remembered that day. "I certainly do. I was a woman. Talk about being bitchy. I was enraged. I went to Crawford and said, 'I want to know why I can't read John Dean.' I was so angry. They ridiculed me for thinking I could be John Dean. I never forgave him for it. Crawford told me, 'They're all men.' I said, 'So what? This is acting. It really doesn't matter who reads the part.' He said, 'Of course it does. Sorry, Toots.' I smoldered."[5]

Even without the smoldering Stahl, the prime-time special won an Emmy that year in the "Special Events" category. Crawford's reputation soared, because we all knew in the bureau that it was his *Morning News* idea, lifted almost entirely into the prime-time special, that nailed CBS its third straight Watergate Emmy.

Within a year or two, Crawford and I began working together as field producer and correspondent. We had already learned for ourselves how being too honest or too confrontational could cause network careers to suddenly plummet — Crawford's for bearding Leiser and mine for publicly disparaging TV news. That common experience not only drew us together, but it also set us apart as a pair who had survived, who knew how things worked, who had their own distinctive ideas about what stories to do and how to do them, and who were willing to tell New York how wrong they were.

During our four-year stretch together Crawford and I did pieces on live television in the Canadian House of Commons; on presidential rhetoric; on the politics of snow; on Bobby Byrd, the front-porch fiddler; on the smothering political influence of Boston's five TV stations; and on the tenth anniversary of Robert Kennedy's death, with a visit to Hickory Hill that focused on his children and their dogs.

One of Crawford's closest friends, Barry Serafin, remembers how tired they got of covering Robert Dole day after day during the 1976 campaign. One morning Crawford said, "The hell with Dole. Let's cover his advance man." They found him handing out posters, paying the locals, laying out the schedule. "It was a one-day quickie," says Serafin, "but it was twice as interesting as Dole."

Crawford's diary reveals a quiet pride in his work, a constant battle with minor health problems, a sometimes fractious home life with an alcoholic wife, and a constant attention to his motorcycle, his farm in West Virginia, and his three children, Maggie, Ken, and Annabel. Little of this did he reveal to me.

I did know that he was the son of Kenneth Crawford, the *Newsweek* columnist, from whom he got his toughs; that he was born in Buffalo or Washington; that he graduated from Beloit College in Wisconsin; and that he had been a CBS man since 1954. He cultivated the very same dark, bristly mustache that his father wore, a mustache that has been described as "Faulknerian." He was a very quick judge of talent. We turned out to be easy travel companions, respecting each other's privacy, enjoying each other's humor, and admiring each other's love of books and politics.

On one of our trips I brought on board David Halberstam's book on the media, *The Powers That Be,* and every few minutes I would say, "Hey, Bill! Listen to this," and then I would read aloud a chunk or two. After about an hour, when I got up to go to the john I left the book at my seat. When I returned, Crawford was reading *my* book and refused to give it back for three days.

CHAPTER 44
AT NOON TOMORROW

After twelve years of running the Washington bureau, Bill Small was gone, gone to New York to become the vice president of news. He took with him, as his praetorian guards, Sylvia Westerman and Don Richardson. He left in February 1974, the very week the House of Representatives cranked up the machinery to impeach Richard Nixon. Many of us wondered how Small could stand not being part of the action in Washington during the country's looming constitutional crisis, but his new job was huge. It put him in line to become the president of CBS News.

To take his place in Washington Small sent forty-two-year-old Sanford Socolow, known by all as "Sandy" or "Soc," and also known by all as Walter Cronkite's closest CBS friend and editorial confidant, and as the driving force behind the *Evening News.* Born in the Bronx of immigrant parents,

Socolow spent his early childhood herding cows on his family's dairy farm in Connecticut. Following his graduation from City College in New York, Socolow was drafted in 1950. He signed on with the International News Service in Japan after his discharge, went to work at CBS in 1956, and hooked up with Cronkite as a writer in 1959. His long history with CBS, his intimate familiarity with newsroom politics, his connections with Cronkite, and his all-encompassing skills as a producer made him a man of noteworthy value.

The bureau Socolow took over in the winter of 1974 was in excellent shape. All the beats had strong, established correspondents and superior backups, the production staff had been beefed up, morale was high, and the bureau was riding on the crest of the Watergate wave. Whether the press liked Nixon or not, to be a political reporter in Washington during those days was to be in a journalistic nirvana — oblivious of everything but the most compelling, breathtaking story most of us had ever covered. We could not wait for the next day to come, the next Nixon lie, the next smoking gun, the next acerbic comment from Barry Goldwater, the next defection on the Hill.

Socolow was no micromanager, as Small

had been. There was no need to be, because the bureau almost ran itself. John Armstrong recalls, "Soc was a great delegator. He never slept. He'd go to lunch, have two martinis, and never miss a trick."

Within a week or two after his arrival in Washington, however, Socolow got hit by his first crisis. It involved Bruce Morton, who had become very prickly about having his copy changed. Morton had just had a story turned down by the Cronkite show. Presenting himself to Socolow, he said, "Well, I guess I'll just have to look for work elsewhere" and walked out. In a panic, Socolow called Bill Small to tell him his best writer had quit. Small started laughing. "Get used to it. That happens once or twice a week."

Socolow had brought with him to Washington as his assistant bureau chief forty-three-year-old Bill Headline, a quiet, well-organized, and efficient former Navy intelligence officer whose speciality in New York had been producing live remotes, space shots, and network pool coverage. It was Headline, along with Bill Galbraith, who ran the bureau after Socolow's wife announced, out of the blue, that she wanted a divorce. "Soc was in such total shock," says Headline, "that he was elsewhere for a long stretch."

Headline was on duty as a pool producer on the day Richard Nixon's presidency effectively came to an end — July 27, 1974. The House Judiciary Committee had voted twenty-one to seventeen to impeach the president. Ron Ziegler, Nixon's press secretary, got the news in San Clemente when his secretary ran to tell him. According to Woodward and Bernstein, she cried out, "The poor president. Oh, the poor man."[1] The secretary's name was Diane Sawyer. Her hiring as a CBS reporter four years later was a public-relations gamble, not because she was without television experience but because she had worked in the Nixon White House and had hung in with the disgraced Nixon for three years after his fall from grace. But the Sawyer gamble turned out to be a triumph. She became one of the brightest media stars to come from Washington, brief as her stay was. She was another Bill Small hire; their connections were from Louisville, where Sawyer's mother had taught Small's eldest daughter.

With the committee's vote, the federal government drifted into chaos, not knowing who was in charge, not knowing how long it would take Nixon before he surrendered. It took him twelve days. On Thursday, August

8, Ziegler told the White House press that the president would address the nation that night at 9 o'clock.

Cronkite was already in town, to originate the *Evening News* from our bureau that night. With Ziegler's announcement, CBS decided to remain on the air beyond the Nixon speech, until 11 PM.

Arthur Taylor, the president of CBS, who had succeeded Frank Stanton only the year before, had also come to Washington and had set up shop in the bureau. To have a corporate president conducting business in a news bureau was not only highly unusual but also a serious strain on the wall that separated the corporation from the news division. According to the accounts by both CBS News President Richard Salant and Daniel Schorr, Taylor was passing along rumors to the management of CBS News in New York that President Nixon was planning to attack the media, especially CBS News. Salant, who remained in New York that day, wrote, "We in CBS News management telephoned the correspondents who would be covering the story that night to remind them that it was not a time, no matter what Nixon decided to do, for gloating or for editorial attacks. We told our reporters, if, as appeared likely, Nixon was going to resign — the first presidential resignation in American history — it was a time for national unity so that the government and the nation could move forward."[2] And Schorr wrote, "While I was reading a news ticker, Socolow came over and urged me not to be 'vindictive.' When I objected that this sounded like a reflection on my professionalism, Socolow assured me I was not being singled out, but that this precautionary word was being passed to all correspondents."[3]

When I read to Socolow Schorr's account of that conversation not long ago, Socolow's response was "Bullshit." Socolow vehemently denied going around the bureau trying to talk us into "going easy on Nixon," but he did say, "I may have said something to Schorr in passing in the corridor about taking it easy. If I did, that was it."

Whether those of us assigned to comment on the Nixon speech ever got such orders or instructions or suggestions or hints or whispers remains unsettled. I did not. At a panel at Duke University, Schorr later said CBS had gone wobbly on Nixon out of deference to management's wishes. Schorr's allegation provoked a letter to *New York* magazine signed by Sevareid, Cronkite, and

Rather (I declined to sign), calling Schorr's comments at Duke a "slander." Their letter went on: "The notion that executive orders at CBS News were handed down to 'go soft on Nixon,' and that those of us who felt constrained from whipping an obviously beaten man behaved in response to such orders, is false."[4] In his book on CBS News, Gary Paul Gates wrote that Schorr said, "The reason Mudd had not gone along with the kid-gloves treatment was that he had flown into Washington late in the day, and thus did not get the word." Gates mentions three possible sources for the Schorr quotation but does not specify which was more likely — the Duke *Chronicle,* the student newspaper; *New York* magazine; or *Media Report,* a Washington newsletter put out by Kevin Phillips.[5] Schorr himself has called the Duke account "inaccurate" and *Media Report*'s version "totally distorted."[6]

I had flown into Washington, all right, but it was the day *before* the Nixon speech. During the day on Thursday, August 8, I was on the Hill all day reporting and putting together a congressional piece for the *Evening News* and did not walk into the bureau on M Street until nearly 5:30 PM. No one at CBS or CBS News ever said a word or a whisper to me that day about what I should say or how I should say it. The implication of the Schorr quote, if accurate, is that had I only gotten "the word" I would have put on the same kid gloves that Cronkite, Sevareid, and Rather supposedly were wearing — a soft slander that has stuck in my craw ever since.

Nixon said that night that he was resigning because "it has become evident to me that I no longer have a strong enough political base in the Congress. . . . With the disappearance of that base . . . there is no longer a need for the process to be prolonged. . . . Therefore, I shall resign the presidency effective at noon tomorrow. . . . I regret deeply any injuries that may have been done in the course of events that led to this decision. I would say only that if some of my judgments were wrong, and some were wrong, they were made in what I believed at the time to be in the best interest of the nation."[7]

When the president finished, Cronkite began: "It was a sixteen-minute speech, in which the president seemed calm but controlling, obviously, with very deep emotion. He did not — and I think my colleagues will agree — confess any crimes. In regard to the Watergate or any other matters, he said that he was guilty perhaps of bad judgment but that was all. Eric?"

Walter's throw to Eric was so quick that it seemed as if he couldn't wait to get rid of a hot potato.

Sevareid: "On the whole, it seemed to me, as effective, as magnanimous a speech as Mr. Nixon has ever made. And, I suppose, there'd be many — even among his critics — who would say that, perhaps, that few things in his presidency became him as much as his manner of leaving the presidency. . . .

Rather: "Walter, I think it may very well go down, when history takes a look at it, as one of Richard Nixon's — if not his finest hour. . . . There is no joy in this for anyone tonight. No decent-thinking American could take any joy out of this. . . . He did give — and I would agree with, Walter, what you said — he gave to this moment a touch of class. More than that — a touch of majesty. . . .

Mudd: "Well, from a — just from a pure congressional point of view, I really wouldn't think that was a very satisfactory speech. It did not deal with the realities of why he was leaving. There was no accounting in the speech of how he got there and why he was leaving that Oval Office. That whole question of Watergate is all anybody in the Congress has had on their minds for the better part of a year. Half the Congress defended him. Half the Congress has gone out on a limb for him. In the absence of any explanation or any acknowledgment of the president's responsibility in the Watergate cover-up, the viewer is left to conclude that it was simply some craven politicians in the Congress who collapsed in their defense of the president, and solely because of that was he having to leave the presidency. I think that it was, from a congressional standpoint, realistic to think that the president would make some bow toward the Hill to accept the blame that he admitted in the last week was his. But there was nothing like that tonight."

I could not believe I was saying all this stuff. Endless ad-libbing has never been one of my strong suits. I do all right in short bursts on subjects I know something about. But there I was, during the nation's gravest sort of constitutional crisis, being uncharacteristically cool, precise, and articulate, without my usual sprinkling of "uh's" and "ah's" and "er's."

Even a question from Cronkite about "binding up the wounds" didn't slow me down.

Mudd: "Well, there is still to be accounted for in the country, it seems to me, a sizable body of opinion that would rightfully ask: Is the president of the United States really to be beyond the law? That, if certain crimes were committed and certain laws violated, then somebody ought to be punished for them. And an awful lot of men have had their families broken up in the last year because of crimes they have committed. . . . And those people were not beyond the law."

Rather, who is competitive if he is anything, now had a problem. With his strong and edgy reporting on Watergate establishing him as the president's adversary, he was now in danger of looking too soft. He could let me — a minor contributor to our Watergate coverage — steal the show, so to speak, or he could come back at me with a trump:

Rather: "Well, history will be weighed.

561

This is going to be the agony of the next few days, if not weeks and months — the agony of weighing what you have said, on the one hand, Roger, in the Congress and in hearts and minds of the American people; weighing that against, on the other hand, the lack of appetite to — more than that, the absolute determination, I think, on the part of most people, not to shoot at lifeboats."

Rather, characteristically I thought, had decided to split it right down the middle. Sevareid, however, made no bones about it — he did not like what I had been saying.

Sevareid: "I don't think it's for any of us to say whether or not he should be prosecuted. . . . I don't know how one passes judgment — because other people have been convicted, he must be tried. I'm not Solomon, and I don't think any of us are. . . ."[8]

None of us said anything to each other after the broadcast. Cronkite remained in the studio, anchoring our coverage until 11 PM, but Sevareid, Rather, and I slipped out. Sevareid, who wrote very little after his last book in 1964, is not on record about that night. Rather, whose 1977 book covers that

period, makes no mention of the resignation night broadcast.[9] He told David Halberstam in 1978, though, that he was "later
aware that he had blown it, that he had
simply gotten it wrong. . . . Rather's own
explanation for the weakness of his commentary was that . . . he had been running
all day long . . . and had had no time to
think in his own mind of what he wanted to
say for Nixon's epitaph. . . ."[10]

The television audience that night was
huge, and the public reaction to our analysis
was explosive. The three of us were praised
and denounced, me for being "crude and
arrogant" or "courageous and incisive;" they
for being "soft and sentimental" or "respectful and patriotic." One viewer wrote to tell
me that in his house they were throwing
food at the TV set during Sevareid and
Rather but were cheering when my turn
came. At a cocktail party soon after, Lauren
Bacall stopped me with: "Goddamn, Roger
Mudd. You were the only one!"

The next week I was back in New York,
again substituting on the *Evening News.*
Walking west on Fifty-eighth Street on my
way to work one morning, I was accosted
by a woman who wordlessly began whack-
ing me on the shoulders with her furled

umbrella. I was clueless about her, whether she was a Nixon lover or what the police call an "EDP" — an "emotionally disturbed person." She could have been both, of course, and probably was.

My relations with Rather did not improve after that night. Despite all the ex post facto denials of corporate meddling, I was convinced that Cronkite, Sevareid, and Rather had indeed gone in the tank for management. Remembering Rather's less than straightforward response to our letter protesting the death of instant analysis, I concluded that he was much too eager to please the bosses.

More than two decades later — a year after Rather's career had ended at CBS — we sat down in a New York hotel room to talk about his time in the bureau. Our conversation, difficult and guarded at first, almost foundered because of a misunderstanding. When I brought up our Nixon resignation broadcast, I told him I thought he had gone in the tank that night and I had always wondered why. Rather did not like the accusation. "I would think as well as you know me that among the many things that I might do that are less than admirable, that going in the tank for anybody is not one of them." With my accusation on the table and on the tape, Rather unburdened himself in highly guarded language with a series of complaints about me — that perhaps I had adopted the minority view that night hoping that Nixon would be impeached, which would have made me look good; that given the high state of competition in the bureau I was one of those among whom there was "questioning, opposition, and in some cases maybe even slight tinges of envy about our Watergate coverage," and that when Watergate was building there was a "reluctance" on the part of me and Paul Greenberg, my Saturday-night news producer, to accept his White House coverage. But then he softened his complaints by acknowledging that he might have been seeing "shadows when no shadows existed." I was left not knowing whether to respond or not.

Rather's litany, however, had been provoked by a misunderstanding. He thought I had accused him of going in the tank for Nixon, when I meant going in the tank for CBS management. His last two complaints, even if he thought them true, were explicable given our growing rivalry for the Cronkite crown. But his claim that I was rooting for Nixon's impeachment so I could look good beggars an answer and revealed in Rather a calculating and suspicious turn of mind.

After Nixon's resignation in 1974, Rather moved to New York to take over *CBS Reports* and then to join *60 Minutes.* We were no longer Washington colleagues, so our paths rarely crossed, although I kept a close watch through the years as his notoriety grew.

Chapter 45
Pancake

If television viewers could not tell that Richard Nixon had been crying the night he resigned the presidency, the credit went to a sixty-year-old woman from Lima, Ohio, who among the politicians and the press was Washington's premier makeup artist.

Lillian Brooks Brown was on duty at CBS that night, August 8, preparing to apply Sevareid's makeup for his nightly commentary when the White House called. Press Secretary Zeigler had already announced that the president would address the nation at 9 PM, and his office wanted her at the White House by 7:30 PM.

Brown had been doing presidential makeup since she met John Kennedy on his many appearances on CBS's *Face the Nation* during the 1960 campaign, and her informal White House contract — about a hundred dollars per makeup — had carried through Johnson and Nixon.

With Ziegler's call she hustled to the White House and was admitted to the Cabinet Room, where the president and his congressional supporters from the Hill had assembled, many of them crying. As the meeting broke up, a Secret Service agent told Brown, "You're going to be alone with him for thirty minutes and he's not in very good shape." When she went with Nixon into the sitting room off the Oval Office, he began crying again, "sobbing, really," she told me recently. She tried her best to brighten him up so she could apply the makeup. "But nothing seemed to work. The makeup kept streaking because of his tears."

Brown, anxious to help Nixon get control of himself, suddenly recalled a laugh they had had at the last White House Christmas party. She reminded him how his excitable Irish setter, King Timahoe, had disrupted the hanging of tree ornaments at the party and how she had suggested putting him in the nearby bathroom. As she led the way, Brown had looked back in surprise to find that it was not an aide but Nixon himself bringing the dog into the bathroom. The door somehow closed and they heard the lock click. For Lillian Brown, it was a first — trapped in a bathroom with the president of the United States and his dog. Remembering the story apparently helped Nixon pull himself out of his self-pity; Brown got the makeup to stay on; the president returned to the Oval Office to do his mike check, makeup check, and lighting check before he began: "Good Evening. This is the thirty-seventh time I have spoken to you from this office. . . ."

Nixon regarded makeup as a necessity, Brown said, because with that beard "there was nothing he could do."

The other presidents she worked on also welcomed the makeup. "They wanted to look professional on the camera, but they didn't want to look made-up," said Brown. "I had a horror that someday somebody would say, 'The president, comma, heavily made-up, comma,' but it never happened with me.

"John Kennedy had these problems — and we didn't know what they were," she said. "But if he had a lot under the chin, I'd walk in and [he'd look] at me and wiggle his fingers under his chin." Apparently it was his Addison's disease, which had caused either some puffiness or skin discoloration.

When the men's jackets rode up, Brown "would just simply — you know, [the] president or whoever — I would just reach up and pull it down and tuck it under.

That's how I came to find out that John Kennedy was wearing that metal brace."

Lyndon Johnson, she said, "wanted makeup. He wanted to look good."

Gerald Ford was anxious to get the shine off his high forehead. "I think I gave more powder compacts to Ford than anybody." Once she decided on a president's skin tone, Brown would keep it in separate compacts. If the president was going to the Hill for a State of the Union speech, for instance and she could not go, Brown would first show the president's special compact to the Secret Service and then hand it to the president himself. That way, she said, "he could go into the bathroom and do a little, tiny bit, maybe just the nose."

Brown did Jimmy Carter dozens of times, she said, especially for White House functions like a big Horowitz concert. Because Carter would be seen on camera or make a speech on camera, Carter wanted to wear makeup at his own party.

With Ronald Reagan, she said, it was more a matter of adjusting what had already been done. "You have to realize that the two actors in the White House wore makeup most all the time."

"You mean when Reagan got up in the morning he would put it on?" I asked.

"I don't know. All I know is that I realized he wore makeup most of his private life. If you looked at the pictures you could tell. The biggest thing was he'd come to the studio and say, 'I'm already made up.'"

Clinton, she said, was eager, "always eager" to be made up. His signed photo, showing his entire staff watching while he went over a speech and while Brown applied the powder, reads:

"To Lillian — Washington's finest plastic surgeon with her most reluctant baggy-eyed patient. Thanks, Bill Clinton."

For TV correspondents, especially ones who had come from newspapers, where makeup was used only by women, whipping out a compact before going on camera was like zipping up your fly in public — it had to be done effectively but in a way no one could see it being done. Cameraman Laurens Pierce, who knew firsthand the fury of the KKK, says, "Hell, you don't know what guts [are] until you have to stand in front of a screaming race mob and put on your pancake makeup."[1]

During my time on the *11 PM Report* on WTOP, I refused to wear makeup. Simply stated, I felt it unmanly. Of course, I was an unblemished and unwrinkled thirty-one-year-old at the time. Even with CBS in the field, we rarely carried a compact, although Dan Rather tells the story on himself that on a flight from Memphis to Birmingham his pancake compact fell out of his briefcase from the overhead rack. The stewardess, of course, couldn't wait to return it to her dashing passenger. When she tried, Rather says, "I gave her an innocent blank stare that said, 'Well, don't look at me. What would I being doing with *that?*' "[2] I would have given her the same answer.

But with the advent of color television and video cameras and the widespread use of newspaper reporters as talking heads, anti-pancake holdouts became hard to find. Occasionally, though, the old *Front Page* contempt for the "pretty boys" would erupt. After years of being ignored by the Sunday talk shows, Jack Germond of the Gannett papers was invited to be a panelist on *Meet the Press,* which was originating from Florida during the 1972 primary. Germond was a political reporter without equal, known to the political crowd around the country, but the TV producers thought he lacked the television look.

Word of the next morning's Germond debut spread quickly among his pals. During the night, two of them — Jules Witcover and Tom Ottenad — rushed into Germond's hotel room carrying huge canisters of talcum powder, shaking powder all over Germond and running around the room, yelling, "Makeup, makeup."

CHAPTER 46
PIKE'S PEEK

The headline read: "THE REPORT ON THE CIA THAT PRESIDENT FORD DOESN'T WANT YOU TO READ." It was the February 16, 1976, issue of the *Village Voice,* the liberal New York weekly. The report, a classified document on the illegal activities of the CIA, came from the House Select Intelligence Committee, otherwise known as the Pike Committee, whose chairman was Otis Pike of New York.

The Pike report had been leaked to Daniel Schorr, but the byline on the newspaper's introduction to the report was Aaron Latham, a freelance writer and the boyfriend of Lesley Stahl. Copies of the *Voice* reached Dan Schorr in the Washington bureau late that morning. He went in to see Sandy Socolow, the bureau chief, and dropped a copy of the *Voice* on his desk. Socolow pointed to the Latham byline and said, "Are you thinking what I'm thinking?"

meaning, says Schorr, that Socolow suspected Stahl might have helped Latham acquire a copy of the report. Schorr says his response to Socolow was "an elaborate shrug."[1]

Socolow maintains it was just the other way around. "Schorr comes into my office and says, 'Shouldn't we look into where Lesley was? Shouldn't we check about Lesley's whereabouts in the days leading up to this?' "

The difference in those two versions almost tore apart the Washington bureau of CBS News.

Schorr, who moved from reporting the Great Society to the Watergate scandal, had created a new intelligence beat and once again was leaving a wake. On January 25, Schorr was leaked a copy of the Pike report. Not wanting to be seen in the bureau Xeroxing a three-hundred-plus-page document, Schorr asked the bureau researcher, Susan Zirinsky, to do the copying. As any good researcher would do, Zirinsky also Xeroxed a copy for herself. But suddenly, she says, "This thing kind of exploded and I realized I'm complicit and I have a copy of it with the source's handwriting in the corner. So I took my copy and buried it in my back yard at Forty-fourth and Warren Street." Zirinsky, who transferred to New York in 1989, never went back to dig it up. It may still be moldering in its back yard grave.

For the next five nights Schorr was on the *Evening News* reporting various angles from the Pike report and holding up his copy on camera to prove, in effect, that he knew what he was talking about. But as the story got thinner and thinner, the broadcast began to lose interest, much to Schorr's frustration. He felt the Pike report certainly ranked near the Pentagon Papers in importance.

A few days later, the House voted to keep the Pike Committee report classified unless President Ford ruled otherwise. For the corporate management of CBS the vote meant that continued pursuit of the story would not only defy the decision of the House but also run the risk that CBS would lose the goodwill of the House, which no TV network can do without.

With his CBS outlets cut off, Schorr felt abandoned by his network. Driven by his belief that the Pike report had to be made public but never would be, Schorr leaked a copy to the *Village Voice*. Five days later the *Voice* published it, under the Latham byline. Stahl says she came under immediate suspicion from Socolow, and "there were actual meetings to determine what to do with me." Of course, Stahl knew exactly who had provided the *Voice* its copy, because Latham had told her. Nonetheless, Schorr continued to spread the Stahl-Latham rumor, according to both Socolow and Stahl. At one point, Stahl says, Zirinsky pulled her aside to tell her Schorr was claiming "you rifled through his desk, found the Pike papers, Xeroxed them, and gave them to Aaron." Stahl says, "Eric Sevareid approached me — I never went to him for advice — he came and said, 'You should never speak to him again until he apologizes.'"

The morning the *Voice* published the Pike report, Richard Salant, the news president, called Socolow and demanded to know what the hell was going on. "Things were getting really hot," says Socolow. "The Congress is threatening to send the whole CBS bureau to jail and . . . as far as they are concerned [the report] was classified and making it public was illegal." Socolow maintains that because of the uproar on the Hill Schorr panicked and tried laying it off on Stahl and Latham.

Salant asked Socolow how many copies of the report there were. "I've got the only existing copy," said Socolow, obviously not being aware of the buried treasure at Forty-fourth and Warren streets.

"Where is it?"

"I've got it in the trunk of my car."

"I want you to get up from your desk right now. I want you to leave the office right now. I don't want you to talk to anybody. I want you to go get in your car. I want you to drive to the airport. I want you to open the trunk, take the copy out and I want you to get on a plane, fly to New York, come to my office, and give me the copy, and I'm going to put it in my safe." Salant told Socolow that if anybody at CBS was going to jail for possessing a classified document, he, Richard S. Salant, would be the one.

Within a few days, Stahl was off the hook, when Schorr acknowledged to the *Washington Post* that he was the source of the *Voice* story.[2] He said it was "pointless" to deny his connection any longer. Socolow never forgave Schorr for misleading him and for damaging, even temporarily, Stahl's reputation.

Now it was Daniel Schorr who was on the hook. CBS affiliates were demanding that Schorr be banished from the air. Salant ordered Schorr off the intelligence beat and put on general assignment. In late February the House voted to investigate the leaking of the Pike report. Salant and the CBS lawyers responded by suspending Schorr from all duties "indefinitely" and requiring him to sign an undated letter of resignation. Despite Schorr's sterling defense of the First Amendment in refusing to divulge his source in his testimony before the House Ethics Committee, despite an outpouring of support from the media, his bonds with CBS had been broken. The night before he was to go to New York for a final meeting with Salant, Schorr called him at home to tell him he had decided to resign. Salant was shocked and unprepared for Schorr's decision, because he had tentatively decided to reinstate Schorr. He had polled various CBS executives and correspondents, including George Herman, who, when asked whether Schorr's return to Washington would demoralize the bureau, said, "No more than it always did."[3]

Small told Schorr's lawyer, Joseph Califano, however, that had Schorr been reinstated Sevareid would have been outraged, Socolow would have been transferred, and Stahl might have resigned.

Schorr cleared out in September. In leaving, he acknowledged that his presence in the bureau would have been "polarizing," a "source of tension," which would have damaged his effectiveness as a correspondent.[4] Those of us who read his statement thought he spoke the truth.

According to Stahl, Schorr called after his resignation and told her, "Lesley, I just want you to know that I'm sorry if I caused you any pain." "Is that an apology?" Stahl asked. "Well, I just want you to know how badly I feel," he said, "that you may have been embarrassed or made to feel uncomfortable."[5] Stahl says she is still waiting for a genuine apology. But while she waited, she got to wait in her new office in the bureau's Front Row. She had been given Schorr's old cubicle.

The Pike story is a chapter that few in the bureau enjoy rereading or talking about. For those who never trusted Schorr or were offended by his journalistic avarice, the role he played only reinforced their opinion of him. For those who admired his tenacity, his pursuit of a story, and his steadiness under congressional fire, his departure was a critical and unnecessary loss to CBS News. The bureau never had another correspondent quite like him.

Few of us knew it then but 1976 marked an imperceptible change at the bureau. The Dan Schorr episode revealed disharmony in the House of Murrow; the election of Jimmy

Carter meant we no longer had Nixon to kick around and to unify us, and the rise of a competitive ABC News lessened our swagger a bit. John Armstrong, who had become the bureau's chief *Evening News* producer, says, "By 1976, everything was winding down. It was going to be a different kind of life. We had done the war, we had done Agnew, we had done Watergate, we had done a couple of campaigns. It was so much fun. It was satisfying." Beyond all that, the huge news division budgets were becoming a thing of the past. Armstrong says the 1972 presidential race was the last in which there were no money restrictions. At one point during the later part of the McGovern campaign, Armstrong was running three three-man crews — that is, camera, sound, and lights. Armstrong himself was gone by 1980, unable to resist the charismatic pull of Roone Arledge at ABC or the double-his-salary offer that was waved in his face.

For me the last years of the 1970s were spent mainly as Cronkite's one-and-only substitute, summer, fall, winter, and spring, an assignment that left me unavailable for great chunks of time to cover the Congress. So I cut loose from Capitol Hill after more than fifteen years to become the national affairs correspondent and float freely with features on a variety of subjects — religious broadcasters, the *Federal Register,* Washington lobbyists, congressional wives, the presidential yacht, the USS *Sequoia.* But when Cronkite called, I went, and went so frequently that I kept a small apartment at the Wyndham Hotel on West Fifty-eighth Street, which the owner, John Mados, equipped with a refrigerator and a toaster oven.

CHAPTER 47
UNCLE WALTER

On the evening of October 20, 1977, a teenage member of my family could not believe what he'd heard Walter Cronkite say. Cronkite had just broadcast a late bulletin that a plane crash in Mississippi had killed Ronnie Van Sant, the leader of the southern rock band Lynyrd Skynyrd. Despite its odd spelling, the band's name was pronounced "Leonard Skinnerd," which without the final "d" was in fact the name of the high school gym teacher of one of the musicians. But my teenager groaned in disbelief when he heard Cronkite pronounce it "Lean-yerd Skeen-yerd." There had not been time, obviously, to supply Cronkite with an accurate pronunciation, and it did reveal that the great man had a few weak spots, among them pop culture. But there were not many.

For those of us in the Washington bureau, it really didn't matter much that he blew Lynyrd Skynyrd's name or that he hadn't heard of Woody Guthrie, although we all snorted about his gaffes behind his back. What mattered to us was that Cronkite believed that almost everything that happened in Washington was important. Some of the reliance on Washington in the sixties and early seventies was because news from the capital was technically so much easier and cheaper to broadcast than stories from London, Paris, and Moscow. Even so, Cronkite regarded Washington as the news center of the world. "Never," says Eric Engberg, "would Cronkite have said, 'Let's move this story out of Washington,' " a phrase Engberg says he heard many times in the 1990s from "New York producers who had decided the capital was boring, tired, and lacking in sufficient glamour."

What was critical in Cronkite's approach to the news was his early training as a wire-service reporter with United Press. Hard facts, strong writing, and breaking stories were what he valued most. Engberg says the CBS newsrooms were run more like a wire service than a broadcasting shop, because of Cronkite's wire-service background.

"God forbid that you missed something that Walter's sacred wires were reporting," says Engberg, a Westinghouse alumnus who was in the Washington bureau for twenty years. "You would get heated calls from New York if your script did not take note of some fact that was in the third paragraph of the AP story."

Aware as we were of Cronkite's standards, few of us in Washington knew him personally. The 1960s was not a time when anchors moved around a lot, so rarely was he in our bureau. Most of us knew him only from a distance. But even up close, he seemed so totally focused on the news and all the other obligations that came with being an anchorman that he held himself apart, though without being condescending or pretentious.

My own relationship with him was uneven and occasionally difficult. Bouncing him from the convention anchor chair in 1964 got us started on an uneven keel. The speech I gave at Washington and Lee University in late 1970, sharply critical of television news, followed a few months later by the "Selling of the Pentagon" documentary, in which we showed him narrating a Pentagon propaganda film, and finally my semipublic complaint about his plugging Pan-Am in one of his radio commentaries must have caused him to wonder whose side I was on.

Then in the summer of 1973, as I began

my summer-long substitution for Cronkite, I ran into a serious problem with one of the show's new writers. She was Carol Ross, a *Time* magazine reporter, who had impressed Cronkite and was hired late in 1972. She says I was "stern, serious, somewhat aloof . . . and most people grumbled. They respected you but the connection was not warm and fuzzy."

We were "oil and water" from the beginning, she says. "There was a chemical imbalance." With the 6:29 PM deadline always getting closer, I would set aside her copy and write my own version, in my own voice. There was no time to argue; there was enough tension already. She tried but, she says, "I could not get your voice in my head."

Finally I complained to Socolow and asked that Ross be taken off the show during my substitutions. That night Ross called Cronkite at his summer home on Martha's Vineyard to tell him what I had done. She says Cronkite told her, "Roger is doing this just to get at me." Ross says she sobbed. "Do you want me to get you back on the show? I can talk to Socolow," Cronkite offered. Ross told him, "No. Roger doesn't want me. So be it."

Carol Ross, now Carol Joynt and the

owner of a very popular restaurant in Georgetown, returned later from time to time as one of my writers, but the episode remained with Cronkite as proof of my contentiousness.

Not until the campaign of 1976 did the tension between us become public. Beginning with the Iowa caucuses, I had been working with a bright, happy young producer named Brian Healy, from New Bedford, Massachusetts, a graduate of Penn State and Columbia's journalism school. Healy was short, bustling, engaging, voluble, and great fun to be with.

We had done profiles of the candidates and pieces on the New Hampshire, Massachusetts, Florida, and Pennsylvania primaries, and in late May Healy and I headed for California to do a story setting up the primary on June 8. But once we got on the ground, I suggested to Healy that this piece would be different. We would not cover Ronald Reagan and Gerald Ford as if their campaigning were real. We would show how everything they did was staged for television. Healy was enthusiastic.

The centerpiece of the story was Ronald Reagan's speech to the California police chiefs convention, a law-and-order audience and a great Reagan photo op if there ever was one. It was a standard speech that he'd made a dozen times to his conservative base. In speaking to two thousand people at most that day, Reagan took no new positions and he broke no new ground. In other words, there was no news in it, but that night on Los Angeles's three early-evening newscasts Reagan was seen and heard by an audience of 1,071,000 for five minutes and fifty-one seconds. That night on the three network newscasts, Reagan was seen and heard for four minutes and four seconds by 37 million people. The combination of Reagan, the police chiefs, and a law-and-order speech proved irresistible to the producers in New York.

Healy headed back to New York to edit our story, and I returned to Washington in time to be at field day at my daughter's school.

When Healy finished editing the next week, he proudly screened the story for the show's producers, who thought it powerful. Late that afternoon Healy called to tell me Cronkite had killed the piece. He had no explanation, only that Cronkite did not like it. For the anchor to kill a story by the network's premier political correspondent was no laughing matter. The news zipped through the halls of CBS on West Fifty-seventh Street in Manhattan.

Healy thought the killing was "outrageous" and told Tom Bettag, one of the producers on the *Morning News,* what had happened. Bettag liked the idea of the piece, told Healy that Walter Cronkite was not his boss, and scheduled the story for the next morning, Friday, June 4.

The next morning — it was Healy's birthday — just minutes after the *Morning News* had ended, Healy's home telephone rang. It was Bud Benjamin calling. Benjamin, one of television's sweetest men, was the executive producer of the Cronkite show.

"Did Roger give that piece to the morning show?" Benjamin wanted to know.

"No, I did," said Healy.

"Thank God," said Benjamin.

Benjamin was thanking God because an angry Cronkite suspected that I had given the story to the *Morning News* and ordered Benjamin to find out. When Healy said it was he who had arranged the handoff, Benjamin knew a major explosion between his anchor and the anchor's so-called heir apparent had been averted.

The story behind the Reagan story was leaked to the *New York Times* by one of Cronkite's own writers. The *Times* reported that Cronkite vetoed the story "because it cast television news in a bad light by allowing itself to be manipulated."[1] Because the *Times* also said there had developed a "rift" between Cronkite and me, management suggested that the two of us meet.

We met in Los Angeles the day before the primary. I didn't know what to expect, whether my ousting of Carol Ross or my unofficial designation as his heir apparent was grating on him and might spill out. But the session was low-key. I had forgotten what a nonaggressive interviewer he was and how he was lambasted for being a patsy in his interview with Chicago's Mayor Daley at the 1968 convention. In a surprisingly quiet voice, Cronkite told me he killed the piece because the Nixon administration's generally hostile attitude toward the networks, including Vice President Agnew's attack in 1969, made it the wrong time to be piling on. I said I thought he was overreacting, that Agnew's speech was eight years ago, that the disgraced Nixon had been out of office almost two years, that I hoped CBS News was mature enough to handle the criticism, and that if we couldn't critique ourselves the wackos would do it for us. Cronkite made no reply. And that was it. We simply agreed to disagree.

Walter Cronkite was a pussycat, when he wanted to be.

CHAPTER 48
TEDDY

Substituting for Walter Cronkite may have set my image with the viewing public, but the assignment I turned to in the fall of 1979 helped establish my worth as an independent journalist, with no strings attached, social or otherwise. It was my last major assignment with CBS News. It was the one-hour documentary on Senator Edward M. Kennedy called simply "Teddy."

Nothing knots the stomach of a TV journalist quicker than to read a denunciation of his work as "snide, contemptuous, laden with innuendo." William A. Henry of the *Boston Globe* wrote that "Roger Mudd raised questions about the seriousness of his journalism."[1] Even the fearsome William Buckley was content with a mere "tasteless."[2]

That was about the worst of it for me but not for the senator. Much of the political press used "Teddy" to tee off on a Kennedy they thought to be an inadequate replacement for his two brothers and a flawed bearer of the torch, and writers who did not admire the senator to begin with were, of course, delighted.

Anthony Lewis of the *New York Times* said Kennedy was "stumbling, inarticulate, unconvincing"[3]; Mary McGrory of the *Washington Star* wrote the senator was not "even coherent"[4]; Patrick Buchanan called the documentary "little short of devastating"[5]; Jimmy Breslin of the *New York Daily News* said he found Kennedy to be "annoying, wanting, and disturbing"[6]; and Evans and Novak wrote that "amateurism" was one deficiency not expected from a Kennedy.[7]

In the understated comment of Patrick Lucey, one of the senator's campaign managers, " 'Teddy' was not the way you'd like to launch the campaign."[8]

"Disaster" was the word that Howard Stringer, Andrew Lack, and I used on September 29, 1979, during a break in the filming at Kennedy's Cape Cod home. The senator had gone inside the house and Stringer, the executive producer of *CBS Reports,* and Lack, the producer of "Teddy," and I walked down the lawn away from the crew toward the water. We had thirty minutes of film, all right, but we agreed that unless the next thirty minutes got a lot better we had a "disaster" on our hands. The senator's answers were halting, incomplete, flat, and totally lacking in color or humor. Stringer and Lack, who were not aware of how tough a Kennedy was to interview, seemed truly worried. The network had given us November 7 as our air date — less than six weeks hence. We had to keep going and pray that the second half would get better. The subject of the second thirty minutes was his car accident at Chappaquiddick Island, and it was an improvement — more spirited, at times even aggressive, because the senator had had, after all, ten years to prepare his answers.

But we were still not sure what we had until the three of us looked at the film a week later in New York. It was a disaster, all right, but not for CBS. For a presidential candidate who could not give a sensible reason for running, who had obviously not thought about why he deserved the nomination, who was still avoiding the truth about his behavior on Chappaquiddick on July 18, 1969, who claimed that night had changed his life but could not say how or why — to see all of that as a viewer would see it, away from the distraction of cables, cameras, crews, lights, monitors, clouds, airplanes, and birds in the quiet of a screening room, with the candidate's handsome, sculptured face filling the screen, his mind groping for answers, his jaws and eyes reflecting a growing irritation — to see all of that added up to a political disaster.

The idea for "Teddy" had come from Bill Leonard, president of the news division, who thought an hour on Kennedy was needed because he would be a major player during the campaign year, whether he ran or not. The hour, he said, would be part of the greatly esteemed *CBS Reports* series, which had been started in 1959 by Fred Friendly and Edward R. Murrow but was currently without a regular chief correspondent. To do Kennedy would mean postponing a *CBS Reports* I was gearing up for, tentatively titled "Biography of an Embassy." We had picked the U.S. Embassy in Riyadh, Saudi Arabia, and the ambassador, former Governor John West of South Carolina, whom I knew and liked from southern politics, had agreed to cooperate. The embassy program would have been unlike anything I had done before.

But an hour on Kennedy was tempting. He had never sat down for a serious interview. The TV audience knew him mostly from clips on the nightly news or his occasional appearances on the Sunday morning talk shows when the issues were what he wanted to discuss.

Whether Leonard wanted me to do it because I was the network's congressional reporter or because I was "a friend of the Kennedys" was not clear. Leonard said later that "Mudd was my personal choice, and I didn't consider any other correspondent. It never occurred to me that he'd be harder or easier because of his relationship with Kennedy."[9]

That relationship was on the same plane I had with many other members of Congress — occasionally social off the Hill but slightly adversarial on the Hill. The only difference in this case stemmed from our friendship with his brother, Robert, and his sister-in-law, Ethel, and our off-and-on presence at Hickory Hill, where the senator was a regular. During the early 1970s there were times when the senator seemed more like a neighbor to us than a political celebrity. After our youngest son, Matthew, was hit by a car and hospitalized with serious injuries, the senator called to offer his help in making sure Matthew was getting the best care from the best doctors. And at the door one Halloween stood the senator and a passel of costumed kids, just dropping by to trick or treat, filling our kitchen and bagging our treats. The senator went off to the library to have his first one-on-one with a Mudd. This Mudd, however, was our son, Daniel, then fifteen years old. Because of these connections, perhaps there was in 1979 an assumption by the senator and his staff that this would be a softball documentary. I'm sure he knew better. I hoped he knew me better.

After a week of doing the pros and cons, I told Leonard I'd do the show. The embassy in Riyadh would still be there, but Kennedy might not.[10] The first step was to lay out to the senator's press secretary, Tom Southwick, what we had in mind — to film him with his family, to cover him at the Senate, to travel with him, and to interview him. Southwick agreed to set up an appointment for Stringer, Lack, and me to see the senator. I remember doing most of the talking, telling him that this was to be a serious undertaking by serious TV journalists, that it would be a better program if he cooperated, but that we were committed to go ahead without his help, if necessary. I explained the dimensions of the show and what would be required from him. I said we wanted two sit-down interviews, one at his

Cape Cod home about family and personal matters and one at his Senate office or at his home in McLean about senatorial matters. He was agreeable.

Stringer and Lack came to lunch at my home on their way back to New York to work out our approach. We knew that to show a complete picture of the man we would need glimpses of his family and his glamorous life as a Kennedy, but we were determined to make the interviews the core of the program. We agreed that his face should fill the frame, that there would be no cutaways during the interviews or voice-overs to illustrate his words, that the camera would stay on him, that we would use generously edited answers to fifteen or twenty questions rather than tightly edited answers to thirty-five or forty questions. I was reluctant to make the program a rehash of Chappaquiddick, but it was apparent to us that we could not come to grips with his veracity without dealing with the issue. Given what Richard Nixon had put the country through, we agreed that character, truthfulness, steadiness, and strength would be critical in the 1980 presidential campaign. We agreed, therefore, because he was no longer just the senior senator from Massachusetts but was about to become a presidential candidate, that he now owed the nation — not just Massachusetts — some further explanation of his actions that night. We would at least give him a chance, but none of us was holding his breath on that one.

Lack went to work with his crews filming the senator on the Hill, at hearings, in his office, on the phone, at Hyannisport, and on the family's annual camping trip into western Massachusetts. I went back to work in New York substituting for Cronkite. The mornings I spent burrowing into the CBS Library's Kennedy file, knowing that unless I could match him on the details of legislation, presidential politics, the Kennedy legacy, and his behavior the night he drove off the bridge at Chappaquiddick, the interview would be a waste.

On Tuesday afternoon, September 5, the Associated Press moved a short item quoting Kennedy as saying his mother and his wife no longer had objections to his running. Knowing that the Kennedys rarely give out such signals, I argued that Kennedy's quote was about as close to an announcement as we would get until he actually announced. I began the *Evening News* with the story, unlike NBC and ABC, which buried it. The senator's statement not only signaled that Leonard's instincts about doing a Teddy show were prescient but it also put pressure on Lack and me to finish the program before Kennedy became an official candidate for president. If we did not, CBS would be subject to the demands of President Carter and all other declared candidates for equal television time.

In late September, I returned to New York to screen Lack's footage and to begin writing. What we needed almost more than a finished script was some realistic estimate on when Kennedy would announce. On September 27, Lack and I had lunch at the Four Seasons in New York with the senator's campaign manager and brother-in-law, Steve Smith, who knew the box we were in if Kennedy announced before we were ready to broadcast the show. Smith said, "It looks like early December. My only problem is trying to hold down the candidate."[11] Based on Smith's guidance, CBS set the program for November 14 but later moved it to November 7, a Wednesday. Through the month of October, I was in and out of New York, writing, screening, and rewriting. On the twenty-fourth, Stringer, Lack, and I showed Leonard the rough cut of the entire show. We got his immediate thumbs-up.

The next night, Steve Smith tracked me down by telephone in my room at the Wyndham Hotel, where I was writing the close. How was the show going? he asked. We joked back and forth about how much alike his answers and the senator's answers were to the same questions. Smith wondered when we were going to broadcast the show. I told him — November 7. That way, I said, we would be on before the announcement and duck the equal-time issue.

Monday I was back in the bureau in Washington and learned that Smith had called an afternoon press conference in a former Cadillac showroom the Kennedy campaign leased for its headquarters. I caught up with Steve just as he was going into the building.

"Are you still announcing in December?" I asked.

"No, no, we're announcing an exploratory committee today," Smith said, "and he's announcing up in Faneuil Hall in Boston next Wednesday."

"God Almighty, Steve, that's the night we're scheduled to go on the air," I said.

"I guess I should have called you," Smith said and turned away to walk into the building.

Lack later told Jules Witcover that he did

not believe the Kennedy campaign had timed the announcement to scuttle the documentary. Not for one minute did I doubt, however, that was what Smith had in mind.

I was furious. I skipped Smith's press conference, ran back to the bureau, and found Bill Leonard having lunch at the Slate Restaurant on Ninth Avenue near the CBS News building. I told him what had happened and how I had visions of this major piece of work going down the drain. But Leonard saved it. He refused to let it be canceled or chopped up, and he insisted that Gene Jankowski, the president of CBS, find a time prior to the Faneuil Hall event. They settled on 10 o'clock Sunday night, November 4, replacing the popular *Trapper John, M.D.* and competing against the first TV showing of *Jaws* on ABC and *MacArthur* on NBC.

At Leonard's direction, CBS launched a full week of promotion for "Teddy" — full-page ads, transcripts, and tapes distributed, and a preview of the show for the press in the Washington bureau. Bob Healy, the *Boston Globe's* bureau chief, came out of the screening room blowing air and flapping his hand as if it had just been burned. The first story, written by Martin Nolan of the *Globe,* called the program a "major political event."[12] Nolan had gotten an early copy of the transcript. I know, because I leaked it to him.

"Teddy" got trampled in the ratings, but no one at CBS complained. They were proud, we were all proud that this original piece of work had remained whole. Senator Robert Dole, always ready with a stinger, said the next day that "seventy-five percent of the country watched *Jaws,* twenty-five percent watched Roger Mudd, and half of them couldn't tell the difference."

What attracted the most attention was the senator's helpless, hopeless answer to the question "Why do you want to be president?" It was probably the slowest pitch I'd ever thrown at a presidential candidate, slow enough that the senator could have seen the stitches on the ball. So basic was the question and so easy should have been the answer that most reporters never asked it, for fear of being labeled pushovers. The question gained notoriety — Daniel Schorr henceforth referred to it as "the Roger Mudd Question" — because of the answer, almost a parody of a politician's circumlocution. If Kennedy had been a southerner, his answer would have come right out of the

603

mouth of Senator Claghorn.

My question, which I asked during our interview in his Senate office on October 12, came after I had gone back over Chappaquiddick, over Judge James Boyle's findings in the case, over whether the public feared he might panic again, and the suggestion in the *Manchester Guardian* that he would choke during a nuclear crisis. The senator's answers were a virtual replay of what he's said to me back in August on Cape Cod. I had again hit the Kennedy stone wall, and there seemed no way to get over, around, under, or through it. So I changed the subject:

MUDD: Why do you want to be president?

KENNEDY: Well, I'm — were I to make the announcement, and to run, the reasons I would run is because I have a great belief in this country. That it is — there's more natural resources than any nation in the world; there's the greatest education population in the world; the greatest technology of any country in the world; the greatest capacity for innovation in the world; and the greatest political system in the world. And yet I see at the current time that most of the industrial nations of the world are exceeding us in terms of productivity and are doing better than us in terms of meeting the problems of inflation; that they're dealing with their problems of energy and their problems of unemployment. It just seems to me that this nation can cope and deal with its problems in a way that it has in the past; we're facing complex issues and problems in this nation at this time and that we have faced similar challenges at other times. And the energies and resourcefulness of this nation, I think, should be focused on these problems in a way that brings a sense of restoration in this country by its people to — in dealing with the problems that we face: primarily the issues on the economy, the problems of inflation, and the problems of — energy. And I would basically feel that — that it's imperative for this country to either move forward; that it can't stand still or otherwise it moves backward. And that leadership for this nation can galvanize a — a — an effort with a team to try and deal with these problems that we're facing in our nation, and can be effective in trying to cope with the problems that we'd face. And I think that'd be the real challenge in — in the 1980s. I think it's a watershed period in our country, from a variety of different points, primarily from an energy point of view and from an economic point of view.[13]

His answer contained 336 words and we used the first 242 of them, stopping with the sentence that ended with "or otherwise it moves backward."

"Oh, my God," I thought. "He doesn't know. He doesn't know why he's running." His sentences did not parse, his words walked over themselves as he kept repeating that the country had problems of energy, and inflation, and unemployment, and inflation, and energy, and unemployment. It never got much better than that.

Throughout his campaign there was a feeling that he had not thought deeply about why he wanted to be president, a feeling he had never gone to the top of the mountain and asked himself, "Why am I doing this? Whom do I want to help? Who are society's enemies?" In his interviews and his speeches rarely was there an articulated sense of what was fueling the Kennedy movement.

It was that answer that gave the campaign

the most trouble explaining. Led by the senator's press secretary, Tom Southwick, they launched their own campaign, accusing me of doing the interviews before Kennedy had decided to run, of tricking the senator into a discussion of Chappaquiddick, and of prying into the most intimate details of his family's personal life. But their claims never stuck, because the transcript disproved them. They claimed they had generously offered us a second interview because he had not done well during the first. The fact was they had agreed to two interviews from the start.

But they did succeed in gulling Tom Shales, the celebrated TV reviewer for the *Washington Post*. In one of his columns, Shales accused me of "willful Mudd-slinging," based on Southwick's claim to him that my question about why he wanted to be president was "filmed before he had really made a move toward it [the nomination]. He had a lot going through his mind about whether or not to run."[14] To swallow Southwick's line, as Shales did, meant believing that presidential candidates don't have to think about why they want to be president until the day they announce their candidacy. Southwick knew he was not telling Shales the truth. Southwick and the entire Kennedy staff knew the senator reached his decision to run over the Labor Day weekend. Not until six weeks later did I ask Kennedy the presidential question. Shales failed to include that critical detail, assuming he made himself aware of it.

Kennedy never got his campaign off the ground. Our interview was certainly not reassuring. On that very same Sunday, a mob in Teheran surrounded the U.S. embassy, demanding that the United States return the ailing Shah of Iran, who was in the U.S. for medical treatment. President Carter broke off campaigning, whereupon Kennedy committed a second political blunder by denouncing the shah as a thief who had stolen "umpteen billion dollars" from Iran.[15]

Despite its faltering start, the expectations for the Kennedy candidacy were so high that the smallest missteps — like his "fam farmlies" spoonerism — became major oratorical blunders. When the convention opened in New York City, President Carter had 315 more votes than he needed for the nomination. Kennedy's only chance was to defeat the rule that bound the delegates to vote on the first ballot for the candidate under whose banner they were elected. When the Kennedy forces lost that fight, the senator announced that he would not have his name put in nomination. Thus, Kennedy brought his first and only presidential campaign to a close.[16]

Today he remains a first-class senator. Both his friends and his enemies respect him, because he is not a flake and because his positions are strong and not far out. He loves politics as a profession that requires generosity, tolerance, compassion, a sense of humor, and a joyful anticipation of a fight without carrying grudges or becoming nasty. As a senator, he practices a version of politics that is the closest to presidential politics one can get without actually being president. For many voters who feel disenfranchised by the political system or are contemptuous of their own senator, he is their man. He has been politically brave on a host of issues. He took a fearsome pounding in Boston on the school busing issue, but he never flinched. And in the aftermath of the "Teddy" broadcast, he never publicly whined, made excuses, or claimed, as his staff did, that he had been tricked.

The broadcast brought all communications from and invitations to Ethel Kennedy and Hickory Hill to an abrupt halt. From time to time I would run into the senator, and although we were no longer on quite the same footing, he was never unfriendly. In fact, his greeting was invariably a quick wiggle of his eyebrows. And at the 1981 Radio-TV Correspondents Dinner he brought down the house with his version of our interview: "Roger Mudd came to MY Cape Cod and sat on MY lawn in one of MY chairs at MY house and then had the nerve to ask me a trick question, like 'Why do you want to be president?' "

Not until election night in 1982, when I was at NBC, did I have the chance to interview him again — he was in Boston and I was in the New York studio, coanchoring with Tom Brokaw. Kennedy had just crushed some hapless Republican in his reelection to the Senate. But I tried again: "Senator, are you closing the door for a run for the presidency in 1984?" He said, sidestepping nicely, that he enjoyed his work in the Senate and would "let the future take care of itself." In 1987 when he read that I had been bumped off the *NBC Nightly News,* there came a warm, generous, and rousing telephone call from the senator.

That call was the last contact I had with him until Easter Sunday, 2005, when E. J. and I were at 10 o'clock Mass at the Church of the Epiphany in Georgetown. We had just returned to our seats after receiving communion when there was the lightest touch on my shoulder. I looked up. In line on his way to communion was the senator. The touch was not the touch of a politician. It was nearly delicate, not meant to intrude on our prayers, but perhaps meant to let me know that after the twenty-six years since "Teddy" we were still somehow connected. Quickly I returned the touch. When I watched him return to his seat, his gait seemed to be more of a shuffle than a stride, his torso and head bent forward, nothing like I remembered him and nothing like his TV image on C-Span. I had hoped to see him after church, but he was gone.

In the spring of 1980, I was in New York for the fortieth annual Peabody Award luncheon at the Pierre Hotel. Charlie Kuralt was to get one for his endearing show, *Sunday Morning,* Robert Trout for fifty years of "excellence," and I for "Teddy."

My Peabody citation read:

Roger Mudd has never lacked for incisiveness in the interviews he has done. His *CBS Reports* with senator and presidential hopeful Edward Kennedy brought a new dimension to his work.

Taking a complete look at Senator Kennedy from every possible angle, the Mudd interview captured instant attention across America. For his interview entitled "Teddy," a Peabody Award to CBS News Correspondent Roger Mudd in recognition of an exceptionally fine effort.

The time had come, I thought, to answer the continuing trashing of "Teddy" by Kennedy's partisans. In my brief remarks at the luncheon I said the program was "conceived and undertaken by honorable men and women. . . . There were no tricks, no deceits, no contrivances. . . . The editing was generous. We were not afraid to let the man be heard. . . . We have nothing to apologize for, clarify, or explain." I praised the "honesty and integrity" of Howard Stringer and Andy Lack. And finally I singled out Bill Leonard for his critical role in repelling the CBS lawyers who at first wanted to cut "Teddy" into pieces to run on the *Evening News.* Leonard's hide, I said, "was never tougher and his back never straighter." Praising Leonard did not come easy. Less than three months earlier, it was Leonard who had flown down to Washington to tell me that Walter Cronkite's replacement as anchor of the *Evening News* would be Dan Rather.

CHAPTER 49
"A COMPELLING MYSTIQUE"

Over the twenty years from 1961 to 1981, CBS assigned four different full-time correspondents to the Pentagon; three to the Congress; two to the State Department; one to the Supreme Court and Justice; and eleven to the White House.

The White House needed five times more help during those years than Foggy Bottom and Capitol Hill for a clutch of reasons: every news broadcast wanted something about the president or his people morning, noon, night, and weekends; the networks generally changed correspondents with a change in administrations; covering the nation's first citizen is stressful and adversarial in ways that covering opinion day at the Supreme Court or a Senate floor debate could never be; the White House was where the press needed extra hands to absorb the spoon-fed briefings, backgrounders, press releases, press conferences, travel schedules, photo ops, and exclusives to the favored; it was the one beat in Washington where TV stars were actually made — Rather, Schieffer, Stahl, Bradley, and Brokaw — and once made, did not stay long; and finally it was and is the instantly recognizable symbol for Washington and a living federal government, certainly more welcoming than the Capitol dome sitting on top of five hundred or so bickering politicians or the remote and shimmering Supreme Court, and absolutely more recognizable than the architecturally nondescript Pentagon and State Department.

John Herbers, who covered Richard Nixon's second term for the *New York Times* found that for most Americans "there is a compelling mystique about the White House . . . and this feeling is shared even by that band of cynical journalists who have a longworn familiarity with the place."[1]

For many journalists the mystique can become intimidating. Bob Pierpoint, who began his long run at the White House in 1960 with Eisenhower, says he was nervous at the start. "After the first two or three days that I had spent at the White House," he says, "I was so upset that I threw up. . . . I was really kind of awed by Eisenhower."

It is no wonder, then, that the White

House TV correspondent has been the first among equals, the one who was a daily presence in breaking news, an automatic on live coverage, a given as a floor reporter during conventions, and the network's lightning rod to receive the bolts of criticism from the president and his followers. The White House was and is the place to be seen.

Was it any wonder, then, that rookies like David Dick would try to make their mark at the White House? Dick tried it by taking on the fabled UPI reporter Merriman Smith. He had been sent over to the White House on an errand — it was November 3, 1966 — to pick up a copy of President Johnson's itinerary. But Press Secretary Bill Moyers corralled everybody into the Cabinet Room and locked the door. He said the president would be coming in to make an important announcement and nobody could leave until he was finished.

"And so Johnson came in," says Dick. "I was so overwhelmed. This was the first time I'd ever been this close to a president of the United States. I got my reporter's notebook going and I said 'I'm going to get this right.'" Johnson announced he would be having two operations, one to remove a small intestinal lump, the other to remove a polyp on his vocal cord. There followed a Q and A with Johnson's doctors, but Dick says he couldn't wait for Moyers to unlock the door.

He burst from the room. "I led the pack. Down the hallway I led the pack. I beat Merriman Smith. I knew this was a net alert. If this was not a net alert there was no such thing as a net alert. I called in and said 'I have a net alert.' 'Oh, really?' 'Yes, I've got it written and I'm ready to go. I was just talking just as clear. . . . I mean, I was rising to this occasion. I was beating everybody, including Merriman Smith."

But whoever handled Dick's phone call on the desk told him there had been no mention of the story on the wires yet. For many insecure desk editors, stories do not exist unless they are on the wires. So David Dick, the man who on his first try had beaten the wires, had beaten Merriman Smith, was told to record the piece for the next hourly newscast. By that time, the wires would have the story, the editor figured, making it legitimate.

Dick says he felt bludgeoned. "I took it," he says. "I didn't scream or yell." But, Lord, how he had tried.

More than any of the city's other beats, the quality of the White House coverage could make or break the reputation of a TV news bureau. State, Defense, the Court, and the Hill could all be brilliantly reported, but unless the White House correspondents were consistently ahead of the competition, the bureau was deficient. Like no other address, 1600 Pennsylvania Avenue is a place of intense competition, not only between and among the correspondents in a bureau, but also against the opposition. The pressure to be first was unrelenting; at the same time there was daily pressure from the White House not to be critical of the president.

The Nixon press office regularly watched the CBS station in Baltimore, which took the early feed off the Cronkite show, so that it could demand a correction in time for the 7 o'clock broadcast, which the Washington affiliate carried. Producer Susan Zirinsky remembers taking a call in the control room from Gerald Warren, the deputy press secretary.

"This is Gerald Warren. Where the hell is Dan?" Zirinsky said he was still on the set. "Well, tell him to call me back. That story is goddamn wrong."

How wrong, if wrong at all, was anybody's guess. It may have been a simple matter of tone.

Unfairly or not, Rather was accused of having what Ed Joyce, the CBS News president in the 1980s, called "scoopitis," defined as a tendency to go with only a piece of a story without taking the time to check it out thoroughly. During Richard Nixon's final days in office in 1974, Rather reported on the *CBS Evening News* that the president's phlebitis had made him limp slightly during his June trip to the Middle East. Rather said in our 2006 interview that in working on the story he found film revealing Nixon "not limping but with a hitch in his giddyup." His story on the *Evening News,* however, did not include the film. Rather told me he had "no idea" why it was not used. The White House confirmed a "mild" case of phlebitis, but denied that Nixon had been limping. The next morning, June 25, the *Washington Post* seemed to go out of its way to undercut Rather by confirming the White House denial, quoting its White House correspondent, Carroll Kilpatrick, that the president reviewed the troops at every stop on his trip, walked to reception lines, and then shook hundreds of hands "without any apparent trouble." Ed Fouhy, the Washington producer and no major admirer of Rather, says, "He'd stick his neck out a lot on stories that nobody else had and sometimes he was not correct. But he had Bob Pierpoint there and Bob was a superb reporter . . . and quite often Bob would have to clean up after Dan."

Pierpoint himself cited the case in 1969 of Rather reporting incorrectly that Nixon had decided to dump FBI Director J. Edgar Hoover.[2] In the midst of Pierpoint's tenth wedding anniversary party, Bill Galbraith on the desk called to send Pierpoint to Hoover's home, where the president was having dinner.

Pierpoint protested. "Wait a minute," he said. "That's not my story. That's Rather's story." But the orders from Bill Small were "to go or else." Pierpoint went and got an interview with Nixon, who denied the whole story. Hoover ran the FBI until his death in 1972.

Fouhy said recently that he suspected the Nixon White House leaked stories to Rather deliberately, because they knew he would get on the air with them. When I mentioned that Donald Rumsfeld, a senior advisor to the president, was thought to be one of Rather's big sources, Fouhy said, "As far as I know, the only one. We had a rule at CBS News that an anonymous source had to be disclosed to the producer and that was usually me."

Never close friends with Pierpoint, Rather says, however, he and Bob did have a "really good working relationship."

"A really good working relationship" were probably not the words Pierpoint would use. After the elections of 1964, he wanted to return to the White House even though Rather was now the chief correspondent. He told Fred Friendly, the president of the news division, he thought there was enough work for two people. Friendly okayed his return. Pierpoint went to Rather with a proposition. "Look, I've lived abroad for ten years and I can do the foreign stories and you can do the domestic stories. Rather said to me very coldly, 'I'll do 'em all.' And that was basically his attitude, and I was sucking hind tit."

Rather's response was qualified years later: "I don't recall that, which is not to say I deny it. I honestly don't recall that conversation. . . . Pierpoint is a truth-teller. I've never known him to say anything that was not true. I don't recall this conversation."

By the time Nixon resigned in 1974, Rather was unquestionably the most famous reporter in America. The Nixon people had helped make him that, because they were smart enough to pick him out as the symbol of everything they thought was liberal, slanted, and untrustworthy. Few have forgotten the 1973 press conference when Rather, prefacing his question with the words "with due respect to your office," got cut off by Nixon with "That would be unusual."

But it was in Houston in March 1974, at the National Association of Broadcasters convention, that Rather's reputation as a Nixonbaiter became engraved in stone. When Rather rose to give his name and ask a question of the president, the audience of station owners and managers gave him a burst of applause.

Nixon, unable to let the moment pass, taunted Rather with, "Are you running for something?" Rather, also unable to let the moment pass, answered in less than a blink, "No, sir, Mr. President, are you?" There followed more applause, some boos, and some gasps.

In talking with me about his celebrated stand-off, Rather said he "certainly felt it was a trap. Right from the get-go I never felt we should have been on that stage. . . . The thing was certainly a set-up, which is to say it was designed to be a paper-the-house and put on a television show in which the president would be at his best and . . .

not being seriously challenged." Nixon was always "looking for ways to throw you off balance," he said, "to knock you off stride."

Whether Rather walked unaware into the traps Nixon laid for him or whether he thought himself too clever to be trapped, the results violated a central rule for journalists: never become more important than the story and never get in the way of the story.

By late 1974, Rather had left the White House to take over *CBS Reports* in New York. In his place had come Bob Schieffer from the Pentagon and not Phil Jones, who for ten months had been covering Gerald Ford as vice president, who had become on August 9 the thirty-eighth president of the United States. Schieffer would be number one, "and not me," says Jones, "and that was a little hard to take because I knew everybody. I'd covered the guy."

So it was with a bittersweet pleasure that Jones watched Schieffer struggle to get recognized at President Ford's first press conference. "Ford had no idea who Bob Schieffer was, and I held back . . . because I knew it was not my role, and finally Bob had made two or three attempts and didn't make it and I ended up standing up and getting in a question."

The next day, Jones says, "the White House phone rings and it's Rather calling for Schieffer. 'Listen, Bob. I just want to call and let you know don't worry about last night. The fact that you didn't get recognized and didn't get in a question, don't worry. Don't pay any attention to what anybody is saying about it. It doesn't make any difference. You're going to do just fine. But don't you worry about what people are saying.' " That call, sending Schieffer off newly worried about what people were saying or not saying about him, was, thought Jones, "typical of Dan."

Once again, it was Bob Pierpoint who got walked on. Under the new assignments at the Ford White House, he became not number two to Schieffer but number two-and-a-half to Jones. Then late in Jimmy Carter's term, when Lesley Stahl arrived to replace Ed Bradley, Pierpoint had had enough. He wanted out. Cronkite got wind of it and called Pierpoint.

"Bob, we need you to stay and train Lesley," he told Pierpoint. "I think she's going to be OK, but we'd rather have you there." When Pierpoint told Cronkite that he'd been training junior reporters for years and he didn't want to train another one to be a White House correspondent while he remained everybody's number two or three, Cronkite guaranteed him a 40 percent raise if he'd stay. With kids in college, 40 percent sounded "pretty darn good . . . and so I stayed. . . . Lesley didn't know where the ladies room was, but she was a hard worker and it worked out well."

In 1980, Pierpoint took a deep breath and finally let go of the White House and moved to the State Department. Schieffer had shifted to New York to anchor the *Morning News*. Stahl was now in a position to be number one at the White House. She kept hearing rumors, however, that Bill Plante, who had done a first-class job covering Reagan during the 1980 campaign, was about to replace her. After less than two years at the White House, Stahl felt insecure, her tenure still tentative. The Plante rumor rattled her and sent her scurrying to New York to beg for her job. Management assured her it liked her work and, of course, she would stay as "chief correspondent." But when the time came, Plante refused to be Stahl's number two and CBS wound up with two chiefs at the White House — Stahl and Plante rotating each week between the *Evening News* and the *Morning News*. It was awkward, but the two made the best of it.

Stahl found Plante to be decent, generally

unflappable, but fastidious. Every Thursday, she says, Plante would sponge down the CBS broadcast booth at the White House with Lysol.[3] Not so, says Plante. "It wasn't every Thursday and it wasn't Lysol. It was '[Formula] 409.' . . . The goddamn place was, and continues to be, a pigpen. People come in and put down their French fries and their soda and leave a ring and a grease stain." Jackie Adams, a new black hire and weekend reporter at the White House, saw Plante cleaning the booth one day and started giggling. "I just love it," she told him, "when white people clean."

After four turns in Vietnam, Plante came to the Washington bureau in 1976. As a native of Chicago, a graduate of Loyola, and the winner of a CBS Fellowship to Columbia, he became along the way the father of six sons and an oenophile with a wine cellar known to be extensive. Except for three years at the State Department covering Secretary James Baker, Plante has been at the White House since 1981. During that quarter century the list of other CBS White House reporters who passed through grew longer and longer — Nelson Benton, Neil Strawser, Terence Smith, John Ferrugia, Deborah Potter, Wyatt Andrews, Norman Robinson, Randall Pinkston, Mark Knoller,

Susan Spencer, Rita Braver, Scott Pelley, John Roberts, and Jim Axelrod.

But Plante stayed — content, always reliable, but perhaps growing a touch cynical through the years. He regards the White House "as probably the most interesting beat in town. . . . You have the luxury of watching it long enough to see that they make the same mistakes whether they are Republican or Democrats. They come in expecting to change things easily or quickly; they can't; they stumble; they get crossways with Congress; venality eventually sets in during most second terms in one form or another."

Approaching his seventieth year, Plante remains the last man standing, the link to the glory years of CBS News at the White House.

CHAPTER 50
"WE'RE GOING WITH RATHER"

By 1978 Walter Cronkite had been anchoring for fifteen years. With his unwavering dedication to hard news and his ferocious sense of competition, he and a first-class corps of correspondents and producers had brought the *CBS Evening News* into first place, outpacing NBC's Huntley and Brinkley, who had dominated the ratings for a decade.

But Cronkite at sixty-two was getting tired and began talking about leaving the anchor chair. For more than a year the management at CBS News kept putting him off, unable to face up to a future without Cronkite. Finally, in late 1979, the front office agreed to let him go and for the next few months the three thousand employees of the news division lived and breathed rumors — the "Who Will Succeed Walter?" rumors.

Would it be me, Cronkite's longtime

substitute, straight news traditionalist, and in-shop favorite? Or would it be Dan Rather, the talented and ambitious White House reporter, who always left a turbulent wake?

CBS Chairman William Paley had told the news president, Bill Leonard: "Choose either one you want but don't lose either one." Leonard first tried to lock me in with a substantial raise but with no promise of succeeding Walter. I turned him down, offended and puzzled that he did not immediately name me as Walter's successor, even though I had been his steady substitute year-in, year-out, summer-in, summer-out for more than six years. He then proposed a Rather-Mudd coanchor — Dan in New York and me in Washington. I turned that down, too, mainly because I saw only trouble in harness with a man about whom I had professional misgivings.

At that point, I told my agent, Bill Cooper, that the next move was up to CBS and that I did not want him calling Leonard. Neither did I want him calling the other networks, shopping me around. Negotiating with the competition while still under contract to CBS struck me as underhanded. I considered myself above the fray and was, in effect, dealing myself out. Leonard said later he never understood why I kept myself apart from the negotiations that so deeply involved my career.

During January and February 1980, there was a rumor a day about major changes. Washington's social circles were buzzing with speculation. The *Chicago Sun-Times* reported the pick was Rather. The *Washington Post* said ABC had offered Rather $8 million for five years. Rather and his agent, Richard Leibner, were obviously working the territory.

During the first week in February, I was on assignment in Boston, finishing a report on the unprecedented amount of money the candidates were spending on TV as they approached the 1980 presidential primary season. Bill Crawford, the producer of most of my political reports, and I had finished up our filming and interviews that February afternoon and were having dinner at Locke-Ober near the Boston Common. With us was a rare guest — my wife, E. J. — who almost never traveled with me when I was working. She was in Boston for a meeting of the Boston College board of trustees and had the evening free.

When we were on the road, Crawford routinely stayed in close touch with the New York assignment desk, making sure they knew our schedule, hotels, and telephone numbers. That night at Locke-Ober, Crawford told me his last call to New York was not routine. He said the desk and the news division on West Fifty-seventh Street were going crazy with rumors about Cronkite's retirement and that Dan Rather's name kept surfacing. Bill figured with all the opening and closing of doors to the executive suites that something big was about to happen. He thought maybe I should call Bill Leonard and find out what was going on.

"No," I said. "If they want me, they know where to find me." And that was that.

Amidst the restaurant's mellow paneled walls and the courtly nineteenth-century service, it was easy for E. J., Crawford, and me to return to our dinner of fish cakes, scalloped potatoes, and a bottle of Crawford's favorite wine, a Wente Brothers Grey Riesling.

As the stiff, unbending son of a stiff, unbending father, I had always been intellectually unwilling to try to sell myself, to take my agent in tow and hustle the network executives. I was uninterested in office politics and wanted to avoid the personal angst that I knew would grow out of a war with Dan.

I had always been ambivalent about anchoring. For all the prestige of the position, the fact is that anchoring is among the most boring jobs in television news. The journalism of it is rarely original, usually second-hand, and mostly one big rewrite of the wire services. Anchors are created personages, public personages, promoted by the network publicists as authoritative, informed, trustworthy, and, above all, likeable. They are hood ornaments for their companies; they must be corporate loyalists and glad-handers with the station affiliates; they are unable to watch over every detail of their broadcasts, because everybody — every vice president, every producer — wants a piece of their time and attention; and therefore they are almost totally dependent on others to create and maintain a reputation for being accurate, fair, and balanced. Of course, the money was beyond belief, the fame and recognition were vast and almost instantaneous, and the thrill of being first with breaking news or running the competition into the ground was exhilarating. But valuing my professional independence and my personal privacy, I remained ambivalent.

I was back in Washington the next week when Leonard called for the first time in months. Could we set aside time for lunch in Washington at "some place private?" I made lunch reservations at Le Lion d'Or, but the next day Leonard's secretary called to cancel. Then, at the request of the CBS Press Office, I posed for pictures for both *Time* and *Newsweek.* The *Newsweek* reporter asked if I had heard that Rather had been chosen for the Cronkite job. I told him I had heard nothing. One by one my bureau colleagues dropped by to tell me they were being questioned by the TV press and that *Time* was putting Rather on its cover.

The next morning, Thursday, Leonard called again. Could we meet in the bureau that very afternoon between 12:30 and 1? I suggested lunch. He agreed, but only perfunctorily. Next came a call that Leonard was running late, that I should forget lunch and wait for him around 2 PM.

What suspense was left came to an end at 2:15 PM when a secretary came to tell me Leonard had arrived. When I walked through the newsroom everybody knew exactly what was about to happen — the desk editors, the film editors, the researchers, the producers. The scene reminded me of *High Noon,* with a clock clicking down toward noon, with the marshal walking down the deserted main street to face down

Frank Miller, and finally with the marshal removing his tin badge and throwing it in the dust. The badge might well have been my plastic-coated CBS News ID.

The meeting with Leonard was not an easy one. I saw to that — a lot of glaring and chunks of silence. Leonard was in a hurry. He had flown down on the company's Gulfstream jet — its only passenger. He had to get back, he said, for his 4:30 PM press conference in New York.

"We're going with Rather," he said. "Of course, we want you to stay, but you won't be substituting for Walter anymore."

"Do you really think I'd want to?" I said.

He had no time for softened words. He wanted to end it.

I told him his decision hurt, because it was such a sudden and public humiliation. His decision had been leaked and was on the radio even before I got the word.

Leonard said he was sorry he hadn't been able to keep me posted but he hadn't known for sure until that morning whether Rather would stay at CBS.

I found out later he had had a handshake deal with Rather's agent for more than a week.

I asked to be released from my contract immediately. He refused.

He suggested that I was bitter. I agreed. He said the bitterness would pass in a week or two. I disagreed.

We shook hands — I don't know why. He was gone in fifteen minutes, jetting back to New York to announce the news. A newspaper reporter asked him at his press conference why there was such a rush. Couldn't he have waited until the next day, Friday? Leonard said it would have then been a weekend story — always the worst time for major press and TV coverage.

In a quiet fury, I went back to my desk, gathered up my personal belongings, and walked out of the bureau for good. I felt white in the face and probably was. There was not a sound in the newsroom as I left. No one looked up. No one said a word. It was eerie. They all knew without being told what had just happened.

It was three o'clock in the afternoon and I needed some time to absorb the shock of the scene with Leonard. So, seeking some serenity and comfort in a world apart, I drove to Georgetown and spent the afternoon in one of my favorite haunts, Larry McMurtry's "Booked Up," hoping to find something to add to my collection of southern fiction. For two hours I browsed in the cozy bookshop, trying to blot out Leonard, Rather, and the years I'd put in helping make CBS News number one in the country.

As I moved from row to row among the books, I tried to rationalize. For someone who thought himself a journalist first and an entertainer last, for someone whom the corporate side regarded with suspicion as a purist, for someone who "hated up," to use Leonard's phrase, I would not have been a good fit. As Cronkite's regular substitute and before that as the anchor of the Saturday news, I knew what life would be like as the full-time Monday-to-Friday anchor, as the anchor on specials, election night, inaugurations, on everything and anything. I was not sure I wanted to lead that life. But as the one who had been considered by so many for so long as Walter's "heir apparent," I thought I deserved better treatment.

For two hours, surrounded by books that were central to my life, I quietly scanned the shelves from Faulkner to Glasgow to Percy to Styron to Welty, looking for a volume I didn't own and wondering whether I should ever have left academia in the first place.

Afraid to admit it even to myself, I wondered whether I wasn't secretly glad I'd been rejected — proof that I was right, proof that I was superior to the values and mores of commercial television.

Finally, I spotted a book I wanted. For forty dollars, I bought a copy of Robert Penn Warren's *World Enough and Time.*

I drove home to McLean not knowing how to tell E. J. what had happened. She had never been an ambitious Washington wife, glorying in my notoriety, working the social scene, parlaying one invitation against another. Back in 1973 when CBS named me as Cronkite's full-time substitute, she had raised objections with me, because she knew what was ahead for her and our four children, then aged nine to fourteen: Missed precious family time, missed birthdays, Christmases, Easters, school plays, field days, ball games. When the children were out of school and on summer vacation, I'd be working Monday to Friday in New York.

But CBS presented it as a rarefied opportunity, and each year management reiterated that substituting for Walter took precedence over all other assignments. Despite her misgivings, I accepted the assignment eagerly.

But the news I brought E. J. that evening outraged her — more than it did me, I think. Not so much the decision itself but the way the whole affair had been handled and the callous disregard for her husband's dignity.

The questions neither of us could answer were: What were all those years of totally loyal service for? Why had I stayed on that ascending escalator for so long only to be pushed off one step short of the top?

We sat together in our kitchen near the big fireplace, stunned and bewildered, trying without much success to comfort one another.

Finally, E. J. stood up and said, "We'll be late for our reservation at the Serbian Crown. Let's go listen to some gypsy music. It's Valentine's Day."

What a sweetheart of a day.

CHAPTER 51
THE PLACE TO BE

I walked out of the CBS bureau on M Street the afternoon of February 14, 1980, and did not go back for twenty-six years. What brought me back was this book. Back then, writing a book about CBS was unthinkable. What I wanted to do was to get even, and the only way to do that was to join the opposition. In late June I signed with NBC.

CBS refused to let me out of my contract early, because they did not want me helping NBC during the 1980 presidential campaign. So I sat out the campaign, the first one I had not covered since 1960. I tried my best to keep up, reading the *Washington Star,* the *Washington Post,* the *New York Times,* and the *Wall Street Journal* and watching my new employer and my old one. But I was missing the camaraderie of the campaign plane, the late and boozy dinners, the jokes, the rumors, the gossip, the asides, the rare privilege of seeing it for yourself.

Without all that, I found myself not quite able to follow what they were saying on the tube and what they meant on the evening news. Everything was so truncated, the sound bites so brief, the reportage so inside, the photo ops so dominating that I soon lost my grip on the Reagan-Carter contest.

My contractual limbo ended the day after Reagan defeated Carter. NBC had given me David Brinkley's office suite, which was empty because an unhappy Brinkley had moved to ABC. The two of us had probably passed in the night.

Rather ascended to the CBS throne a few months later to begin a troubled and difficult twenty-four-year run as anchor of the *CBS Evening News.*

In the end, with the newspapers plastered with accounts of his fall from grace and the implosion at CBS News, the columnists and editorial writers coast to coast pummeling him and the House that Murrow Built, I could not but feel empathy for my former competitor.

In the midst of Rather's humiliation, a reporter for the *Washington Times* called me for lunch. "Nothing special," he said. "I've lost track of you and thought I might catch up." We met at my favorite restaurant in McLean and talked about how poor the television coverage of the Hill had gotten, how the chairman of CBS had declared the "voice of God" anchor to be out of date, and how one of the CBS News vice presidents had proclaimed that a reporter didn't have to live in Moscow to cover Moscow. And then, of course, he asked me about Rather. I heard myself saying, "Dan has gone more places and worked harder and done more in that job than any of the other anchors."[1] It wasn't a calculated response; I truly thought he was due some recognition for the career he had led. He had done everything that CBS had asked of him and more. He had tried hard, worked all hours, and gone everywhere there was to go. But he fell short, because he was a complicated, guarded, tightly wound, and driven man, whose personality quirks left him lacking the essential quality every successful anchor needs — personal believability.

A month after the *Washington Times* article appeared, I received a very personal, handwritten note from Rather. After forty years of the ups and downs we had both been through, I found it hard, if not impossible, not to be touched by his letter. Perhaps I should have stayed and not have walked out when Leonard picked Rather to succeed Cronkite. Lord knows, they offered me everything and anything I wanted to do except anchoring. But the hurt was too great and the fall too sudden. If I had stayed, perhaps the Kalb brothers would not have jumped ship to NBC, and perhaps we could have helped keep the *CBS Evening News with Dan Rather* in first place. Perhaps, perhaps. Too late then and too bad now.

In 1986, I left NBC to join the *MacNeil/Lehrer NewsHour* on PBS for five happy and rewarding years. What followed that were ten years as the documentary host at the History Channel, interspersed with visiting professorships at Princeton University and Washington and Lee University.

But never was there a doubt during those years about where my heart lay. It lay with the Washington bureau of CBS News.

Ed Fouhy once called it "the perfect storm." It was a rare combination of principled leadership at the top; talented and honest journalists; and dedicated and skilled producers, editors, photographers, and couriers, with all of us locked in on twenty years of stories unequalled for their importance, their drama, and their violence. We felt unique to have been a part of it. Why else would we have spent so much time and energy arguing about our stories, screening the footage, writing and rewriting our copy, losing our tempers over mistakes or blown feeds, competing for air time, arguing about being passed over? We had no doubts about how good we were; we had no doubts about our values; we had no doubts that our mission was to cover the news without flattering or tricking the viewer. Most of us thought ourselves chosen. It was as if we had been lifted up by a journalistic deity and dropped down in the middle of the Washington bureau to serve our country by doing God's work.

Even during the six years I spent at NBC, trying my best to beat CBS, there was always a little hitch, perhaps a slight choke, in saying, "I'm Roger Mudd, NBC News, Washington."

I had never truly ceased being a CBS man.

It was, indeed, the place to be.

WHERE ARE THEY NOW?

Martin Agronsky left CBS to anchor *Agronsky & Company* for eighteen years. He died in 1999 at age eighty-four.

John Armstrong left CBS in 1979 to join the Washington bureau of ABC News as a senior producer. He retired in 1993 and lives in Bethesda, Maryland.

Nelson Benton joined the bureau in 1968. He left CBS in 1982, anchored the local news at WBAL in Baltimore, reported on Mutual Radio, and freelanced with the Voice of America until his death in 1988 at age sixty-four.

Tom Bettag left CBS in 1991 to produce *Nightline* at ABC. He is now the executive producer for the Koppel Group and lives in Washington, D.C.

Ed Bradley, after four years in the bureau, moved to New York in 1981 to go to *60 Minutes.* He died in 2006 at age sixty-five.

Rita Braver went from desk editor to field

producer to law correspondent to White House correspondent and is now national correspondent for *Sunday Morning.* She lives in Washington, D.C.

Lillian Brown's last presidential makeup client was Bill Clinton. Now in her midnineties, she continues to speak, teach, and write on how to appear on television. She lives in McLean, Virginia.

Connie Chung left CBS in 1976 and during the next thirty years moved from KNXT in Los Angeles to NBC, CBS, ABC, CNN, and MSNBC. She lives in Middleton, New Jersey.

Wells "Ted" Church joined the Washington bureau in 1954 as a correspondent and retired in 1966. He died in 1974 at the age of seventy-two.

Bill Crawford moved to New York in 1980 to become Dan Rather's senior producer on the *Evening News.* He retired in 1991 and died in 1999 at age seventy.

Walter Cronkite left the anchor chair of the *Evening News* in 1981 at age sixty-five. He has remained active as a TV narrator, syndicated columnist, and occasional freelance correspondent. He lives in New York City.

David Dick left CBS in 1985, taught at the University of Kentucky for ten years, and since 1992 has run the Plum Lick Publishing Company in Paris, Kentucky.

Nancy Hanschman Dickerson moved from CBS to NBC in 1963 and from NBC to freelancing in 1970. She died in 1997 at age seventy.

Bill Downs, one of the original Murrow's Boys, left CBS for ABC in 1963. He died in 1978 at the age of sixty-three.

Eric Engberg joined the bureau in 1981. There were thirty-three reporters in the bureau when he came. When he retired in 2002, there were only nine. He lives in Palmetto, Florida.

Ed Fouhy left CBS in 1974 for three years at NBC, came back to CBS for four years, then went to ABC for three years, and finally was at NBC again until 1987. He is the founder of the Center for Civic Journalism. He retired in 2004 and lives in Chatham, Massachusetts.

Bill Galbraith retired in 1985 after twenty-five years in the bureau. He lives in Fernandina Beach, Florida.

Fred Graham left CBS in 1987 to anchor the news at WKRN-TV in Nashville, Tennessee. In 1989 he became the chief anchor of Court TV and is now its senior editor. He lives in Washington, D.C.

Carol Hamedy spent ten years at CBS, leaving in 1983 for a kidney transplant. In 1990 she resumed work as a freelance editor. She lives in Wilmington, North Carolina.

Bill Headline left the bureau in 1982 and ran CNN's Washington bureau for fifteen years. He headed the Voter News Service for two years and retired in 2000. He lives in Bethesda, Maryland.

Brian Healy started with CBS in New York in 1972, was assigned to the bureau in 1979, and is now the Washington producer for *Sunday Morning.* He lives in Kensington, Maryland.

George Herman worked at CBS for forty-three years, retiring in 1987. He moderated *Face the Nation* for fourteen years. He died in 2005 at age eighty-five.

Phil Jones retired in 2001 after forty years with CBS. He is currently a contributing correspondent for "Religion and Ethics" on PBS. He lives in Naples, Florida.

Bernard Kalb joined brother Marvin in the 1980 move to NBC. In 1985 and 1986 he was the spokesman for Secretary of State George Schultz. He finished his TV career as moderator of CNN's *Reliable Sources.* He lives in Bethesda, Maryland.

Marvin Kalb left CBS in 1980 for NBC. In 1987 he became the Murrow Professor of

Press and Publicity at Harvard, and in 2007 became an emeritus professor. He lives in Chevy Chase, Maryland.

Peter Kendall left CBS in 1988 and became the executive producer in CNN's Washington bureau. He retired in 2001. He lives in Washington, D.C.

Bill Leonard from CBS after thirty-seven years as a reporter, broadcaster, producer, and executive. He died in 1994 at age seventy-eight.

Cal Marlin was a CBS Washington cameraman for thirty-one years. In 1995 he retired at age sixty-five and moved to Santa Barbara, California.

Marya McLaughlin retired from CBS in 1988. She died in 1998.

Jim McManus left CBS in 1987, worked briefly at the Voice of America and NPR, taught at Georgia State University in Atlanta, and retired to Madison, Georgia.

Elizabeth Midgley spent eighteen years in the bureau, retiring in 1987. She lives in Washington, D.C.

Bruce Morton spent almost thirty years in the bureau before moving to CNN. He retired in 2006 and lives in Washington, D.C.

Ike Pappas left CBS in 1987. He formed his own production company in 1991 and retired in 2000. He lives in McLean, Virginia.

Bob Pierpoint spent forty years at CBS. He retired in 1990 and lives in Santa Barbara, California.

Bill Plante has been a CBS White House correspondent, on and off, for almost a quarter of a century. He lives in Washington, D.C.

Dan Rather resigned in 2005 after more than forty years with CBS. He is now the anchor of HDNet. He lives in New York City.

Harry Reasoner was in the Washington bureau for less than a year. For most of the 1970s he anchored at ABC, but he returned to CBS in 1979 and joined *60 Minutes.* He died in 1991 at age sixty-eight.

Don Richardson moved to CBS in New York with Bill Small in 1974, retired in 1986, and died in 2003 at age seventy-nine.

Cindy Samuels worked for CBS on and off until 1976. She was a *Today* producer for NBC from 1980 to 1986 and since then has worked for Whittle Communications and NPR, and as an internet consultant. She lives in Washington, D.C.

Tony Sargeant left CBS after fourteen years

to become economics correspondent for ABC radio. He retired in 1996 and lives in Vienna, Virginia.

Bob Schieffer, the long-time moderator of *Face the Nation,* is also CBS's chief Washington correspondent. He is the bureau's senior survivor. He lives in Washington, D.C.

David Schoenbrun left CBS in 1963 and then worked in New York as a news analyst for radio and Metromedia TV. He died in 1988 at age seventy-three.

Daniel Schorr resigned from CBS in 1976 and has since been a news analyst at CNN and NPR. He lives in Washington, D.C.

David Schoumacher left CBS in 1972 for ABC. He later anchored the local news for WMAL-TV, the Washington, D.C., affiliate of ABC, until he retired in 1989. He lives in Hume, Virginia.

Barry Serafin left CBS in 1979. After twenty-five years at ABC, he retired in 2004 and moved back to his home state of Oregon.

Eric Sevareid retired from CBS in 1977 at age sixty-five but continued working freelance on documentaries for syndication and for PBS. He died in 1992.

Bernard Shaw left CBS in 1977. After three years at ABC, he anchored at CNN until he retired in 2001. He lives in Takoma Park, Maryland.

Bill Small left the bureau in 1974 for New York as vice president for news. In 1979, he moved to NBC, as president for news. In 1982 he became president of UPI and in 1985 began almost ten years as professor and dean of the Fordham Graduate School of Business. He retired in 1999. He lives in New York City.

Howard K. Smith left CBS in 1961 and joined ABC in 1962; he became a coanchor with Frank Reynolds in 1969 and later with Harry Reasoner. He retired in 1978 at age sixty-five and died in 2002.

Sanford Socolow returned to New York in 1978 to become executive producer of the *CBS Evening News* and later was reassigned as London bureau chief. He left CBS in 1988 and ran Cronkite Productions until retiring in 1993. He lives in New York City.

Susan Spencer joined the bureau in 1977, covered the White House in 1980 and 1981, became the medical correspondent in 1984, and joined *48 Hours* in 1993. She lives in Washington, D.C.

Lesley Stahl became a *60 Minutes* correspondent in 1991. She lives in New York City.

Neil Strawser, hired at CBS in 1952, retired in 1987. He was the press secretary for the House Budget Committee from 1987 to 1994. He died on New Year's Eve 2006 at age seventy-eight.

Peter Sturtevant, who joined the bureau in 1967, spent two years in Vietnam and five years in New York as national editor before joining CNN and then helping to create CNBC. He retired in 1997 and lives in New York City.

Bob Vitarelli retired after almost forty years at CBS, most of them directing the Washington stories for the *Evening News* and *Face the Nation.* He retired in 1992 and lives in Chevy Chase, Maryland.

Charles Von Fremd came to the bureau in 1951 and covered Eisenhower for eight years. He died suddenly in 1966 at age forty. His son, Mike, carries on, but at ABC.

Hal Walker left CBS in 1980 for ABC, where he worked until retirement in 1995. He died in 2003 at age seventy.

Sylvia Westerman joined the bureau in 1963 and then worked with Bill Small at CBS in New York and at NBC, UPI, and Fordham University. She died in 1995 at age sixty-two.

Susan Zirinsky spent almost twenty years in

the bureau before moving to New York, where she is now the producer of *48 Hours.* She lives in New York City.

ACKNOWLEDGMENTS

Writing this book was anything but lonely. It became instead a happy reunion with the men and women who brightened my life a quarter century ago and brought credit and fame to CBS News.

It began as a full-blown memoir. At first I wrote in fits and starts but with no real narrative arc — chapters on growing up in Washington, on summer camp, on college, on Dan Rather, on NBC. A telephone call to one of Washington's most successful lawyer-agents nearly caused me to abandon the project. He told me there was no market for a journalist's memoirs unless I dished about the famous and powerful. Otherwise, he said, only the academic press would be interested.

But when Jim Lehrer interceded with his magic touch, Peter Osnos of Public Affairs agreed to take a look. "Send me fifty pages," he said. A week or two later, Osnos told me he did not want to publish a story that was so familiar. "Everybody knows what's happened to the networks," he said. "Why don't you write about how great network news used to be? Why don't you write about that great Washington bureau you were part of?"

Oh, my God! There it was, handed to me.

Within the month I was off in a brand-new direction with a creative publisher, a narrative arc, a book title, and the enthusiastic response of everybody I called.

Equipped with a microcassette recorder, I started interviewing as many of the past and present Washington staff as I could locate. With the invaluable help of John Armstrong, the keeper of our flame, I found forty-six of them. They were all delighted finally to be asked to talk about a central experience in their lives — their stories, their hurts, their rivalries, their best and worst memories. The tapes of those interviews are punctuated with bursts of wild laughter as the recollections of our glory years came flooding back.

To each of them I am deeply indebted. Without them, this book would be limp. My hope is that it measures up to the standards they set. The names of my colleagues are gratefully listed in "Where Are They Now?"

Of the sixty men and women who figure in the book, fourteen had died well before I started writing. My interview with a fifteenth, Ed Bradley, came just five months before his death.

My thanks extend to many others who gave me critical help: Ken Crawford, a producer at the Newseum, who unearthed the diaries of his father, Bill Crawford; Don Ritchie, the associate historian, and Beth Koed, the assistant historian, at the Senate Historical Office, who promptly tracked down obscure but needed facts; Laura Koepnick at the CBS Library in New York, who generously supplied an unpublished and internal history of CBS News; David Lombard at CBS Photo Archives, who uncomplainingly handled my repeated requests; and Jessica Tallant, whose digital artistry at the Langley Photo Shop in McLean, Virginia, salvaged the unsalvageable.

To those at PublicAffairs, my debts are obvious. First, to Peter Osnos, who gave me a second career; Melissa Raymond and Niki Papadopoulos, the shepherds of manuscripts, endnotes, and galleys, who kept it all moving; the fact-checker, Katherine Whitworth, who saved me again and again from the pitfalls of a wobbly memory; and finally my editor, the gentle Bill Whitworth, whose love of words and knowledge of grammar made the rough edges smooth and the obscure clear.

Our four children, Daniel, Maria, Jonathan, and Matthew grew up with, and occasionally in, the bureau and, given the generosity of bureau chief Bill Small, found themselves from time to time on the CBS payroll as convention and election-night gofers. In the early stages of the book, Maria and Jonathan both gave me such praise, encouragement, and editorial help that I was bound not to let them down.

E. J.'s support, patience, faith, and understanding never wavered. If writing *The Place to Be* was not lonely for me, it surely must have been for her. But she knew to give me the most valuable gift a writer could have — A Room of One's Own.

McLean, Virginia
October 9, 2007

BIBLIOGRAPHY

Associated Press. *The Torch Is Passed.* Washington, D.C.: Associated Press, 1963.

Eric Barnouw. *The Golden Web.* New York: Oxford University Press, 1968.

Gwenda Blair. *Almost Golden.* New York: Simon & Schuster, 1988.

Robert O. Blanchard, ed. *Congress and the Media.* New York: Hastings House, 1974.

Peter J. Boyer. *Who Killed CBS?* New York: Random House, 1988.

Robert A. Caro. *Means of Ascent.* New York: Knopf, 1990.

Stanley Cloud and Lynne Olsen. *The Murrow Boys.* New York: Houghton Mifflin, 1996.

Congressional Quarterly. *Guide to U.S. Elections,* 2nd ed. Washington, D.C.: Congressional Quarterly, Inc., 1985.

David Dick. *Follow the Storm.* Middletown, Ky.: Plum Lick Publishing, 2002.

Elizabeth Drew. *Portrait of an Election.* New York: Simon & Schuster, 1981.

Corydon B. Dunham. *Fighting for the First Amendment.* Westport, Conn.: Praeger, 1997.

Fred W. Friendly. *Due to Circumstances Beyond Our Control.* New York: Random House, 1967.

———. *The Good Guys, the Bad Guys and the First Amendment.* New York: Random House, 1976.

Gary Paul Gates. *Air Time.* New York: Harper & Row, 1978.

Jack W. Germond. *Fat Man Fed Up.* New York: Random House, 2004.

Jack W. Germond and Jules Witcover. *Blue Smoke & Mirrors.* New York: Viking, 1981.

Fred Graham. *Happy Talk.* New York: Norton, 1990.

David Halberstam. *The Powers That Be.* New York: Knopf, 1979.

John Herbers. *No, Thank You, Mr. President.* New York: Norton, 1976.

Nick Kotz. *Judgment Days.* Boston: Houghton Mifflin, 2005.

Bill Leonard. *In the Eye of the Storm.* New York: Putnam, 1987.

Neil MacNeil. *Dirksen.* New York: World, 1972.

Martin Plissner. *The Control Room.* New York: Free Press, 1999.

Daniel Rapoport. *Inside the House.* Chicago: Follett, 1975.

Dan Rather. *The Camera Never Blinks.* New York: Morrow, 1977.

Walt Whitman Rostow. *Conflict and Controversy.* Austin: University of Texas Press, 2003.

Richard Salant. *Salant, CBS, and the Battle for the Soul of Broadcast Journalism.* Boulder, Col.: Westview, 1999.

Bob Schieffer. *This Just In.* New York: Putnam, 2003.

Arthur M. Schlesinger Jr. *A Thousand Days.* Boston: Houghton Mifflin, 1965.

Daniel Schorr. *Clearing the Air.* Boston: Houghton Mifflin, 1977.

William Small. *To Kill a Messenger.* New York: Hastings House, 1970.

Sally Bedell Smith. *In His Glory.* New York: Simon & Schuster, 1990.

Richard Norton Smith. *Uncommon Man.* New York: Simon & Schuster, 1984.

Lesley Stahl. *Reporting Live.* New York: Simon & Schuster, 1999.

Alexis de Tocqueville. *Democracy in America.* New York: D. Appleton, 1904.

U.S. Congress. *Congressional Record, 88th Congress, 2nd Session.* Washington, D.C.:

Government Printing Office, 1964.

————. *Congressional Record, 92nd Congress, 1st Session.* Washington, D.C.: Government Printing Office, 1971.

Warren Weaver Jr. *Both Your Houses.* New York: Praeger, 1972.

Alan Weisman. *Lone Star.* Hoboken, N.J.: Wiley, 2006.

Theodore White. *Breach of Faith.* New York: Atheneum, 1975.

————. *America in Search of Itself.* New York: Harper & Row, 1982.

Jules Witcover and Richard Cohen. *A Heartbeat Away.* New York: Viking, 1974.

Jules Witcover. *85 Days.* New York: Putnam, 1969.

————. *White Knight.* New York: Random House, 1972.

————. *The Year the Dream Died.* New York: Warner, 1977.

Bob Woodward and Carl Bernstein. *All the President's Men.* New York: Simon & Schuster, 1974.

————. *The Final Days.* New York: Simon & Schuster, 1976.

NOTES

Prologue

1. David Halberstam, *The Powers That Be,* pp. 17–18.
2. Radio program listings, the *New York Times,* November 16, 1933.
3. Eric Barnouw, *The Golden Web,* p. 78.

Chapter 5: You'll Be Local the Rest of Your Life

1. Sally Bedell Smith, *In His Glory,* pp. 370–372, 417.

Chapter 6: Take Two, Take Three

1. Dale P. Harper, "Axis Sally," *World War II,* November 1995.

Chapter 7: Old Four Fingers

1. All quotations that are not endnoted were either taken from interviews with the source or from the author's own notes and papers.

Chapter 10: The Front Row
1. Alan Weisman, *Lone Star,* pp. 21, 28–31.
2. Halberstam, *The Powers That Be,* p. 437.
3. *Ibid.,* p. 386.

Chapter 11: The Back Row
1. Bob Schieffer, *This Just In,* p. 123.

Chapter 12: The Four Rules of Sevareid
1. Stanley Cloud and Lynne Olsen, *The Murrow Boys,* p. 367.

Chapter 14: Wanted by the FBI
1. Nick Kotz, *Judgment Days,* pp. 82–83.
2. FBI memo, unclassified March 4, 1982. Author's papers.
3. University of Texas Web site — journalism.utexas.edu/awards/prize/ogri.html
4. Letter to the author, dated May 6, 2005.
5. FBI memo.
6. *Ibid.*
7. Robert A. Caro, *Means of Ascent,* p. 87, 100.
8. *Ibid.,* p. 88.

Chapter 15: Nothing Could Be Finer
1. Arthur M. Schlesinger Jr., *A Thousand Days,* pp. 707–711.

Chapter 16: "The Hunkies Have Run Amok"

1. Martin Plissner, *The Control Room,* p. 72.
2. Theodore F. White, *America in Search of Itself,* p. 171.

Chapter 17: The Useful Pest

1. CBS News transcript, "The Washington Report," June 2, 1963.
2. "The Washington Report," May 19, 1963.
3. "The Washington Report," September 1, 1963.
4. "The Washington Report," June 2, 1963.
5. "The Washington Report," September 8, 1963.

Chapter 18: The March on Washington

1. Peter Jennings, "I Have a Dream," ABC News, August 28, 2003.
2. Richard Norton Smith, *Uncommon Man,* p. 137.
3. Jennings, "I Have a Dream."

Chapter 19: The Rumormonger

1. CBS News transcript, "Case History of a Rumor," November 13, 1963, p. 19.
2. Richard Severo, "Jessica Mitford, Incisive Critic of American Ways and a British Upbringing, Dies at 78," the *New York Times,* July 24, 1996.

3. "Case History of a Rumor," pp. 20–22.

4. *Ibid.*, pp. 23–24.

5. *James B. Utt* v. *CBS,* February 24, 1964, U.S. District Court for the Southern District of New York.

6. *Guide to U.S. Elections,* 2nd ed., pp. 977–1017.

7. Goodbyemag.com.

Chapter 20: Where Were You When. . . . ?

1. CBS News transcript, "The Assassination of President John F. Kennedy as Broadcast on the CBS Network," November 22, 1963, Vol. 1, p. 24.

2. "Making History with Roger Mudd," the History Channel, October 29, 2004.

3. CBS News, "Assassination of the President," p. 97.

4. CBS News, "Assassination of the President," Vol. 2, p. 241.

5. CBS News, "Assassination of the President," Vol. 3, p. 44.

6. CBS News, "Assassination of the President," Vol. 4, p. 79.

7. William Small, *To Kill a Messenger,* p. 146.

8. CBS News, "Assassination of the President," Vol. 3, p. 137.

9. The Associated Press, *The Torch Is Passed,* p. 91.

10. CBS News, "Assassination of the Presi-

dent," Vol. 4, p. 257.

Chapter 21: "A Sad, Sorry Mess"
1. Words and music by Saxie Dowell, 1939.

Chapter 22: "What Do We Do Now, Dick?"
1. Halberstam, *The Powers That Be,* p. 136.
2. Small, *To Kill a Messenger,* pp. 257–258.
3. *CBS Morning News* transcript, March 30, 1964, author's papers.
4. Small, *To Kill a Messenger,* p. 257.
5. *CBS Morning News,* March 30, 1964.
6. All quotes in this chapter are from author's notes and scripts, March 30–June 20, 1964.
7. "Mudd into Gold," *Newsweek,* June 22, 1964.
8. John Horn, "Meanwhile, Back in Reality," the *New York Herald Tribune,* April 26, 1964.
9. *Congressional Record,* June 10, 1964.
10. *Guide to U.S. Elections, op. cit.,* p. 623.
11. Kotz, *Judgment Days,* p. 153.
12. Small, *To Kill a Messenger,* p. 258.
13. Author's papers.
14. CBS News transcript, June 20, 1964, author's papers.

Chapter 23: "Will You Wave, Sir?"

1. Gary Paul Gates, *Air Time,* p. 112.
2. William Leonard, *In the Eye of the Storm,* p. 112.
3. Fred W. Friendly, *Due to Circumstances Beyond Our Control,* pp. 185–187.
4. Gates, *Air Time,* p. 115.
5. Rex Reed, "Two Against Huntley and Brinkley," the *New York Times,* August 23, 1964.
6. Charles Strum, "A Model Anchor Can't Escape the Microphone," the *New York Times,* March 12, 2000.
7. Jack Gould, "TV: Stylish Punch of C.B.S. News," the *New York Times,* August 24, 1964.
8. Barbara Delatiner, "First Returns Go to New CBS Duo," *Newsday,* August 24, 1964.
9. Jack Gould, "TV: Convention Ratings," the *New York Times,* August 26, 1964.

Chapter 24: The Minnesota Twins

1. Gates, *Air Time,* pp. 232–237.
2. CBS News, Humphrey transcript, March 12, 1965.
3. Author's papers, August 1977.
4. *Ibid.,* February 7, 1978.

Chapter 25: Mister Ev, the Talking Horse

1. Kotz, *Judgment Days,* pp. 310–311.
2. Author's papers.
3. Warren Weaver Jr., *Both Your Houses,* p. 12.
4. CBS News transcript, "Everett Dirksen — A Self Portrait," June 6, 1965.
5. Jack Gould, "TV: Dirksen Portrait," the *New York Times,* June 7, 1965.
6. Neil MacNeil, *Dirksen,* pp. 257–258.
7. *Ibid.,* p. 304.
8. *Ibid.,* p. 230.
9. *Ibid.,* pp. 385–386.
10. Author's conversation with Brad Dye, October 9, 2004.
11. CBS News transcript, "Everett McKinley Dirksen 1896–1969," September 7, 1969.
12. *Ibid.*

Chapter 26: "Not While I'm Around"

1. Robert O. Blanchard, ed., *Congress and the Media,* pp. 70–78.
2. Lesley Stahl, *Reporting Live,* p. 19.

Chapter 27: "Of Course, It's a Great Body"

1. Jack Germond, *Fat Man Fed Up,* p. 207.
2. Author's papers.
3. Author's papers.
4. Alexis de Tocqueville, *Democracy in*

America, p. 213.

5. Roger Mudd, CBS Radio, "Byline," March 17, 1972.

6. Weaver, *Both Your Houses,* p. 8.

Chapter 28: "Who the Hell Is Alexander Kendrick?"

1. To be certain my memory had not failed me, I e-mailed Rostow's widow, Elspeth Rostow, the former dean of the LBJ School of Public Affairs in Austin, Texas. She referred me to page 15 of her husband's last book, *Conflict and Controversy:* "One of my campers was Roger Mudd, later the well-known TV news anchor and commentator. He was then a charming eight-year-old. At swimming periods he would hold his breath and swim with me underwater, his hands on my shoulders. He came down suddenly with pneumonia. There were no antibiotics in the thirties. Roger's temperature rose. The doctor said there was nothing to do but keep cold compresses on him regularly, make sure he had enough liquids, and count on his constitution to see him through. We stayed up with him during several nights of great anxiety with this primitive system. At last his temperature broke, and he recovered." I remember the pneumonia and being

pulled out of camp and taken to Children's Hospital in Washington, D.C., where I was diagnosed with double pneumonia. My mother was furious, and brought a formal complaint to the D.C. Medical Society against the camp doctor, who, in addition to Rostow's claim that he drank and did drugs, did not have a license to practice. In her e-mail, Professor Rostow said her husband had mentioned having to pull me out of the water hastily because for some reason I had panicked. "This came up," she wrote, "when we were listening to you saying such sensible things on the tube that Walt remarked: 'Glad I saved Roger Mudd's life.' An exaggeration? No idea . . . but he felt a special tie to you." And yet for all the turbulent years we worked in the same city — he as one of President Johnson's hawks on the Vietnam War and me as a correspondent for a television network that was at times adversarial toward the administration — Walt Rostow never let it be known that he had a "special tie" to me or never once called in his chits with me or suggested even delicately that CBS News might back off a bit on the war.

2. John Hart, a rare TV man because of his minimal ego, moved to NBC in the late

seventies and is now retired. Of all the men and women who moved through the bureau in the sixties and seventies, Hart was the only one who declined to talk to me about his days in Washington. His e-mail to me, characteristic of his personal modesty, read as follows: "It's good of you to include me but I'm going to decline. The time in the bureau was relatively short for me and so far in the past that it's more like a good book I read long ago, retaining a sense of it but without the details."

3. Peter Boyer, *Who Killed CBS?*, p. 124.

Chapter 29: "How about Bobbsie?"

1. Descriptions of Kennedy's travels and appointments between March 13 and 15, 1967, have been taken directly from the author's papers.

2. Jules Witcover in his 1997 book, *The Year the Dream Died,* writes that on May 6, 1968, at a courthouse rally in LaPorte, Indiana, Blackburn's hometown, Kennedy, in a playful spirit, introduced him to the crowd "in terms that advertised Blackburn as the nonpareil giant of American journalism." Witcover described Blackburn as a "friendly and conscientious young man to whom Kennedy took a lik-

ing," pp. 197–198. My only explanation for Kennedy's turnaround on Blackburn is that in 1968, he was a presidential candidate and could not afford to alienate Blackburn and decided to swallow leeches and all.

Chapter 30: "I Don't Know — I Don't Know"

1. All quotes, on and off the record, are from the author's papers.
2. CBS News transcript, *CBS Reports: Robert F. Kennedy,* June 20, 1967.
3. Unedited transcripts, *CBS Reports: Robert F. Kennedy.*
4. *Ibid.*

Chapter 31: Too Deep a Hole

1. Author's papers.
2. *Ibid.*
3. Swainson lost both legs when he stepped on a land mine in 1944 during the fighting in Alsace-Lorraine. After the war, at Chapel Hill, Swainson regaled us with his unlikely story of unstrapping his uncomfortable artificial legs and putting them in the wastebasket of his study carrel while he hit the books. After an hour or so, he put his head on his desk and fell asleep. When he awoke his legs were gone —

gathered up by the library janitor making his rounds. Not until his classmates pawed through the garbage did the future governor of Michigan get his legs back.

4. Author's papers.
5. Wikipedia, "George W. Romney."
6. *Guide to U.S. Elections,* p. 211.

Chapter 32: "Ma'am, I've Been Hit, Too"

1. Jules Witcover, *85 Days,* p. 44.
2. *Ibid.,* p. 68.
3. *Ibid.,* p. 258.
4. CBS News transcript.

Chapter 33: "Nixon's the One What?"

1. Jules Witcover, *White Knight,* p. 300.
2. Agnew speech text, author's papers.
3. Small, *To Kill a Messenger,* p. 248.
4. From the author's papers.

Chapter 34: Hitting Our Stride

1. Gwenda Blair, *Almost Golden,* p. 216.
2. Blair, *Almost Golden,* p. 250.

Chapter 35: The Hand That Feeds You

1. Author's papers.
2. *Ibid.*
3. *Ibid.*
4. Gates, *Air Time,* pp. 266–268.
5. Halberstam, *The Powers That Be,* p. 151.

The Murrow reference is to his 1968 speech in which he charged the networks with "decadence, escapism and insulation from the realities of the world." CBS Chairman William Paley was enraged by Murrow's speech. The fallout ultimately led to Murrow's retirement.

Chapter 36: Yes, No, and Just a Little Bit

1. Richard Salant, *Salant, CBS, and the Battle for the Soul of Broadcast Journalism,* Susan and Bill Buzenberg, eds., p. 87.
2. Peter Davis e-mail to author, April 1, 2005.
3. *Ibid.*
4. CBS News transcript, "The Selling of the Pentagon," February 23, 1971, p. 9.
5. Davis, e-mail to author, April 23, 2005.
6. *Newsweek,* March 8, 1971.
7. Davis, e-mail to author, April 1, 2005.
8. Assistant Secretary of Defense Daniel Z. Henkin to Representative F. Edward Hébert, of Louisiana. Letter dated March 3, 1971, author's papers.
9. Daniel Rapoport, *Inside the House,* p. 109.
10. Salant, *Salant, CBS, and the Battle,* p. 88.
11. Claude Witze, *Air Force Magazine,* March 15, 1971.

12. Robert Sherrill, *New York Times Magazine,* May 16, 1971.
13. Salant script, March 23, 1971, author's papers.
14. Salant, *ibid.,* p. 95.
15. Minnesota Public Radio, "The Memoirs of Frank Stanton," January 20, 2003.
16. *Congressional Record,* Ninety-second Congress, First Session, July 13, 1971.
17. Smith, *In His Glory,* p. 475.
18. *Congressional Record,* 92nd Congress, 1st session, July 23, 1971.
19. *Ibid.*
20. *Ibid.*
21. Salant, *Salant, CBS, and the Battle,* p. 97.
22. Fred Friendly, *The Good Guys, the Bad Guys and the First Amendment,* p. 207.
23. Salant, *Salant, CBS, and the Battle,* p. 96.
24. Corydon B. Dunham, *Fighting for the First Amendment,* p. 159–161.
25. Friendly, *The Good Guys,* footnote, p. 207.
26. Salant, *Salant, CBS, and the Battle,* p. 93.
27. Minnesota Public Radio, "Memoirs of Frank Stanton."
28. Davis, e-mail to author, April 1, 2005.
29. Minnesota Public Radio, "Memoirs of

Frank Stanton."

30. Davis, e-mail to author, April 1, 2005.

31. *The Weekly Standard,* "Dan Rather's Day of Reckoning," October 4, 2004.

32. Smith, *In His Glory,* pp. 475–476.

33. *Ibid.,* p. 479.

Chapter 37: The Stakeout Queens

1. James Naughton, e-mail, May 13, 2007.

2. Stahl, *Reporting Live,* p. 13.

3. Walter's "magic number" is a reference to Cronkite's insistence that he be seen and/or heard for a minimum of five and a half minutes on each broadcast.

Chapter 38: "I Think I Got It — I Hope I Got It"

1. David Dick, *Follow the Storm,* p. 23.

2. *Ibid.,* p. 23.

Chapter 40: "We Could Have Done Better"

1. Vanderbilt Television News Archives, June 17–21, 1972.

2. *Ibid.,* August 29–October 31, 1972.

3. Stahl, *Reporting Live,* p. 20, 26.

4. Bob Woodward and Carl Bernstein, *All the President's Men,* p. 105.

5. Gates, *Air Time,* p. 305.

6. Stahl, *Reporting Live,* pp. 26–27.

Chapter 41: Nattering Nabobs

1. Smith, *In His Glory*, p. 493.

Chapter 42: The Legal Eagles

1. Fred Graham, *Happy Talk*, pp. 148–149.
2. Jules Witcover and Richard Cohen, *A Heartbeat Away*, footnote, p. 259. The authors say Petersen "could not recall making such a statement. It was reported by Fred Graham, who apparently was told of Petersen's comment by someone who had overheard it."
3. Graham, *Happy Talk*, pp. 152–153.
4. Woodward and Bernstein, *The Final Days*, footnote, p. 171.

Chapter 43: "Voices from Hell"

1. William B. Crawford, 1974 Diary. Property of Ken Crawford.
2. Gates, *Air Time*, p. 249.
3. Schieffer, *This Just In*, p. 210.
4. Crawford diary, May 1, 1974.
5. Stahl, *Reporting Live*, pp. 38–39.

Chapter 44: At Noon Tomorrow

1. Woodward and Bernstein, *The Final Days*, pp. 292–293.
2. Salant, *Salant, CBS, and the Battle*, pp. 114–115.

3. Daniel Schorr, *Clearing the Air,* p. 112–113.

4. Gates, *Air Time,* p. 389.

5. *Ibid.,* p. 388.

6. Schorr, *Clearing the Air,* p. 117.

7. Theodore White, *Breach of Faith,* pp. 349–350.

8. CBS News transcript, author's papers.

9. Dan Rather, *The Camera Never Blinks,* pp. 245–246.

10. Halberstam, *The Powers That Be,* pp. 703–704.

Chapter 45: Pancake

1. Rather, *The Camera Never Blinks,* p. 64.

2. *Ibid.,* p. 65.

Chapter 46: Pike's Peek

1. Daniel Schorr, *Clearing the Air,* pp. 204–205.

2. Laurence Stern, "Schorr Says He Leaked Material," the *Washington Post,* February 14, 1976.

3. Schorr, *Clearing the Air,* p. 252.

4. *Ibid.,* pp. 256–257.

5. Stahl, *Reporting Live,* p. 54.

Chapter 47: Uncle Walter

1. Lee Dembart, "A Mudd Report on Candidates Rejected by Cronkite Pro-

gram," the *New York Times,* June 8, 1976.

Chapter 48: Teddy

1. William A. Henry III, "Objectivity Wasn't There," the *Boston Globe,* November 6, 1979. Apparently Henry's editor found some of Henry's review unfit for the *Globe.* The phrase "raised questions about the seriousness of his journalism" originally read "proved himself unfit for journalism," and the phrase "obsessed with sex" was deleted altogether.
2. William F. Buckley Jr., "Senator Kennedy and Mr. Mudd," the *Washington Star,* November 13, 1979.
3. Anthony Lewis, "Policy and Press," the *New York Times,* November 8, 1979.
4. Mary McGrory, "Ted Kennedy Doesn't Speak in the Rousing Language of His Brothers," the *Washington Star,* November 5, 1979.
5. Patrick J. Buchanan, "Where Do Reporters Draw the Line?" the *St. Louis Globe-Democrat,* November 20, 1979.
6. Jimmy Breslin, "Now Teddy Comes to a Bridge He'll Have to Cross," the *New York Daily News,* November 6, 1979.
7. Rowland Evans and Robert Novak, "Ted Kennedy's Amateur Hour," the *Washington Post,* December 6, 1979.

8. Fred Barnes, "Kennedy Bid Off to a Slow Start," the *Baltimore Sun,* November 30, 1979.

9. "Who, er, Picked, uh, Roger Mudd?" *New York,* January 14, 1980.

10. My account of the Kennedy documentary in this chapter is taken largely from a 1980 interview with Jules Witcover. It formed the basis of Chapter 3 in a book he coauthored with Jack Germond, *Blue Smoke & Mirrors.* It is the most authoritative published account of the events surrounding "Teddy," and because the quotes are mine and are accurate, I feel free to use them.

11. *Ibid.,* p. 60.

12. Martin Nolan, "Kennedy's Chappaquiddick Strategy," the *Boston Globe,* October 31, 1979.

13. Kennedy transcript, author's papers.

14. Tom Shales, "On the Air," the *Washington Post,* November 22, 1979. According to Elizabeth Drew, in *Portrait of an Election,* p. 33, Kennedy told her on November 5, 1979, "I made up my mind this summer."

15. Witcover, *Blue Smoke & Mirrors,* p. 87.

16. *Guide,* pp. 429–434.

Chapter 49: "A Compelling Mystique"

1. John Herbers, *No Thank You, Mr. President,* pp. 34–35.
2. A search of the Vanderbilt University TV Archives revealed no mention of the Hoover story by either Rather or Cronkite on the *CBS Evening News* from September 29 through October 3, 1969.
3. Stahl, *Reporting Live,* pp. 119–124.

Chapter 51: The Place to Be

1. Chris Baker, "Former Reporter Mudd Upon News," *Washington Times,* February 2, 2005.

ABOUT THE AUTHOR

Roger Mudd was most recently the primary anchor for the History Channel. Previously, he was weekend anchor of *CBS Evening News,* coanchor of the weekday *NBC Nightly News,* and host of NBC's *Meet the Press* and *American Almanac.* He is the recipient of numerous awards, including the George Foster Peabody Award, the Joan Shorenstein Award for Distinguished Washington Reporting, and five Emmy Awards. He lives in McLean, Virginia.

The employees of Thorndike Press hope you have enjoyed this Large Print book. All our Thorndike and Wheeler Large Print titles are designed for easy reading, and all our books are made to last. Other Thorndike Press Large Print books are available at your library, through selected bookstores, or directly from us.

For information about titles, please call:
(800) 223-1244

or visit our Web site at:
http://gale.cengage.com/thorndike

To share your comments, please write:
Publisher
Thorndike Press
295 Kennedy Memorial Drive
Waterville, ME 04901